BARRON'S

FRENCH

Fourth Edition

THE EASY WAY

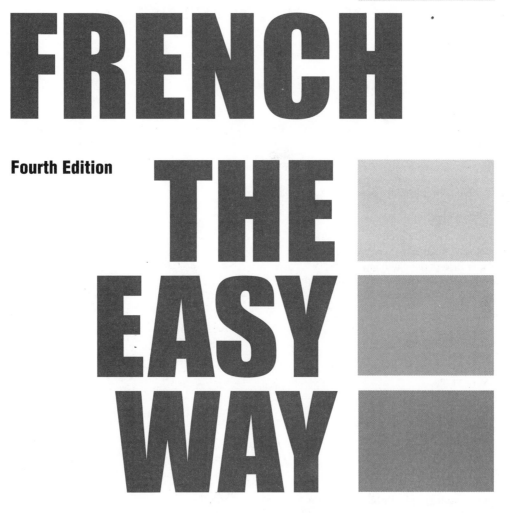

For students of French 1 and 2 in schools and colleges and for self-instruction in review.

Christopher Kendris

B.S., M.S., Columbia University, New York, New York
M.A., Ph.D., Northwestern University, Evanston, Illinois

Diplômé, Faculté des Lettres, Université de Paris
(en Sorbonne) et Institut de Phonétique, Paris

Former Assistant Professor, Department of French
and Spanish, State University of New York, Albany,
New York

Theodore Kendris

M.A., Northwestern University, Evanston, Illinois
Ph.D., Université Laval, Québec, Canada

BARRON'S

For St. Sophia Greek Orthodox Church of Albany,
New York, our parish

and

to the eternal memory of our beloved
YOLANDA FENYO KENDRIS
who is always by our side
with love

All inquiries should be addressed to:
Barron's Educational Series, Inc.
250 Wireless Boulevard
Hauppauge, New York 11788
http://www.barronseduc.com

ISBN-13: 978-0-7641-3411-1
ISBN-10: 0-7641-3411-6

Library of Congress Catalog Card No. 2006045736

Library of Congress Cataloging-in-Publication Data

Kendris, Christopher.
French the easy way / by Christopher Kendris and Theodore Kendris. —4th ed.
p. cm. — (The easy way series)
English and French.
Includes index.
ISBN-13: 978-0-7641-3411-1
ISBN-10: 0-7641-3411-6
1. French language—Textbooks for foreign speakers—English. 2. French language—
Self-instruction. 3. French language—Grammar. I. Kendris, Theodore. II. Title.
III. Series: Easy way.

PC2129.E5K43   2006
448.2'421—dc22   2006045736

PRINTED IN THE UNITED STATES OF AMERICA
9 8 7 6 5 4 3

 Paper contains a minimum of 15%
post-consumer waste (PCW).

Contents

About the Authors

Dr. Christopher Kendris has worked as an interpreter and translator for the U.S. State Department at the American Embassy in Paris.

Dr. Kendris earned his B.S. and M.S. degrees at Columbia University, where he held a New York State scholarship, and his M.A. and Ph.D. degrees at Northwestern University in Evanston, Illinois. He also earned two diplomas with *Mention très Honorable* at the Université de Paris (en Sorbonne), Faculté des Lettres, École Supérieure de Préparation et de Perfectionnement des Professeurs de Français à l'Etranger, and at the Institut de Phonétique, Paris.

He has taught French at the College of the University of Chicago as visiting summer lecturer and at Northwestern University, where he held a teaching assistantship and tutorial fellowship for four years. He has also taught at Colby College, Duke University, Rutgers—The State University of New Jersey, and the State University of New York at Albany. He was chairman of the Foreign Languages Department at Farmingdale High School, Farmingdale, New York, where he was also a teacher of French and Spanish.

He is the author of numerous school and college books, workbooks, and other language guides. Among his most popular works are *501 French Verbs* and *501 Spanish Verbs Fully Conjugated in All the Tenses* (both books in Sixth Edition), *French Now! Level 1, Write It in French, Write It in Spanish* (both composition workbooks with answers), *Master the Basics: French* (Second Edition), *Master the Basics: Spanish* (Second Edition), *Pronounce It Perfectly in French* (with three CDs of listening comprehension including tests with answers), *Spanish Now! Level 2* (Second Edition), and many others, all published by Barron's. He is listed in *Contemporary Authors* and in the *Directory of American Scholars*.

Dr. Theodore Kendris earned his B.A. degree in modern languages at Union College, Schenectady, New York, where he received the Thomas J. Judson Memorial Award for modern language study. He went on to earn his M.A. degree in French language and literature at Northwestern University, Evanston, Illinois, where he held a teaching assistantship. He earned his Ph.D. degree in French literature at Université Laval in Quebec City, where he studied the Middle Ages and Renaissance. While at Université Laval he taught French writing skills as *chargé de cours* in the French as a Second Language program and, in 1997, he was awarded a doctoral scholarship by the Fondation de l'Université Laval. He has also taught in the Department of English and Foreign Languages at the University of St. Francis in Joliet, Illinois, as well as at the Hazleton campus of Penn State University.

A Guide to Pronunciation of French Sounds

Pure Vowel Sounds

IPA Phonetic Symbol	pronounced as in the French word	English word*
a	la	similar to the vowel sound in Tom
a	pas	father, Ah!
e	été	ate
ε	ère	egg
i	ici	see
o	hôtel	over
ɔ	donne	bun
u	ou	too
œ	leur	urgent
ø	deux	pudding
y	tu	cute
ə	le	ago

Nasal Vowel Sounds

ɶ̃	un	similar to sung
ɔ̃	bon	similar to song
ɛ̃	vin	similar to sang
ã	blanc	similar to throng

Semi-consonant Sounds

w	oui	west
ɥ	huit	you eat
j	fille, yeux	yes, see ya later

Consonant Sounds

IPA Phonetic Symbol	pronounced as in the French word	English word*
b	bonne	bun
d	dans	done
f	fou	first, pharmacy
g	gare	go
ʒ	je	measure
ʃ	chose	shake
k	café, qui	cap, key
l	le	let
m	mette	met
n	nette	net
ɲ	montagne	canyon, onion, union
ŋ	le camping	camping, sleeping
p	père	pear
r	rose	rose
s	silence, garçon	see, sit
t	te	lot
v	vous	vine
z	zèbre	zebra

*English words contain sounds that only approximate French sounds.

NOTE: The French letter **c** in front of a, o, or u is pronounced as **k**; in front of e, i, or y, it is pronounced as **s**. The French letter **g** in front of a, o, or u is pronounced hard as in **go**; in front of e, i, or y, it is pronounced as in **je** and the English word **measure**.

Abbreviations

adj.	adjective	*fam.*	familiar	*par.*	paragraph
adv.	adverb	*i.e.*	that is, that is to say	*part.*	participle
advl.	adverbial	*illus.*	illustration	*per.*	personal
art.	article	*indef.*	indefinite	*pers.*	person
conj.	conjunction	*indic.*	indicative	*pl.*	plural
def.	definite	*indir.*	indirect	*poss.*	possessive
dem.	demonstrative	*inf.*	infinitive	*prep.*	preposition
dir.	direct	*interj.*	interjection	*pres.*	present
disj.	disjunctive	*interrog.*	interrogative	*pron.*	pronoun
e.g.	for example	*m.* or *masc.*	masculine	*refl.*	reflexive
etc.	et cetera, and so on	*n.*	noun	*rel.*	relative
exclam.	exclamation	*no.*	number	*s.* or *sing.*	singular
expr.	expression	*obj.*	object	*subj.*	subject
f. or *fem.*	feminine	*p.*	page	*v.*	verb

Introduction

This fourth edition of *French the Easy Way* is for you if you are studying beginning French in school or in a college course. You can use this book as a supplement to the book you are using in the classroom for a fresh review because it has the advantages of a textbook and workbook all in one.

This book is also intended for self-instruction if you are an adult studying French on your own at home or with a private tutor. It is very suitable for review if you have already studied French and would like to refresh your memory of the basics of the language. Answers to the exercises, review tests, and major tests are in the back pages of the book so you can check your work. The book is strong in a commonsense approach to the study of French. It contains all essential basic elements of the language. Many of the stories and dialogues tell of the adventures of an imaginary French family: Claire and François Paquet, their two children, Janine and Pierre, and their dog, Coco.

This new edition focuses on French for communication. The primary objective is to help you communicate freely in French by providing exercises that encourage you to participate in speaking, listening, reading, and writing.

The exercises in this edition focus on practical situations, such as meeting people, socializing, providing and obtaining information, talking about what you see in pictures, expressing personal feelings, asking for help, giving advice, helping others, becoming familiar with announcements and advertisements, shopping, sports, educational and cultural topics, and much more.

The traditional exercises in this book provide you with a solid foundation in the basic structures of the French language, including a thorough presentation of a wide range of vocabulary, idiomatic expressions, grammar, and verbs in the present tense and in the past (le passé composé), the two most important and commonly used tenses in beginning French.

Other helpful features include verb tables, in the back pages of the book, for easy and quick reference, and a section on definitions of basic grammatical terms with examples to help you achieve a better understanding of the different parts of speech and elements of sentence structure. There is also a comprehensive index.

The language content in this book meets the minimum standards and sequence of an introductory course of study in French.

We want to thank Françoise Lapouille, friend and colleague of Christopher Kendris. Mme Lapouille was born and educated in France and has been a teacher of French for many years. She holds the degree of *Licence ès Lettres* from the Université de Paris (La Sorbonne). She read the draft of this book to make certain that the French is *juste et comme il faut*, correct and as it should be.

We hope you find the stories, dialogues, situations for speaking and writing, artwork, photographs, the variety of exercises, word games, and puzzles interesting and fun to do.

The Guide to Pronunciation of French Sounds on the preceding page contains French and English words as examples to illustrate sounds that are approximately like those in acceptable standard speech. It is merely a guide. If you want to improve your fluency and pronunciation of French, we recommend *Pronounce It Perfectly in French*, Second Edition, also issued by Barron's Educational Series, Inc. The book comes with three CDs. You can listen to the beautiful French language spoken by professional French radio commentators and imitate what you hear during the pauses.

Travaillez bien!/Work well! **Et bon courage!**/And good luck!

Christopher Kendris, Ph.D.
Theodore Kendris, Ph.D.

How to Use This Book

1. First, become familiar with the entire book from cover to cover. Start with the table of contents, and read it to get an idea of what is in the book. Turn the pages, and look at the pictures, stories, and exercises. Take a close look at the vocabulary in the back of the book, and browse through the Answer Key.

2. The preliminary lessons on pages 1 to 17 are very important because you are introduced to certain basic elements of the French language. Use the vocabulary beginning on page 400.

3. Each unit contains a story or dialogue. First, study the vocabulary at the end of each story. Take a 3 × 5 card or an envelope, and try to cover the English. Read the French words on the vocabulary list aloud. Move the card down so you can see the English meaning. Then move the card up to cover the English. Try to recall the English for the French words. Do this as often as you need to, until you can associate the French word with the English word. In your mind try to see a picture of what the word represents. Then do the opposite. Try to recall the French for the English.

4. You can also use a stack of 3 × 5 blank cards. On one side of a card write the French word, and on the other side write the English equivalent. Then test yourself. Look at the French word, and try to remember the English meaning. Then flip the card to see the English meaning. You can also look at the English word on one side of the card and try to recall the French, flipping the card as often as you need to, until you know the word in both languages. Carry around with you about 10 cards of words, and when you have a few minutes, for example, while waiting for a bus or while on a bus, study the words on both sides of the cards

5. Do all the exercises in order from the beginning to the end of the book. Use a pencil so you can erase mistakes. Do not skip around here and there because the language progresses. Then check your answers in the Answer Key. If you have any wrong answers, draw a line through your answer, and write it correctly. Then, after you have studied your errors, erase all your answers on a page, and do the exercises again until your answers are correct. That is how you make progress.

Remember that you will get out of this book whatever you put into it. Work steadily, and follow our suggestions.

Bonne chance!/Good luck!

Suggestions for Independent Study

1. Speaking Proficiency

A. Read aloud the stories and model sentences that introduce the exercises.

B. If you are alone, say aloud not only the role you are playing in the situational dialogues but also what the other persons in the dialogues are saying.

C. The dialogues provide material for dramatizations. You and your tutor or a friend or relative can switch roles to practice speaking another person's lines.

D. If you have a cassette recorder at home, make a recording of what you say in French. Play it back and listen to yourself. Ask your tutor or a relative or friend who pronounces French well to listen to it to help you improve your pronunciation.

2. Reading and Writing Proficiency

A. There is a major review test at the end of every five work units. There are five major tests in all.

B. Do not skip the review tests. You must take them because they will help you determine your strengths and weaknesses. Answers to the five major tests are also in the back pages of the book.

3. Repetition

A. You can strive for proficiency in speaking, reading, and writing by repeating words and statements in French as often as possible.

B. When you check your written work in the Answers section, repeat the correct words or statements aloud, then write them. Repeat them again, aloud, while you write them a second and third time.

Leçons Préliminaires
Preliminary Lessons

(Answer Key, pp. 426–427)

I. La famille Paquet: Présentation

Salut! *Hi!*

Nous sommes la famille Paquet.

We are the Paquet family.

Je suis Claire Paquet. Je suis la mère. J'ai un bon mari

I am Claire Paquet. I am the mother. I have a good husband.

Je suis François Paquet. Je suis le père. J'ai une bonne épouse.

I am François Paquet. I am the father. I have a good wife.

Je suis Janine. Je suis la fille. J'ai un bon frère.

I am Janine. I am the daughter. I have a good brother.

Je suis Pierre. Je suis le fils. J'ai une bonne soeur.

I am Pierre. I am the son. I have a good sister.

Je suis Coco. Je suis le chien. J'ai une bonne famille.

I am Coco. I am the dog. I have a good family.

Present Tense		Present Tense	
être *(to be)*		**avoir** *(to have)*	
je suis	I am	**j'ai**	I have
tu es	you are	**tu as**	you have
il est	he *or* it is	**il a**	he *or* it has
elle est	she *or* it is	**elle a**	she *or* it has
nous sommes	we are	**nous avons**	we have
vous êtes	you are	**vous avez**	you have
ils sont	they are	**ils ont**	they have
elles sont	they are	**elles ont**	they have

Exercises

I. Fill in the missing French words on the blank lines. Refer to the preceding page if you have to.

1. Je suis François Paquet. Je suis _____ _____. J'ai _____

    _____ _____.

2. Je suis Claire Paquet. Je _____ la _____. J' _____ un

    _____ mari.

3. Je suis Pierre. Je _____ le fils. J'ai _____ bonne _____.

4. Je suis Janine. Je suis _____ _____. J'ai un _____ frère.

5. Je suis Coco. Je _____ _____ chien. _____ une bonne

    _____.

II. Match the following.

1. I am the daughter.   _____ Je suis le fils.

2. I am the father.   _____ Je suis la mère.

3. I am the son.   _____ Je suis la fille.

4. I am the mother.   _____ Je suis le chien.

5. I am the dog.   _____ Je suis le père.

III. And match these.

1. the son   _____ la mère

2. the father   _____ la fille

3. the mother   _____ le père

4. the dog   _____ le fils

5. the daughter   _____ le chien

IV. And these.

1. a good sister   _____ un bon mari

2. a good family   _____ un bon frère

3. a good husband   _____ une bonne épouse

4. a good brother   _____ une bonne soeur

5. a good wife   _____ une bonne famille

V. Qui est-ce? (Who is it?) On the blank line write in French the name of the person described. **C'est . . .** (It's . . .)

1. Je suis la fille. J'ai un bon frère.

    Qui est-ce? C'est_____.

2. Je suis la mère. J'ai un bon mari.

    Qui est-ce? C'est_____.

3. Je suis le père. J'ai une bonne épouse.

    Qui est-ce? C'est_____.

4. Je suis le chien. J'ai une bonne famille.

    Qui est-ce? C'est_____.

5. Je suis le fils. J'ai une bonne soeur.

    Qui est-ce? C'est_____.

VI. Choose the correct answer and write the letter on the blank line.

1. Janine est   (a) la mère.   (b) le père.   (c) la fille.   (d) le fils.   _____

2. Pierre est   (a) le père.   (b) la mère.   (c) la soeur.   (d) le frère.   _____

3. Claire Paquet est   (a) le père.   (b) la mère.   (c) la fille.   (d) le fils.   _____

4. Coco est   (a) le fils.   (b) la fille.   (c) la soeur.   (d) le chien.   _____

5. François Paquet est (a) le frère.   (b) le fils.   (c) le père.   (d) la mère.   _____

II. Choses (Things)

The pictures are arranged alphabetically by word.

	l'arbre	Est-ce un arbre?	Oui, c'est un arbre. Il est grand.
	le ballon	Est-ce un ballon?	Oui, c'est un ballon. Il est rond.
	la banane	Est-ce une orange? Est-ce une banane?	Non, ce n'est pas une orange. Oui, c'est une banane. Elle est bonne.
	la chaise	Est-ce une table? Est-ce une chaise?	Non, ce n'est pas une table. Oui, c'est une chaise. Elle est petite.

Exercises

I.   Fill in the missing words (adjectives). Refer to the statements next to the pictures on the previous page.

1. L'arbre est _____ .   3. La banane est _____ .

2. Le ballon est _____ .   4. La chaise est _____ .

II.   Choose the correct adjective. Refer to the statements on the previous page.

1. La chaise est   (a) petite.   (b) ronde.   (c) grande.   (d) bonne.   _____

2. La banane est   (a) ronde.   (b) grande.   (c) petite.   (d) bonne.   _____

3. Le ballon est   (a) rond.   (b) grand.   (c) bon.   (d) petit.   _____

4. L'arbre est   (a) grand.   (b) petit.   (c) rond.   (d) bon.   _____

III.   Match the following.

1. the chair   _____ la banane

2. the ball   _____ l'arbre

3. the tree   _____ la chaise

4. the banana   _____ le ballon

le chapeau   Est-ce un chapeau?   Oui, c'est un chapeau. Il est joli.

la commode   Est-ce une chaise?   Non, ce n'est pas une chaise.
                    Est-ce une commode?   Oui, c'est une commode. Elle est belle.

le crayon   Est-ce un stylo?   Non, ce n'est pas un stylo.
                    Est-ce un crayon?   Oui, c'est un crayon. Il est long.

la fleur   Est-ce une fleur?   Oui, c'est une fleur. Elle est jolie.

Exercises

I.   Fill in the missing words (adjectives). Refer to the statements next to the pictures above.

1. Le chapeau est _____ .   3. Le crayon est _____ .

2. La commode est _____ .   4. La fleur est _____ .

II. Match the following. Refer to the statements on the previous page.

1. the pencil   _____ la fleur

2. the hat   _____ le crayon

3. the flower   _____ la commode

4. the dresser   _____ le chapeau

III. Choose the correct adjective. Refer to the statements on the previous page.

1. Le chapeau est (a) joli.   (b) long.   (c) bon.   (d) petit.   _____

2. La commode est (a) belle. (b) ronde. (c) longue. (d) bonne.   _____

3. Le crayon est (a) joli.   (b) rond.   (c) bon.   (d) long.   _____

4. La fleur est (a) jolie. (b) ronde. (c) grande. (d) longue.   _____

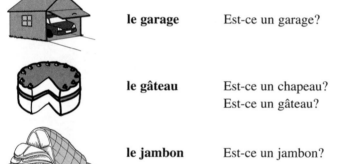

le garage	Est-ce un garage?	Oui, c'est un garage. Il est grand.
le gâteau	Est-ce un chapeau? Est-ce un gâteau?	Non, ce n'est pas un chapeau. Oui, c'est un gâteau. Il est délicieux.
le jambon	Est-ce un jambon?	Oui, c'est un jambon. Il est beau.
le journal	Est-ce un journal?	Oui, c'est un journal. Il est intéressant.

Exercises

I. Fill in the missing words (adjectives). Refer to the statements next to the pictures above.

1. Le garage est _____ .   3. Le jambon est _____ .

2. Le gâteau est _____ .   4. Le journal est _____ .

II. Choose the correct adjective. Refer to the statements above.

1. Le garage est (a) intéressant. (b) délicieux. (c) grand.   _____

2. Le gâteau est (a) long. (b) intéressant. (c) délicieux.   _____

3. Le jambon est (a) beau. (b) grand. (c) intéressant.   _____

4. Le journal est (a) rond. (b) intéressant. (c) beau.   _____

III. Fill in the missing words. Refer to the statements next to the pictures on the previous page.

1. Est-ce un garage? Oui _____ _____ _____ . Il _____ grand.

2. Est-ce un chapeau? Non, ce _____ _____ un chapeau. C'est _____ gâteau.

3. Est-ce un jambon? Oui, _____ un jambon. Il est _____ .

4. Est-ce un journal? Oui, _____ un journal. Il _____ intéressant.

une lampe	Est-ce une lampe?	Oui, c'est une lampe. Elle est splendide.
un lit	Est-ce une commode?	Non, ce n'est pas une commode.
	Est-ce un lit?	Oui, c'est un lit. Il est confortable.
une maison	Est-ce un garage?	Non, ce n'est pas un garage.
	Est-ce une maison?	Oui, c'est une maison. Elle est charmante.
un oeuf	Est-ce un ballon?	Non, ce n'est pas un ballon.
	Est-ce un oeuf?	Oui, c'est un oeuf. Il est blanc.

Exercises

I. Choose the correct adjective. Refer to the statements next to the pictures above.

1. Le lit est   (a) blanc.   (b) délicieux.   (c) intéressant.   (d) confortable.   _____

2. La lampe est   (a) confortable. (b) splendide.   (c) bonne.   (d) longue.   _____

3. La maison est   (a) délicieuse.   (b) bonne.   (c) charmante.   (d) ronde.   _____

4. L'oeuf est   (a) blanc.   (b) charmant.   (c) confortable.   (d) beau.   _____

II. Match the following.

1. a house   _____ un oeuf

2. a lamp   _____ un lit

3. a bed   _____ une maison

4. an egg   _____ une lampe

	un parapluie	Est-ce un parapluie?	Oui, c'est un parapluie. Il est ouvert.
	une pomme	Est-ce une banane? Est-ce une pomme?	Non, ce n'est pas une banane. Oui, c'est une pomme. Elle est magnifique.
	une robe	Est-ce un chapeau? Est-ce une robe?	Non, ce n'est pas un chapeau. Oui, c'est une robe. Elle est mignonne.
	un sandwich	Est-ce un gâteau? Est-ce un sandwich?	Non, ce n'est pas un gâteau. Oui, c'est un sandwich. Il est délicieux.

Exercises

I. Fill in the missing words (adjectives). Refer to the sentences next to the pictures above.

1. Le parapluie est _____ .   3. La robe est _____ .

2. La pomme est _____ .   4. Le sandwich est _____ .

II. Fill in the missing words. Refer to the sentences above.

1. Est-ce un parapluie? Oui, c'est _____ _____ . Il _____ ouvert.

2. Est-ce une banane? Non, ce _____ _____ une banane. C' _____ une pomme.

3. Est-ce un chapeau? Non, _____ _____ _____ un chapeau. C'est _____ robe.

4. Est-ce un sandwich? Oui, c'est _____ sandwich. Il est _____ .

	un stylo	Est-ce un crayon?	Non, ce n'est pas un crayon.
		Est-ce un stylo?	Oui, c'est un stylo. Il est long.
	un téléphone	Est-ce une radio?	Non, ce n'est pas une radio.
		Est-ce un téléphone?	Oui, c'est un téléphone. Il est noir.
	un téléviseur	Est-ce un téléviseur?	Oui, c'est un téléviseur. Il est beau.
	un ordinateur	Est-ce un ordinateur?	Oui, c'est un ordinateur. Il est grand.

Exercises

I.   Choose the correct adjective. Refer to the sentences next to the pictures above.

1.   Le stylo est   (a) blanc.   (b) délicieux.   (c) ouvert.   (d) long.   _____

2.   Le téléphone est   (a) confortable.   (b) joli.   (c) rond.   (d) noir.   _____

3.   Le téléviseur est   (a) délicieux.   (b) beau.   (c) charmant.   (d) confortable. _____

4.   L'ordinateur est   (a) long.   (b) grand.   (c) noir.   (d) délicieux.   _____

II.   Match the following.

1.   a television set   _____ un stylo

2.   a chair   _____ un téléphone

3.   a flower   _____ un téléviseur

4.   a pen   _____ un oeuf

5.   a telephone   _____ une chaise

6.   an egg   _____ une fleur

III. Personnes (People)

Que fait-il?	Que fait-elle?	Que font-ils?
(What is he doing?)	(What is she doing?)	(What are they doing?)

Le garçon boit du lait.   Que fait-il?   Il boit du lait.

La petite fille danse.   Que fait-elle?   Elle danse.

Le garçon lit un livre.   Que fait-il?   Il lit un livre.

La petite fille et le garçon courent.   Que font-ils?   Ils courent.

Exercises

I.   Fill in the missing words. Refer to the sentences next to the pictures above.

1. Le garçon boit du lait. Que fait-il? Il _____ du _____ .

2. La petite fille danse. Que fait-elle? Elle _____ .

3. Le garçon lit un livre. Que fait-il? Il lit _____ _____ .

4. La petite fille et le garçon courent. Que font-ils? Ils _____ .

II.   The following sentences are scrambled. **Write them in the correct word order.** Refer to the sentences next to the pictures above.

1. Le / lait / du / garçon / boit / _____ .

2. La / danse / jeune / fille / _____ .

3. Le / livre / un / garçon / lit / _____ .

4. La / fille / jeune / et / garçon / le / courent / _____ .

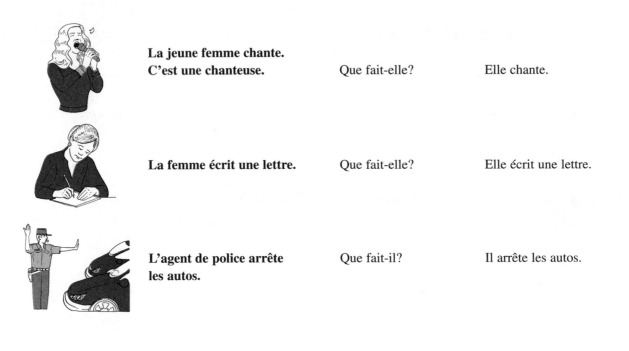

La jeune femme chante.
C'est une chanteuse.   Que fait-elle?   Elle chante.

La femme écrit une lettre.   Que fait-elle?   Elle écrit une lettre.

L'agent de police arrête
les autos.   Que fait-il?   Il arrête les autos.

Exercises

I. Fill in the missing words. Refer to the sentences next to the pictures above.

1. La jeune femme chante. Que fait-elle? Elle _____ .

2. La femme écrit une lettre. Que fait-elle? Elle _____ une lettre.

3. L'agent de police arrête les autos. Que fait-il? Il _____ les _____ .

II. Choose the correct answer. Refer to the sentences next to the pictures above.

1. La jeune femme   (a) arrête les autos.   (b) chante.   (c) écrit une lettre.   _____

2. La femme   (a) écrit une lettre.   (b) arrête les autos.   (c) danse.   _____

3. L'agent de police (a) boit du lait.   (b) lit un livre.   (c) arrête les autos.   _____

IV. L'École: la salle de classe (The School: the classroom)

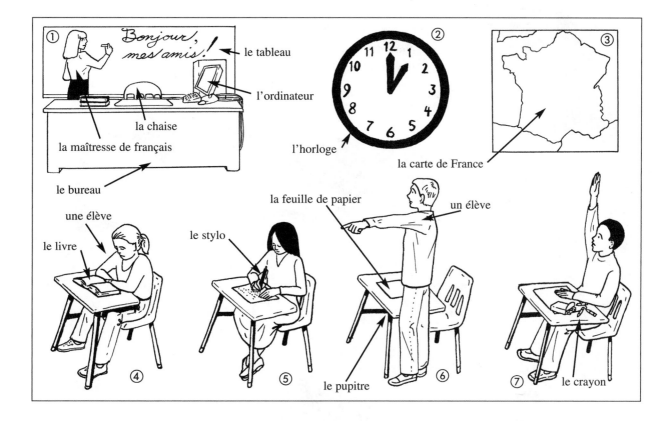

le tableau

l'ordinateur

la chaise

la maîtresse de français

le bureau

une élève

le livre

l'horloge

la carte de France

la feuille de papier

un élève

le stylo

le pupitre

le crayon

Exercises

I. Choose the sentence in Column A that corresponds to the picture and write it on the line next to the number of the picture in Column B. If you have to, look up the French words in the vocabulary at the end of the book.

Column A	Column B
Le garçon est debout.	1. _____
La jeune fille lit un livre.	2. _____
Il y a une carte de France sur le mur.	3. _____
Madame Duval est derrière le bureau.	4. _____
Le garçon lève la main.	5. _____
La jeune fille écrit une composition.	6. _____
Il est une heure.	7. _____

II.   Answer each question following the example in the box.

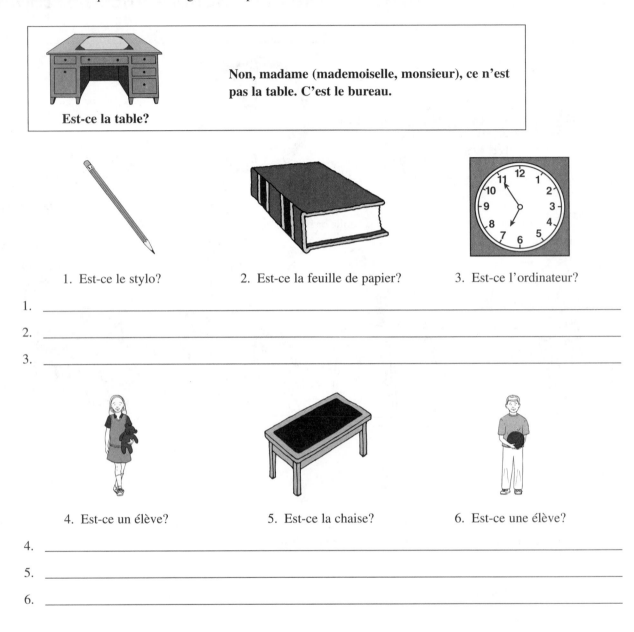

Non, madame (mademoiselle, monsieur), ce n'est pas la table. C'est le bureau.

Est-ce la table?

1. Est-ce le stylo?

2. Est-ce la feuille de papier?

3. Est-ce l'ordinateur?

1. _____

2. _____

3. _____

4. Est-ce un élève?

5. Est-ce la chaise?

6. Est-ce une élève?

4. _____

5. _____

6. _____

V. La Maison: la salle à manger
(The House: the dining room)

Exercises

I. Answer each question following the example in the box.

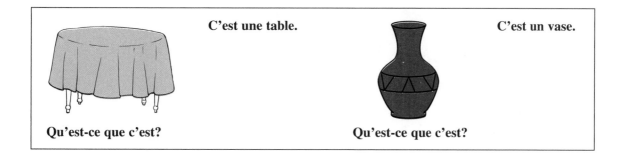

C'est une table.

C'est un vase.

Qu'est-ce que c'est?

Qu'est-ce que c'est?

1. Qu'est-ce que c'est?   2. Qu'est-ce que c'est?   3. Qu'est-ce que c'est?

4. Qu'est-ce que c'est?   5. Qu'est-ce que c'est?   6. Qu'est-ce que c'est?

1. _____

2. _____

3. _____

4. _____

5. _____

6. _____

II.   Fill in the missing letters of these French words.

1. UNE CHA__SE   6. UNE NAP__E

2. UNE AS__IET__E   7. UN VER__E

3. UN TAPI__   8. UN__ TAS__E

4. UNE FO__RCHET__E   9. UNE CU__LLER

5. UN COU__EAU   10. UN__ FL__U__

VI. La Ville: dans la rue (The City: in the street)

le métro

ENTRÉE

un immeuble

un autobus

un agent de police

un garçon

une voiture

un feu

une petite fille

une valise

le trottoir

une dame

le passage clouté

un homme

un petit chien

un petit garçon

—la rue—

le trottoir

Exercises

I. Answer each question following the example in the box.

C'est une dame.

C'est un homme.

Qui est-ce?

Qui est-ce?

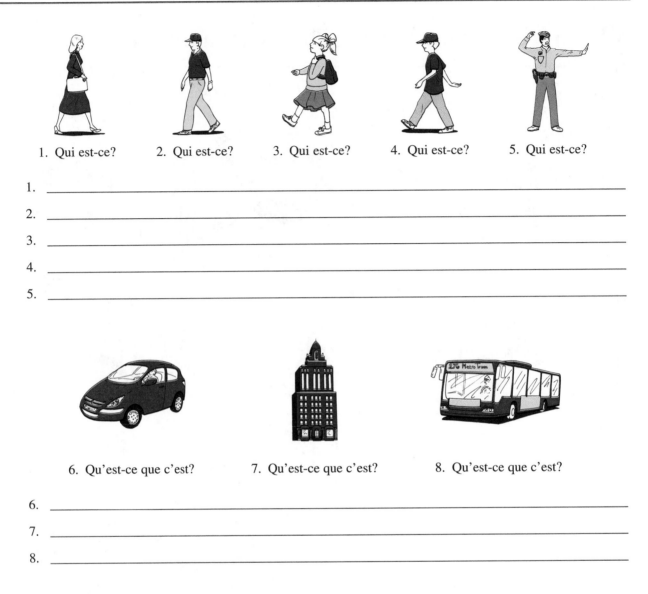

1. Qui est-ce?   2. Qui est-ce?   3. Qui est-ce?   4. Qui est-ce?   5. Qui est-ce?

1. _____

2. _____

3. _____

4. _____

5. _____

6. Qu'est-ce que c'est?   7. Qu'est-ce que c'est?   8. Qu'est-ce que c'est?

6. _____

7. _____

8. _____

II. Fill in the missing letters of these French words.

1. UN__   VA__IS__

2. UN PETI__   CH__EN

3. L__   TROT__OI__

4. LE MÉT__O

VII. Summary of two very common irregular verbs: avoir and être in the present tense, affirmative, and negative.

For speaking practice, say aloud the verb forms, with the subject pronouns, of **avoir** and **être** in the present tense, affirmative, and negative.

avoir (to have)

affirmative		negative	
j'ai	I have	**je n'ai pas**	I don't have
tu as	you have (*familiar*)	**tu n'as pas**	you don't have
il a	he *or* it has	**il n'a pas**	he *or* it doesn't have
elle a	she *or* it has	**elle n'a pas**	she *or* it doesn't have
nous avons	we have	**nous n'avons pas**	we don't have
vous avez	you have	**vous n'avez pas**	you don't have
ils ont	they have	**ils n'ont pas**	they don't have
elles ont	they have	**elles n'ont pas**	they don't have

être (to be)

affirmative		negative	
je suis	I am	**je ne suis pas**	I am not
tu es	you are (*familiar*)	**tu n'es pas**	you are not
il est	he *or* it is	**il n'est pas**	he *or* it isn't
elle est	she *or* it is	**elle n'est pas**	she *or* it isn't
nous sommes	we are	**nous ne sommes pas**	we are not
vous êtes	you are	**vous n'êtes pas**	you are not
ils sont	they are	**ils ne sont pas**	they are not
elles sont	they are	**elles ne sont pas**	they are not

Note that the subject pronoun **vous** is singular or plural. Use it when speaking to an adult you do not know or, if you do know the person, use it for courtesy, politeness, and respect. Examples:

Singular

Vous êtes Monsieur Paquet?
You are Mr. Paquet?

Plural

Vous êtes Monsieur et Madame Paquet?
You are Mr. and Mrs. Paquet?

Note also that the subject **tu**, which also means *you*, is used in the singular when speaking to a child, a relative, a friend, or an animal. The plural of **tu** is **vous**. Examples:

Singular

Tu es Janine? Tu es Pierre?
You are Janine? You are Pierre?

Plural

Vous êtes Janine et Pierre?
You are Janine and Pierre?

Structures and Verbs

Saint-Tropez. French city on the Mediterranean Sea.

The Noun and the Definite and Indefinite Articles (Singular)

Le chapeau échappé

Have you ever looked high and low for something you lost?

Madame Paquet cherche dans l'armoire, Janine cherche dans la commode, et Pierre cherche sous le lit.

Monsieur Paquet cherche son chapeau. Madame Paquet cherche le chapeau dans l'armoire. Janine cherche dans la commode, et Pierre cherche sous le lit. Le chien est sous le lit.

Monsieur Paquet:	Où est mon chapeau?
Janine:	Je cherche dans la commode, papa. Tiens! J'ai trouvé mon téléphone portable.
Pierre:	Nous cherchons partout, papa. Je cherche sous le lit maintenant. Hé! J'ai trouvé mon iPod!
Madame Paquet:	Je cherche aussi, François. Je cherche dans l'armoire. Oh! Je suis fatiguée de chercher le chapeau!
Monsieur Paquet:	Je cherche sous la chaise maintenant. Cherchons dans la cuisine, dans le salon, dans la salle de bains, dans la cave, sous le lit, sous la commode, dans l'armoire, dans le garage. Partout dans la maison!
Janine:	Tiens! Papa! Coco mange le chapeau. Il est sous la commode maintenant!
Monsieur Paquet:	Ah, non! Quelle horreur!
	(Monsieur Paquet quitte la chambre vite.)
Madame Paquet:	Où vas-tu, François?
Monsieur Paquet:	Je vais en ville acheter un nouveau chapeau. Zut, alors!
Madame Paquet:	Attends, attends! Je vais avec toi. J'aimerais acheter une nouvelle robe.

Vocabulaire

acheter *v.*, to buy

aimer *v.*, to like, to love

l'armoire *n. f.*, the closet, the wardrobe

aussi *adv.*, also, too

avec *prep.*, with

la cave *n.*, the cellar

la chaise *n.*, the chair

la chambre *n.*, the room

le chapeau *n.*, the hat

chercher *v.*, to look for, to search for

le chien *m.*, **la chienne** *f.*, *n.*, the dog

la commode *n.*, the dresser, the chest of drawers

la cuisine *n.*, the kitchen

dans *prep.*, in

de *prep.*, of

échappé *m.*, **échappée** *f.*, *adj.* escaped

elle *pron.*, she, it

en *prep.*, in, into

et *conj.*, and

être *v.*, to be

la famille *n.*, the family

fatigué *m.*, **fatiguée** *f.*, *adj*, tired

la fille *n.*, the daughter

le fils *n.*, the son

le garage *n.*, the garage

l'horreur *n. f.*, the horror

il *pron.*, he, it

iPod *m.*, iPod

je *pron.*, I

le *m.*, **la** *f.*, *def. art.*, the

le lit *n.*, the bed

madame *n.*, Mrs., madam

maintenant *adv.*, now

la maison *n.*, the house

manger *v.*, to eat

la mère *n.*, the mother

mon *m.*, **ma** *f.*, *poss. adj.*, my

monsieur *n.*, Mr., sir

nous *pron.*, we, us

nouveau *m.*, **nouvelle** *f.*, *adj.*, new

où *adv.*, where

partout *adv.*, everywhere

le père *n.*, the father

petit *m.*, **petite** *f.*, *adj.*, small

placard *n.m.*, closet

quel *m.*, **quelle** *f.*, *adj.*, what

qui *pron.*, who

quitter *v.*, to leave

la robe *n.*, the dress

la salle de bains *n.*, the bathroom

le salon *n.*, the living room

son *m.*, **sa** *f.*, *poss. adj.*, his, her

sous *prep.*, under

le téléphone portable *n.*, cell phone

tiens! *exclam.*, look!

toi *pron.*, you

un *m.*, **une** *f.*, *indef. art.*, a, an

la ville *n.*, the town, the city

vite *adv.*, quickly

le vocabulaire *n.*, the vocabulary

zut alors! *exclam.*, darn it!

Verb forms used in this dialogue:

j'aimerais I'd like, I'd love
attends wait
je cherche I look (for), I am looking (for)
il cherche, elle cherche he is looking (for), she is looking (for)

qui cherche who is looking (for)
nous cherchons we are looking (for)
cherchons let's look (for)
est is
il est he is, it is
il mange he eats, he is eating

il quitte he leaves, he is leaving
J'ai trouvé ... I found ...
je suis I am
je vais I am going
vas-tu? are you going?

Exercises

Review the dialogue and vocabulary before starting these exercises.

I. **Choose the correct answer based on the dialogue in this unit.**

1. Monsieur Paquet cherche
   (a) dans la commode.   (b) sous le lit.   (c) le chapeau.   (d) dans l'armoire.   _____

2. Janine cherche
   (a) sous le lit.   (b) dans le salon.   (c) sous la commode.   (d) dans la commode.   _____

3. Pierre cherche
   (a) sous la chaise.   (b) dans le garage.   (c) dans la salle de bains.   (d) sous le lit.   _____

4. Le chapeau est
   (a) dans la commode.   (b) sous la commode.   (c) sous le lit.   (d) dans la cuisine.   _____

5. Coco mange le chapeau sous
   (a) le lit.   (b) la chaise.   (c) l'armoire.   (d) la commode.   _____

II. Answer the following questions in complete sentences.

Model: Qui cherche sous le lit?   **Answer: Pierre cherche sous le lit.**
    (Who is searching under the bed?)   (Pierre is searching under the bed.)

1. Qui cherche dans la commode? _____

2. Qui cherche dans l'armoire? _____

3. Qui cherche sous la chaise? _____

III. Answer the following questions in complete sentences.

Model: Qui est Monsieur Paquet?   **Answer: Monsieur Paquet est le père.**
    (Who is Mr. Paquet?)   (Mr. Paquet is the father.)

1. Qui est Madame Paquet? _____

2. Qui est Janine? _____

3. Qui est Pierre? _____

4. Qui est Coco? _____

IV. Un acrostiche (an acrostic). Complete the French words in the squares across.

1. definite article (*fem. sing.*)

2. and

3. to search, to look for

4. horror

5. closet

6. father

7. she

8. to love, to like

9. indefinite article (*masc. sing.*)

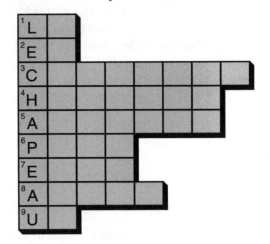

Structures de la Langue

A. The definite articles

MASCULINE NOUNS			
le père	the father	**l'homme**	the man
le garçon	the boy	**l'ami**	the friend (boy)
le frère	the brother	**le fils**	the son

FEMININE NOUNS			
la mère	the mother	**la femme**	the woman, wife
la jeune fille	the girl	**l'amie**	the friend (girl)
la soeur	the sister	**la fille**	the daughter

Rules and observations:

1. Nouns are classified by gender, which means that they are either masculine or feminine. A noun is a word that refers to a person, thing, place, or quality; *e.g.*, **la mère, la chaise, le salon, la beauté** (beauty).

2. Nouns denoting persons of the male sex are naturally of the masculine gender.

3. Nouns denoting persons of the female sex are naturally of the feminine gender.

4. Animals that are male or female are naturally of the masculine or feminine gender; *e.g.*, **le chat, la chatte** (the cat).

5. Things are also either masculine or feminine, but there is no easy way to determine their gender. You must learn the gender of a noun when you learn the noun by putting **le** or **la** in front of it! **Le** is masculine, **la** is feminine.

6. Some nouns, whether masculine or feminine, take **l'** in front, if they begin with a vowel or a silent **h**. The **e** in **le** drops and the **a** in **la** drops. You're left with **l'**.

7. Some nouns are sometimes masculine, sometimes feminine, in which case the meaning changes; *e.g.,* **le livre** (the book), **la livre** (the pound)

8. To sum it up, French has three forms for the definite article in the singular: **le, la, l'**—they all mean **the**.

A FEW MORE COMMON MASCULINE NOUNS	
l'arbre the tree	**le fils** the son
le beurre the butter	**le garage** the garage
le café the coffee, the café	**le mari** the husband
le chapeau the hat	**le nom** the name
le chef the chief, the chef	**l'ordinateur** the computer
l'enfant the child (boy)	**le téléphone portable** the cell phone

A FEW MORE COMMON FEMININE NOUNS	
la bouche the mouth	**l'heure** the hour
la calculatrice the calculator	**la maison** the house
la campagne the countryside	**la montre** the watch
la chaise the chair	**la porte** the door
l'enfant the child (girl)	**la souris** the mouse
la famille the family	**la table** the table

Exercises

Review the preceding material before starting these exercises.

I. Use the appropriate definite article in the singular: **le, la,** or **l'.**

1. _____ garçon
2. _____ mère
3. _____ père
4. _____ jeune fille
5. _____ ami
6. _____ homme
7. _____ café
8. _____ chapeau
9. _____ enfant
10. _____ commode
11. _____ nom
12. _____ arbre
13. _____ lit
14. _____ porte
15. _____ amie

II. Word Hunt. Can you find these 10 words in French in this puzzle?

1. the woman

2. the man

3. the boy

4. the girl

5. the sister

6. the tree

7. the child

8. the brother

9. the book

10. the mother

L	A	M	L	E	L	I	V	R	E	P	L
O	L	E	G	A	R	Ç	O	N	F	G	A
J	H	I	L	A	M	È	R	E	A	E	S
A	U	O	I	L	H	O	M	M	E	E	O
L	A	J	E	U	N	E	F	I	L	L	E
E	B	L	E	F	R	È	R	E	A	E	U
L	E	J	O	U	R	L	A	I	R	O	R
A	L	A	F	E	M	M	E	M	B	O	Y
L	E	L	E	N	F	A	N	T	R	U	E
Z	Y	L	E	L	A	M	O	I	E	N	A

III. Substitute the word in parentheses for the noun in italics. Use the appropriate definite article. Then rewrite the sentence.

Model:	**Le livre est là-bas.**	**(femme)**	**La femme est là-bas.**
	(The book is over there.)		(The woman is over there.)

A. La *maison* est là-bas.   (The house is over there.)

1. (père) _____

2. (mère) _____

3. (garçon) _____

4. (jeune fille) _____

5. (ami) _____

Le professeur parle beaucoup.

B. Le *professeur* parle beaucoup.   (The professor talks a lot.)

1. (femme) _____

2. (homme) _____

3. (frère) _____

4. (soeur) _____

5. (famille) _____

C. La *porte* est ici.   (The door is here.)

1. (table) _____

2. (chapeau) _____

3. (maison) _____

4. (arbre) _____

5. (café) _____

IV. Write the answers to the question in complete French sentences. Use the noun in parentheses with the appropriate definite article: **le, la, l'**.

Question: Où est le chapeau?	Model answer: (salon) Le chapeau est dans le salon.
(Where is the hat?)	(The hat is in the living room.)

1. (cuisine) _____

2. (armoire) _____

3. (maison) _____

4. (commode) _____

5. (garage) _____

B. The indefinite articles

MASCULINE NOUNS		FEMININE NOUNS	
un père	a father	**une mère**	a mother
un garçon	a boy	**une jeune fille**	a girl
un frère	a brother	**une soeur**	a sister
un homme	a man	**une femme**	a woman
un ami	a friend (boy)	**une amie**	a friend (girl)
un parapluie	an umbrella	**une orange**	an orange

Rules and observations:

1. The indefinite article has two forms: **un** and **une**. The first is masculine and the second is feminine. Each means **a** or **an**. e.g., **un père**, **une mère**.

2. **Un** is used with a masculine noun whether it begins with a consonant, a vowel, or a silent **h**; e.g., **un garçon**, **un ami**, **un homme**.

3. **Une** is used with a feminine noun whether it begins with a consonant, a vowel, or a silent **h**; e.g., **une femme**, **une orange**, **une horreur**.

Exercises

Review the preceding material before starting these exercises.

I. Use the appropriate indefinite article in the singular: **un** or **une**.

1. _____ garçon   6. _____ homme   11. _____ arbre

2. _____ mère   7. _____ café   12. _____ orange

3. _____ père   8. _____ chat   13. _____ porte

4. _____ ami   9. _____ chatte   14. _____ famille

5. _____ amie   10. _____ nom   15. _____ parapluie

II.   Word Hunt. Can you find these five words in French in this puzzle?

1. a tree

2. an orange

3. a boy

4. an umbrella

5. a girl

U	N	E	J	E	U	N	E	F	I	L	L	E	A
N	E	F	I	L	M	O	A	U	V	O	U	S	S
A	R	B	E	A	U	N	G	A	R	Ç	O	N	S
R	O	U	G	E	P	L	U	S	E	R	S	T	U
B	L	U	N	P	A	R	A	P	L	U	I	E	R
R	J	O	I	N	D	R	E	E	T	R	E	S	E
E	U	N	E	O	R	A	N	G	E	U	N	A	N

III.   Substitute the word in parentheses for the noun in italics. Use the appropriate indefinite article. Then rewrite the sentence.

Model: Une *femme* cherche dans l'armoire.
(A woman is searching in the closet.)

Une femme cherche dans l'armoire.

A. Une *femme* cherche dans l'armoire.   (A *woman* is searching in the closet.)

1. (homme) _____

2. (garçon) _____

3. (fils) _____

4. (mère) _____

5. (père) _____

B. Un *homme* mange dans la cuisine.   (A *man* is eating in the kitchen.)

1. (femme) _____

2. (jeune fille) _____

3. (ami) _____

4. (chien) _____

5. (fille) _____

C. Une *femme* quitte la chambre.   (A *woman* is leaving the room.)

1. (homme) _____

2. (mère) _____

3. (père) _____

4. (garçon) _____

5. (jeune fille) _____

IV.   Comment dit-on en français…?   (How do you say in French…?)

Find the following statements in the dialogue at the beginning of this work unit and write them in French.

1. Mr. Paquet is looking for his hat. _____

2. The dog is under the bed. _____

3. We are searching everywhere. _____

4. I'm going downtown to buy a new hat. _____

5. Coco is eating the hat. _____

V.   Fill in the blanks with an appropriate singular definite or indefinite article.

Coco, _____ chien, est sous _____ commode. Madame Paquet, _____ mère, cherche dans
　　　　　　　1　　　　　　　　　　　　2　　　　　　　　　　　　　　　　3

_____ armoire. Janine cherche dans _____ commode, et Pierre cherche sous _____ lit. Madame
　　4　　　　　　　　　　　　　　　5　　　　　　　　　　　　　　　　　　　6

Paquet est fatiguée de chercher _____ chapeau. Monsieur Paquet, _____ père, va en ville acheter
　　　　　　　　　　　　　　　　7　　　　　　　　　　　　　　8

_____ nouveau chapeau et Madame Paquet va acheter _____ nouvelle robe.
　　9　　　　　　　　　　　　　　　　　　　　　　　10

VI. Où est mon passeport?   Proficiency in Speaking and Writing.

Situation: You and a friend have just visited the Centre Pompidou in Paris. While pausing for refreshment at a sidewalk café, you notice your passport is missing.

You are playing the role of *Toi*. Let's say your friend's name is Janine. You may use your own words and ideas or follow this guided dialogue. After you make your statements, write them on the lines. First, review the story in this work unit.

Janine:	**Qu'est-ce que tu cherches?**/*What are you looking for?*
Toi:	_____
	Where is my passport?
Janine:	**Tu cherches ton passeport?**
Toi:	_____
	Yes, I'm looking for my passport.
Janine:	**Je cherche sous la table.**
Toi:	_____
	*I'm looking under the chair. Here it is!/***Le voici!**

Centre Pompidou, Paris

WORK UNIT 2

The Noun and the Definite and Indefinite Articles (Plural)

Vive le quatorze juillet!

In this scene, Claire and François Paquet are with their friends from Martinique, Joséphine and Alphonse Banluc, who are living in Paris. They are all with their children at the Bois de Boulogne, a park near Paris, to celebrate **La Fête Nationale** on July 14.

Quel déjeuner!

Claire Paquet:	Venez, tout le monde. Venez! Nous pouvons déjeuner sur l'herbe maintenant. Nous allons commencer par la viande. Janine, as-tu les sandwichs?
Janine:	Les sandwichs? Quels sandwichs? Je n'ai pas les sandwichs. J'ai seulement les gâteaux et les petits fours glacés. C'est pour le dessert.
Claire Paquet:	Tu n'as pas les sandwichs? Bon, bon. Pierre, tu as apporté les sandwichs, j'espère.
Pierre:	Mais non! J'ai seulement les éclairs.
Claire Paquet:	François, tu as sûrement apporté la viande: le rosbif, le veau, le porc, le jambon, et le poulet.
François Paquet:	Mais non, ma chérie. J'ai apporté la glace.
Claire Paquet:	Joséphine, tu as sûrement apporté la viande, j'espère.
Joséphine Banluc:	Mais non. J'ai apporté un gâteau!
Claire Paquet:	Alphonse, tu as les saucisses et les saucissons, j'espère.
Alphonse Banluc:	Mais non, Claire. J'ai apporté un grand gâteau et les brioches au chocolat! C'est pour le dessert. J'ai apporté aussi une bouteille d'eau minérale pour notre santé.
Claire Paquet:	Quel déjeuner!
Tous les enfants:	C'est merveilleux! Nous aimons mieux les desserts!
Claire Paquet:	Eh, bien! C'est la Fête Nationale et, dans l'espirt de ce grand jour de fête, moi, je dis: Mangeons les brioches—et les gâteaux!

Vocabulaire

l'an *n.m.*, the year
apporter *v.*, to bring
bien *adv.*, well
le bois *n.*, the woods
bon *m.*, **bonne** *f.*, *adj.*, good
la bouteille *n.*, the bottle
la brioche *n.*, bread with a slightly sweet taste
ce *dem. adj.*, this
chéri *m.*, **chérie** *f.*, *adj.*, darling, dearest
le chocolat *n.*, the chocolate; **au chocolat** (with) chocolate; **un gâteau au chocolat** *n.*, a chocolate cake
commencer *v.*, to begin
déjeuner *v.*, to have lunch
le déjeuner *n.*, the lunch
le dessert *n.*, the dessert
dire *v.*, to say

l'eau *n. f.*, the water; **l'eau minérale** *n.*, mineral water
l'éclair *n. m.*, the eclair
eh bien! *exclam.*, oh, well!
espérer *v.*, to hope
l'espirt *n. m.*, the spirit
la femme *n.*, the wife
la fête *n.*, the holiday
le gâteau *n.*, the cake
la glace *n.*, the ice cream
glacé *m.*, **glacée** *f.*, *adj.*, glazed, frosted
l'herbe *n. f.*, the grass
le jambon *n.*, the ham
le jour *n.*, the day
juillet *n. m.*, July
les *def. art.*, *pl.*, the
mais non! *exclam.*, why no!
le mari *n.*, the husband
merveilleux *m.*, **merveilleuse** *f.*, *adj.*, marvelous, wonderful

mieux *adv.*, better
moi *pron.*, me
non *adv.*, no
ou *conj.*, or
oui *adv.*, yes
le parc *n.*, the park
la pâtisserie *n.*, the pastry
le petit four *n.*, the little cake
le porc *n.*, the pork
le poulet *n.*, the chicken
pour *prep.*, for
pouvoir *v.*, to be able
près (de) *adv.*, near (to)
quatorze *adj.*, fourteen
le quatorze juillet *n.*, July 14;
    La Fête Nationale the French national holiday
quel *m.*, **quelle** *f.*, *adj.*, what; **quel déjeuner!** what a lunch!
le rosbif *n.*, the roast beef

le sandwich *n.*, the sandwich
la santé *n.*, health
la saucisse *n.*, the sausage
le saucisson *n.*, bologna
seulement *adv.*, only
sur *prep.*, on
sûrement *adv.*, surely
tous *m.*, **toutes** *f.*, *adj.*, *pl.*, all, every
tous les enfants, all the children
tout *m.*, **toute** *f.*, *adj. sing.*, all, every
tout le monde everybody
tu *per. pron.*, you
le veau *n.*, the veal
venir *v.*, to come

la viande *n.*, the meat
vivre *v.*, to live

Verb forms used in this dialogue:
j'ai I have
je n'ai pas I do not have
tu as you have
tu n'as pas you do not have
as-tu? have you?
nous aimons we like, we love
nous allons we are going
j'ai apporté I brought
il a apporté, elle a apporté he
   brought, she brought

je dis I say
j'espère I hope
c'est it is
mangeons! let's eat!
nous pouvons we can, we are able
il va, elle va he goes, she goes (is
   going)
venez! come!
ils viennent (de) they come (from)
vive —! long live —!

Exercises

Review the dialogue and vocabulary before starting these exercises.

I.   Choose the correct answer based on the dialogue in this unit.

1.   Le déjeuner dans le parc est sur
     (a) les gâteaux.   (b) le dessert.   (c) les petits fours glacés.   (d) l'herbe.   _____

2.   Joséphine et Alphonse Banluc viennent
     (a) du Bois de Boulogne.   (b) de la Bastille.   (c) de la Martinique.   (d) du parc.   _____

3.   Le rosbif et le porc sont des
     (a) viandes.   (b) gâteaux.   (c) desserts.   (d) sandwichs.   _____

4.   Tout le monde a apporté
     (a) de la viande.   (b) des sandwichs.   (c) de l'eau minérale.   (d) de la pâtisserie.   _____

5.   Tout le monde mange
     (a) du gâteau et de la glace.   (b) des saucisses.   (c) du veau.   (d) des sandwichs.   _____

II.   **Oui ou Non?**

1.   François est le mari de Claire Paquet.   _____

2.   Joséphine est la femme de François.   _____

3.   La Fête Nationale est le 14 juillet.   _____

4.   Le Bois de Boulogne est un parc près de Paris.   _____

5.   La pâtisserie est un dessert.   _____

III. Mots croisés (crossword puzzle). Give the French words for the English clues.

Horizontalement

1. I
4. good (*masc. sing.*)
6. also
8. the (*pl.*)
9. definite article (*fem. sing.*)
11. the sandwiches
13. with
16. definite article (*masc. sing.*)
17. to bring
18. you (*fam. sing.*)
19. at, to
20. my (*fem. sing.*)
21. and

Verticalement

2. the ice cream
3. is
5. only
7. the cakes
10. year
12. on
14. she
15. for

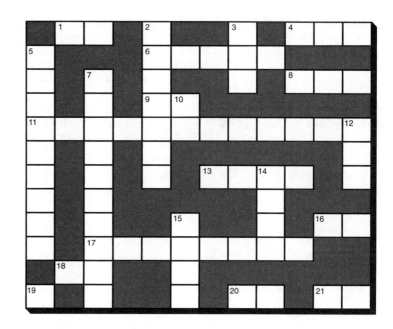

IV. Un acrostiche. Complete the French words in the squares across.

1. the cakes
2. and
3. dessert
4. eclair
5. day
6. to hope
7. indefinite article (*fem. sing.*)
8. no
9. spirit
10. roast beef

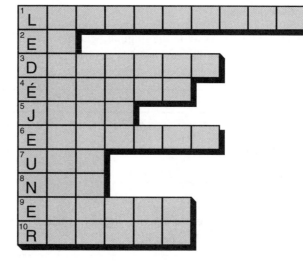

Structures de la Langue

A. Formation of regular plural of nouns

MASCULINE AND FEMININE NOUNS			
Singular		*Plural*	
la mère	the mother	**les mères**	the mothers
le père	the father	**les pères**	the fathers
la jeune fille	the girl	**les jeunes filles**	the girls
la fille	the daughter	**les filles**	the daughters
l'homme	the man	**les hommes**	the men
l'arbre	the tree	**les arbres**	the trees

Rules and observations:

1. To form the plural of a noun, whether masculine or feminine, ordinarily just add **s** to the singular form.

2. Change the definite article **the** from **le** to **les**, **la** to **les**, and **l'** to **les**.

3. In sum, French has only one form for the definite article in the plural: **les**.

B. Formation of irregular plural of nouns

Rules and observations:

1. Nouns that end in **-s**, **-x**, **-z** in the singular, whether masculine or feminine, do not normally change in the plural. They remain the same. See examples in the box below. You can tell the noun is singular or plural from **le** or **la**, or **les**.

Singular		*Plural*	
le fils	the son	**les fils**	the sons
la voix	the voice	**les voix**	the voices
le nez	the nose	**les nez**	the noses

2. Nouns that end in **-au**, **-eu**, **-ou** in the singular, whether masculine or feminine, ordinarily add **-x** to form the plural. See examples in the box below.

Singular		*Plural*	
le gâteau	the cake	**les gâteaux**	the cakes
le jeu	the game	**les jeux**	the games
le genou	the knee	**les genoux**	the knees

3. Nouns that end in **-al** or **-ail** in the singular ordinarily drop that ending and add **-aux** to form the plural. See examples in the box below.

Singular		Plural	
le journal	the newspaper	**les journaux**	the newspapers
le travail	the work	**les travaux**	the works

4. There are other irregular plurals of nouns. Study the examples in the box below.

Singular		Plural	
le ciel	the sky, heaven	**les cieux**	the skies, heavens
l'oeil	the eye	**les yeux**	the eyes
madame	Mrs., madam	**mesdames**	ladies
mademoiselle	miss	**mesdemoiselles**	misses
monsieur	mister, sir, gentleman	**messieurs**	sirs, gentlemen

Exercises

Review the preceding material before starting these exercises.

I. Write the plural form for each noun.

1. le garçon _____
2. le fils _____
3. le chapeau _____
4. le journal _____
5. le ciel _____

6. l'oeil _____
7. le père _____
8. la voix _____
9. la mère _____
10. le chat _____

II. Write the singular form for each noun.

1. les tables _____
2. les nez _____
3. les genoux _____
4. les voix _____
5. les yeux _____

6. les messieurs _____
7. les hommes _____
8. les jeunes filles _____
9. les enfants _____
10. les arbres _____

III. Change to the singular or to the plural, depending on which is given.

1. les pères _____

2. les hommes _____

3. l'eau _____

4. le fils _____

5. la table _____

6. les journaux _____

7. le cheval _____

8. l'oiseau _____

9. les élèves _____

10. le pays _____

C. Contraction of the definite article with à and de

à + **le** *changes to* **au**	de + **le** *changes to* **du**
à + **les** *changes to* **aux**	de + **les** *changes to* **des**

Rules and observations:

1. When the preposition **à** (*at, to*) is in front of the definite article **le** or **les**, it changes to the forms given in the box above.

2. When the preposition **de** (*from, of*) is in front of the definite article **le** or **les**, it changes to the forms given in the box above.

3. There is no contraction of **à** followed by **l'** or **la**. It remains **à l'** or **à la**.

4. There is no contraction of **de** followed by **l'** or **la**. It remains **de l'** or **de la**.

Janine va au café.

Madame Paquet va aux grands magasins.

Janine va à la gare.

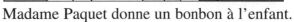

Madame Paquet donne un bonbon à l'enfant.

Pierre vient du restaurant.

Madame Paquet vient des grands magasins.

Pierre vient de l'école.

Janine vient de la bibliothèque.

Exercises

Review the preceding material before starting these exercises.

I.   Match the following.

1.   Janine is going to the station.   _____ Janine va au café.

2.   Pierre is coming from the restaurant.   _____ Madame Paquet va aux grands magasins.

3.   Mr. Paquet is coming from the department stores.   _____ Pierre vient de l'école.

4.   Janine is coming from the library.   _____ Monsieur Paquet vient des grands magasins.

5.   Pierre is coming from the school.   _____ Madame Paquet donne un bonbon à l'enfant.

6.   Mrs. Paquet is giving candy to the child.   _____ Pierre vient du restaurant.

7.   Janine is going to the café.   _____ Janine va à la gare.

8.   Mrs. Paquet is going to the department stores.   _____ Janine vient de la bibliothèque.

II.   Fill in the missing words. Choose **au**, **aux**, **à l'**, or **à la**.

1.   Janine va _____ café.   3.   Madame Paquet va _____ grands magasins.

2.   Pierre va _____ gare.   4.   Hélène va _____ école.

III.   Fill in the missing words. Choose **du**, **de l'**, **de la**, or **des**.

1.   Pierre vient _____ restaurant.   3.   Monique vient _____ bibliothèque.

2.   Janine vient _____ école.   4.   Marie vient _____ grands magasins.

D. Use of the definite article with **de** for possession

le livre **du** maître	the teacher's book
le livre **de la** maîtresse	the teacher's book
les livres **des** garçons	the boys' books
le livre **de** Janine	Janine's book
le livre **de l'**élève	the pupil's book

Rules and observations:

1.   The preposition **de** is used to express possession, as shown in the examples in the above box.

2.   The preposition **de** changes to **du** or **des**, as shown in the examples in the above box.

Exercises

Review the preceding material before starting the exercises.

I.   Match the following.

1. le parapluie de Pierre   _____ the boy's hat

2. les robes des jeunes filles   _____ the boys' dogs

3. les cheveux de Janine   _____ the girl's skirt

4. le chapeau du garçon   _____ the girls' dresses

5. le journal de Pierre   _____ the pupil's pencil

6. les chiens des garçons   _____ the pupils' pens

7. la jupe de la jeune fille   _____ Janine's eyes

8. les yeux de Janine   _____ Janine's hair

9. les stylos des élèves   _____ Pierre's newspaper

10. le crayon de l'élève   _____ Pierre's umbrella

II.   Fill in the missing words. Use **du**, **des**, **de**, **de l'**, or **de la**.

1. J'ai les crayons _____ jeunes filles.

2. J'ai le journal _____ femme.

3. J'ai les livres _____ Pierre.

4. J'ai les cahiers _____ garçon.

5. J'ai le stylo _____ élève.

6. J'ai le chapeau _____ homme.

7. J'ai le jeu _____ Janine.

8. J'ai les journaux _____ père.

9. J'ai les bonbons _____ enfant.

10. J'ai le parapluie _____ mère.

BRAVO! NOW GO BACK AND REVIEW!

III. Food and Drink.   Proficiency in Speaking and Writing.

First, review the story and vocabulary at the beginning of this work unit. After you read Situations A and B, say aloud the three short sentences you plan to write for each situation. Then write them on the lines below.

A. Situation: You and your friends are planning a picnic in the park. You call your friend to discuss what you will each bring. In three sentences tell your friend what food you would like to have at the picnic. Then ask your friend which of these he/she would like to bring. You may use your own ideas or ideas suggested by the following: **avoir, apporter, les sandwichs, les desserts, les éclairs, la glace, le gâteau, le poulet, la viande, le veau, le jambon, la saucisse.**

B. Situation: You are at a restaurant and your friend asks you why you like mineral water: **Pourquoi aimes-tu l'eau minérale?** Begin your response with: **Pour moi.** In three sentences tell why you like it. You may use your own ideas or ideas suggested by the following: **c'est bon, la santé, aimer mieux, le café.**

A. _____

_____

_____

B. _____

_____

_____

Avignon, France

The Noun and the Definite and Indefinite Articles (Conclusion)

La grande décision

Some people always know what to order in a restaurant and some don't. Have you ever done what Pierre does in this scene?

Avez-vous de la viande? Avez-vous des saucisses? Avez-vous du café?

Le Serveur:	Bonjour. Vous désirez?
Pierre:	Bonjour. Avez-vous de la viande?
Le Serveur:	Oui. Nous avons de la viande.
Pierre:	Avez-vous des saucisses?
Le Serveur:	Oui. Nous avons de belles saucisses.
Pierre:	Non, je ne veux pas de viande. Je ne veux pas de saucisses.
Le Serveur:	Nous avons du poisson.
Pierre:	Je ne veux pas de poisson … Avez-vous de l'eau minérale?
Le Serveur:	Oui. Nous avons de l'eau minérale.
Pierre:	Non, je ne veux pas d'eau minérale … Avez-vous du café?
Le Serveur:	Oui. Nous avons du café.
Pierre:	Non, je ne veux pas de café.
Le Serveur:	Aimez-vous les éclairs et les tartes?
Pierre:	Oui, oui. J'aime les éclairs et les tartes.
Le Serveur:	Je regrette. Nous n'avons ni éclairs, ni tartes.

Vocabulaire

aimer *v.*, to like, to love; **aimez-vous?** do you like? **j'aime** I like

avoir *v.*, to have; **avez-vous?** do you have? **nous avons** we have; **nous n'avons ni éclairs, ni tartes** we have neither eclairs nor tarts

beau *m.*, **belle** *f., adj.*, beautiful

bonjour *salutation,* good day

la décision *n.*, decision

désirer *v.*, to wish, to desire; **vous désirez?** you wish?

l'école *n. f.*, the school

grand *m.*, **grande** *f., adj.*, great, big

ni … ni *conj.*, neither … nor

parle *v.*, form of **parler** (to talk, to speak); **Pierre parle** Pierre is talking

le poisson *n.*, the fish

regretter *v.*, to regret, to be sorry; **je regrette** I'm sorry

le restaurant *n.*, restaurant

le serveur *n.*, server, waiter

la serveuse *n.*, server, waitress

veux *v.* form of **vouloir** (to want); **je ne veux pas** I do not want; **Pierre veut** Pierre wants

vous *pron.*, you

Exercises

Review the dialogue and vocabulary before starting these exercises.

I. Choose the correct answer based on the dialogue in this unit.

1. Pierre est dans
   (a) une école.   (b) un parc.   (c) la maison.   (d) un restaurant.   _____

2. Pierre parle avec
   (a) un ami.   (b) une amie.   (c) une femme.   (d) un serveur de restaurant.   _____

3. Pierre aime
   (a) la viande.   (b) le poisson.   (c) les éclairs et les tartes.   (d) les saucisses.   _____

II. Oui ou Non?

1. Pierre est dans un restaurant.   _____

2. Pierre veut du café.   _____

3. Pierre aime les éclairs et les tartes.   _____

III. Word Hunt.   Can you find these words in French in this puzzle? Circle them.

1. I like

2. some fish

3. we have

4. the meat

5. some coffee

6. sir

7. some water

D	U	C	A	F	É	D	E	S
U	M	O	N	S	I	E	U	R
P	D	U	O	D	E	L	A	O
O	C	A	U	J	A	I	M	E
I	D	C	S	P	O	I	D	U
S	E	L	A	V	O	S	N	E
S	L	A	V	I	A	N	D	E
O	E	D	O	E	L	A	E	A
N	A	E	N	A	U	E	A	E
D	U	L	S	O	M	O	N	S

Structures de la Langue

A. The Partitive

Essentially, the plural of the indefinite articles **un** and **une** is **des**. The partitive denotes a part of a whole; or in other words, *some*. It can be plural or singular in form.

1. SIMPLE AFFIRMATIVE	
J'ai **du** café.	I have *some* coffee.
J'ai **de la** viande.	I have *some* meat.
J'ai **de l'**eau.	I have *some* water.
J'ai **des** bonbons.	I have *some* candies.

2. SIMPLE NEGATIVE	
Je n'ai pas **de** café.	I don't have *any* coffee.
Je n'ai pas **de** viande.	I don't have *any* meat.
Je n'ai pas **d'**eau.	I don't have *any* water.
Je n'ai pas **de** bonbons.	I don't have *any* candies.

3. WITH AN ADJECTIVE	
J'ai **du** bon café.	I have *some* good coffee.
J'ai **de** jolis chapeaux.	I have *some* pretty hats.
J'ai **de** jolies jupes.	I have *some* pretty skirts.

Observations based on the examples given in the three boxes above:

1. Use **du**, **de la**, **de l'**, or **des** in front of the noun, depending on whether the noun is masculine or feminine, singular or plural. Study the examples in the first box above.

2. The form **du** is used in front of a masculine singular noun beginning with a consonant, as in **j'ai du café**. See the first box above.

3. The form **de la** is used in front of a feminine singular noun beginning with a consonant, as in **j'ai de la viande**. See the first box above.

4. The form **de l'** is used in front of a feminine or masculine singular noun beginning with a vowel or a silent *h*, as in **j'ai de l'eau**. See the first box above.

5. The form **des** is used in front of all plural nouns.

6. To express *any* in front of a noun, when the verb is negative, use **de** in front of the noun. The noun can be feminine or masculine, singular or plural, but it *must* begin with a consonant, as in **je n'ai pas de café**. See the second box.

7. To express *any* in front of a noun, when the verb is negative, use **d'** in front of the noun. The noun can be feminine or masculine, singular or plural, but it *must* begin with a vowel or silent *h*, as in **je n'ai pas d'eau**. See the second box.

8. When the noun is preceded by an adjective, use **de**, as in **j'ai de jolis chapeaux**. See the third box.

9. When the noun is preceded by an adverb or noun of quantity or measure, use **de**, as in **j'ai beaucoup de choses**/I have many things.

10. When the noun is modified by another noun, use **de**, as in **une école de filles** / a girls' school.

11. The partitive is not used with **sans** or **ne ... ni ... ni**.

    Examples: Je quitte la maison **sans argent**.
                      (I'm leaving the house *without any money*.)

                      Nous **n'**avons **ni** éclairs, **ni** tartes.
                      (We have *neither* eclairs *nor* tarts.)

Exercises

Review the preceding material before starting these exercises.

I.   Answer the following questions in the affirmative.

Model:	**Avez-vous du café?**	**Answer:**	**Oui, j'ai du café.**
	(Do you have any coffee?)		(Yes, I have some coffee.)

1. Avez-vous du pain? _____

2. Avez-vous de la viande? _____

3. Avez-vous de l'eau? _____

4. Avez-vous des bonbons? _____

5. Avez-vous du beurre? _____

Avez-vous des bonbons?

II.   Answer the following questions in the negative.

Model: Avez-vous du café?   **Answer: Non, je n'ai pas de café.**
            (Have you any coffee?)   (No, I haven't any coffee.)

1.   Avez-vous du café? _____

2.   Avez-vous de la viande? _____

3.   Avez-vous de l'eau? _____

4.   Avez-vous des bonbons? _____

5.   Avez-vous du beurre? _____

III.   Answer the following questions in the affirmative.

Model: Avez-vous du bon café?   **Answer: Oui, j'ai du bon café.**
            (Do you have [any] good coffee?)   (Yes, I have [some] good coffee.)

1.   Avez-vous du bon café? _____

2.   Avez-vous de jolis chapeaux? _____

3.   Avez-vous de jolies jupes? _____

4.   Avez-vous du bon vin? _____

5.   Avez-vous de jolies cravates? _____

IV.   Answer the following questions in the negative.

Model: Avez-vous du bon café?   **Answer: Non, je n'ai pas de bon café.**
            (Do you have [any] good coffee?)   (No, I don't have any good coffee.)

1.   Avez-vous du bon café? _____

2.   Avez-vous de jolis chapeaux? _____

3.   Avez-vous de jolies jupes? _____

4.   Avez-vous du bon vin? _____

5.   Avez-vous de jolies cravates? _____

B. The definite article with parts of body and clothing

J'ai **les** mains sales.	My hands are dirty.
J'ai **les** yeux bruns.	My eyes are brown.
J'ai **les** cheveux noirs.	My hair is black.
J'ai **le** chapeau sur **la** tête.	I have my hat on my head.

Rule: Use the definite article instead of the possessive adjective when you know without a doubt who the possessor is.

Exercises

I.   Answer the following questions in the affirmative.

Model: **Avez-vous les mains sales?**	**Answer:** **Oui, j'ai les mains sales.**
(Are your hands dirty?)	(Yes, my hands are dirty.)

1. Avez-vous les mains sales? _____

2. Avez-vous le visage sale? _____

3. Avez-vous les pieds grands? _____

4. Avez-vous les yeux bruns? _____

5. Avez-vous les cheveux noirs? _____

II.   Answer the following questions in the negative.

Model: **Avez-vous les pieds grands?**	**Answer:** **Non, je n'ai pas les pieds grands.**
(Are your feet big?)	(No, my feet are not big.)

1. Avez-vous les pieds grands? _____

2. Avez-vous le visage sale? _____

3. Avez-vous les mains sales? _____

4. Avez-vous le chapeau sur la tête? _____

5. Avez-vous les cheveux noirs? _____

C. The definite article with parts of the day

Je vais à l'école **les** matins.	I go to school *in the* mornings.
Je joue **les** après-midi.	I play *in the* afternoons.
J'étudie **les** soirs.	I study *in the* evenings.

Rule: Use the definite article with parts of the day. It can also be used in the singular. In English it means *in the*.

Je vais à l'école le matin.

Je joue l'après-midi.

J'étudie le soir.

Exercises

I. Answer the following questions in the affirmative.

Model:	**Allez-vous à l'école les matins?**	**Answer:**	**Oui, je vais à l'école les matins.**
	(Do you go to school in the mornings?)		(Yes, I go to school in the mornings.)

1. Allez-vous à l'école les matins? _____

2. Allez-vous à la bibliothèque les après-midi? _____

3. Allez-vous au restaurant les soirs? _____

4. Allez-vous au parc les après-midi? _____

5. Allez-vous au café les soirs? _____

II.   Answer the following questions in the negative.

Model:	**Allez-vous au cinéma les soirs?** (Do you go to the movies in the evenings?)	**Answer:**	**Non, je ne vais pas au cinéma les soirs.** (No, I don't go to the movies in the evenings.)

1.   Allez-vous au cinéma les soirs? _____

2.   Allez-vous à l'école les matins? _____

3.   Allez-vous à la bibliothèque les soirs? _____

D. Omission of the definite article with **parler, de,** and **en**

Janine est **de** France.	Elle **parle** français.	Elle **prononce** bien **le français**.
Janine is from France.	She speaks French.	She pronounces French well.

Julie répond **en** français dans la classe **de** français.
Julie answers in French in the French class.

Rules and observations:

1.   Do not use the definite article in front of the name of a language if the verb **parler** directly precedes it.

2.   Do not use the definite article in front of the name of a language if the preposition **de** or **en** directly precedes it.

3.   **De** indicates *concerned with* in expressions such as the following:
     la classe de français (the French class), **la leçon de français** (the French lesson), **le professeur d'anglais** (the English teacher), **le maître de musique** (the music teacher).

4.   Change **de** to **d'** if the word that follows starts with a vowel or a silent *h*. Example: **le professeur d'anglais**.

E. Omission of the indefinite article with **cent** and **mille**

J'ai **cent dollars**.	I have *one hundred dollars*.
J'ai **mille dollars**.	I have *one thousand dollars*.

Rule: Do not use the indefinite article **un** or **une** in front of **cent** (100) or **mille** (1,000).

Exercises

Review the preceding material before starting these exercises.

I. Write two sentences using the word (language name) given in italics. Begin the first sentence with **il** (he) or **elle** (she) and use the verb **parle** (speaks). Begin the second sentence with the appropriate subject pronoun (**il** *or* **elle**) and use the verb **prononce** (pronounces) and the adverb **bien** (well).

Model:	**Pierre est de France.**	**You write:**	**Il parle français.**
	(Peter is from France.)		(He speaks French.)
			Il prononce bien le français.
			(He pronounces French well.)

1. Louis est de France.

   le français _____

2. María est d'Espagne.

   l'espagnol _____

3. Madame Belini est d'Italie.

   l'italien _____

4. Monsieur Armstrong est d'Angleterre.

   l'anglais _____

5. Hilda est d'Allemagne.

   l'allemand _____

II. Answer the following questions in the affirmative.

Model:	**Avez-vous cent dollars?**	**Answer:**	**Oui, j'ai cent dollars.**
	(Have you 100 dollars?)		(Yes, I have 100 dollars.)

1. Avez-vous cent dollars? _____

2. Avez-vous mille euros? _____

3. Avez-vous cent livres? _____

4. Avez-vous mille amis? _____

III. Complete with an appropriate selection: **le**, **la**, **l'**, or **les**. Use a dash (—) if no definite article is required.

Le maître de _____ musique à _____ école est aussi professeur de _____ français. Il parle _____
              1   2   3   4

français dans _____ classe de français, et il prononce bien _____ français. Il a _____ yeux bleus et
             5   6   7

_____ cheveux noirs.
  8

IV. Change the words in italics to either the singular or plural, depending on which is given.

Model:	J'ai le gâteau.	Answer:	J'ai les gâteaux.
	(I have the cake.)		(I have the cakes.)

1. J'ai *le sandwich*. _____

2. J'ai *l'éclair*. _____

3. J'ai *les saucisses*. _____

4. J'ai *un dollar*. _____

5. J'ai *des jupes*. _____

6. J'ai *le chapeau*. _____

7. J'ai *les desserts*. _____

8. J'ai *des gâteaux*. _____

V. Jeu de mots (Word game) Translate these 14 words into French to fill in the squares.

1. the newspapers
2. water
3. health
4. dress
5. children
6. on
7. works (*noun*)
8. afternoon
9. indefinite article (*fem. sing.*)
10. roast beef
11. tree
12. nose
13. head
14. evening

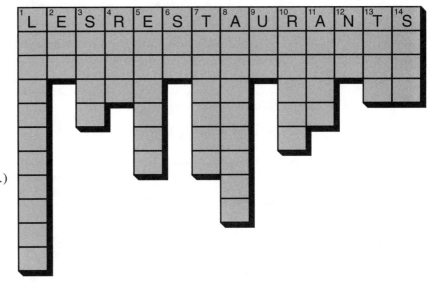

VI. Physical Characteristics. Proficiency in Writing.

Situation: You are filling in an application for a student visa to France. You are asked to write a short paragraph in French containing four or five sentences stating a few of your physical characteristics.

Before you begin, you may want to review this topic and the exercises in section **B** in this work unit.

You may use your own ideas and words or the following: *I have blue (brown, gray, green) eyes*/**J'ai les yeux bleus (bruns, gris, verts).** *I have black (brown, blond, red) hair*/**J'ai les cheveux noirs (bruns, blonds, roux).** *I have big (small) feet*/**J'ai les pieds grands (petits).** *I have a round (long) face*/**J'ai le visage rond (long).** *I have big (small) hands*/**J'ai les mains grandes (petites).**

Practice writing the paragraph here:

_____

_____

_____

_____

VII. Eating Out. Proficiency in Speaking and Writing.

Situation: You are in a small café-restaurant (**un bistro**) in Paris. In this guided dialogue, you are playing the role of *Vous*. You may address the waiter (**le serveur**) as **Monsieur**/*Sir*.

You may use your own words and ideas or those suggested below. After you say the words aloud, write them on the lines. Before you start you may want to review the dialogue and vocabulary at the beginning of this lesson. You may also want to use the vocabulary at the end of the book.

Le serveur: **Bonjour, madame (mademoiselle, monsieur). Vous désirez?**

Vous: _____

Respond with a greeting and ask: Have you any fish today?

Le serveur: **Oui, nous avons du poisson aujourd'hui.**

Vous: _____

Do you have any meat?

Le serveur: **Oui, nous avons du bifteck et du rosbif aux pommes frites**/*steak and roast beef with French fries.*

Vous: _____

Do you have any sausages?

Le serveur: **Oui, nous avons de belles saucisses.**

Vous: _____

No, sir. I'm sorry. I don't want any meat. I don't want any sausages.

Le serveur: **Vous désirez du poisson?**

Vous: _____

No, sir, I don't want any fish. I'm sorry.

Le serveur: **Vous désirez du café?**

Vous: _____

No, sir, I don't want any coffee.

Le serveur: **Aimez-vous les éclairs et les tartes?**

Vous: _____

Yes, yes. I like eclairs and tarts.

Le serveur: **Je regrette. Nous n'avons ni éclairs, ni tartes.**

VIII. Shopping.   Proficiency in Speaking and Writing.

Situation: You are in a pastry shop **(une pâtisserie)** in Paris. In this guided dialogue, you're playing the role of *Vous*. When you greet the clerk, use **Madame**.

You may use your own words and ideas or those suggested below. After you say the words aloud, write them on the lines. Say **J'aimerais** for *I would like*. Before you start, review the dialogue and vocabulary at the beginning of Work Units 2 and 3.

Madame: **Bonjour, madame (mademoiselle, monsieur). Vous désirez?**

Vous: _____

 I would like a big chocolate cake **(un grand gâteau au chocolat).**

Madame: **Et avec ceci?**/*And with this?*

Vous: _____

 I would like two eclairs and two apple tarts **(deux tartes aux pommes).**

Madame: **C'est tout?**

Vous: _____

 Yes, that's all, thank you.

Madame: **Vous pouvez payer à la caisse. Merci.** *(You may pay at the cashier's desk. Thank you.)*

IX.   Socializing.   Proficiency in Speaking and Writing.

Situation: You are at a party with five new foreign exchange students. Janine and Pierre Paquet are there. You are introducing them to the new students.

On the lines below, write three short statements in French about each of the new students. You may use your own words and ideas or those under the lines. First, you may need to review Exercise I under section **E** in this lesson.

1. _____

 Jacques is from France. He speaks French. He pronounces French well.

2. _____

 María is from Spain. She speaks Spanish. She pronounces Spanish well.

3. _____

 Rosa is from Italy. She speaks Italian. She pronounces Italian well.

4. _____

 Ian is from England. He speaks English. He pronounces English well.

5. _____

 Marlena is from Germany. She speaks German. She pronounces German well.

Present Indicative Tense of Regular Verbs Ending in *-er*

La beauté ou la violence?

Can Janine and Pierre live without violence on television for one evening?

Maman, papa, notre téléviseur ne marche pas!

Janine et Pierre allument le téléviseur, mais il ne marche pas. Tous les deux sont inquiets parce que l'émission ce soir est "La violence triomphe!" La mère et le père entrent dans le salon et Pierre et Janine s'exclament:

—Maman, papa, notre téléviseur ne marche pas!

—Bon! Vous regardez trop de violence à la télévision, vous deux, dit la mère.

—Mais l'émission ce soir est très importante! C'est "La violence triomphe!" s'exclament Janine et Pierre.

—La violence ne triomphe pas dans cette maison! Je regrette, dit le père.

—Est-ce que nous allons faire réparer le téléviseur? demandent Janine et Pierre.

—Allons-nous faire réparer le téléviseur?! répètent la mère et le père. Oh! s'exclament-ils. Oh, non! Aujourd'hui, non!

Pierre et Janine regardent dans les journaux. L'émission "Les oeuvres d'art du Louvre" est à la télévision ce soir avant l'émission "La violence triomphe!" Alors, ils s'exclament:

—Papa, maman, c'est l'émission "Les oeuvres d'art du Louvre" à la télévision ce soir!

—Quoi?! Vite! Allons au magasin! Nous allons acheter un téléviseur à écran plasma!

Vocabulaire

aller *v.,* to go; **nous allons** we are going; **Allons au magasin!** Let's go to the store!

allumer *v.,* to turn on (a machine or device)

alors *adv.,* then

après *prep.,* after

aujourd'hui *adv.,* today

avant *prep.,* before

la beauté *n.,* beauty

cet *m.,* **cette** *f., adj.,* this

demander *v.,* to ask

deux *adj.,* two; **tous les deux** both

dire *v.,* to say, to tell; **dit la mère** says the mother

un écran *n.* **plasma** plasma screen, plasma display

l'émission *n.f.,* the show, the television program

entrer *v.,* to enter

s'exclamer *v., refl.,* to exclaim

faire *v.,* to do, to make

inquiet *m.,* **inquiète** *f., adj.,* upset, worried

mais *conj.,* but

marcher *v.,* to walk; to run, to work (a machine or device)

l'oeuvre *n. f.,* **d'art** *n. m.,* the work of art

parce que *conj.,* because

quoi *interr. pron.,* what

regarder *v.,* to look (at), to watch

réparer *v.,* to repair; **faire réparer** to have (something) repaired

répéter *v.,* to repeat

le soir *n.,* the evening

le téléphone *n.,* the telephone

le téléviseur *n.,* the television set

un téléviseur à écran plasma *n.,* a plasma screen television set

la télévision, la télé *n.,* television

tout de suite *adv.,* right away, immediately, at once

très *adv.,* very

triompher *v.,* to triumph

trop (de) *adv.,* too much (of)

la violence *n.,* violence

Exercises

Review the story and vocabulary before starting these exercises.

I. Answer the following questions in complete sentences. They are based on the story "La beauté ou la violence?"

1. Qui allume le téléviseur? _____

2. Qui entre dans le salon? _____

3. Qui regarde dans les journaux? _____

II. Oui ou Non?

1. Janine et Pierre allument le téléviseur.   _____

2. Le téléviseur marche très bien.   _____

3. L'émission ce soir est "La violence triomphe!"   _____

4. L'émission "Les oeuvres d'art dans le Louvre" est à la télévision ce soir après
    "La violence triomphe!"   _____

5. Le téléviseur va être réparé.   _____

III. Choose the correct answer based on the story in this unit.

1. Janine et Pierre allument
    (a) la radio.   (b) le téléviseur.   (c) l'émission.   _____

2. Janine et Pierre regardent dans
    (a) le téléviseur.   (b) le téléphone.   (c) les journaux.   _____

3. Madame et Monsieur Paquet entrent dans
    (a) la cuisine.   (b) le salon.   (c) le garage.   _____

IV. Complete by writing the missing French words. Find them in the story in this unit.

Janine et Pierre _____ le téléviseur mais il ne _____ pas. La mère et le père _____ dans le salon et Pierre et Janine s'_____ .

—Maman, papa, notre téléviseur ne _____ pas!

La mère dit: Bon! Vous _____ trop de violence à la télévision, vous deux.

—Est-ce que nous allons faire réparer le téléviseur? _____ Janine et Pierre.

—Oh! Oh, non! Aujourd'hui, non! s'exclament la _____ et le _____ .

Structures de la Langue

A. Introduction

A verb is a word that expresses an action *(to dance)* or a state of being *(to think)*. Tense means time. French and English verb tenses are divided into three main groups of time: past, present, and future. A verb tense shows if an action took place (past), is taking place (present), or will take place (future). Here we will study the present tense.

French verbs are divided into three main conjugations (types) according to the infinitive ending, which can be either **-er**, **-ir**, or **-re**. You might say that these endings mean *to* in English; for example, **danser** means "*to* dance." In this unit, we will concentrate on the first conjugation (**-er** ending).

You must memorize the personal endings for the **-er** verbs because they indicate the subject. You must also memorize the personal subject pronouns in French because each one is used with its own personal ending on the verb. These are all given in boldface letters in the following chart.

FIRST CONJUGATION

			-er
Infinitive		→	**danser** *to dance*
			I dance, *or* I do dance, *or* I am dancing; you dance, etc.
Required subject pronouns			
PERSON		SINGULAR	
1. **je**		I	dans**e**
2. **tu**		you *(familiar only)*	dans**es**
3. **il** **elle**	}	he *or* it she *or* it	dans**e**
		PLURAL	
1. **nous**		we	dans**ons**
2. **vous**		you	dans**ez**
3. **ils** **elles**	}	they	dans**ent**

Rules and observations:

1. To form the present tense of a regular verb ending in **-er**, drop the **-er**. What remains is called the *stem*. Add to the stem the correct personal ending: **-e**, **-es**, **-e**, **-ons**, **-ez**, or **-ent**.

2. Note that *do, am, are, does, is* (which are used in English in the present tense) are *not translated* into French. Therefore, **je danse** can mean *I dance*, or *I do dance*, or *I am dancing*. The same applies to the rest of the conjugation, for example, *you dance*, or *you do dance*, or *you are dancing*, etc.

SINGULAR	
With noun	With pronoun
Janine danse tous les soirs. (Janine dances every night.)	**Elle danse tous les soirs.** (She dances every night.)
L'ours danse. (The bear is dancing.)	**Il danse.** (It (or he) is dancing.)
PLURAL	
Janine et Marie dansent souvent. (Janine and Mary dance often.)	**Elles dansent souvent.** (They dance often.)
Janine et Pierre dansent beaucoup. (Janine and Peter dance a lot.)	**Ils dansent beaucoup.** (They dance a lot.)
Les ours dansent. (The bears are dancing.)	**Ils dansent.** (They are dancing.)

B. The subject pronouns

1. Study the subject pronouns in the first conjugation chart.

2. The subject pronoun is placed in front of the verb in an affirmative statement: **Je danse tous les soirs**. I dance every night.

3. The subject pronoun is always used with the verb.

4. In French, there are two subject pronouns that mean *you*:

    (a) **tu** is used when you are speaking to a member of your family, a close friend, a classmate, someone younger than you, or an animal.

    (b) **vous** is the polite form of *you*; it is used at all other times.

    (c) **vous** is also the plural of **tu**; when you are speaking to two or more members of your family at the same time, or two or more close friends at the same time, use **vous**.

5. If the first letter of a verb is a vowel, drop **e** in **je** and add an apostrophe: **j'aime la glace**. I like ice cream.

6. The subject pronouns **il**, **elle**, **ils**, and **elles** are used to take the place of a noun, whether it is a person, place, thing, or animal.

7. The subject pronoun **il** is used to take the place of a masculine singular noun.

8. The subject pronoun **elle** is used to take the place of a feminine singular noun.

9. The subject pronoun **ils** is used to take the place of two or more masculine nouns. It is also used to take the place of one masculine and one feminine noun. Any number of feminine nouns could be subjects, but as long as at least one masculine noun is mixed in with the subjects, the pronoun must be **ils**.

10. The subject pronoun **elles** is used to take the place of two or more feminine nouns *only*.

C. Some common regular verbs of the first conjugation

aimer to love, to like; **apporter** to bring; **chanter** to sing; **chercher** to look for; **demander** to ask (for); **désirer** to desire, to wish; **donner** to give; **écouter** to listen (to); **étudier** to study; **fermer** to close; **jouer** to play; **montrer** to show; **oublier** to forget; **parler** to talk, to speak; **porter** to carry, to wear; **regarder** to look (at), to watch; **réparer** to fix, to repair; **trouver** to find

D. The uses of the present tense

This tense is used much of the time in both French and English. It indicates:

(a) An action or a state of being at the present time.

Examples:
1. **Je vais** à l'école maintenant. *I am going* to school now.
2. **Je pense**; donc, **je suis**. *I think;* therefore, *I am.*

(b) Habitual action.

Example:
1. **Je vais** à la bibliothèque tous les jours. *I go* to the library every day.

(c) A general truth, something that is permanently true.

Example:
1. Deux et deux **font** quatre. Two and two *are* four.

(d) Vividness when talking or writing about past events. This is called the *historical present*.

Example:
1. Marie-Antoinette **est** condamnée à mort. Elle **entre** dans la charrette et **est** en route pour la guillotine. Marie-Antoinette *is* condemned to die. She *goes* into the cart and *is* on her way to the guillotine.

(e) The near future.

Example:
1. Il **arrive** demain. He *arrives* tomorrow.

(f) An action or state of being that occurred in the past and *continues up to the present*. In English, this tense is the *present perfect*.

Examples:
1. Je **suis** ici depuis dix minutes. I *have been* here for ten minutes. (meaning: I am still here.)
2. Elle **est** malade depuis trois jours. She *has been* sick for three days. (meaning: She is still sick.)

E. The verb in the negative

1.   To use a verb in the negative, place **ne** in front of the verb and **pas** after it:

Je **ne** danse **pas**.   I do not dance (or, I am not dancing).

---

2.   If the first letter of a verb is a vowel, drop **e** in **ne** and add an apostrophe:

Je **n'**aime **pas** le café.   I do not like coffee.

F. The verb in the interrogative

1.   To use a verb in a question, put **est-ce que** in front of the subject:

Est-ce que vous dansez?   Do you dance?

Est-ce que Janine danse?   Is Janine dancing?

---

2.   If the first letter of the subject is a *vowel* or *silent h*, drop **e** in **que** and add an apostrophe:

Est-ce qu'Albert danse?   **Est-ce qu'**il danse?
Is Albert dancing?   Is he dancing?

Est-ce qu'Hélène danse?   **Est-ce qu'**elle danse?
Is Helen dancing?   Is she dancing?

---

3.   To use a verb in a question, there is something else you can do instead of using the **est-ce que** form. You can use the *inverted form.* Move the subject pronoun and put it after the verb, joining it with a hyphen:

Dansez-vous?   Do you dance?

---

4.   If the subject pronoun is **je**, do not use the inverted form. Use the **est-ce que** form. The inverted form with **je** is used only with certain verbs.

5. In the inverted form, when the last letter of the verb is a vowel in the third person singular, insert **-t-** in front of **il** or **elle**:

Danse-t-il?	Does he dance?
	Is he dancing?
Danse-t-elle?	Does she dance?
	Is she dancing?

6. In the inverted form, if the subject is a noun, mention the noun first and use the pronoun of the noun:

Pierre danse-t-il?	Does Pierre dance?
Janine danse-t-elle?	Does Janine dance?
Le garçon danse-t-il?	Is the boy dancing?
La jeune fille danse-t-elle?	Is the girl dancing?

G. The verb in the negative interrogative

1. To use a verb in a question that is negative, first use the interrogative form you learned above (section **F**).

2. Put **ne** in front of the verb.

3. Put **pas** after the verb if you use the **est-ce que** form.

4. Or, if you use the inverted form, put **pas** after the subject pronoun:

Est-ce que vous ne dansez pas?	Don't you dance?
Est-ce qu'Albert ne danse pas?	Doesn't Albert dance?
Est-ce qu'elle ne danse pas?	Doesn't she dance?
Ne dansez-vous pas?	Don't you dance?
Ne danse-t-il pas?	Doesn't he dance?
Janine ne danse-t-elle pas?	Doesn't Janine dance?
Le garçon ne danse-t-il pas?	Doesn't the boy dance?

Exercises

I.   Match the following, keeping in mind that you are supposed to choose one subject pronoun to take the place of the noun or nouns as given.

(a)

1. il   _____ Janine

2. elles   _____ Pierre et moi

3. nous   _____ le garçon

4. ils   _____ Alice et elle

5. elle   _____ Paul et Robert

(b)

1. elles   _____ Roger et moi

2. elle   _____ le chien

3. ils   _____ Marie et sa mère

4. nous   _____ la télévision

5. il   _____ Alice et Pierre

II. Substitute only one appropriate subject pronoun for the word or words in italics and rewrite the entire sentence in French.

Model:	**Janine allume le téléviseur.**	**You write:**	**Elle allume le téléviseur.**
	(Janine turns on the television set.)		(She turns on the television set.)

1. *Madame Paquet* entre dans le salon. _____

2. *Pierre* cherche le journal. _____

3. *Marie et Alice* chantent bien. _____

4. *Robert et Georges* jouent à la balle. _____

5. *Janine et Pierre* regardent trop de violence à la télévision. _____

_____

Janine et Pierre regardent trop de violence à la télévision.

III. Use the subject pronoun in parentheses to take the place of the subject in italics. Rewrite each sentence in French, making the required changes in the verb forms.

Model:	**Nous regardons la télévision.**	**(Je)**	**You write:**	**Je regarde la télévision.**
	(We watch television.)			(I watch television.)

Nous dansons beaucoup.

1. (Tu) _____

2. (Il) _____

3. (Elle) _____

4. (Vous) _____

5. (Ils) _____

6. (Elles) _____

IV. Use the subject pronoun in parentheses to take the place of the subject in italics. Rewrite each sentence in French, making the required changes in the verb forms. Keep them all in the negative.

Model:	**Tu ne danses pas.**	**(Je)**	**You write:**	**Je ne danse pas.**
	(You don't dance.)			(I don't dance.)

Nous ne danson pas.

1. (Je) _____

2. (Tu) _____

3. (Il) _____

4. (Vous) _____

5. (Ils) _____

6. (Elles) _____

V. Answer the following questions in the affirmative in complete French sentences. In answer (a) use **oui**. In answer (b) use **aussi** (also). Study the models. Use subject pronouns in your answers.

Models:	**(a) Chantez-vous les matins?**	**You write:**	**(a) Oui, je chante les matins.**
	(Do you sing in the mornings?)		(Yes, I sing in the mornings.)
	(b) Et Simone?	**You write:**	**(b) Elle chante aussi.**
	(And Simone?)		(She sings also.)

1. (a) Dansez-vous les matins? _____

   (b) Et François? _____

2. (a) Pierre cherche-t-il le chapeau? _____

   (b) Et Janine? _____

3. (a) Hélène étudie-t-elle la leçon? _____

   (b) Et vous? _____

VI. Answer the following questions in the negative in complete French sentences. In answer (a) use **non**. In answer (b) use **non plus** (either). Study the models carefully. Use subject pronouns in your answers.

Models: **(a) Est-ce que vous dansez?**   You write: **(a) Non, je ne danse pas.**
   (Do you dance?)   (No, I don't dance.)
(b) Et Charles?   You write: **(b) Il ne danse pas non plus.**
   (And Charles?)   (He doesn't dance either.)

1. (a) Est-ce que vous dansez? _____

   (b) Et Paul? _____

2. (a) Est-ce qu'il étudie? _____

   (b) Et Monique? _____

3. (a) Est-ce que Paul cherche la balle? _____

   (b) Et les enfants? _____

4. (a) Est-ce que la femme écoute la musique? _____

   (b) Et vous? _____

5. (a) Est-ce que tu fermes la fenêtre? _____

   (b) Et nous? _____

VII. Choose the correct verb form and write it with its subject on the blank line.

1. Je (fermes, ferme, fermons) la porte.   *Je ferme*
   _____

2. Tu (apportes, apportez, apportent) le gâteau.   _____

3. Il (étudient, étudions, étudie) les devoirs.   _____

4. Elle (parlent, parle, parlez) bien.   _____

5. Nous (marche, marchez, marchons) lentement.   _____

6. Vous (donner, donnez, donnons) des fleurs à la maîtresse.   _____

7. Ils (joue, jouent, jouons) dans la rue.   _____

8. Elles (chante, chantent, chantes) doucement.   _____

9. Vous (cherchez, cherches, cherchent) le chapeau.   _____

10. J' (aimes, aime, aimons) la glace.   _____

VIII. Word Search. Can you find these verb forms with their subject pronouns *in French* in this puzzle? Circle them.

1. I dance.

2. You (*familiar form*) study.

3. She plays.

4. We love.

5. They (*m.*) are singing.

6. I love.

7. He arrives.

8. He talks.

9. He forgets.

J	E	D	A	N	S	E	N	T	C	O
A	J	A	I	M	E	J	I	U	N	I
I	L	P	A	R	L	E	O	É	O	E
I	L	O	U	B	L	I	E	T	U	A
E	L	L	E	J	O	U	E	U	S	U
J	E	J	O	U	E	A	L	D	A	O
I	L	A	R	R	I	V	E	I	I	I
E	L	L	E	A	R	R	I	E	M	E
N	O	U	S	J	O	U	O	S	O	A
I	L	S	C	H	A	N	T	E	N	T
A	E	I	O	U	I	L	S	P	S	L

IX. Change the following affirmative statements to negative sentences.

Model:	**Je danse.**	**You write:**	**Je ne danse pas.**
	(I dance.)		(I don't dance.)

1. Je parle. _____

2. Tu chantes. _____

3. Il écoute. _____

4. Elle oublie. _____

5. Nous jouons. _____

6. Vous désirez. _____

X. Family Life. Proficiency in Speaking and Writing.

Situation: You are at home. Your mother and father want to watch a TV show about French art. You and your brother (or sister) were planning on watching a sports program. Both shows are at the same time.

In three sentences try to persuade your parents to let you watch the sports program. You may use your own ideas and words, those in this lesson, or any or all of the following: **Nous désirons regarder le programme de sports**/*We want to watch the sports program*. **Nous aimons les sports**/*We like sports*. **Si nous avons la permission de regarder le programme de sports, nous promettons de laver la voiture et nettoyer la salle de bains**/*If we have permission to watch the sports program, we promise to wash the car and clean the bathroom.*

Before you begin, organize your thoughts and the words you are going to use, say them aloud, then practice writing them on the lines below.

1. _____

2. _____

3. _____

XI. Entertainment. Proficiency in Speaking and Writing.

Situation: You and your friend (**ami**, *masc.*; **amie**, *fem.*) are talking about what to do this evening. You want to dance but your friend wants to see a movie.

Your friend is *ton ami(e)*. What would you say? What would your friend say? After you say the words aloud, write them on the lines. You may want to review the vocabulary in this lesson and at the end of the book, as well as the verb tables. Use **Je désire** for *I want*.

Toi: _____

Ton ami(e): _____

XII. Daily Activities. Proficiency in Writing.

Situation: You are corresponding with Maryvonne, a pen pal in France. She wants to know about your daily activities.

Write a note telling her three activities that you do every day. You may use your own words and ideas or the following: **Je vais à la bibliothèque tous les jours**/*I go to the library every day*. **Je regarde la télé tous les soirs**/*I watch TV every evening*. **J'étudie mes leçons de français**/*I study my French lessons*.

Before you write the note, pretend you are talking to her. Then write your three sentences.

le premier janvier, 2007

Chère Maryvonne,

_____

_____

_____

Ton ami(e),

_____

XIII. List of French Words.   Proficiency in Writing.

Situation: You and your friend are looking at pictures in an album. Your friend wants you to say and write the French words for what you see in the picture below.

For example, find the French words for *new books;* find the expression for *at* (**à**) *reduced prices;* the French word for *salesman*. In addition, you may want to say **beaucoup de livres/***many books;* **beaucoup de personnes/***many persons*. Which three verbs come to mind as you look at the picture? For example, *to look at, to buy, to talk*. Do you see anything else in the picture?

First, say the French words aloud; then write them on the lines that are provided.

1. _____   3. _____   5. _____   7. _____

2. _____   4. _____   6. _____   8. _____

WORK UNIT 5

Present Indicative Tense of Regular Verbs Ending in *-ir*

Tout est bien qui finit bien

Have you ever received a note from a boy or girl in class at school? If you are an adult using this book, do you remember your school days when notes were passed from one student to another? In this episode, Pierre is reading a note that was just passed to him.

Au revoir, Monsieur!

Pierre est en classe de mathématiques. Il lit un petit mot caché dans les pages de son livre. Voici le mot:

Pierre, mon chéri:

Je déteste ce cours et je déteste le professeur. Il est très mauvais prof. Il choisit des leçons difficiles et il punit les élèves quand ils ne finissent pas leurs devoirs.

Je t'aime et je t'adore.

Anne-Marie

Le professeur dit à Pierre:

—Tu ne finis pas tes devoirs! Tu as un mot caché dans les pages de ton livre! De qui est ce mot? Donne-moi le mot!

Pierre rougit. Il regarde la belle Anne-Marie et elle lui dit tendrement de ses beaux yeux bleus de ne pas révéler leur amour secret et de ne pas donner le petit mot au professeur.

A ce moment-là, le signal retentit. Le cours est fini! Tous les élèves quittent la salle de classe immédiatement et Pierre aussi, avec le petit mot caché dans les pages de son livre.

Quand il est à la porte, Pierre s'exclame:

—Au revoir, monsieur!

Dans le couloir, Anne-Marie dit à Pierre:

—Chéri, tu es formidable! Tu es vraiment un homme.

Pierre dit:

—Ouf! Je l'ai échappé belle! Tout est bien qui finit bien!

Vocabulaire

à *prep.,* to, at

adorer *v.,* to adore

aimer *v.,* to love, to like; **je t'aime** I love you

au revoir *salutation,* good-bye

cacher *v.,* to hide; **caché** hidden

la calculatrice *n.,* calculator

choisir *v.,* to choose; **il choisit** he chooses

le cours *n.,* the course

détester *v.,* to detest

les devoirs *n. m. pl.,* the homework, the assignments

dit *v. form of* **dire** (to say, to tell); **le professeur dit** the teacher says

donner *v.,* to give; **donne-moi** give me

échapper *v.,* to escape; **je l'ai échappé belle!** I had a narrow escape!

l'élève *n. m. f.,* the student, the pupil; **tous les élèves** all the students

fini, finis, finit, finissent *v. forms of* **finir** (to finish); **fini** finished; **tu ne finis pas** you are not finishing; **ils ne finissent pas** they do not finish; **tout est bien qui finit bien!** all's well that ends well!

formidable *adj.,* terrific

ils *subject pron. m.,* **elles** *subject pron. f.,* they

immédiatement *adv.,* immediately

la leçon *n.,* the lesson

leur, leurs *poss adj.,* their

lit *v. form of* **lire** (to read); **il lit** he is reading

le livre *n.,* the book

lui *indir. obj. pron.,* to him, to her; **elle lui dit** she says to him

mauvais *adj. m. s.,* bad

le moment *n.,* moment; **à ce moment-là** at that moment

le mot *n.,* the word, the note; **un petit mot** a note

ne pas révéler not to reveal; **ne pas**

donner not to give

ouf! *interj.,* whew!

la porte *n.,* the door

le professeur *n.,* the teacher

punit *v. form of* **punir** (to punish); **il punit** he punishes

quand *adv.,* when

qui *pron.,* who, whom, which; **de qui** from whom

quittent *v. form of* **quitter** (to leave); **tous les élèves quittent la salle de classe** all the students leave the classroom

retentit *v. form of* **retentir** (to resound, to ring); **le signal retentit** the signal sounds, the bell rings

rougit *v. form of* **rougir** (to blush); **Pierre rougit** Pierre blushes

la salle *n.,* the room; **la salle de classe** the classroom

son *poss. adj. m. sing.,* his

ton *poss. adj. m. sing.,* your

voici here is

Exercises

Review the story and vocabulary before starting these exercises.

I. Choose the correct answer based on the story in this unit.

1. Pierre est dans
   (a) le restaurant.   (b) le garage.   (c) l'école.   (d) la bibliothèque.   _____

2. Pierre lit
   (a) un journal.   (b) un livre.   (c) un menu.   (d) un petit mot.   _____

3. Le petit mot est caché dans les pages du livre
   (a) du professeur.   (b) de son ami.   (c) de Pierre.   (d) de son amie.   _____

II. **Oui ou Non?**

1. Le professeur choisit des leçons faciles.   _____

2. Pierre ne finit pas les devoirs.   _____

3. Anne-Marie déteste le cours de mathématiques.   _____

4. Pierre ne rougit pas.   _____

5. Le professeur punit les élèves quand ils ne finissent pas les devoirs.   _____

6. Anne-Marie aime Pierre.   _____

III. Choose the appropriate French word and write it on the blank line. Base your choice only on the content of the story in this unit.

rougit	**finit**	**retentit**	**choisit**	**finissent**

1. Le professeur _____ des leçons difficiles.

2. Pierre _____ .

3. Tout est bien qui _____ bien.

4. Les élèves ne _____ pas les devoirs.

5. Le signal _____ .

Structures de la Langue

A. Introduction

Go back to Work Unit 4 and reread section **A. Introduction.**
Here are the personal endings for verbs of the second conjugation **(-ir).**

SECOND CONJUGATION

	-ir
Infinitive →	**finir** *to finish*
	I finish, *or* I do finish, *or* I am finishing; you finish, etc.

Required subject pronouns

PERSON	SINGULAR	
1. **je**	I	fin**is**
2. **tu**	you (*familiar only*)	fin**is**
3. **il** **elle** }	he *or* it she *or* it	fin**it**
	PLURAL	
1. **nous**	we	fin**issons**
2. **vous**	you	fin**issez**
3. **ils** **elles** }	they	fin**issent**

Rules and observations:

1. To form the present tense of a regular verb ending in **-ir**, drop the **-ir**. What remains is called the *stem*. Add to the stem the personal endings shown in the above chart: **-is, -is, -it, -issons, -issez, -issent.**

2. Note that *do, am, are, does, is* (which are used in English in the present tense) are *not translated* into French. Therefore, **je finis** can mean *I finish,* or *I do finish,* or *I am finishing*. The same applies to the rest of the conjugation, for example, *you finish,* or *you do finish,* or *you are finishing*, etc.

B. The subject pronouns

Go back to Work Unit 4 and reread section **B. The subject pronouns.**

C. Some common regular verbs of the second conjugation

accomplir to accomplish; **bâtir** to build; **bénir** to bless; **choisir** to choose; **désobéir (à)** to disobey; **obéir (à)** to obey; **punir** to punish; **remplir** to fill; **réussir (à)** to succeed (in); **rougir** to blush; **saisir** to seize; **salir** to soil, to dirty

Exercises

Review the preceding material before starting these exercises.

I. Match the following, keeping in mind that you are supposed to choose one subject pronoun to take the place of the noun or nouns as given.

(a)

1. il _____ Anne-Marie

2. elles _____ Joseph

3. ils _____ Hélène et Janine

4. elle _____ Pierre et Anne

(b)

1. ils _____ le chien

2. elle _____ les maisons

3. il _____ la France

4. elles _____ les chiens

II. Substitute only one appropriate subject pronoun for the word or words in italics and rewrite the entire sentence in French.

Model: **Le signal retentit.**   **You write:** **Il retentit.**
             (The signal sounds.)   (It sounds.)

1. *Le professeur* choisit des leçons difficiles. _____

2. *La jeune fille* saisit la balle. _____

3. *Madame Berty* punit les élèves. _____

4. *Madame et Monsieur Banluc* choisissent une nouvelle automobile. _____

_____

5. *Les élèves* finissent toujours les devoirs. _____

6. *Anne et Monique* rougissent facilement. _____

Madame Berty punit les élèves.

III. Use the subject pronoun in parentheses to take the place of the subject pronoun in italics. Rewrite each sentence in French, making the required changes in the verb forms.

Model: *Nous* **finissons la leçon.**   **(Je)**   **You write:**   **Je finis la leçon.**
        (We are finishing the lesson.)   (I am finishing the lesson.)

1. (Ils) _____   4. (Elle) _____

2. (Tu) _____   5. (Vous) _____

3. (Il) _____   6. (Elles) _____

IV. Use the subject pronoun in parentheses to take the place of the subject pronoun in italics. Rewrite each sentence in French, making the required changes in the verb forms. Keep them all in the negative.

Model: *Elle* **ne finit pas le dîner.**   **(Je)**   **You write:**   **Je ne finis pas le dîner.**
        (She is not finishing the dinner.)   (I am not finishing the dinner.)

1. (Vous) _____   4. (Elles) _____

2. (Il) _____   5. (Ils) _____

3. (Tu) _____   6. (Nous) _____

V. Answer the following questions in the affirmative in complete French sentences, using subject pronouns in your answers. In answer (a) use **Oui**. In answer (b) use **aussi**.

Models: **(a) Henri finit-il la leçon?**   **You write:**   **(a) Oui, il finit la leçon.**
            (Is Henry finishing the lesson?)   (Yes, he is finishing the lesson.)

         (b) Et vous?   **You write:**   **(b) Je finis la leçon aussi.**
            (And you?)   (I am finishing the lesson also.)

1. (a)   Henri finit-il le livre? _____

    (b)   Et vous? _____

2. (a)   Les professeurs punissent-ils les mauvais élèves? _____

         _____

    (b)   Et Monsieur Fouchy? _____

3. (a)   Monsieur Banluc choisit-il une nouvelle automobile? _____

         _____

    (b)   Et Madame et Monsieur Paquet? _____

         _____

4. (a)   Le chien obéit-il au garçon? _____

    (b)   Et les chats? _____

5. (a)   Finissez-vous la leçon aujourd'hui? _____

    (b)   Et Janine? _____

VI. Answer the following questions in the negative in complete sentences in French, using subject pronouns in your answers. In answer (a) use **Non**. In answer (b) use **non plus** (either).

Models: **(a) Est-ce que vous finissez la leçon?**   You write: **(a) Non, je ne finis pas la leçon.**
(Are you finishing the lesson?)   (No, I am not finishing the lesson.)

(b) Et Charles?   You write: **(b) Il ne finit pas la leçon non plus.**
(And Charles?)   (He isn't finishing the lesson either.)

1. (a) Est-ce qu'Henri désobéit? _____

    (b) Et vous? _____

2. (a) Est-ce que tu finis la leçon? _____

    (b) Et Pierre? _____

3. (a) Est-ce que Monsieur Paquet choisit une auto? _____

    (b) Et Madame Paquet? _____

4. (a) Est-ce que nous bâtissons une maison? _____

    (b) Et Monsieur et Madame Banluc? _____

5. (a) Est-ce que vous rougissez? _____

    (b) Et les jeunes filles? _____

VII. Choose the correct verb form and write it with its subject on the blank line.

1. Je (finissons, finis, finissez) la leçon.   _____

2. Tu (saisis, saisit, saisissons) la balle.   _____

3. Il (accomplis, accomplit, accomplissez) les devoirs.   _____

4. Elle (bâtit, bâtissons, bâtissent) une maison.   _____

5. Nous (choisissons, choisissez, choisissent) un dessert.   _____

6. Vous (punis, punit, punissez) le chien.   _____

7. Ils (rougit, rougissez, rougissent) facilement.   _____

8. Elles (désobéissent, désobéit, désobéissez) à leurs parents. _____

9. Je (remplis, remplit, remplissons) le vase.   _____

10. Vous (finis, finissons, finissez) les devoirs.   _____

VIII. Word Search. Can you find these verb forms with their subject pronouns *in French* in this puzzle? Circle them.

1. We finish.

2. You (*polite form*) succeed.

3. I choose.

4. You (*familiar form*) obey.

5. He seizes.

6. I finish.

7. She punishes.

8. He blesses.

9. I build.

A	E	I	O	J	E	C	H	O	I	S	I	S	J
E	A	E	L	L	E	P	U	N	I	T	A	E	O
I	L	B	É	N	I	T	A	E	O	U	I	F	B
V	O	U	S	R	É	U	S	S	I	S	S	E	Z
F	O	T	N	Z	Z	S	S	I	L	F	I	N	I
N	O	U	S	F	I	N	I	S	S	O	N	S	E
J	E	O	E	L	J	E	L	L	A	N	O	U	S
E	L	B	S	J	E	B	Â	T	I	S	F	I	N
I	S	É	S	S	F	O	N	S	S	I	T	S	T
V	O	I	U	R	I	U	E	S	I	S	E	Z	S
J	E	S	F	O	N	L	M	O	T	N	L	L	E
I	L	C	H	O	I	M	N	A	E	I	U	A	N
B	N	E	I	T	S	N	O	U	S	P	A	L	R

IX. Activities.   Proficiency in Speaking and Writing.

After you read Situations A and B, say your statements aloud; then write them on the lines provided.

A. **Situation A:** You are in French class. All the students have finished an exercise in writing except you. The teacher approaches and asks you why you have not finished the assignment: **Pourquoi ne finis-tu pas le devoir?** In two sentences tell your teacher why. You may use your own words, those in this lesson, or the following: **finir, accomplir, choisir, la leçon, l'exercice, parce que, difficile.**

B. **Situation B:** You and a friend are in the school cafeteria talking about homework. In three sentences tell your friend about an assignment one of your teachers gave your class. Explain why the assignment was given. You may use your own words, those in this lesson, or the following: **punir, choisir, les exercices, faciles, difficiles, parce que.**

A. _____

_____

B. _____

_____

Review Test: Work Units 1–5

I. Write the appropriate definite article in front of each noun.

1. _____ jeune fille   4. _____ livres
2. _____ garçon   5. _____ homme
3. _____ arbre   6. _____ parapluies

II. Write the appropriate indefinite article in front of each noun.

1. _____ soeur   4. _____ porte
2. _____ frère   5. _____ café
3. _____ amie   6. _____ orange

III. Change the following nouns in the singular to the plural.

Model: le garçon   **les garçons**

1. la mère _____   4. le monsieur _____
2. le journal _____ 5. l'oeil _____
3. la voix _____   6. le fils _____

IV. Change the following nouns to the singular or to the plural, depending on which is given.

1. les tables _____   4. le genou _____
2. l'eau _____   5. les journaux _____
3. les nez _____   6. le pays _____

V. Fill in the missing words. Choose either **au, aux, à l', or à la.**

1. _____ restaurant   4. _____ magasins
2. _____ hôtel   5. _____ école
3. _____ bibliothèque   6. _____ maison

VI. Match the following.

1. les stylos des élèves   _____ the girl's dresses
2. la jupe de la jeune fille   _____ the pupils' pens
3. les chiens des garçons   _____ the pupil's pencil
4. les robes de la jeune fille   _____ the boys' dogs
5. le crayon de l'élève   _____ the girl's skirt

VII. Write the French for the following sentences.

1. I have some coffee. _____

2. I have some meat. _____

3. I don't have any coffee. _____

4. I don't have any candies. _____

VIII. Write the missing letters in the following words.

1. J____ V A I____ A L'E ____O____E L____S MAT ____N____ .

2. JANINE V____ENT D____ FRA____C____ .

3. M____N____IEU____ ARMSTRONG P____RLE A____GLA____S.

IX. Change the following statements into questions using **Est-ce que.**

Model: Janine danse. <u>Est-ce que Janine danse?</u> (Does Janine dance?)

1. Vous parlez français. _____

2. Jacqueline regarde la télévision. _____

3. Ils étudient la leçon. _____

X. Change the following statements into questions using the inverted form.

Model: Pierre danse. <u>Pierre danse-t-il?</u> (Does Pierre dance?)

1. Odette et Yvette chantent bien. _____

2. Robert et Pierre jouent à la balle. _____

3. Vous regardez trop de télévision. _____

XI. Choose the correct verb form and write it in with its subject.

Model: Elle (parlent, parle, parlez) français. <u>Elle parle français.</u> (She speaks French.)

1. J' (aimes, aimons, aime) la glace au chocolat. _____

2. Vous (donner, donnez, donne) des fleurs à la dame. _____

3. Je (fermons, fermez, ferme) la porte. _____

4. Michelle (choisis, choisit, choisissez) une jolie robe. _____

5. Vous (finissez, finis, finissent) les devoirs. _____

6. Nous (bâtis, bâtissons, bâtissent) une maison. _____

XII. Proficiency in Reading.

Directions: In the following passage there are ten numbered spaces. Each space represents a missing word. Four possible completions are provided for each. Only one of them is grammatically correct and makes sense in the context of the passage.

First, read the passage in its entirety to determine its general meaning. Then read it a second time. Choose the completion that makes the best sense and is grammatically correct, and write its letter in the space provided.

Pierre _____ la belle Anne-Marie et elle _____ dit tendrement de ses

1.	A. regarde	2.	A. le
	B. choisit		B. la
	C. apporte		C. lui
	D. punit		D. les

beaux _____ bleus de ne pas révéler leur _____ secret et de ne

3.	A. cheveux	4.	A. classe
	B. yeux		B. livre
	C. pieds		C. amour
	D. mains		D. cours

pas _____ le petit mot _____ professeur. A ce moment-là, le signal _____ .

5.	A. cacher	6.	A. au	7.	A. choisit
	B. quitter		B. à		B. donne
	C. parler		C. aux		C. finit
	D. donner		D. des		D. retentit

Le cours est _____! Tous les élèves _____ la salle de classe

8.	A. fini	9.	A. quitte
	B. finissons		B. quittons
	C. finissez		C. quittez
	D. finissent		D. quittent

immédiatement et Pierre aussi, avec le petit mot _____ dans

10.	A. caché
	B. cachons
	C. cachez
	D. cachent

les pages de son livre.

Present Indicative Tense of Regular Verbs Ending in *-re*

Le vase extraordinaire

Have you ever bought anything at a flea market? Sometimes you can pick up something interesting.

Pour combien vendez-vous ce vase, madame?

Aujourd'hui Janine est au marché aux puces avec son amie Monique. Elles passent la journée au marché parce que c'est un endroit très intéressant.

—Oh, Monique! Regarde! Un joli vase. Il est superbe! s'exclame Janine.

—Pour combien vendez-vous ce vase, madame? demande Monique.

—Je vends ce vase pour dix euros, mademoiselle, répond la marchande. Il est vraiment très joli.

—Il est d'une beauté très rare! dit Janine. Mais je n'ai pas dix euros sur moi. J'ai deux euros. Monique, as-tu huit euros?

—Non, Janine, je n'ai pas huit euros, répond Monique.

—Je vais retourner à la maison pour demander à ma mère les huit euros. Je veux avoir ce vase. Il est extraordinaire, dit Janine à la femme. Viens, Monique!

Après une heure, Janine et Monique reviennent avec l'argent. Quand elles arrivent à la boutique où la femme vend le vase, Janine s'exclame:

—Oh! Le vase n'est pas ici! Où est le vase extraordinaire, madame? Le vase rare! Le joli vase!

—Je regrette, mademoiselle, mais il est vendu, répond la femme.

Janine et Monique vont partir et après un moment, la femme ajoute:

—Attendez! Attendez! Attendez, mesdemoiselles! J'ai beaucoup de vases exactement comme l'autre.

La marchande ouvre une grande boîte et elle met sur la table quinze vases exactement comme l'autre.

—Choisissez, mademoiselle! dit la femme.

Vocabulaire

ai, as *v. forms of* **avoir** (to have); **j'ai** I have; **je n'ai pas** I don't have; **as-tu?** do you have?

ajoute *v. form of* **ajouter** (to add); **la femme ajoute** the woman adds

l'argent *n. m.,* money

arrivent *v. form of* **arriver** (to arrive); **elles arrivent** they arrive

attendez *v. form of* **attendre** (to wait); **attendez!** wait!

aujourd'hui *adv.,* today

autre *adj., pron.,* other; **l'autre** the other one

la boîte *n.,* the box

la boutique *n.,* the shop

c'est it's, it is

choisissez *v. form of* **choisir** (to choose); **choisissez!** choose!

combien *adv.,* how much

comme *adv.,* like, as

dix *adj.,* ten

l'endroit *n. m.,* the place

un euro euro, eurodollar

exactement *adv.,* exactly

extraordinaire *adj.,* extraordinary, unusual

huit *adj.,* eight

ici *adv.,* here

intéressant *adj.,* interesting

joli *m.,* **jolie** *f., adj.,* pretty

la journée *n.,* the day

le marchand *n.,* **la marchande** *n.,* the merchant, shopkeeper

le marché *n.,* the market; **au marché aux puces** at the flea market

met *v. form of* **mettre** (to put); **elle met** she puts

ouvre *v. form of* **ouvrir** (to open); **elle ouvre** she opens

partir *v.,* to leave

passent *v. form of* **passer** (to spend time); **elles passent** they are spending

la puce *n.,* the flea

quinze *adj.,* fifteen

rare *adj.,* rare

regarde *v. form of* **regarder** (to look, to look at); **regarde!** look!

répond *v. form of* **répondre** (to reply, to answer); **répond la marchande** answers the shopkeeper

retourner *v.,* to return, to go back

reviennent *v. form of* **revenir** (to return, to come back); **elles reviennent** they return

vais *v. form of* **aller** (to go); **je vais** I'm going

le vase *n.,* the vase

vend, vendez, vends, vendu *v. forms of* **vendre** (to sell); **la femme vend** the woman is selling; **vendez-vous?** are you selling?; **je vends** I am selling; **vendu** sold

veux *v. form of* **vouloir** (to want); **je veux** I want

viens *v. form of* **venir** (to come); **viens!** come!

vont *v. form of* **aller** (to go); **elles vont** they are going

vraiment *adv.,* really

Exercises

Review the story and vocabulary before starting these exercises.

I. Oui ou Non?

1. Aujourd'hui Janine est au marché aux puces. _____

2. La marchande vend le vase pour quinze euros. _____

3. Monique n'a pas huit euros. _____

4. Janine et Monique retournent à la maison. _____

5. Quand elles retournent à la boutique avec l'argent, le vase est vendu. _____

II. Complete the dialogue between Janine and the merchant. Refer to the dialogue in this unit if you have to.

1. Janine: Pour combien _____-vous ce vase, madame?

2. La Marchande: Je _____ ce vase pour _____ euros, mademoiselle.

3. Janine: Oh! Il est _____ très rare!

4. La Marchande: Oui, et il est très _____ aussi.

III. The words in the following boxes are scrambled. Unscramble them to find a meaningful sentence. Write the sentences on the lines provided.

Model:

combien	pour	madame?
vase	ce	vendez-vous

You write: *Pour combien vendez-vous ce vase, madame?*
                   (For how much are you selling this vase, madam?)

1.

vends	vase	pour
dix euros	ce	je

You write: _____

2.

marchande	de	la
vend	beaucoup	vases

You write: _____

3.

moment	un	après
ajoute	femme	la

You write: _____

Structures de la Langue

A. Introduction

Go back to Work Unit 4 and reread section **A. Introduction.** Here are the personal endings for verbs of the third conjunction (**-re**).

THIRD CONJUGATION

	-re
Infinitive →	**vendre** *to sell*
	I sell, *or* I do sell, *or* I am selling; you sell, etc.

Required subject pronouns

PERSON	SINGULAR	
1. **je**	I	vend**s**
2. **tu**	you (*familiar only*)	vend**s**
3. **il** } **elle** }	he *or* it she *or* it	vend
	PLURAL	
1. **nous**	we	vend**ons**
2. **vous**	you	vend**ez**
3. **ils** } **elles** }	they	vend**ent**

Rules and observations:

1. To form the present tense of a regular verb ending in **-re**, drop the **-re**. What remains is called the *stem*. Add to the stem the personal endings shown in the chart on the previous page: **-s, -s, -, -ons, -ez, -ent**.

2. Note that for an **-re** verb there is normally no ending to add in the third person singular. The last letter of the stem is often **d**, so the verb form remains the same as the stem, for example, **il** or **elle vend**. However, there are some **-re** verbs whose last letter in the stem is not **d**. In that case, you have to add **t**:

interrompre *to interrupt*	**rompre** *to break*
il, elle interromp**t**	il, elle romp**t**

3. In the plural, note that the personal endings for an **-re** verb are the same as those for an **-er** verb.

4. Finally, note also that *do, am, are, does, is* (which are used in English in the present tense) *are not translated* into French. Therefore, **je vends** can mean *I sell*, or *I do sell*, or *I am selling*. The same applies to the rest of the persons, for example, *you sell*, or *you do sell*, or *you are selling*, etc.

B. The subject pronouns

Go back to Work Unit 4 and reread section **B. The subject pronouns.**

C. Some common regular verbs of the third conjugation

attendre to wait (for); **défendre** to defend, to forbid; **descendre** to go (come) down, to descend; **entendre** to hear; **interrompre** to interrupt; **perdre** to lose; **rendre** to give back, to return; **répondre (à)** to answer, to reply; **rompre** to break

Exercises

Review the preceding material before starting these exercises.

I. Substitute only one appropriate subject pronoun for the word or words in italics and rewrite the entire sentence in French.

Model:	*La dame* **répond au téléphone.**	**You write:**	**Elle répond au téléphone.**
	(The lady is answering the phone.)		(She is answering the telephone.)

1. *Le soldat* défend sa patrie. _____

2. *La marchande* vend des vases. _____

3. *Anne et Georges* entendent la musique. _____

4. *L'homme et la femme* vendent leur maison. _____

5. *Le grand chien* rompt la petite barrière. _____

II. Use the subject pronoun in parentheses to take the place of the subject pronoun in italics. Rewrite each sentence in French, making the required changes in the verb forms.

> **Model:** *Nous* **vendons des livres.**   **(Je)**   **You write:**   **Je vends des livres.**
> (We are selling books.)   (I am selling books.)

1. (Elle) _____
2. (Tu) _____
3. (Vous et moi) _____

4. (Ils) _____
5. (Vous) _____
6. (Elles) _____

III. Use the subject pronoun in parentheses to take the place of the subject pronoun in italics. Rewrite each sentence in French, making the required changes in the verb forms. Keep them all in the negative.

> **Model:** *Vous* **ne vendez pas la voiture.**   **(Elle)**   **You write:**   **Elle ne vend pas la voiture.**
> (You are not selling the car.)   (She is not selling the car.)

1. (Nous) _____
2. (Je) _____
3. (Tu) _____

4. (Il) _____
5. (Elles) _____
6. (Ils) _____

IV. Answer the following questions in the affirmative in complete French sentences, using subject pronouns in your answers. In answer (a) use **oui**. In answer (b) use **aussi** (also). Make the required changes in the verb forms.

> **Models:**   **(a) La dame répond-elle au téléphone?**   **You write:**   **(a) Oui, elle répond au téléphone.**
> (Is the lady answering the phone?)   (Yes, she is answering the phone.)
>
>   **(b) Et les dames?**   **You write:**   **(b) Elles répondent au téléphone aussi.**
> (And the ladies?)   (They're answering the phone too.)

1. (a) Pierre répond-il à la lettre? _____

   (b) Et vous? _____

2. (a) Monsieur Coty vend-il la maison? _____

   (b) Et Monsieur Dupont? _____

3. (a) Le soldat défend-il la patrie? _____

   (b) Et vous? _____

4. (a) Le vase est-il joli? _____

   (b) Et le parapluie? _____

5. (a) Janine est-elle au marché aux puces? _____

   (b) Et Monique? _____

V. Change the following affirmative statements to interrogative sentences. Use the inverted form only.

Model:	**Pierre danse tous les soirs.**	**You write:**	**Pierre danse-t-il tous les soirs?**
	(Pierre dances every evening.)		(Does Pierre dance every evening?)

1. Janine étudie dans la bibliothèque. _____

2. Elle cherche le chapeau. _____

3. Il finit la leçon. _____

4. Elle choisit une jolie robe. _____

5. Nous répondons à la lettre. _____

6. Ils vendent la maison. _____

VI. Change to the plural or singular, according to what is given.

Models:	**Il vend.** (He sells.)	**You write:**	**Ils vendent.** (They sell.)
	Elles chantent. (They sing.)		**Elle chante.** (She sings.)

1. Elle attend. _____

2. Je vends. _____

3. Nous dansons. _____

4. Il écoute. _____

5. Tu finis. _____

6. Ils répondent. _____

VII. Change the following affirmative statements to interrogative sentences. Use the **est-ce que** form only.

Model:	**Pierre étudie.**	**You write:**	**Est-ce que Pierre étudie?**
	(Pierre studies.)		(Does Pierre study?)

1. Elle finit le livre. _____

2. Monsieur Berty vend la voiture. _____

3. Elle choisit un joli chapeau. _____

4. Il défend la patrie. _____

5. Hélène ouvre la boîte. _____

VIII. Write the French word opposite each picture. Use the definite article with the word.

1.

_____

2.

_____

3.

_____

4.

_____

5.

_____

6.

_____

IX. Complete each verb form in the present indicative by writing the correct letter or letters on the blank lines.

1. J'aim _____ le français.

2. Vous chant _____ bien.

3. Janine étudi _____ beaucoup.

4. Je chois _____ un chapeau.

5. Ils attend _____ l'autobus.

6. Je vend _____ l'automobile.

7. Vous chois _____ une leçon facile.

8. Nous fin _____ les devoirs.

X. Give the three English translations for each of the following French verb forms in the present indicative.

1. Je danse. _____ _____ _____

2. Vous finissez. _____ _____ _____

3. Nous vendons. _____ _____ _____

XI.   Word Search. Can you find these verb forms with their subject pronouns *in French* in this puzzle? Circle them.

1.   He sells.

2.   She waits.

3.   We answer.

4.   They (*m.*) lose.

5.   You (*familiar*) forbid.

6.   They (*f.*) lose.

7.   I give back.

8.   You answer.

N	N	O	I	L	V	E	N	D	O	U	I	N
I	L	S	P	E	R	D	E	N	T	I	C	I
E	L	L	E	S	I	M	P	O	R	T	A	N
L	U	I	E	L	L	E	A	T	T	E	N	D
E	L	L	E	S	P	E	R	D	E	N	T	O
E	J	E	R	E	N	D	S	A	L	O	R	S
V	O	S	S	E	T	M	O	I	S	O	N	T
N	O	U	S	R	É	P	O	N	D	O	N	S
U	E	A	I	P	N	A	C	E	G	L	I	L
A	E	I	T	U	D	É	F	E	N	D	S	T
V	O	U	S	R	É	P	O	N	D	E	Z	U

XII.   Friendly Persuasion.   Proficiency in Speaking and Writing.

Situation: You want to go to a county fair in the suburbs of the city where you live, but your parents don't like the idea. In four sentences, persuade them to let you go. You may use your own words, those in this lesson, or the following: **aller, vendre, attendre, acheter, beaucoup de choses** (*many things*), **entendre, perdre, j'aimerais aller à la foire** (*I would like to go to the fair*).

Say aloud the four short sentences you have in mind; then write them on the lines below. Remember to use the Answers section beginning on page 426. The sentences given there are samples. They may not be exactly the same as the ones you write.

1.   _____

2.   _____

3.   _____

4.   _____

WORK UNIT 7

Formation and Use of Reflexive Verbs in the Present Indicative

Surprise! Surprise!

Are you as eager as Pierre to play in a soccer game?

Pierre aime les sports. Son sport favori est le football.

Pierre aime les sports. Son sport favori est le football. Il veut être toujours en forme parce qu'il est gardien de but dans son équipe à l'école. Il veut être toujours prêt à bien jouer. Il est au régime. Il mange seulement des aliments qui sont bons pour la santé. Pendant la saison de football, il évite les glaces, les pommes frites, et les pâtisseries. C'est un brave garçon.

Il se couche de bonne heure, il se lève avec le soleil, il se lave soigneusement, il s'habille vite, et il prend le petit déjeuner.

Il annonce à ses parents:

—C'est le grand match de football aujourd'hui! C'est après les classes.

Pierre dit à Janine:

—Janine, tu vas jouer dans l'équipe avec les garçons et les jeunes filles aussi, n'est-ce pas?

—Oui, répond Janine. Les jeunes filles aiment les sports aussi. Je vais être au stade pour jouer avec les garçons et les jeunes filles cet après-midi.

Pierre se dépêche pour arriver tôt dans la grande cour de l'école. Il court un kilomètre sur la piste avant d'entrer dans l'école.

Pour Pierre, le football est tout. Il se rappelle les bons conseils de son entraîneur de football:

—Attention au filet, Pierre! Attention au filet! Garde le but! Le but!

Pierre joue extrêmement bien. C'est un très bon garçon, bon étudiant, bon joueur. Ses camarades aiment beaucoup Pierre.

Après la dernière classe, Pierre va au gymnase. Il se prépare pour le grand match. Il met sa tenue d'exercice. Il fait de la gymnastique avant de commencer le match.

Pierre fait de la gymnastique pendant quelques heures. Maintenant il est prêt pour le grand match!

Pierre court à toute vitesse au stade. Quand il arrive au stade, il voit que tout le monde est là.

—Pierre! Pourquoi es-tu en retard? demande l'entraîneur.

Pierre ne répond pas. Il est à bout de souffle.

—Le match commence tout de suite, dit l'entraîneur.

—Je ne peux pas jouer au football aujourd'hui, s'exclame Pierre.

—Pourquoi pas? demande l'entraîneur.

—Je suis trop fatigué!

Vocabulaire

l'aliment *n. m.,* food
annoncer *v.,* to announce
l'après-midi *n.m.,* the afternoon
attention à watch out for
à bout de souffle out of breath
brave *adj., m. f.,* good, fine, honest (when **brave** follows a noun, it means *brave;* **une femme brave, un homme brave** a brave woman, a brave man)

le but *n.,* the goal; **gardien de but** goalie
c'est ... it's (*sometimes* he's ... (or) she's ...)
le conseil *n.,* advice
se coucher *refl. v.,* to go to bed
la cour *n.,* the yard
court *v. form of* **courir** (to run); **Pierre court** Pierre runs
se dépêcher *refl. v.,* to hurry

dernier *m.,* **dernière** *f., adj.,* last
l'entraîneur *n. m.,* the coach, sports instructor
l'équipe *n. f.,* the team
éviter *v.,* to avoid
fais, fait *v. forms of* **faire** (to do, to make); **il fait de la gymnastique** he does gymnastics
fatigué *adj., m. s.,* tired
le filet *n.,* the net

le football *n.,* soccer (in the U.S.A.)

la forme *n.,* the shape, the form; **en forme** in good shape

garder *v.,* to guard; **gardien de but** goalie

le gymnase *n.,* the gymnasium; **la gymnastique** *n.,* gymnastics

s'habiller *refl. v.,* to get dressed

jouer *v.,* to play; **le joueur** *m.,* **la joueuse** *f., n.,* the player

le kilomètre *n.,* kilometer (about 0.62 miles)

là *adv.,* there

se laver *refl. v.,* to wash oneself

se lever *refl. v.,* to get up

le match *n.,* the game, the match (sport)

mettre *v.,* to put, to put on (wear); **il met** he puts on

n'est-ce pas? isn't it so? aren't you?

le petit déjeuner *n.,* breakfast

peux *v. form of* **pouvoir** to be able; **Je ne peux pas …** I can't …

la piste *n.,* the track

les pommes frites *n. f.,* fried potatoes, French fries (You can also say **les frites** for French fries.)

prendre *v.,* to take; **prendre le petit déjeuner** to have breakfast

se préparer *refl. v.,* to prepare oneself, to get ready

prêt *m.,* **prête** *f., adj.,* ready, prepared

que *interrog. pron.,* what; *as a conj.,* that

quel *adj., m. s.,* what (which); **quel sport?** what (which) sport?

se rappeler *refl. v.,* to remember, to recall

le régime *n.,* diet; **au régime** on a diet

se *refl. pron.,* himself, herself, oneself, itself, themselves

soigneusement *adv.,* carefully

le soleil *n.,* the sun

son *poss. adj., m. s.,* **ses** *pl.,* his

le stade *n.,* the stadium

tard *adv.,* late

la tenue d'exercice gym suit

tôt *adv.,* early

toujours *adv.,* always

tout de suite *adv.,* immediately, right away

trop *adv.,* too

veut *v. form of* **vouloir** (to want); **il veut** he wants

la vitesse *n.,* speed; **à toute vitesse** very fast

voit *v. form of* **voir** (to see); **il voit** he sees

Exercises

Review the story and vocabulary before starting these exercises.

I.   Answer the following questions in complete sentences. They are based on the story, "Surprise! Surprise!"

1.   Quel est le sport favori de Pierre? _____

2.   Pourquoi veut-il être toujours en forme? _____

3.   Quels aliments mange-t-il? _____

4.   Se lève-t-il tôt ou tard? _____

5.   Est-ce que Janine va jouer dans le match aussi? _____

II.   Answer the following questions in complete sentences. They are personal questions and require answers of your own.

1.   Aimez-vous les sports? _____

2.   Est-ce que vous vous couchez tôt ou tard? _____

3.   Vous dépêchez-vous pour arriver à l'école? _____

4.   Est-ce que vous vous lavez soigneusement? _____

5.   Vous habillez-vous vite? _____

III. Oui ou Non?

1. Le sport favori de Pierre est le tennis. _____

2. Pierre est gardien de but. _____

3. Janine aime les sports aussi. _____

4. Pierre se lève tard. _____

5. Janine va au stade pour jouer avec les garçons et les jeunes filles. _____

IV. Un acrostiche. Complete the French words in the squares across.

1. slowly
2. to avoid
3. to go to bed
4. to get up
5. for
6. or
7. to answer
8. late
9. to wash oneself

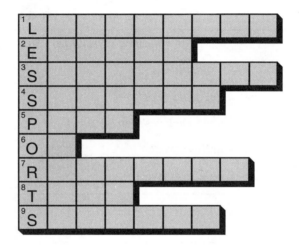

Structures de la Langue

A. Formation and use of reflexive verbs in the present indicative; all four forms: Affirmative, Negative, Interrogative, and Negative Interrogative

se laver   *to wash oneself*

AFFIRMATIVE

I wash myself, I am washing myself, I do wash myself, etc.			
Singular		*Plural*	
je	**me lave**	nous	**nous lavons**
tu	**te laves**	vous	**vous lavez**
il	**se lave**	ils	**se lavent**
elle	**se lave**	elles	**se lavent**

NEGATIVE

I am not washing myself, I do not wash myself, etc.

Singular		*Plural*	
je	**ne** me lave **pas**	nous	**ne** nous lavons **pas**
tu	**ne** te laves **pas**	vous	**ne** vous lavez **pas**
il	**ne** se lave **pas**	ils	**ne** se lavent **pas**
elle	**ne** se lave **pas**	elles	**ne** se lavent **pas**

INTERROGATIVE WITH **est-ce que** FORM

Am I washing myself? Do I wash myself? etc.

Singular	*Plural*
est-ce que je me lave?	**est-ce que** nous nous lavons?
est-ce que tu te laves?	**est-ce que** vous vous lavez?
est-ce qu'il se lave?	**est-ce qu'**ils se lavent?
est-ce qu'elle se lave?	**est-ce qu'**elles se lavent?

INTERROGATIVE WITH *INVERTED FORM*

Am I washing myself? Do I wash myself? etc.

Singular	*Plural*
*****est-ce que** je me lave?	**nous** lavons-nous?
te laves-tu?	**vous** lavez-vous?
se lave-t-il?	**se** lavent-ils?
se lave-t-elle?	**se** lavent-elles?

*The inverted form is ordinarily used in the first person singular *only* with certain verbs.

Observe that the subject pronoun shifts in the interrogative when using the inverted form; it is joined to the verb with a hyphen:

Affirmative:	Tu te laves.	Nous nous lavons.
Interrogative:	Te laves-tu?	Nous lavons-nous?

Est-ce que je ne me lave pas?

NEGATIVE INTERROGATIVE WITH **est-ce que** FORM

Am I not washing myself? Don't I wash myself? etc.

Singular	*Plural*
est-ce que je **ne** me lave **pas**?	**est-ce que** nous **ne** nous lavons **pas**?
est-ce que tu **ne** te laves **pas**?	**est-ce que** vous **ne** vous lavez **pas**?
est-ce qu'il **ne** se lave **pas**?	**est-ce qu'**ils **ne** se lavent **pas**?
est-ce qu'elle **ne** se lave **pas**?	**est-ce qu'**elles **ne** se lavent **pas**?

NEGATIVE INTERROGATIVE WITH *INVERTED FORM*

Am I not washing myself? Don't I wash myself? etc.

Singular	*Plural*
*****est-ce que** je **ne** me lave **pas**?	**ne** nous lavons-nous **pas**?
ne te laves-tu **pas**?	**ne** vous lavez-vous **pas**?
ne se lave-t-il **pas**?	**ne** se lavent-ils **pas**?
ne se lave-t-elle **pas**?	**ne** se lavent-elles **pas**?

*The inverted form is ordinarily used in the first person singular *only* with certain verbs.

Observe that the subject pronoun shifts in the negative interrogative when using the inverted form; it is joined to the verb with a hyphen:

Negative:	Tu ne te laves pas.	Nous ne nous lavons pas.
Negative Interrogative:	Ne te laves-tu pas?	Ne nous lavons-nous pas?

Rules and observations:

1. To form the present tense of a reflexive verb in a simple affirmative sentence, put the reflexive pronoun in front of the verb. Study the first box (Affirmative).

2. A reflexive verb expresses an action that is turned back upon the subject; for example, I wash *myself* (je **me** lave). The reflexive pronoun in the English sentence is *myself*; in the French sentence it is **me**.

3. The reflexive pronouns in French are **me**, **te**, **se**, **nous**, and **vous**.

4. The reflexive pronouns in English are **myself**, **yourself**, **herself**, **himself**, **itself**, **ourselves**, **yourselves**, and **themselves**.

REFLEXIVE PRONOUNS

Singular		*Plural*	
me	myself	**nous**	ourselves
te	yourself	**vous**	yourselves (yourself)
se	himself, herself, itself	**se**	themselves

5. Be careful to use the appropriate reflexive pronoun, the one that matches the subject pronoun. You already know the subject pronouns, but here they are again, next to the reflexive pronouns.

Singular	*Plural*
1. **je me…**	1. **nous nous…**
2. **tu te…**	2. **vous vous…**
3. **il se…**	3. **ils se…**
elle se…	**elles se…**

6. Note that in the third person singular and third person plural, the relfexive pronoun is the same: **se** (himself, herself, itself, themselves).

7. Note that in the first person plural, the reflexive pronoun is the same as the subject pronoun: **nous** (ourselves).

8. Note that in the second person plural, the reflexive pronoun is the same as the subject pronoun: **vous** (yourself, yourselves).

9. Most of the time, a verb that is reflexive in French is also reflexive in English. Here's one example of a verb that is not reflexive in English but is in French.

se dépêcher   to hurry

je me dépêche   I hurry, *or* I do hurry, *or* I am hurrying

10. Note the position of the reflexive pronouns and the **ne** and **pas** in the boxes above.

11.   The reflexive pronouns **me**, **te**, and **se** become **m'**, **t'**, and **s'** when they are in front of a verb beginning with a vowel or silent *h*, as in the following example:

s'appeler   to be called, named

je **m'appelle** Marie.	My name is Mary.
tu **t'appelles** Hélène.	Your name is Helen.
il **s'appelle** Henri.	His name is Henry.
elle **s'appelle** Jeanne.	Her name is Jeanne.

B.   Formation of some irregular reflexive verbs

<table>
<tr><td colspan="2">s'asseoir   to sit down</td><td colspan="2">s'endormir   to fall asleep</td></tr>
<tr><td>je m'assieds</td><td>nous nous asseyons</td><td>je m'endors</td><td>nous nous endormons</td></tr>
<tr><td>tu t'assieds</td><td>vous vous asseyez</td><td>tu t'endors</td><td>vous vous endormez</td></tr>
<tr><td>il s'assied</td><td>ils s'asseyent</td><td>il s'endort</td><td>ils s'endorment</td></tr>
<tr><td>elle s'assied</td><td>elles s'asseyent</td><td>elle s'endort</td><td>elles s'endorment</td></tr>
<tr><td colspan="2">se servir   to use</td><td colspan="2">se souvenir   to remember</td></tr>
<tr><td>je me sers</td><td>nous nous servons</td><td>je me souviens</td><td>nous nous souvenons</td></tr>
<tr><td>tu te sers</td><td>vous vous servez</td><td>tu te souviens</td><td>vous vous souvenez</td></tr>
<tr><td>il se sert</td><td>ils se servent</td><td>il se souvient</td><td>ils se souviennent</td></tr>
<tr><td>elle se sert</td><td>elles se servent</td><td>elle se souvient</td><td>elles se souviennent</td></tr>
</table>

C.   Some other reflexive verbs

s'amuser to enjoy oneself, to have a good time; **se coucher** to go to bed, to lie down; **s'habiller** to get dressed, to dress oneself; **se lever** to get up; **se rappeler** to remember, to recall; **se regarder** to look at oneself; **se reposer** to rest; **se trouver** to be situated, to be located

Exercises

Review the preceding material before starting these exercises.

I.   Fill in the missing reflexive pronouns.

1. Je _____ lave.

2. Je ne _____ dépêche pas.

3. Tu _____ amuses.

4. Il _____ couche.

5. Elle _____ habille.

6. Nous _____ levons.

7. Vous _____ rappelez.

8. Ils _____ amusent.

9. Elles _____ reposent.

10. Il _____ regarde.

II.   Match the following.

1. Je me dépêche.

2. Je m'appelle Yves.

3. Vous vous couchez de bonne heure.

4. Tu t'amuses ici.

5. Il s'habille.

6. Est-ce que je ne me lave pas?

7. Je m'assieds.

8. Elle s'endort.

9. Te laves-tu?

10. Vous ne vous lavez pas.

_____ She is falling asleep.

_____ You are having a good time here.

_____ Are you washing yourself?

_____ Aren't I washing myself?

_____ My name is Yves.

_____ I sit down.

_____ I hurry.

_____ You go to bed early.

_____ He is getting dressed.

_____ You don't wash yourself.

III.   Word Search. Can you find the following five verb forms in French with their subject pronouns in this puzzle?

1. I am getting dressed.

2. You are washing yourself.

3. He is hurrying.

4. They (*m.*) are enjoying
    themselves.

5. I am resting.

D	E	I	P	T	E	C	H	E	J
J	E	L	A	U	L	A	V	R	E
D	I	S	D	T	E	J	A	U	M
I	L	S	U	E	L	O	I	N	E
A	S	A	I	L	M	A	N	G	R
J	E	M	H	A	B	I	L	L	E
I	D	U	O	V	E	E	O	A	P
I	É	S	S	E	M	E	T	S	O
O	P	E	I	S	S	E	L	V	S
J	Ê	N	A	P	P	E	L	E	E
U	C	T	I	L	S	E	M	E	L
A	H	J	E	I	U	O	I	L	T
J	E	M	E	R	E	G	A	R	E

IV.   Fill in the missing subject pronouns.

1. _____ m'amuse.

2. _____ t'habilles.

3. _____ vous regardez.

4. _____ (or) _____ se servent.

5. _____ (or) _____ se souvient

6. _____ nous couchons.

7. _____ vous levez.

8. _____ (or) _____ s'assied.

9. _____ (or) _____ se reposent.

10. _____ m'endors.

V.   Answer the following questions in the affirmative.

Model: Vous lavez-vous?	**You write: Oui, je me lave.**
(Do you wash yourself?)	(Yes, I wash myself.)

1. Vous amusez-vous? _____

2. Vous couchez-vous? _____

3. Vous reposez-vous? _____

4. Vous habillez-vous? _____

5. Vous asseyez-vous? _____

VI. Answer the following questions in the negative.

> **Model:** **Vous lavez-vous tous les jours?**   You write: **Non, je ne me lave pas tous les jours.**
> (Do you wash yourself every day?)   (No, I do not wash myself every day.)

1. Vous amusez-vous ici? _____

2. Vous couchez-vous de bonne heure tous les soirs? _____

_____

3. Vous habillez-vous vite tous les matins? _____

_____

4. Vous appelez-vous Jean-Jacques? _____

5. Vous asseyez-vous ici? _____

VII. Change each sentence by replacing the verb in italics with the proper form of the verb in parentheses. Keep the same subject. Rewrite the entire sentence in French.

> **Model:** **Se dépêche-t-il tous les matins? (s'habiller)**   You write: **S'habille-t-il tous les matins?**
> (Does he hurry every morning [to get dressed]?)   (Does he get dressed every morning?)

1. *Se lave*-t-il tous les soirs? (se dépêcher) _____

2. Je *m'assieds* sur cette chaise. (s'endormir) _____

3. Nous *nous couchons* de bonne heure. (se lever) _____

4. Il *s'habille* vite. (se laver) _____

5. Je *me lave* tous les jours. (s'amuser) _____

VIII. The words in the following boxes are scrambled. Unscramble them to find a meaningful sentence. Write the complete sentences on the lines provided.

Model:

nous	café	maintenant
servons	du	nous

You write: **Nous nous servons du café maintenant.**
(We are serving ourselves coffee now.)

1.

m'	ma	habille
dans	je	chambre

2.

ils	samedis	théâtre
au	tous les	s'amusent

3.

tu	reposes	te
dîner	après	le

4.

me	heure	bonne
couche	je	de

5.

dépêchons	pour	à l'école
nous	aller	nous

6.

je	tous	matins
les	lave	me

1. _____

2. _____

3. _____

4. _____

5. _____

6. _____

IX.   Change the following statements into questions. Use the **est-ce-que** form only.

Model:	**Elle s'appelle Hélène.**	**You write:**	**Est-ce qu'elle s'appelle Hélène?**
	(Her name is Helen.)		(Is her name Helen?)

1. Robert s'amuse. _____

2. Vous vous endormez vite. _____

3. Ils se couchent tard. _____

4. Henri est absent aujourd'hui. _____

5. Alice se dépêche pour aller à l'école. _____

X.   Change the following statements into questions. Use the inverted form only.

Model:	**Il se lave avant de manger.**	**You write:**	**Se lave-t-il avant de manger?**
	(He washes himself before eating.)		(Does he wash himself before eating?)

1. Elle se repose. _____

2. Vous vous levez très tard le matin. _____

3. Elle s'assied devant la porte. _____

4. Nous nous dépêchons. _____

5. Ils se couchent tard. _____

XI. Change the following statements into negative interrogative sentences. Use the **est-ce que** form or the inverted form.

Model: **Pierre se lève avec le soleil.**   **You write:**   **Pierre ne se lève-t-il pas avec le soleil?**
(Pierre gets up with the sun.)   **Or:**   **Est-ce que Pierre ne se lève pas avec le soleil?**
(Doesn't Pierre get up with the sun?)

1. Pierre se couche de bonne heure. _____

2. Il se lave soigneusement. _____

3. Il s'habille vite. _____

4. Il se dépêche. _____

5. Il se prépare à jouer au football. _____

XII. Choose the correct form and write it on the blank line. Write the verb form with the subject.

1. Je (me lave, vous lavez, se lavent) tous les matins. _____

2. Vous (vous amusez, s'amusent, nous amusons) tout le temps. _____

3. Il (s'endorment, s'endort, vous endormez) vite. _____

4. Elle (s'habille, s'habillent, nous habillons) dans la chambre. _____

5. Nous (me couche, vous couchez, nous couchons) de bonne heure. _____

6. Tu (t'amuses, s'amuse, s'amusent) tous les jours! _____

7. Ils (se sert, se servent, nous servons) du café noir. _____

8. Elles (s'endort, vous endormez, s'endorment) tranquillement. _____

9. Je (s'amuse, m'amuse, nous amusons) tous les soirs au café. _____

10. Madame Paquet (se dépêche, nous dépêchons, vous dépêchez) pour sortir. _____

XIII. Providing and Obtaining Information.   Proficiency in Speaking and Writing.

Situation: You have just arrived in Paris and a representative of the airline wants to have some information for a survey.

Imagine a conversation. You are playing the role of *Vous*. First, say aloud the statements you plan to make; then write them on the lines provided. You may use your own words and ideas or follow the guided conversation.

Le représentant: **Bonjour. Est-ce que vous connaissez déjà la France?**

1. *Vous:* _____

Le représentant: **Le voyage est agréable?**

2. *Vous:* _____

Le représentant: **Pourquoi faites-vous ce voyage en France?**

3. *Vous:* _____

Le représentant: **Est-ce que vous voyagez seul?**

4. *Vous:* _____

Le représentant: **Est-ce que vous avez des suggestions pour le service?**

5. *Vous:* _____

XIV. Daily Activities.   Proficiency in Writing.

Situation: You are studying French in a summer session at the Alliance Française Institute in Paris. Before you left for France, you promised your best friend Robert that you would send him a postcard about your daily activities.

On the lines below, write a note telling him at least five things you do every day. Use a few of the reflexive verbs you studied in this lesson. For example, you may want to say that you go to bed early, you fall asleep easily, you get up with the sun, you dress quickly, and you are enjoying yourself in Paris. You may add other words and ideas.

le deux avril, 2007

Cher Robert,

_____

_____

_____

_____

_____

Ton ami(e)

_____

XV. Obtaining Information.   Proficiency in Writing.

Situation: You also promised to write to Diane during your summer studies in Paris. This time you are going to ask her questions using reflexive verbs with **est-ce que** or the inverted form. Use the familiar *tu* form because she is your friend. Ask at least three questions. For example, **Est-ce que tu t'amuses? T'amuses-tu?**/*Are you having a good time?*

le trois avril, 2007

Chère Diane,

_____

_____

_____

_____

_____

Ton ami(e)

_____

XVI. Sports. Proficiency in Writing.

Situation: You spent a wonderful afternoon at an indoor swimming pool in Paris. A picture of the pool is shown below. It's something to write home about.

Write at least four sentences. You may use your own ideas and words or the following: **la piscine**/*swimming pool*; **voici une photo de la piscine**/*here is a photo of the swimming pool*; **nager**/*to swim*; **j'aime nager**/*I like to swim*; **je nage tous les jours**/*I swim every day*; **la natation**/*swimming*; **j'aime la natation**/*I like swimming*; **c'est mon sport favori**/*it's my favorite sport*.

Practice writing your sentences on these lines:

_____

_____

_____

_____

Cardinal and Ordinal Numbers

Ch! Ch! Filez! Filez!

Have you ever been at a public auction? Let's see what happens to Madame Paquet.

—Ch! Ch! Filez! Filez! Oh, ces mouches! s'exclame Madame Paquet.

Madame et Monsieur Paquet quittent la maison pour aller à une vente aux enchères. Madame Paquet aime beaucoup les ventes aux enchères. Elle veut acheter une petite table ronde pour le salon de sa maison.

Ils arrivent et ils entrent dans la salle des ventes. Ils entendent le commissaire-priseur qui parle à un groupe de personnes:

Le Commissaire-priseur: Mesdames, Messieurs, attention! S'il vous plaît!

> *(Monsieur et Madame Paquet prennent deux places au cinquième rang près de la porte.)*

Le Commissaire-priseur: J'ai ici, mesdames et messieurs, un très, très beau fauteuil. Qui offre cinquante euros?

> *(Monsieur Paquet parle à sa femme à voix basse: —Tout est si élégant ici. Très élégant.)*
> *(Madame Paquet répond à voix basse: —Oui, mais je n'aime pas les mouches! Et le fauteuil est très laid!)*

Le Commissaire-priseur: Merci, monsieur! J'ai cinquante euros pour ce beau fauteuil. Qui offre soixante euros? … Soixante euros, ce n'est pas beaucoup pour ce beau fauteuil! Qui offre soixante euros?

> *(Madame Paquet dit à son mari à voix basse: —Les mouches dans cette salle sont terribles!)*

Le Commissaire-priseur: Merci, madame! Merci! J'ai soixante euros de la dame au premier rang. Qui offre soixante-dix euros?

> *(Madame Paquet demande à son mari à voix basse: —François, qui est la dame au premier rang qui offre soixante euros pour ce fauteuil monstrueux? Elle doit être folle!)*
> *(Monsieur Paquet répond: —Je ne sais pas, ma chérie.)*

Le Commissaire-priseur: Merci encore, madame! J'ai une offre de soixante-dix euros! Qui offre quatre-vingts?… Merci, monsieur! J'ai une offre de quatre-vingts euros. Qui offre quatre-vingt-dix euros? … Merci, madame! J'ai quatre-vingt-dix euros de la dame là-bas au troisième rang. Qui offre cent euros? Cent euros? Qui offre cent euros?

> *(Madame Paquet lève la main pour chasser les mouches de son nez. —Ch! Ch! Filez! Filez! Oh, ces mouches!)*

Le Commissaire-priseur: Merci, madame! J'ai cent euros de la dame au cinquième rang près de la porte! J'ai cent euros! C'est la dernière mise! Une fois, deux fois, trois fois. C'est fini! Vendu à la charmante dame avec son mari au cinquième rang près de la porte! Vous pouvez payer à la caisse, s'il vous plaît, madame.

> *(Tout le monde regarde Madame Paquet.)*

Madame Paquet: Qui? Moi?

Vocabulaire

ai *v. form of* **avoir** (to have); **j'ai** I have

assister à *v.,* to be present at, to attend

beau *m.,* **belle** *f., adj.,* beautiful, handsome

la caisse *n.,* the cash box; **à la caisse** at the cash desk

Ch! Ch! *interj.,* Shoo! Shoo!

charmant *m.,* **charmante** *f., adj.,* charming

chasser *v.,* to chase away

le commissaire-priseur *n.,* the auctioneer

doit *v. form of* **devoir** (to owe, ought to, must); **elle doit être folle** she must be crazy

l'enchère *n. f.,* the bid, the bidding

l'euro *n.m.,* the euro; unit of money used by several countries in Europe

le fauteuil *n.,* the armchair

filez! *exclam.,* go away!

fois *n. f.,* time; **une fois** one time, once; **deux fois** two times, twice

folle *f.,* **fou, fol** *m., adj.,* crazy

le franc *n.,* the franc, the former French unit of money

là-bas *adv.,* over there

laid *m.,* **laide** *f., adj.,* ugly

lève *v. form of* **lever** (to raise, to lift); **elle lève la main** she raises her hand

la mise *n.,* the bid; **la dernière mise** the last bid

moi *pron.,* me

monstrueux *m.,* **monstrueuse** *f., adj.,* monstrous

la mouche *n.,* the fly

le nez *n.,* the nose

offre *v. form of* **offrir** (to offer); **une offre** an offer; **qui offre?** who offers?

payer *v.,* to pay

la place *n.,* the seat, the place

pouvez *v. form of* **pouvoir** (to be able, can, may); **vous pouvez** you can, you may

prennent *v., form of* **prendre** (to take); **ils prennent** they take

le rang *n.,* the row

rond *m.,* **ronde** *f., adj.,* round

sais *v. form of* **savoir** (to know); **je sais** I know; **je ne sais pas** I don't know

la salle *n.,* the (large) room; **la salle des ventes** the auction sales room

si *adv.,* so; *conj.,* if

s'il vous plaît please

tout *pron.,* everything, all; **tout le monde** everybody

vendu *v. form of* **vendre** (to sell) sold

la vente *n.,* the sale; **la vente aux enchères** the auction

la voix *n.,* the voice; **à voix basse** in a low voice

Exercises

Review the story and vocabulary before starting these exercises.

I. Answer the following questions in complete sentences. They are based on the story in this unit.

1. Qui aime beaucoup les ventes aux enchères? _____

2. Qui entre dans la salle des ventes? _____

3. Pourquoi Madame Paquet lève-t-elle la main? _____

4. Qui offre cent euros pour le fauteuil? _____

5. Qui regarde Madame Paquet? _____

II. Answer the following questions in complete sentences. They are personal questions and require answers of your own.

1. Aimez-vous les ventes aux enchères? _____

2. Avez-vous un salon dans votre maison? _____

3. Avez-vous une jolie petite table ronde dans votre maison? _____

_____

III. Comment dit-on en français ...? (How do you say in French ...?) Find these statements in the story and write them in French.

1. Mr. Paquet talks to his wife in a low voice. _____

_____

2. Mrs. Paquet raises her hand to chase away the flies from her nose. _____

_____

3. I have one hundred euros. _____

IV. The words in the following boxes are scrambled. Unscramble them to find a meaningful sentence. Write the sentence in French on the line provided.

Model:

de	ils	maison
la	bonne heure	quittent

You write: **Ils quittent la maison de bonne heure.**

(They leave the house early.)

1.

salle	ils	la
dans	des ventes	entrent

3.

est	élégant	dans
cette salle	si	tout

2.

n'aime	je	ce
fauteuil	pas	monstrueux

4.

veux	une	je
ronde	table	jolie petite

1. _____

2. _____

3. _____

4. _____

Structures de la Langue

A. Cardinal Numbers 1 to 1,000

0	zéro	13	treize	**40**	**quarante**
1	un, une	14	quatorze	41	quarante et un
2	deux	15	quinze	42	quarante-deux, etc.
3	trois	16	seize	**50**	**cinquante**
4	quatre	17	dix-sept	51	cinquante et un
5	cinq	18	dix-huit	52	cinquante-deux, etc.
6	six	19	dix-neuf	**60**	**soixante**
7	sept	**20**	**vingt**	61	soixante et un
8	huit	21	vingt et un	62	soixante-deux, etc.
9	neuf	22	vingt-deux, etc.	**70**	**soixante-dix**
10	**dix**	**30**	**trente**	71	soixante et **onze**
11	onze	31	trente et un	72	soixante-douze, etc.
12	douze	32	trente-deux, etc.	**80**	**quatre-vingts**

81	quatre-vingt-un	**300**	**trois cents**	602	six cent deux, etc.
82	quatre-vingt-deux, etc.	301	trois cent un	**700**	**sept cents**
90	**quatre-vingt-dix**	302	trois cent deux, etc.	701	sept cent un
91	quatre-vingt-onze	**400**	**quatre cents**	702	sept cent deux, etc.
92	quatre-vingt-douze, etc.	401	quatre cent un	**800**	**huit cents**
100	**cent**	402	quatre cent deux, etc.	801	huit cent un
101	cent un	**500**	**cinq cents**	802	huit cent deux, etc.
102	cent deux, etc.	501	cinq cent un	**900**	**neuf cents**
200	**deux cents**	502	cinq cent deux, etc.	901	neuf cent un
201	deux cent un	**600**	**six cents**	902	neuf cent deux, etc.
202	deux cent deux, etc.	601	six cent un	**1,000**	**mille**

Rules and observations:

1. Learning numbers in French is easy. It's very much like the way we form numbers in English.

2. From 0 to 16 it's a matter of learning new vocabulary because there is, naturally, a word for each number. Study the simple words in French from 0 to 16 in the table.

3. Next, notice that numbers 17, 18, and 19 are based on 10 plus 7, 8, and 9. The word for 10 (**dix**) is joined with a hyphen to the word for 7 (**sept**), 8 (**huit**), and 9 (**neuf**). Examine these three numbers in the table.

4. The compound numbers actually start with 20. From 20 to 29, just state the word for 20 (**vingt**) and add to that word the cardinal numbers from 1 to 9. This is how we form the numbers in English too. There is one exception: You are supposed to use the word **et** (*and*) with **un** (*one*). The **et** is omitted after one: vingt-deux, vingt-trois, etc. Don't forget to join the added word with a hyphen.

5. Next, it's a matter of learning new vocabulary after 20: **vingt** (20), **trente** (30), **quarante** (40), and so on. To each whole number add **un** through **neuf**. Don't forget to use **et** (*and*) with **un** only and drop it from **deux** to **neuf**. Study these numbers in the table.

6. The word 100 is also new vocabulary for you: **cent**, with no **un** in front of it for one hundred. It's just plain **cent**.

7. From 200 to 900, you're using words you have already learned: 200 is **deux cents**, 300 is **trois cents**, just as in English. Notice the **s** on **cents**. The **s** drops with compound numbers in the hundreds; **deux cent un** (201), **trois cent un** (301), and so on. In brief, there is an **s** on **cents** only in the round whole number in the hundreds: 200 (**deux cents**), 300 (**trois cents**), 400 (**quatre cents**), and so on. In the hundreds, never use **et** (*and*). Any multiple, any other number added to the round whole number drops the **s** on **cents**: cent un (101), cent deux (102), and so on.

B. Simple arithmetical expressions

deux **et** deux **font** quatre	$2 + 2 = 4$
trois **fois** cinq **font** quinze	$3 \times 5 = 15$
douze **moins** dix **font** deux	$12 - 10 = 2$
dix **divisés par** deux **font** cinq	$10 \div 2 = 5$

Rules and observations:

1. In French you need to state **et** (*and*) as we do in English when adding. Besides saying two *and* two are four, we can say two *plus* two are four. In French, we say **et** (*and*).

2. The symbol × (meaning *times*) is expressed by **fois** in French.

3. In French, we use the word **moins** to express *minus* or *less*.

4. In French, we say **divisés par** to express *divided by*.

5. In French, we use the word **font** (meaning *make*) to express *are* or *make*.

C. Fractions

½	**un demi**	a (one) half
⅓	**un tiers**	a (one) third
¼	**un quart**	a (one) fourth
⅕	**un cinquième**	a (one) fifth

D. Approximate amounts

une dizaine	about ten
une quinzaine	about fifteen
une vingtaine	about twenty
une trentaine	about thirty
une quarantaine	about forty
une cinquantaine	about fifty
une soixantaine	about sixty
une centaine	about a hundred
un millier	about a thousand

Observations:

1. Notice that each of the approximate amounts listed above is based on a cardinal number.

2. Did you notice that **une quarantaine** (*about forty*) is related to the English word *quarantine*, which means a period of *forty* days?

E. Ordinal numbers: first to twentieth

first	**premier, première**	1st	**1ᵉʳ, 1ʳᵉ**
second	**deuxième (second, seconde)**	2nd	**2ᵉ**
third	**troisième**	3rd	**3ᵉ**
fourth	**quatrième**	4th	**4ᵉ**
fifth	**cinquième**	5th	**5ᵉ**
sixth	**sixième**	6th	**6ᵉ**
seventh	**septième**	7th	**7ᵉ**
eighth	**huitième**	8th	**8ᵉ**
ninth	**neuvième**	9th	**9ᵉ**
tenth	**dixième**	10th	**10ᵉ**
eleventh	**onzième**	11th	**11ᵉ**
twelfth	**douzième**	12th	**12ᵉ**
thirteenth	**treizième**	13th	**13ᵉ**
fourteenth	**quatorzième**	14th	**14ᵉ**
fifteenth	**quinzième**	15th	**15ᵉ**
sixteenth	**seizième**	16th	**16ᵉ**
seventeenth	**dix-septième**	17th	**17ᵉ**
eighteenth	**dix-huitième**	18th	**18ᵉ**
nineteenth	**dix-neuvième**	19th	**19ᵉ**
twentieth	**vingtième**	20th	**20ᵉ**

Rules and observations:

1. You must learn the difference between a **cardinal** number and an **ordinal** number. If you have trouble distinguishing between the two, just remember that we use the cardinal numbers most of the time: **un**, **deux**, **trois** (one, two, three), and so on.

2. Use the *ordinal* numbers to express a certain *order*: premier (première, if the noun following is feminine), deuxième, troisième (first, second, third), and so on.

3. **Premier** is the masculine singular form and **première** is the feminine singular form. Examples: **le premier homme** (*the first man*), **la première femme** (*the first woman*).

4. The masculine singular form **second**, or the feminine singular form **seconde**, is used to mean *second* when there are only two. When there are more than two, **deuxième** is used. Examples: **le Second Empire** because there were only two empires in France; however, **la Deuxième République** because there have been more than two republics in France.

5. The superscript letters in **1ᵉʳ** are the last two letters in the word **premier**; it is equivalent to our *st* in *1st*. The superscript letters in **1ʳᵉ** are the last two letters in the word **première**, which is the *feminine* singular form of *first*.

6. The superscript letter **e** after an ordinal number (for example, **2ᵉ**) stands for the **ième** ending of a French ordinal number.

7. When referring to sovereigns or rulers, the only ordinal number used is **Premier**. For all other designations, the cardinal numbers are used. The definite article (*the*) is used in English but not in French. Examples:

but:	François Iᵉʳ	François Premier	Francis the First
	Louis XIV	Louis Quatorze	Louis the Fourteenth

F. Weights, Measures, Values* (Poids, mesures, valeurs)

un gramme = 0.035274 ounce (1 gram)

28.3 grammes = 1 ounce

100 grammes = 3.52 ounces

453.6 grammes = 1 pound

500 grammes = 17.63 ounces (about 1.1 pounds)

1000 grammes = 1 kilogram

un kilogramme = 2.2 pounds (1 kilogram)

une livre = 17.63 ounces (about 1.1 pounds)

un litre = 1.0567 quarts (0.26417 gallon)

---

un euro = $1.20

5 euros = $6.00

20 euros = $24.00

50 euros = $60.00

---

un kilomètre = 0.62137 mile (about ⅝ mile or 1000 meters)

1.61 kilomètres = 1 mile

10 kilomètres = 6.21 miles

---

un centimètre = 0.39 inch (1 centimeter)

2.54 centimètres = 1 inch

30.5 centimètres = 1 foot

91.4 centimètres = 1 yard

un mètre = 39.37 inches (100 centimeters)

0.9144 mètre = 1 yard

---

1. To convert Fahrenheit degrees into Celsius (Centigrade): subtract 32, multiply by 5, and divide by 9.

2. To convert Celsius (Centigrade) into Fahrenheit: multiply by 9, divide by 5, and add 32.

3. A Fahrenheit degree is smaller than a Celsius degree. One F degree is ⁵/₉ of a C degree.

4. France uses the Celsius scale.

---

*All the equivalents given are approximate. To obtain the current rate of exchange of American dollars for euros inquire at a commercial bank or check online.

Exercises

A. Cardinal numbers

I. Complete the following by writing in the French word or words.

1. Deux et deux font _____

2. Trois et quatre font _____

3. Cinq et sept font _____

4. Six et quatre font _____

5. Huit et neuf font _____

6. Neuf et trois font _____

II. Write the French word or words for the following cardinal numbers.

1. 2 _____   6. 20 _____   11. 61 _____

2. 4 _____   7. 21 _____   12. 69 _____

3. 6 _____   8. 22 _____   13. 70 _____

4. 8 _____   9. 30 _____   14. 80 _____

5. 10 _____   10. 37 _____   15. 100 _____

III. Match the following.

1. seize   _____ seventeen   6. quatre-vingts   _____ one hundred

2. dix-sept   _____ twenty   7. soixante   _____ ninety

3. dix-neuf   _____ eighteen   8. cent   _____ eighty

4. vingt   _____ nineteen   9. quatre-vingt-dix _____ seventy

5. dix-huit   _____ sixteen   10. soixante-dix   _____ sixty

IV. Choose the correct answer and write the word on the line.

1. Deux et cinq font   (a) quatre   (b) six   (c) sept   (d) neuf.   _____

2. Trois fois cinq font   (a) quinze   (b) vingt   (c) dix-sept   (d) huit.   _____

3. Douze moins dix font   (a) vingt-deux   (b) cent vingt   (c) deux   (d) vingt.   _____

4. Dix divisés par deux font   (a) douze   (b) cinquante   (c) six   (d) cinq.   _____

5. Douze divisés par six font   (a) douze   (b) dix-huit   (c) deux   (d) dix.   _____

B. Ordinal numbers

I. Match the following.

1. troisième   _____ first   6. vingtième   _____ fifteenth

2. cinquième   _____ second   7. quinzième   _____ seventeenth

3. premier   _____ third   8. dix-neuvième   _____ twentieth

4. deuxième   _____ fourth   9. seizième   _____ nineteenth

5. quatrième   _____ fifth   10. dix-septième   _____ sixteenth

II. Write the French word or words for the following ordinal numbers.

1. first (feminine) _____

2. first (masculine) _____

3. second (of only 2, masculine) _____

4. second (of only 2, feminine) _____

5. second (of more than 2) _____

6. fourth _____

7. fifth _____

8. ninth _____

9. tenth _____

10. third _____

III. Match the following.

1. Henri Quatre   _____ Francis I

2. Louis Seize   _____ Louis XIV

3. François Premier   _____ Henry V

4. Henri Cinq   _____ Louis XVI

5. Louis Quatorze   _____ Henry IV

C. Cardinals, fractions, approximate amounts, ordinals, simple arithmetical expressions, weights and measures

I. Complete the following by writing in the French word or words.

1. Six moins quatre font _____

2. Vingt et quarante font _____

3. Cinquante divisés par deux font _____

4. Trois cents moins cent font _____

5. Mille moins deux cents font _____

II. Word Search. Find these seven words *in French* in this puzzle and circle them.

1. one hundred

2. thirty

3. third

4. one thousand

5. fifty

6. five

7. twelve

U	N	M	I	C	T	R	E	N	T	E	X
N	D	E	C	I	N	Q	U	A	N	T	E
M	T	R	C	C	E	N	T	A	I	N	E
T	R	O	I	S	I	È	M	E	U	N	E
O	M	I	N	L	D	O	U	Z	E	L	L
Q	C	I	Q	N	T	R	M	I	L	L	E

III. Match the following.

1.	four	_____ un quart
2.	about a thousand	_____ une centaine
3.	eighty	_____ quatorze
4.	one half	_____ quatre
5.	fourteenth	_____ soixante-neuf
6.	about a hundred	_____ quatre-vingts
7.	one fourth	_____ quatorzième
8.	fourteen	_____ un demi
9.	ninety	_____ quatre-vingt-dix
10.	sixty-nine	_____ un millier

IV. Transcribe the following into French words.

Model: $2 \times 5 = 10$ **You write: Deux fois cinq font dix.**

1. $3 \times 9 = 27$ _____

2. $8 - 6 = 2$ _____

3. $20 \div 5 = 4$ _____

4. $7 \times 100 = 700$ _____

5. 80 et $10 = 90$ _____

V. Transcribe the following French words into simple arithmetical expressions using symbols and figures.

Model: Deux fois dix font vingt.   **You write: $2 \times 10 = 20$.**

1. Trois fois cinq font quinze. _____

2. Douze moins dix font deux. _____

3. Dix divisés par deux font cinq. _____

4. Deux et deux font quatre. _____

5. Neuf fois dix font quatre-vingt-dix. _____

VI. Match the following.

1. un kilogramme

2. une livre

3. un centimètre

4. un kilomètre

5. un mètre

6. un litre

7. 5 euros

8. 10 kilomètres

9. 1,000 grammes

10. 0.9144 mètre

_____ 0.62137 mile

_____ 39.37 inches

_____ $6.00

_____ 1.0567 quarts

_____ 1.1 pounds

_____ 6.21 miles

_____ 0.39 inch

_____ 2.2 pounds

_____ 1 yard

_____ 1 kilogram

VII. Expressing Personal Feelings.   Proficiency in Writing.

Situation: You are at an auction with a friend. You are not making any bids and you want to leave immediately. Your friend asks why you want to leave: **Pourquoi veux-tu partir?** In five sentences give your reasons for wanting to leave. You may use your own words, those in this unit, or any of the following: **aller, partir, être, les choses, laid, monstrueux, le fauteuil, les meubles** (furniture), and any of the numbers given in this lesson.

_____

_____

_____

_____

_____

Trois fois cinq font quinze.

Time Expressions, Telling Time, Dates, Age, Months, Days, Seasons

Bon voyage! Bon retour!

In this scene, Monsieur and Madame Paquet, Janine, and Pierre are going through security at Charles de Gaulle Airport. What an experience!

Monsieur Paquet dit: L'avion va partir sans nous!

La famille Paquet fait des préparations pour un voyage par avion aux États-Unis. Madame Paquet a une soeur qui habite à La Nouvelle-Orléans avec son mari et ses trois enfants. Maintenant, ils font les valises et dans quelques minutes ils vont quitter la maison pour aller à l'aéroport Charles de Gaulle.

—Quelle heure est-il? demande Monsieur Paquet.

—Il est huit heures, répond sa femme.

—Il faut se dépêcher, dit Pierre. L'avion va partir dans deux heures.

Madame Paquet est très heureuse parce qu'elle va revoir sa soeur. Janine et Pierre sont heureux aussi parce qu'ils vont voir leurs cousins pour la première fois. Monsieur Paquet est heureux parce qu'il va voir la Louisiane.

Ils montent dans le taxi et dans quelques minutes ils arrivent à l'aéroport. Ils ont acheté leurs billets électroniques en ligne. Ils vont au guichet pour l'enregistrement.

—Votre nom, s'il vous plaît, demande la jeune dame au guichet.

—Paquet. Nous allons aux États-Unis pour quelques semaines, à La Nouvelle-Orléans, en Louisiane.

—Vous êtes sûr que c'est pour aujourd'hui, monsieur? demande la jeune dame.

—Oui, oui. Quelle est la date aujourd'hui? C'est le premier juillet, n'est-ce pas? demande Monsieur Paquet.

—Oui, c'est bien ça, répond-elle. Voilà! Quel âge ont les deux enfants?

—Janine, dis à la dame ton âge, dit la mère.

—J'ai quinze ans, répond Janine.

—Pierre, dis ton âge à la dame.

—J'ai dix ans, répond Pierre.

—Bien, dit la dame. Vos passeports, s'il vous plaît.

Monsieur Paquet donne les passeports à la dame.

—Parfait. C'est parfait, dit la dame au guichet. Voici vos cartes d'embarquement. L'avion va partir dans quelques minutes. Veuillez passer par le contrôle de sécurité. Bon voyage et bon retour!

—Merci, merci, merci, merci, répondent-ils.

Ils passent au contrôle de sécurité où il y a un détecteur de métal et une machine à rayons X. Quand le sac de vol de Monsieur Paquet passe par la machine à rayons X, ils entendent un signal d'alarme assourdissant. Un agent arrive vite.

—Halte! crie-t-il. Il faut chercher dans le sac, dit l'agent.

—Quel embarras! C'est très ennuyeux, dit monsieur Paquet. L'avion va partir sans nous. Il est dix heures moins deux!

—Je regrette, monsieur, mais les règles sont les règles.

L'agent de police cherche dans le sac de Monsieur Paquet.

—Ah! Ha! Un pistolet! Vous êtes arrêté! s'exclame l'agent.

—Mais ce n'est pas une arme! s'exclame Pierre. C'est mon pistolet à eau!

L'agent ferme le sac.

—Vous pouvez passer. Mais nous gardons le pistolet à eau, le coupe-ongles, et les allumettes, dit l'agent.

—Ils nous volent toutes nos affaires, dit Monsieur Paquet à Madame Paquet.

—Notre vol! Vite! crie Madame Paquet. L'avion va partir sans nous!

Vocabulaire

l'aéroport *n. m.,* the airport

les allumettes *f.,* matches

l'arme *n. f.,* the weapon

arrêter *v.,* to stop; **l'arrêt** *n. m.,* the stop, the arrest; **vous êtes arrêté** you are under arrest

assourdir *v.,* to deafen; **assourdissant** *adj.,* deafening

avez *v. form of* **avoir** (to have); **vous avez** you have

l'avion *n. m.,* the airplane

le billet *n.,* the ticket; **le billet électronique** electronic ticket, e-ticket

bon retour! *exclam.,* have a good return (trip)!

bon voyage! *exclam.,* have a good trip!

la carte d'embarquement boarding pass

cela *dem. pron.,* that (**ça** is short for **cela**); **c'est ça** that's it; **c'est bien ça** that's quite right

le contrôle de sécurité security check (travel)

le coupe-ongles nail clippers

crie *v. form of* **crier** (to shout, to cry out); **crie-t-il** he shouts

déjà *adv.,* already

dis *v. form of* **dire** (to tell, to say); **dis à la dame …** tell the lady …

la douane *n.,* customs

en ligne online

ennuyer *v.,* to annoy; **ennuyeux** annoying

l'enregistrement *m.,* check-in

Les États-Unis *n. m.,* the United States; **aux États-Unis** to (in) the United States

fait, font *v. forms of* **faire** (to do, to make); **faire un voyage** to take a trip

falloir *v.,* to be necessary; **il faut** it is necessary

le guichet *n.,* the ticket window

habiter *v.,* to live, to reside

l'heure *n. f.,* the hour (used in telling time); **quelle heure est-il?** what time is it?

heureux *m.,* **heureuse** *f., adj.,* happy

il est dix heures moins deux it's two minutes to ten

il y a there is, there are

j'ai quinze ans I'm fifteen years old; **j'ai dix ans** I'm ten years old

leurs *poss. adj. pl.,* their

la Louisiane *n.,* Louisiana

la machine à rayons X X-ray machine (travel)

merci thank you

monter *v.,* to climb up or into, to ascend, to get into; **ils montent dans le taxi** they get into the taxi

le nom *n.,* the name

La Nouvelle-Orléans *n.,* New Orleans

l'objet *n. m.,* the object

par *prep.,* by

parfait *adj.,* perfect

passent *v. form of* **passer** (to pass, to go by); **ils passent à la douane** they go to customs

le pistolet à eau water pistol

quel âge ont les deux enfants? how old are the two children? **quelle est la date aujourd'hui?** what's the date today? **quelle heure est-il?** what time is it?

quelque *adj.,* some, any; **quelque chose** something

le sac de vol carry-on bag

le signal *n.,* the signal; **le signal d'alarme** the alarm

sûr *adj.,* sure, certain; **bien sûr** of course, certainly

ton *poss. adj. m. s.,* your

va, vont *v. forms of* **aller** (to go); **elle va** she is going; **ils vont** they are going

voir *v.,* to see

le vol the flight

voler to fly; also to steal **Ils nous volent toutes nos affaires!** They're stealing all our things!

le voyage *n.,* the trip

Exercises

Review the story and vocabulary before starting these exercises.

I. Choose the correct answer based on the story.

1. La famille Paquet va faire un voyage à
   (a) Paris.   (b) Chicago.   (c) La Nouvelle-Orléans.   (d) New York.   _____

2. Madame Paquet est heureuse parce qu'elle va revoir
   (a) son frère.   (b) sa mère.   (c) ses cousins.   (d) sa soeur.   _____

3. Janine et Pierre sont heureux parce qu'ils vont voir
    (a) leur chien.   (b) leurs amis.   (c) leurs cousins.   (d) l'aéroport.   _____

4. Janine a
    (a) douze ans.   (b) treize ans.   (c) quatorze ans.   (d) quinze ans.   _____

5. Pierre a
    (a) treize ans.   (b) douze ans.   (c) onze ans.   (d) dix ans.   _____

II. Oui ou Non?

1. Monsieur Paquet est heureux parce qu'il va voir la Louisiane.   _____

2. L'avion va partir à dix heures.   _____

3. Monsieur Paquet a un revolver dans sa poche.   _____

4. L'agent de police trouve une clef dans la poche de Monsieur Paquet.   _____

5. La famille Paquet va faire un voyage par avion aux États-Unis.   _____

III. Scrambled sentences. Unscramble each sentence so that it is meaningful. Write them in the proper word order. Look for them in the story.

1. Quinze ans j'ai. _____

2. Heure est quelle il? _____

3. Aujourd'hui date la est quelle? _____

4. Huit heures est il. _____

5. Chercher sac le faut dans il. _____

IV. Answer the following questions in complete sentences. They are personal questions and require answers of your own.

1. Aimez-vous faire des voyages? _____

    _____

2. Aimez-vous les avions ou les trains? _____

    _____

3. Aimez-vous regarder un avion dans le ciel? _____

    _____

Structures de la Langue

A. Telling Time

TIME EXPRESSIONS

Quelle heure est-il?	What time is it?
Il est une heure.	It is one o'clock.
Il est une heure dix.	It is ten minutes after one.
Il est une heure et quart.	It is a quarter after one.
Il est deux heures et demie.	It is half past two; it is two-thirty.
Il est trois heures moins vingt.	It is twenty minutes to three.
Il est trois heures moins le quart.	It is a quarter to three.
Il est midi.	It is noon.
Il est minuit.	It is midnight.
à quelle heure?	at what time?
à une heure	at one o'clock
à une heure précise	at exactly one o'clock
à trois heures précises	at exactly three o'clock
à neuf heures du matin	at nine in the morning
à trois heures de l'après-midi	at three in the afternoon
à dix heures du soir	at ten in the evening
à l'heure	on time
à temps	in time
vers trois heures	around three o'clock
un quart d'heure	a quarter of an hour
une demi-heure	a half hour
Il est midi et demi.	It is twelve-thirty.

Il est une heure.

Il est une heure dix.

Il est une heure et quart.

Il est deux heures et demie.   **Il est trois heures moins vingt.**   **Il est trois heures moins le quart.**

Rules and observations:

1. In telling time, **Il est** is used plus the hour, whether it is one or more than one (e.g., **Il est une heure**, **Il est deux heures**).

2. If the time is *after* the hour, state the hour, then the minutes (e.g., **Il est une heure dix**).

3. The conjunction **et** is used with **quart** after the hour and with **demi** or **demie** (e.g., **Il est une heure et quart**, **Il est une heure et demie**, **Il est midi et demi**).

4. The masculine form **demi** is used after a masculine noun (e.g., **Il est midi et demi**). The feminine form **demie** is used after a feminine noun (e.g., **Il est deux heures et demie**).

5. **Demi** remains **demi** when *before* a feminine or masculine noun, and it is joined to the noun with a hyphen (e.g., **une demi-heure**).

6. If the time expressed is *before* the hour, **moins** is used (e.g., **Il est trois heures moins vingt**).

7. A quarter *after* the hour is **et quart**; a quarter *to* the hour is **moins le quart**.

8. To express A.M. use **du matin**; to express P.M. use **de l'après-midi** if it is the afternoon or **du soir** if it is the evening.

9. The 24-hour system of telling time is used by the French government on radio and TV, in railroad and bus stations, and at airports. In this system, **quart** and **demi** or **demie** are not used. **Moins** and **et** are not used. When you hear or see the stated time, subtract 12 from the number that you hear or see. If the number is less than 12 it is A.M. time, except for **24 heures**, which is midnight (**zéro heure** is also midnight).

   Examples: **Il est treize heures.** / It is 1 P.M.
   Il est quinze heures. / It is 3 P.M.
   Il est vingt heures trente. / It is 8:30 P.M.
   Il est vingt-quatre heures. / It is midnight.
   Il est zéro heure. / It is midnight.
   Il est seize heures trente. / It is 4:30 P.M.
   Il est dix-huit heures quinze. / It is 6:15 P.M.
   Il est vingt heures quarante-cinq. / It is 8:45 P.M.
   Il est vingt-deux heures cinquante. / It is 10:50 P.M.

The abbreviation for **heure** or **heures** is **h**.

   Examples: **Il est 20 h. 20.** / It is 8:20 P.M.
   Il est 15 h. 50. / It is 3:50 P.M.
   Il est 23 h. 30. / It is 11:30 P.M.

B. Asking the date, giving the date

Quelle est la date aujourd'hui?	
Quel jour du mois est-ce aujourd'hui?	What's the date today?
Quel jour du mois sommes-nous aujourd'hui?	
C'est aujourd'hui le premier mai.	Today is May first.
C'est aujourd'hui le deux mai.	Today is May second.

Rule:

In giving the date, use the cardinal numbers except for the first of the month, which is always **le premier**.

C. Asking your age, giving your age

Quel âge avez-vous?	How old are you?
J'ai quinze ans.	I am fifteen (years old).

Rules:

1. In giving your age, use the cardinal numbers.

2. The verb **avoir** is used in French; the verb *to be* is used in English.

D. Months of the year

Les mois de l'année sont **janvier, février, mars, avril, mai, juin, juillet, août, septembre, octobre, novembre, décembre**.

The months of the year are January, February, March, April, May, June, July, August, September, October, November, December.

Rules:

1. The months are not ordinarily capitalized.

2. They are all masculine in gender.

E. Days of the week

> Les jours de la semaine sont **dimanche**, **lundi**, **mardi**, **mercredi**, **jeudi**, **vendredi**, **samedi**.
>
> The days of the week are Sunday, Monday, Tuesday, Wednesday, Thursday, Friday, Saturday.
>
> **Le samedi nous faisons des achats.**   (On Saturdays we go shopping.)
>
> **Quel jour est-ce aujourd'hui?**   **C'est aujourd'hui lundi.**
>
> (What day is it today?)   (Today is Monday.)

Rules:

1. The days are not capitalized.

2. They are also all masculine in gender.

F. Seasons of the year

> Les saisons de l'année sont **le printemps**, **l'été**, **l'automne**, **l'hiver**.
>
> The seasons of the year are spring, summer, fall, winter.

Rules:

1. The seasons are not capitalized.

2. They are masculine in gender.

Exercises

Review the preceding material before starting these exercises.

I.   Match the following.

1. Quelle heure est-il?   _____ It is 9 o'clock.

2. Est-il deux heures?   _____ It is noon.

3. Il est neuf heures.   _____ Is it 2 o'clock?

4. Il est midi.   _____ What time is it?

5. Il est minuit.   _____ It is midnight.

6. Il est une heure.   _____ It is 1 o'clock.

II.   Quelle heure est-il? Write the answer in a complete sentence (in French) on the line provided under each clock.

Model:

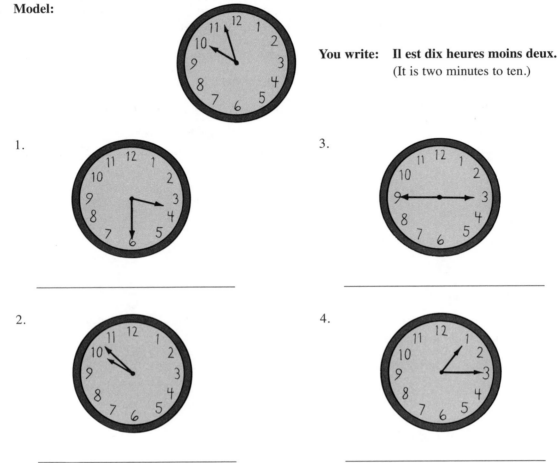

You write: **Il est dix heures moins deux.**
(It is two minutes to ten.)

1.

3.

2.

4.

III.   Quelle est la date aujourd'hui? Write the answer in a complete sentence on the line provided under each calendar.

Model:

SEPTEMBRE

D	L	M	M	J	V	S
	1	2	3	4	5	6
7	8	9	10	11	12	13
14	15	⑯	17	18	19	20
21	22	23	24	25	26	27
28	29	30				

You write: **C'est aujourd'hui le seize septembre.**
(Today is September 16.)

1.

OCTOBRE

D	L	M	M	J	V	S
		①	2	3	4	
5	6	7	8	9	10	11
12	13	14	15	16	17	18
19	20	21	22	23	24	25
26	27	28	29	30	31	

2.

NOVEMBRE

D	L	M	M	J	V	S
						1
2	3	4	5	6	7	8
9	⑩	11	12	13	14	15
16	17	18	19	20	21	22
23/30	24	25	26	27	28	29

IV. **A quelle heure?** (At what time?) Answer the following questions in complete sentences (in French) using the time given in parentheses. Be sure to use one of the following with each time stated: **du matin**, **de l'après-midi**, **du soir**.

Model:	A quelle heure étudiez-vous? (8 P.M.)	You write:	J'étudie à huit heures du soir.
	(At what time do you study?)		(I study at 8 o'clock in the evening.)

1. A quelle heure vous levez-vous? (6:30 A.M.) _____

2. A quelle heure allez-vous à l'école? (8 A.M.) _____

3. A quelle heure regardez-vous la télévision? (4 P.M.) _____

4. A quelle heure dînez-vous? (6 P.M.) _____

5. A quelle heure vous couchez-vous? (10:30 P.M.) _____

V. Answer the following questions in complete sentences.

1. Quels sont les mois de l'année? _____

    _____

2. Quels sont les jours de la semaine? _____

    _____

3. Quelles sont les saisons de l'année? _____

    _____

VI. Answer the following questions in complete sentences. You will write two sentences. In your first sentence (a) answer the question in the negative. In your second sentence (b) give the day that **precedes** the day asked in the question.

Model:	Est-ce dimanche aujourd'hui?	You write:	(a) **Non, ce n'est pas dimanche.**
	(Is today Sunday?)		(No, it's not Sunday.)
			(b) **C'est aujourd'hui samedi.**
			(Today is Saturday.)

1. Est-ce lundi aujourd'hui?

    (a) _____   (b) _____

2. Est-ce mardi aujourd'hui?

    (a) _____   (b) _____

3. Est-ce mercredi aujourd'hui?

    (a) _____   (b) _____

4. Est-ce vendredi aujourd'hui?

    (a) _____   (b) _____

5. Est-ce jeudi aujourd'hui?

   (a) _____   (b) _____

6. Est-ce samedi aujourd'hui?

   (a) _____   (b) _____

7. Est-ce dimanche aujourd'hui?

   (a) _____   (b) _____

VII. Write in French the questions that would have been asked.

Model:	**Elle a vingt-huit ans.**	**You write:**	**Quel âge a-t-elle?**
	(She is twenty-eight years old.)		(How old is she?)

1. Il a cinquante ans. _____

2. Il est trois heures. _____

3. Elle a trente ans. _____

4. C'est aujourd'hui le premier mai. _____

5. Il est minuit. _____

6. C'est aujourd'hui le cinq avril. _____

7. Elles ont quinze ans. _____

8. Il est midi. _____

9. J'ai vingt ans. _____

10. C'est aujourd'hui lundi. _____

VIII. Friendly Persuasion.   **Proficiency in Writing.**

Situation: You and your friend have saved enough money to go on a vacation by plane. Your friend isn't sure about going. You telephone to persuade your friend to go. Begin with **Salut! C'est moi** and end with **à bientôt!** (*See you soon!*) In six statements or questions, persuade your friend to travel with you. You may use your own ideas or ideas suggested by the following: a good season or month to travel, where you want to go, what you two are to see there, what you are going to do in the evening and in the daytime, doesn't he or she want to spend the vacation there.

Practice writing your six statements on the following lines.

1. _____

2. _____

3. _____

4. _____

5. _____

6. _____

Le Train à Grande Vitesse (TGV)/high-speed train.

WORK UNIT 10

Formation and Use of the Imperative (Command)

Le concours de talents à l'école

Who do you suppose wins the big talent show prize?

Tout d'un coup, Coco arrive en courant dans la grande salle. Sur la tête, il a le chapeau haut-de-forme, dans la gueule le bâton et la cape, et sur le dos le lapin!

C'est aujourd'hui vendredi. C'est le grand jour du concours de talents dans la grande salle de l'école. Il y a des étudiants qui vont chanter, danser, faire des tours de force et des tours de main, jouer d'un instrument de musique, et raconter des contes drôles. Janine et Pierre sont dans le concours de talents aussi. Pierre est le magicien et Janine l'assistante. Ils préparent leur représentation.

—Donne-moi mon chapeau haut-de-forme, dit Pierre à Janine.

—Je n'ai pas ton chapeau haut-de-forme, répond Janine.

—Apporte-moi mon bâton, dit Pierre à Janine.

—Je n'ai pas ton bâton, répond Janine.

—Donne-moi ma cape, dit Pierre.

—Je n'ai pas ta cape, répond Janine.

—Apporte-moi le lapin, dit Pierre.

—Je n'ai pas le lapin, répond Janine.

A ce moment-là, quelques spectateurs dans la grande salle s'écrient:

—Dansez! Chantez! Faites quelque chose!

Ce sont les étudiants et les professeurs.

—Zut, alors! Ne finissons pas, Janine. Nous n'avons ni chapeau haut-de-forme, ni bâton, ni cape, ni lapin.

—Ne choisis pas cette alternative, dit Janine à Pierre.

—Alors, restons-nous ou partons-nous? demande Pierre. Il faut faire quelque chose!

—Allez-vous faire quelque chose, enfin?! demandent tous les spectateurs.

—Ne réponds pas, Janine, dit Pierre.

Tout d'un coup, Coco arrive en courant dans la grande salle. Sur la tête il a le chapeau haut-de-forme, dans la gueule le bâton et la cape, et sur le dos le lapin!

—Viens ici, Coco! s'exclame Pierre.

—Assieds-toi, Coco! s'exclame Janine.

—C'est merveilleux! dit Pierre. Maintenant, finissons la représentation.

Janine et Pierre finissent leur représentation. Les autres étudiants finissent leurs représentations aussi. Et qui gagne le grand prix? Coco, naturellement! Parce qu'il a beaucoup de talent!

Vocabulaire

apporte! bring!; **apporte-moi** bring me

assieds-toi! sit down!

le bâton *n.*, the wand, stick, baton

ce sont ... they are ..., it's ...

le chapeau haut-de-forme *n.*, the top hat

la chose *n.*, thing; **quelque chose** something

le concours de talents the talent show

le conte *n.*, the story, tale

courant *pres. part. of* **courir**; **en courant** (while) running

donne-moi give me

le dos *n.*, the back

drôle *adj.*, funny, droll, odd

faites *v. form of* **faire** (to do, to make); **faites quelque chose!** do something!

finissons! let's finish!; **ne finissons pas!** let's not finish!

gagner *v.,* to win
la grande salle *n.,* the auditorium
la gueule *n.,* the mouth of an animal
le lapin *n.,* the rabbit
le magicien, la magicienne *n.,* the magician
le maître, la maîtresse *n.,* the teacher
naturellement *adv.,* naturally

partons-nous? are we leaving?
le prix *n.,* the price, the prize; **le grand prix** the grand prize
reconter *v.,* to tell, to relate
la représentation *n.,* the presentation, performance, show
restons-nous? are we staying?
le spectateur, la spectatrice *n.,* the spectator

la tête *n.,* the head
tour de force feat of strength; **tour de main** sleight of hand, hand trick
tous *adj. m. pl.,* all
tout d'un coup all of a sudden
viens ici! come here!
zut, alors! darn it!

Exercises

Review the story and vocabulary before starting these exercises.

I.   Answer the following questions in complete sentences. They are based on the story.

1.   Quel jour est-ce aujourd'hui? _____

2.   Dans le concours de talents, qui va jouer le rôle de magicien? _____

_____

3.   Qui est l'assistante de Pierre? _____

4.   Est-ce que Pierre et Janine ont le chapeau haut-de-forme, le bâton, la cape, et le lapin? _____

_____

5.   Qui arrive dans la grande salle avec le chapeau, le bâton, la cape, et le lapin?

_____

6.   Qui gagne le grand prix? _____

II.   Answer the following questions in complete sentences. They are personal questions that require answers of your own.

1.   Avez-vous du talent? Dansez-vous? Chantez-vous? _____

_____

2.   Est-ce que vous jouez d'un instrument de musique? _____

3.   Aimez-vous le français? _____

4.   Quel jour de la semaine allez-vous au cinéma? _____

III. **Comment dit-on en français …?**

Find these statements in the story and write them in French.

1. Today is Friday. _____

2. It's the big day of the talent show. _____

3. Bring me my wand; bring me the rabbit. _____

4. I don't have your cape. _____

5. And who wins the grand prize? Coco, naturally! Because he has a lot of talent. _____

    _____

Structures de la Langue

A. Formation and use of the imperative (command) in the three regular conjugations (-er, -ir, -re)

AFFIRMATIVE

	2nd person singular (**tu**)	2nd person plural (**vous**)	1st person plural (**nous**)
DANSER	**danse!**	**dansez!**	**dansons!**
to dance	*dance!*	*dance!*	*let's dance!*
FINIR	**finis!**	**finissez!**	**finissons!**
to finish	*finish!*	*finish!*	*let's finish!*
VENDRE	**vends!**	**vendez!**	**vendons!**
to sell	*sell!*	*sell!*	*let's sell!*

NEGATIVE

DANSER	**ne** danse **pas!**	**ne** dansez **pas!**	**ne** dansons **pas!**
	don't dance!	*don't dance!*	*let's not dance!*
FINIR	**ne** finis **pas!**	**ne** finissez **pas!**	**ne** finissons **pas!**
	don't finish!	*don't finish!*	*let's not finish!*
VENDRE	**ne** vends **pas!**	**ne** vendez **pas!**	**ne** vendons **pas!**
	don't sell!	*don't sell!*	*let's not sell!*

Rules and observations:

1. In the two boxes above, the second person singular and the second person plural are right next to each other so that you can compare the forms. The first person plural stands alone at the right.

2. To form the *imperative* in the affirmative, use the same verb form as in the present indicative, which you have already learned. Drop the subject pronoun **tu**, **vous**, or **nous**.

3. There is one exception. You must drop the final **s** in the second person singular of an **-er** verb. This is done in the affirmative and negative, as shown on the previous page, as in **danse!** For more about this, see Work Unit 11.

4. To form the negative of the imperative, place **ne** in front of the verb and **pas** after it, as you learned to do when forming the negative of the present indicative.

Exercises

Review the preceding material before starting these exercises.

I.   Write the three forms of the imperative in the affirmative.

Model: danser	**You write:**	**danse** (2nd pers., sing.)	**dansez** (2nd pers., pl.)	**dansons** (1st pers., pl.)

A. -ER verbs

1. donner

2. apporter

3. chercher

4. aider

5. chanter

B. -IR verbs

1. finir

2. choisir

3. bâtir

4. punir

5. obéir

C. -RE verbs

1. vendre

2. attendre

3. descendre

4. répondre

5. rendre

II. Change the following imperative sentences to the negative.

Model:	**Danse, mon enfant!**	You write:	**Ne danse pas, mon enfant!**
	(Dance, my child!)		(Don't dance, my child!)

1. Chantez, Janine! _____

2. Finissons le travail maintenant! _____

3. Vendez la maison, Monsieur Paquet! _____

4. Écoute la musique, Pierre! _____

5. Attendez l'autobus! _____

B. Formation and use of reflexive verbs in the imperative

AFFIRMATIVE

	2nd person singular (**tu**)	2nd person plural (**vous**)	1st person plural (**nous**)
S'ASSEOIR	**assieds-toi!**	**asseyez-vous!**	**asseyons-nous!**
to sit down	*sit down!*	*sit down!*	*let's sit down!*
SE LEVER	**lève-toi!**	**levez-vous!**	**levons-nous!**
to get up	*get up!*	*get up!*	*let's get up!*
SE LAVER	**lave-toi!**	**lavez-vous!**	**lavons-nous!**
to wash oneself	*wash yourself!*	*wash yourself!* or *wash yourselves!*	*let's wash ourselves!*

NEGATIVE

S'ASSEOIR	**ne** t'assieds **pas!**	**ne** vous asseyez **pas!**	**ne** nous asseyons **pas!**
	don't sit down!	*don't sit down!*	*let's not sit down!*
SE LEVER	**ne** te lève **pas!**	**ne** vous levez **pas!**	**ne** nous levons **pas!**
	don't get up!	*don't get up!*	*let's not get up!*
SE LAVER	**ne** te lave **pas!**	**ne** vous lavez **pas!**	**ne** nous lavons **pas!**
	don't wash yourself!	*don't wash yourself!* or *don't wash yourselves!*	*let's not wash ourselves!*

Rules and observations:

1. To form the negative of a reflexive verb in the affirmative, use the same verb as in the present indicative, unless the form is irregular in the imperative.

2. Drop the subject pronouns **tu**, **vous**, and **nous**.

3. You must drop the **s** in the second person singular of an **-er** verb. This is done in the affirmative and negative, as shown. See **se lever** and **se laver** in the second person singular.

4. Keep the reflexive pronouns **te**, **vous**, and **nous**. They serve as direct object pronouns. **Vous** and **nous** are reflexive pronouns as well as subject pronouns.

5. The reflexive pronoun is placed *after* the verb in the affirmative of the imperative. The verb and pronoun are joined with a hyphen. **Te** becomes **toi** when it is placed *after* the verb with a hyphen. This happens only in the affirmative.

6. To form the imperative of a reflexive verb in the negative, keep the reflexive pronoun *in front of* the verb form. **Te** becomes **t'** in the negative imperative when the verb right after it starts with a vowel or a silent *h*, as in **ne t'assieds pas**.

7. To form the negative imperative, place **ne** before the reflexive pronoun and **pas** after the verb.

Exercises

Review the preceding material before starting these exercises.

I. Choose the correct verb form and write it on the line.

1. Wash yourself! (lavez-vous, lavons-nous, vous vous lavez) _____

2. Sit down! (asseyons-nous, assieds-toi, vous vous asseyez) _____

3. Get up! (levons-nous, nous nous levons, levez-vous) _____

4. Sit down! (asseyez-vous, asseyons-nous, levez-vous) _____

5. Let's wash ourselves! (lavez-vous, vous vous lavez, lavons-nous) _____

6. Get up! (lève-toi, levons-nous, lave-toi) _____

7. Don't wash yourself! (ne te lave pas, ne te lève pas, lave-toi) _____

8. Let's not get up! (ne nous levons pas, ne vous levez pas, levez-vous) _____

II. Change the following affirmative imperatives to the negative imperative.

Model: **Levez-vous!**	**You write:** **Ne vous levez pas!**
(Get up!)	(Don't get up!)

1. Lavons-nous! _____   4. Assieds-toi! _____

2. Asseyez-vous! _____   5. Lavez-vous! _____

3. Lave-toi! _____   6. Lève-toi! _____

III.   Match the following.

1. Ne vous lavez pas.

2. Assieds-toi.

3. Ne te lève pas.

4. Levez-vous.

5. Asseyons-nous.

_____ Sit down.

_____ Get up.

_____ Let's sit down.

_____ Don't wash yourself.

_____ Don't get up.

IV.   Fill in the missing letters to form the imperative.

Model: Dance!	**Answer: DANSE _Z_ !**

1.   Listen!   ÉCOUTE ___ !

2.   Give!   DONN ___ ___ !

3.   Sing!   CHANTE ___ !

4.   Finish!   FIN ___ ___ ___ EZ !

5.   Choose!   CHOISISS ___ ___ !

6.   Let's not sell!   NE VEND ___ ___ ___ PAS!

7.   Don't wait!   N'ATTEN ___ ___ ___ PAS!

8.   Answer!   RÉ ___ ___ N ___ ___ Z!

9.   Wait!   ATT ___ ___ D ___ ___ !

10. Sit down!   A ___ ___ EY ___ ___ -VOUS!

11. Get up!   LEV ___ ___ -VOUS!

12. Wash yourself!   L ___ VE ___ -VOUS!

V.   **Expressing Personal Feelings.   Proficiency in Speaking and Writing**

Situation: You are in a florist shop (**chez un fleuriste**) because you want to buy a plant for a friend. You are talking with the florist. Use your own ideas and words or follow the guided conversation. To know what to say and write on the lines, you must read what the florist says before and after your lines.

Le fleuriste: **Bonjour! Vous désirez?**

1.   _Vous:_ _____

Le fleuriste: **C'est pour vous? Ou c'est pour offrir comme cadeau?**

2.   _Vous:_ _____

Le fleuriste: **Ah, bon! C'est pour une occasion spéciale?**

3.   _Vous:_ _____

Le fleuriste: **Aimez-vous cette plante rouge? Elle est très jolie.**

4.   _Vous:_ _____

Le fleuriste: **C'est trente euros.**

5.   _Vous:_ _____

VI. Storytelling. **Proficiency in Speaking and Writing.**

Situation: Alice, one of your classmates, was absent when this lesson was covered in class. She wants you to tell her what is going on in the picture at the beginning of this work unit about the talent show in your school. It was summarized in class.

You may use your own words and the vocabulary words on the pages following the picture. When you tell her, make at least five statements. Then practice writing them here:

1. _____

2. _____

3. _____

4. _____

5. _____

VII. Health. **Proficiency in Speaking and Writing.**

Situation: Pretend that you are a dentist (**le, la dentiste**), telling your patient what to do.

Use the imperative (command) in the polite **vous** form as practiced in this lesson. For example, you may want to say: **Asseyez-vous**/*Sit down*; **ouvrez la bouche**/*open your mouth*; **fermez les yeux**/*close your eyes*; **fermez la bouche**/*close your mouth*; **ouvrez les yeux**/*open your eyes*; **levez-vous**/*get up*. Don't forget to add **s'il vous plaît** (*please*) after each command!

Say aloud at least six statements in the imperative that you would say to your patient. Then practice writing them here:

1. _____

2. _____

3. _____

4. _____

5. _____

6. _____

VIII. Girl Talk. **Proficiency in Speaking, Reading, and Writing.**

Situation: Look at the photo of the three French girls talking. From left to right, they are Claudette, Yvette, and Odette. The photo is on the next page.

Let's imagine what they are saying. You may use your own ideas and words or those in the following guided conversation. Say and write the words on the blank lines. Use the *tu* form of a verb (2nd pers., sing.) because they are friends.

A note of cultural interest: the young women are wearing the typical Pont-Aven costume of Bretagne, a region of France located in the northwest. See Brest and Rennes on the map in the preceding work unit. Original features of the Breton costume include the headdress/**la coiffe** and the large collar made of starched lace.

Claudette: **Moi? Oh, non, je ne chante pas bien!**

Yvette: _____

But you dance very well.

Odette: **Claudette danse très bien quand elle danse avec son ami Roger. N'est-ce pas, Claudette?/***Isn't that so, Claudette?*

Claudette: _____

*Yes. It's true./***Oui, c'est vrai.**

Yvette: _____

Are you going to the big dance in town with Roger tonight?

Claudette: **Oui, je vais au grand bal en ville avec Roger ce soir. Viens avec nous, Yvette/***Come with us, Yvette.*

Yvette: _____

With my friend Pierre?

Claudette: **Bien sûr, avec ton ami Pierre. Et toi, Odette, tu viens avec nous? Avec Gérard?**

Odette: **Gérard et moi nous allons au cinéma ce soir. Nous allons voir le film *Les Parapluies de Cherbourg.*** **C'est un vieux film, mais excellent.**

Claudette: _____

*It's a fascinating film!/***C'est un film passionnant!**

*Cherbourg is a French seaport located in the northwest on the English Channel/**La Manche.**
Find it on the map in the preceding work unit.

Review Test: Work Units 6–10

I.   The words in the boxes are scrambled. Unscramble them to find a meaningful sentence.

Monique	puces	aux	est	marché
au	Janine	amie	son	avec

II.   Choose the correct verb form and write it with its subject. _____

  1.   Monsieur et Madame Durant (vend, vendent, vendons) leur maison. _____

  2.   Le petit chien (romps, rompt, rompent) la grande barrière. _____

  3.   Le professeur (interrompt, interrompez, interrompent) l'étudiant. _____

  4.   Janine (rend, rends, rendent) le livre à la bibliothèque. _____

  5.   Nous (entendons, entendez, entendent) la musique. _____

III.   Complete each verb form in the present indicative by adding the correct letter or letters.

  1.   Nous aim _____ parler français.

  2.   Odette chant _____ bien.

  3.   Pauline chois _____ une jolie jupe.

  4.   J'attend _____ l'autobus.

  5.   Tu parl _____ bien le français.

  6.   Les élèves fin _____ les devoirs.

IV.   Write the appropriate reflexive pronoun.

  1.   Tous les matins je _____ lave.

  2.   Joseph, pourquoi ne _____ laves-tu pas?

  3.   Est-ce que les enfants _____ lavent?

  4.   Je _____ dépêche pour aller à lécole.

  5.   Nous _____ amusons quand nous allons au cinéma.

V.   Choose the correct answer and write the word.

  1.   Trois et quatre font   (a) cinq   (b) six   (c) sept   (d) huit   _____

  2.   Six fois deux font   (a) douze   (b) treize   (c) huit   (d) trois   _____

  3.   Treize moins neuf font   (a) sept   (b) huit   (c) neuf   (d) quatre   _____

  4.   Cinquante divisés par deux font   (a) cinquante-deux   (b) vingt-cinq
        (c) trente-cinq   (d) trente   _____

VI. For each clock, write the time shown in French.

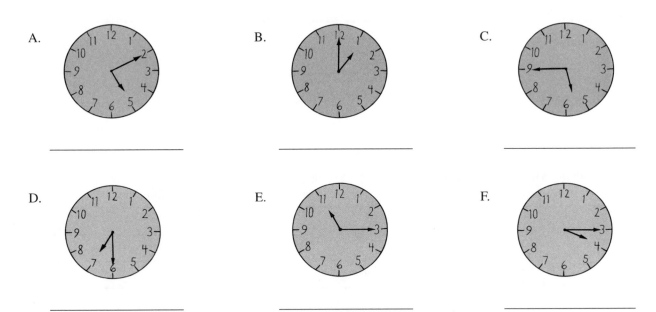

A. _____

B. _____

C. _____

D. _____

E. _____

F. _____

VII. Each of the following sentences contains a blank. Of the four choices given, select the one that can be inserted in the blank to form a sensible and grammatically correct sentence and circle the letter of your choice.

1. Quelle est la date aujourd'hui? C'est aujourd'hui _____ février.

   (a) l'un   (b) le premier de   (c) le premier   (d) la première

2. Quel jour précède lundi? C'est _____ .

   (a) samedi   (b) dimanche   (c) mardi   (d) jeudi

3. Il y a _____ saisons dans l'année.

   (a) cinq   (b) quart   (c) quatre   (d) quarante

4. Les fleurs poussent _____ printemps.

   (a) en   (b) dans   (c) dans le   (d) au

5. En général, _____ hiver il fait froid à New York.

   (a) en   (b) dans   (c) dans l'   (d) à l'

VIII. Write the English for the following commands in French.

   Model: Asseyez-vous!   **You write: Sit down!**

1. Lavez-vous! _____

2. Asseyons-nous! _____

3. Levez-vous! _____

IX. Fill in the missing letters to form the imperative.

| Model: **Dance!** | Answer: DANSE __Z__ ! |

1. Sit down!   A _____ _____ EY _____ _____ -VOUS!

2. Get up!   LEV _____ _____ -VOUS!

3. Choose!   CHOIS _____ _____ _____ _____ _____ !

X. Write in French the questions that would have been asked.

Model: Elle a vingt-huit ans.   (She is twenty-eight years old.)
You write the question that would have been asked: **Quel âge a-t-elle?**   (How old is she?)

1. Monsieur Durand a quarante ans. _____

2. J'ai dix-huit ans. _____

3. Il est quatre heures et demie. _____

4. C'est aujourd'hui vendredi. _____

5. C'est le premier janvier. _____

XI. Proficiency in Reading.

Directions: In the following passage there are ten numbered blank spaces. Each space represents a missing word. Four possible completions are provided for each. Only one of them is grammatically correct and makes sense in the context of the passage.

First, read the passage in its entirety to determine its general meaning. Then read it a second time. Choose the completion that makes the best sense and is grammatically correct, and write its letter in the space provided.

Aujourd'hui Janine _____ au marché _____ puces avec son amie Monique.

1. A. suis	2. A. au
B. es	B. à
C. est	C. à la
D. sont	D. aux

Elles _____ la journée au marché parce que c'est un endroit très intéressant.

3. A. passe
    B. passons
    C. passez
    D. passent

—Oh, Monique! Regarde! Un _____ vase. Il est superbe! s'exclame Janine.

4. A. joli
    B. jolie
    C. jolis
    D. jolies

—Pour combien _____ -vous ce vase, madame? demande Janine.

    5. A. vends
        B. vend
        C. vendons
        D. vendez

—Je _____ ce vase pour dix euros, mademoiselle, répond la marchande.

    6. A. vends
        B. vend
        C. vendons
        D. vendez

—Je n'ai pas dix euros sur moi. J'ai deux euros. Monique, _____ -tu huit euros?

    7. A. a
        B. as
        C. avez
        D. ont

—Non, Janine, je n'ai pas huit euros, répond Monique.

—Je _____ retourner à la maison pour demander à ma mère les huit euros.

    8. A. vais
        B. va
        C. vont
        D. aller

Je veux _____ ce vase. Il est extraordinaire, dit Janine à la femme.

    9. A. être
        B. avoir
        C. vendre
        D. rompre

Monique, _____ avec moi!

    10. A. venir
         B. viens
         C. venons
         D. viennent

XII. Proficiency in Writing.

Directions: Of the following six situations, select four and write your statements on the lines on the next page. For each situation, write at least three sentences.

Situation 1: You want to go to a county fair in the suburbs of the city where you live, but your parents don't like the idea. Persuade them to let you go. You may use your own ideas and words, those in Work Unit 6, and/or the following; **j'aimerais aller à la foire; vendre, acheter, beaucoup de choses.**

Situation 2: You are studying French in a summer session at the Alliance Française Institute in Paris. Before you left for France, you promised your best friend Robert that you would send him a postcard about your daily activities. Use the reflexive verbs you practiced in Work Unit 7.

Situation 3: You spent a wonderful afternoon at a beautiful indoor swimming pool in Paris. It's something to write home about.

Situation 4: You are at an auction with a friend. You are not making any bids and you want to leave immediately. Your friend wants to know why you want to leave. Express your feelings. You may use your own ideas and words, those in Work Unit 8, and/or the following: **désirer, partir, aimer, les choses, les meubles** (furniture), **laid, monstrueux, le fauteuil, la petite table ronde, les chaises.**

Situation 5: You are on vacation in France. You and a friend are planning a trip from Paris to Lyon. Your friend wants to go by plane. You want to go by train, in particular, **le TGV**. Persuade your friend to go on the **TGV** by giving three reasons. You may use your own ideas and words, those in Work Unit 9 where you saw a picture of the **TGV** and consulted the map of France, and/or the following: **Le TGV va très vite**/*The TGV goes very fast*; **C'est un train extraordinaire**/*It's an extraordinary train*; **C'est plus amusant**/*It's more fun.*

Situation 6: Pretend that you are a dentist. You are telling your patient what to do. Use the imperative (command) in the polite **vous** form as practiced in Work Unit 10. For example, you may want to say: *Sit down, please; open your mouth; close your eyes; close your mouth; open your eyes; rinse out your mouth* (**se rincer; rincez-vous la bouche**); *get up, please.*

Select four of the six situations just described, and write your sentences on the following lines.

Situation 1

1. _____
2. _____
3. _____

Situation 2

1. _____
2. _____
3. _____

Situation 3

1. _____
2. _____
3. _____

Situation 4

1. _____
2. _____
3. _____

Situation 5

1. _____
2. _____
3. _____

Situation 6

1. _____
2. _____
3. _____

Notre-Dame de Paris

Arc de triomphe de l'Étoile

WORK UNIT 11

Irregular Verbs in the Present Indicative and Imperative

Qu'est-ce que c'est?

Have you ever played guessing games in English? In French? Here are some in French.

Qu'est-ce que c'est?

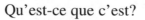

Qu'est-ce que c'est?

Qu'est-ce que c'est?

Qu'est-ce que c'est?

Qu'est-ce que c'est?

A brief description is given of something and then you are asked, "Qu'est-ce que c'est?" (What is it?) See how many you can do. The answers are upside down following the descriptions.

1. C'est quelque chose à boire. Il peut avoir le goût d'orange, ananas, pamplemousse, raisin, ou tomate. Il peut être en boîte ou en bouteille. C'est toujours délicieux. Qu'est-ce que c'est?

2. C'est un meuble. Vous vous asseyez sur ce meuble. Qu'est-ce que c'est?

3. C'est quelque chose à manger. Elle est toujours froide et crémeuse. Elle peut être au chocolat, à la vanille, aux fraises. Elle est toujours délicieuse. Qu'est-ce que c'est?

4. C'est un fruit. Il a la couleur rouge ou jaune ou verte. Qu'est-ce que c'est?

5. C'est une machine qui a un moteur et quatre roues. Elle peut aller vite ou lentement. Elle est dangereuse si le conducteur ne fait pas attention. Elle ne peut pas marcher sans essence. Qu'est-ce que c'est?

6. C'est un appareil. Une personne peut parler dans cet appareil et peut entendre une autre personne parler. Quand une personne veut parler, cet appareil sonne. Qu'est-ce que c'est?

7. C'est un animal qui a des plumes et des ailes. Il vole comme un avion. Qu'est-ce que c'est?

8. C'est un appareil que vous utilisez pour travailler et pour surfer. Il a une souris. Qu'est-ce que c'est?

9. C'est un appareil. Il sonne tous les matins quand vous dormez, et vous vous levez. Qu'est-ce que c'est?

10. C'est une partie du corps humain. Elle a cinq doigts. Qu'est-ce que c'est?

11. C'est un objet d'habillement. C'est pour la tête. Qu'est-ce que c'est?

	11. un chapeau	10. une main	9. un réveille-matin
8. un ordinateur	7. un oiseau	6. un téléphone	5. une automobile ou une voiture
4. une pomme	3. une glace	2. une chaise	1. un jus de fruit

Vocabulaire

l'aile *n. f.,* the wing
l'ananas *n. m.,* the pineapple
l'appareil *n. m.,* the apparatus, the instrument
boire *v.,* to drink
la boîte *n.,* the box, tin can
la bouteille *n.,* the bottle
le conducteur, la conductrice *n.,* the driver
le corps *n.,* body; **le corps humain** the human body
crémeux *m.,* **crémeuse** *f., adj.,* creamy
dangereux *m.,* **dangereuse** *f., adj.,* dangerous
délicieux *m.,* **délicieuse** *f., adj.,* delicious
le doigt *n.,* the finger
entendre *v.,* to hear
l'essence *n. f.,* gasoline

faire attention *v.,* to pay attention, to be careful
la fraise *n.,* the strawberry
froid *m.,* **froide** *f., adj.,* cold
le goût *n.,* the taste, flavor
l'habillement *n. m.,* clothing
jaune *adj.,* yellow
le jus *n.,* juice; **jus d'orange** orange juice
le meuble *n.,* piece of furniture
le moteur *n.,* motor, engine
le pamplemousse *n.,* the grapefruit
la partie *n.,* the part (of a whole)
la personne *n.,* the individual, person
peut *v. form of* **pouvoir** (can, be able to); **elle peut aller** it can go; **il peut avoir** it can have; **il peut être** it can be
qu'est-ce que c'est? what is it?

le raisin *n.,* the grape
la roue *n.,* the wheel
rouge *adj.,* red
sans *prep.,* without
sonner *v.,* to ring
la souris *n.,* the mouse
surfer *v.,* to surf (the Internet); you can also use **naviguer** to navigate, to surf (the Internet)
la tomate *n.,* the tomato
la vanille *n.,* vanilla
veut *v. form of* **vouloir** (to want); **une personne veut** a person wants
la voiture *n.,* the car, automobile
voler *v.,* to fly

Exercises

Review the preceding material before starting these exercises.

I. Choose the correct answer based on the guessing game at the beginning of this unit.

1. Un jus de fruit est quelque chose à
   (a) manger.   (b) boire.   (c) conduire.   (d) pouvoir.   _____

2. La glace est toujours   (a) charmante.   (b) froide.   (c) ennuyeuse.   (d) ronde.   _____

3. Une voiture peut être dangereuse si le conducteur ou la conductrice ne fait pas
   (a) sa leçon.   (b) ses devoirs.   (c) son stylo.   (d) attention.   _____

4. Un téléphone est un   (a) objet d'habillement.   (b) jus.   (c) appareil.   (d) moteur.   _____

5. Un chapeau est un   (a) jus.   (b) goût.   (c) appareil.   (d) objet d'habillement.   _____

II. Answer the following questions in complete sentences. They are personal questions and require answers of your own.
   Model: Mon fruit favori est l'orange.   (My favorite fruit is the orange.)

1. Quel est votre fruit favori? _____

2. Quel est votre dessert favori? _____

3. Quel est votre sport favori? _____

III. Un acrostiche.   Complete the French words in this puzzle.

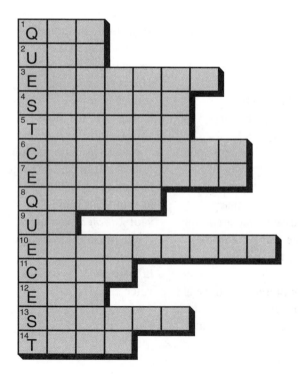

1. who
2. indefinite article (*f., sing.*)
3. gasoline
4. to ring
5. tomato
6. creamy (*f.*)
7. annoying (*m.*)
8. when
9. indefinite article (*m., sing.*)
10. United States
11. key
12. water
13. mouse
14. head

Structures de la Langue

A. Irregular verbs in the present indicative tense

1. **aller** *to go* je vais tu vas il, elle va nous allons vous allez ils, elles vont	2. **apprendre** *to learn* j'apprends tu apprends il, elle apprend nous apprenons vous apprenez ils, elles apprennent	3. **avoir** *to have* j'ai tu as il, elle a nous avons vous avez ils, elles ont
4. **boire** *to drink* je bois tu bois il, elle boit nous buvons vous buvez ils, elles boivent	5. **comprendre** *to understand* je comprends tu comprends il, elle comprend nous comprenons vous comprenez ils, elles comprennent	6. **courir** *to run* je cours tu cours il, elle court nous courons vous courez ils, elles courent
7. **devenir** *to become* je deviens tu deviens il, elle devient nous devenons vous devenez ils, elles deviennent	8. **devoir** *have to, must, should* je dois tu dois il, elle doit nous devons vous devez ils, elles doivent	9. **dire** *to say, tell* je dis tu dis il, elle dit nous disons vous dites ils, elles disent
10. **écrire** *to write* j'écris tu écris il, elle écrit nous écrivons vous écrivez ils, elles écrivent	11. **être** *to be* je suis tu es il, elle est nous sommes vous êtes ils, elles sont	12. **faire** *to do, make* je fais tu fais il, elle fait nous faisons vous faites ils, elles font
13. **lire** *to read* je lis tu lis il, elle lit nous lisons vous lisez ils, elles lisent	14. **mettre** *to put, place, put on* je mets tu mets il, elle met nous mettons vous mettez ils, elles mettent	15. **ouvrir** *to open* j'ouvre tu ouvres il, elle ouvre nous ouvrons vous ouvrez ils, elles ouvrent

16. **partir** *to leave, depart*	17. **pouvoir** *can, to be able*	18. **prendre** *to take*
je pars tu pars il, elle part nous partons vous partez ils, elles partent	je peux *or* puis tu peux il, elle peut nous pouvons vous pouvez ils, elles peuvent	je prends tu prends il, elle prend nous prenons vous prenez ils, elles prennent
19. **revenir** *to come back*	20. **savoir** *to know (how)*	21. **sortir** *to go out, leave*
je reviens tu reviens il, elle revient nous revenons vous revenez il, elles reviennent	je sais tu sais il, elle sait nous savons vous savez ils, elles savent	je sors tu sors il, elle sort nous sortons vous sortez ils, elles sortent
22. **venir** *to come*	23. **voir** *to see*	24. **vouloir** *to want*
je viens tu viens il, elle vient nous venons vous venez ils, elles viennent	je vois tu vois il, elle voit nous voyons vous voyez ils, elles voient	je veux tu veux il, elle veut nous voulons vous voulez ils, elles veulent

Exercises

Review the preceding material before starting these exercises.

I. Answer the following questions in the affirmative in complete sentences. In answer (a) use **oui**; in answer (b) use **aussi**. Study the models.

> Models: **(a) Allez-vous au cinéma?**   You write: **(a) Oui, je vais au cinéma.**
> **(b) Et Pierre?**   **(b) Il va au cinéma aussi.**

1. (a) Lisez-vous beaucoup? _____

   (b) Et Janine? _____

2. (a) Apprenez-vous le français? _____

   (b) Et Pauline? _____

3. (a) Avez-vous de la glace? _____

   (b) Et Dominique? _____

4. (a) Buvez-vous du jus d'orange? _____

   (b) Et Robert? _____

5. (a) Comprenez-vous la leçon? _____

   (b) Et Joséphine? _____

6. (a) Les garçons courent-ils à l'école? _____

   (b) Et vous et Pierre? _____

7. (a) Hélène et Jeanne doivent-elles écrire des compositions? _____

   _____

   (b) Et vous? _____

8. (a) Monsieur Paquet dit-il la vérité? _____

   (b) Et Madame Paquet et Janine? _____

9. (a) Gabrielle écrit-elle une lettre? _____

   (b) Et Françoise et Béatrice? _____

10. (a) Etes-vous dans le concours de talents à l'école? _____

   _____

   (b) Et Pierre et Janine? _____

II. Answer the following statements in the negative in complete sentences. In answer (a) use **Non**. In answer (b) use **non plus**. Study the models.

Models:	(a) **Est-ce que Pierre fait attention en classe?**	You write:	(a) **Non, il ne fait pas attention en classe.**
	(b) **Et vous?**		(b) **Je ne fais pas attention en classe non plus.**

1. (a) Est-ce que Robert lit beaucoup? _____

   (b) Et vous? _____

2. (a) Est-ce que Monique met le vase sur la table? _____

   (b) Et Jacques? _____

3. (a) Est-ce que vous ouvrez la porte? _____

   (b) Et Charles? _____

4. (a) Est-ce que Marie part à huit heures? _____

   (b) Et l'avion? _____

5. (a) Pouvez-vous aller au cinéma ce soir? _____

   (b) Et Madame et Monsieur Paquet? _____

6. (a) Prenez-vous le petit déjeuner à sept heures? _____

   (b) Et Simone? _____

7. (a)   Savez-vous quelle heure il est? _____

    (b)   Et Pierre? _____

8. (a)   Est-ce que Monsieur et Madame Paquet sortent ce soir? _____

    _____

    (b)   Et Janine? _____

9. (a)   Est-ce que vous venez ici tous les jours? _____

    (b)   Et votre ami? _____

10. (a)   Voyez-vous l'avion dans le ciel? _____

    (b)   Et votre amie? _____

III.   Change each sentence by replacing the verb in the sentence with the proper form of the verb in parentheses. Keep the same subject, of course. Rewrite the entire sentence in French.

Model: Ouvre-t-il la fenêtre?   (fermer)   You write: Ferme-t-il la fenêtre?

1. *Ferme*-t-il la porte?   (ouvrir) _____

2. Est-ce qu'elle *écrit* la lettre?   (lire) _____

3. *Buvez*-vous du café?   (prendre) _____

4. Il ne *comprend* pas la leçon.   (faire) _____

5. *Savez*-vous la date?   (écrire) _____

IV.   Write the French equivalent for the English words given. Write the entire sentence in French.
Model: Marie et Janine *understand* la question.   You write: Marie et Janine comprennent la question.

1. Henri et Robert *understand* la réponse. _____

2. *I have* beaucoup de devoirs à faire. _____

3. Hélène et Marie *are they* présentes aujourd'hui? _____

4. Michel et Jacques *do they do* leurs leçons? _____

5. *I don't see* un taxi. _____

V.   Choose the correct verb form.

1. Nous (vois, voyons, voient) la mer.   _____

2. Je (savez, savent, sais) la réponse.   _____

3. Ils (fait, faisons, font) leur travail.   _____

4. Ils (part, partent, partez) maintenant. _____

5. Tu (bois, buvez, boivent) du lait. _____

6. Janine (deviens, devient, deviennent) docteur. _____

VI. Answer the following questions in complete sentences in the affirmative, substituting the subject pronoun **Ils** or **Elles** for the noun **frères** or **soeurs**. Add **aussi**.

Model: **François apprend bien. Et vos frères?** **You write:** **Ils apprennent bien aussi.**

1. Pierre comprend bien. Et vos frères? _____

2. Guillaume écrit bien. Et vos soeurs? _____

3. Michel va bien. Et vos frères? _____

4. Guy lit bien. Et vos soeurs? _____

5. Alfred voit bien. Et vos frères? _____

B. The imperative of some common irregular verbs

Infinitive	2nd pers. sing. (**tu**)	2nd pers. pl. (**vous**)	1st pers. pl. (**nous**)
aller	**va** *go!*	**allez** *go!*	**allons** *let's go!*
apprendre	**apprends** *learn!*	**apprenez** *learn!*	**apprenons** *let's learn!*
avoir	**aie** *have …!*	**ayez** *have ….!*	**ayons** *let's have…!*
boire	**bois** *drink!*	**buvez** *drink!*	**buvons** *let's drink!*
dire	**dis** *say!*	**dites** *say!*	**disons** *let's say!*
écrire	**écris** *write!*	**écrivez** *write!*	**écrivons** *let's write!*
être	**sois** *be …!*	**soyez** *be …!*	**soyons** *let's be …!*
faire	**fais** *do!* (or) *make!*	**faites** *do!* (or) *make!*	**faisons** *let's do!* (or) *let's make!*

lire	**lis** *read!*	**lisez** *read!*	**lisons** *let's read!*
mettre	**mets** *put ...!*	**mettez** *put ...!*	**mettons** *let's put ...!*
ouvrir	**ouvre** *open ...!*	**ouvrez** *open ...!*	**ouvrons** *let's open ...!*
partir	**pars** *leave!*	**partez** *leave!*	**partons** *let's leave!*
prendre	**prends** *take!*	**prenez** *take!*	**prenons** *let's take!*
revenir	**reviens** *come back!*	**revenez** *come back!*	**revenons** *let's come back!*
sortir	**sors** *go out!*	**sortez** *go out!*	**sortons** *let's go out!*
venir	**viens** *come!*	**venez** *come!*	**venons** *let's come!*
voir	**vois** *see!*	**voyez** *see!*	**voyons** *let's see!*

Rules and observations:

1. In the boxes, the second person singular (**tu**) and the second person plural (**vous**) are right next to each other so you can compare the forms of the second persons. The first person plural (**nous**) stands alone at the right.

2. It was pointed out previously that the final **s** drops in the second person singular on an **-ER** verb in the imperative. However, when the pronouns **y** and **en** are linked to it, the **s** is retained in all regular **-ER** verbs and in the verb **aller**. Examples: **donnes-en** (*give some!*); **manges-en** (*eat some!*); **vas-y** (*go there!*). The reason for this is that it makes it easier to link the two elements by pronouncing the **s** as a **z**.

Exercises

Review the preceding material before starting these exercises.

I.   Choose the correct verb form in the imperative.

1.   Drink! (buvez, partez, faites) _____

2.   Come! (pars, viens, vois) _____

3.   Say! (dites, faites, voyez) _____

4.   Write! (mettez, ayez, écrivez) _____

5.   Read! (soyez, sortez, lisez) _____

6.   Open! (ouvrons, ouvre, écris) _____

7.   Let's go out! (sortez, sortons, voyons) _____

8.   Let's be …! (soyez, soyons, ayons) _____

9.   Let's drink! (allons, buvons, buvez) _____

10.   Come back! (revenez, sortez, venez) _____

Dis la vérité.

II. Change each sentence by replacing the verb in the sentence with the proper form of the verb in parentheses. Keep the imperative form, of course. Rewrite the entire sentence in French. The verb form you write must be in the same person as the one you are replacing.

Model:	**Dites la vérité.**	**You write:**	**Ecrivez la vérité.**
	(Tell the truth. [Write])		(Write the truth.)

1. *Ecrivez* la phrase. (dire) _____

2. *Prends* le lait. (boire) _____

3. *Venez* tout de suite. (partir) _____

4. *Ouvre* la fenêtre. (fermer) _____

5. *Mets* la valise là-bas. (prendre) _____

6. *Lisons* la lettre. (écrire) _____

7. *Apprenez* le poème. (lire) _____

8. *Partons* maintenant. (sortir) _____

9. *Soyez* à l'heure. (revenir) _____

10. *Voyons* la leçon. (faire) _____

III. Match the following.

1. Close the door.

2. Take your time.

3. Let's open the windows.

4. Eat some if you want.

5. Leave right away.

6. Put the suitcases here.

7. Give some to the boy.

8. Go there.

9. Come back tomorrow.

10. Tell the truth.

_____ Donnes-en au garçon.

_____ Manges-en si tu veux.

_____ Mettez les valises ici.

_____ Vas-y.

_____ Ouvrons les fenêtres.

_____ Revenez demain.

_____ Ferme la porte.

_____ Dis la vérité.

_____ Pars tout de suite.

_____ Prenez votre temps.

IV. For each sentence write a response in the imperative.

A. Model: **Je veux manger maintenant.**   **You write:** **Bon! Alors, mangez maintenant!**
          (I want to eat now.)   (Good! Then eat now!)

Je veux partir maintenant. (I want to leave now.)

1. Je veux partir maintenant. _____

2. Je dois ouvrir la fenêtre. _____

3. Je désire faire la leçon. _____

4. Je vais écrire une lettre. _____

5. Je vais lire le journal. _____

B. Model: **Nous voulons boire de l'eau**   **You write:** **Bon! Alors, buvez de l'eau**
          maintenant.   **maintenant!**
          (We want to drink water now.)   (Good! Then drink water now!)

1. Nous désirons sortir maintenant. _____

2. Nous voulons être ici à dix heures. _____

3. Nous allons faire le travail ce soir. _____

4. Nous désirons apprendre l'anglais. _____

5. Nous voulons parler français. _____

V. Socializing. Proficiency in Speaking.

Situation: You are at a party. To entertain your friends, play two guessing games in French. After each one, ask: **Qu'est-ce que c'est?** You may use your own ideas and words and/or those at the beginning of this work unit.

The following is a summary of **avoir** and **être** in the present indicative affirmative and negative, and in the interrogative and negative interrogative with **est-ce que** and the inverted form.

AVOIR		ÊTRE	
Affirmative		**Affirmative**	
j'ai	nous avons	je suis	nous sommes
tu as	vous avez	tu es	vous êtes
il *or* elle a	ils *or* elles ont	il *or* elle est	ils *or* elles sont
Negative		**Negative**	
je n'ai pas	nous n'avons pas	je ne suis pas	nous ne sommes pas
tu n'as pas	vous n'avez pas	tu n'es pas	vous n'êtes pas
il n'a pas	ils n'ont pas	il n'est pas	ils ne sont pas
elle n'a pas	elles n'ont pas	elle n'est pas	elles ne sont pas

AVOIR	ÊTRE
Interrogative	**Interrogative**
(a) with **est-ce que**	(a) with **est-ce que**
Est-ce que j'ai?	Est-ce que je suis?
Est-ce que tu as?	Est-ce que tu es?
Est ce qu'il a?	Est-ce qu'il est?
Est-ce qu'elle a?	Est-ce qu'elle est?
Est-ce que nous avons?	Est-ce que nous sommes?
Est-ce que vous avez?	Est-ce que vous êtes?
Est-ce qu'ils ont?	Est-ce qu'ils sont?
Est-ce qu'elles ont?	Est-ce qu'elles sont?
(b) **Inverted form**	(b) **Inverted form**
ai-je?	suis-je?
as-tu?	es-tu?
a-t-il?	est-il?
a-t-elle?	est-elle?
avons-nous?	sommes-nous?
avez-vous?	êtes-vous?
ont-ils?	sont-ils?
ont-elles?	sont-elles?

AVOIR	ÊTRE
Negative interrogative	**Negative interrogative**
(a) with **est-ce que**	(a) with **est-ce que**
Est-ce que je n'ai pas?	Est-ce que je ne suis pas?
Est-ce que tu n'as pas?	Est-ce que tu n'es pas?
Est-ce qu'il n'a pas?	Est-ce qu'il n'est pas?
Est-ce qu'elle n'a pas?	Est-ce qu'elle n'est pas?
Est-ce que nous n'avons pas?	Est-ce que nous ne sommes pas?
Est-ce que vous n'avez pas?	Est-ce que vous n'êtes pas?
Est-ce qu'ils n'ont pas?	Est-ce qu'ils ne sont pas?
Est-ce qu'elles n'ont pas?	Est-ce qu'elles ne sont pas?
(b) **Inverted form**	(b) **Inverted form**
n'ai-je pas?	ne suis-je pas?
n'as-tu pas?	n'es-tu pas?
n'a-t-il pas?	n'est-il pas?
n'a-t-elle pas?	n'est-elle pas?
n'avons-nous pas?	ne sommes-nous pas?
n'avez-vous pas?	n'êtes-vous pas?
n'ont-ils pas?	ne sont-ils pas?
n'ont-elles pas?	ne sont-elles pas?

VI. Newspaper Advertisement.   Proficiency in Reading and Writing.

Situation: You are looking for an apartment in the classified ads of a French newspaper. Read the following ad and answer the questions in complete sentences.

BEL APPARTEMENT
belle vue
2 pièces, salle de bains
cuisine moderne, petit balcon
à Montparnasse
tél. 45-04-55-14

1. Combien de pièces y a-t-il? _____

2. Est-ce que l'appartement est grand ou petit? _____

3. Quel est le numéro de téléphone? _____

VII. Sharing.   Proficiency in Reading and Writing.

Situation: Look at the picture below of two children playing together. Answer the questions in complete sentences on the lines provided.

1.   **Combien d'enfants y a-t-il dans cette photo?** _____

_____

2.   **Qu'est-ce qu'ils font ensemble/***together?* **Jouent-ils?** _____

_____

3.   **Où sont-ils? Dans un parc? Dans une chambre?** _____

_____

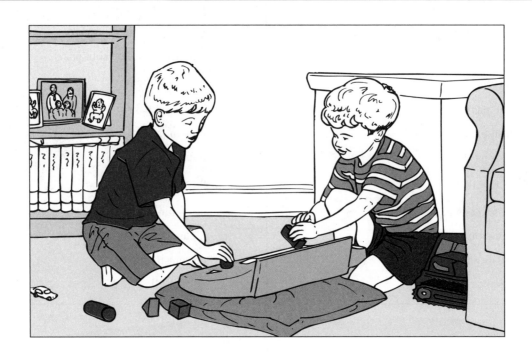

La basilique du Sacré-Coeur, Paris

WORK UNIT 12

The Passé Composé

L'autographe spécial

Have you ever asked someone for an autograph? That's what Janine did while she was at the Paris Opera House during intermission.

Oh! Monsieur! Votre autographe, s'il vous plaît! Voici mon programme et voici mon stylo.

Hier soir la famille Paquet est allée à l'opéra. Ils ont vu la représentation de *Faust*. Ils ont quitté la maison à sept heures et demie et ils sont arrivés à l'opéra à huit heures. Ils sont entrés dans le théâtre et ils ont pris leurs places à huit heurs et quart. La représentation a commencé à huit heures et demie.

Pendant l'entracte, Madame Paquet est allée parler avec quelques dames. Monsieur Paquet est allé faire un appel sur son téléphone portable, Pierre est allé acheter du chocolat, et Janine est allée boire un jus d'orange.

Madame Paquet a parlé avec les dames, et, puis, elle est retournée à sa place. Monsieur Paquet a fait son appel et il est retourné à sa place aussi. Pierre a mangé son chocolat et il est retourné à sa place. Janine a bu son jus d'orange, mais avant de retourner à sa place, elle a vu un homme et elle a dit:

—Oh! Monsieur! vous êtes le grand acteur Philippe Jirard!

—Mais … mademoiselle … a répondu le monsieur.

—Oh! Monsieur! Votre autographe, s'il vous plaît! Voici mon programme et voici mon stylo. Vous pouvez écrire votre autographe sur mon programme, a dit Janine.

—Mais … Mais … a dit le monsieur.

—Vous êtres très modeste, a dit Janine.

—Mais … Ce n'est pas que je suis modeste, mademoiselle … Mais si vous insistez … Voilà mon autographe! a dit le monsieur.

—Merci, monsieur. Merci mille fois, monsieur! a dit Janine.

Janine est retournée à sa place.

L'opéra se termine et tout le monde quitte le théâtre.

Dehors, Janine a annoncé:

—Regardez mon programme! J'ai l'autographe de Philippe Jirard!

—Philippe Jirard?! Vraiment? Incroyable! a dit la mère.

Janine a donné son programme à sa mère et elle a lu: "Je ne suis pas Philippe Jirard. Je m'appelle Jean Leblanc."

—Ce n'est pas possible! Oh! J'ai fait une bêtise! a dit Janine.

—Ce n'est pas si bête. Tu as l'autographe de Jean Leblanc. Tou le monde n'a pas l'autographe de Jean Leblanc sur un programme! a répondu Pierre.

—Qui est Jean Leblanc? a demandé le père.

—C'est une personne ordinaire, comme toi et moi! a répondu la mère. Maintenant nous avons un autographe spécial!

Et ils ont ri.

Vocabulaire

l'acteur *m.,* **l'actrice** *f., n.,* the actor, the actress

allé *past part. of* **aller** (to go); **la famille Paquet est allée** the Paquet family went

un appel a phone call

s'appeler *v.,* to be named, to call oneself; **Je m'appelle Jean Leblanc** My name is John Leblanc

arrivé *past part. of* **arriver** (to arrive); **ils sont arrivés** they arrived

bête *adj.,* foolish, dumb; **une bêtise** a foolish mistake

bu *past part. of* **boire** (to drink); **Janine a bu** Janine drank

commencé *past part. of* **commencer** (to begin); **la représentation a commencé** the performance began

la dame *n.,* the lady

dehors *adv.,* outside

demandé *past part. of* **demander** (to ask); **le père a demandé** the father asked

dit *past part. of* **dire** (to say, to tell); **a dit Janine** said Janine

donné *past part. of* **donner** (to give); **Janine a donné** Janine gave

l'entracte *n. m.,* intermission

entré *past part. of* **entrer** (to enter, to go in); **ils sont entrés** they entered

faire un appel to make a phone call
fait *past part. of* **faire** (to do, to make); **j'ai fait** I did
hier *adv.,* yesterday
incroyable *adj.,* unbelievable
insistez *v. form of* **insister** (to insist); **vous insistez** you insist
leurs *poss. adj. pl.,* their; **leurs places** their seats
lu *past part. of* **lire** (to read); **elle a lu** she read
mangé *past part. of* **manger** (to eat); **il a mangé** he ate
modeste *adj.,* modest

parlé *past part. of* **parler** (to talk, to speak); **elle a parlé** she talked
pouvez *v. form of* **pouvoir** (can, to be able); **vous pouvez écrire** you can write
pris *past part. of* **prendre** (to take); **ils ont pris** they took
le programme *n.,* the program
quitté *past part. of* **quitter** (to leave); **tout le monde a quitté le théâtre** everybody left the theater
répondu *past part. of* **répondre** (to reply); **a répondu Pierre** replied Pierre

retourné *past part. of* **retourner** (to return, go back); **elle est retournée** she returned
ri *past part. of* **rire** (to laugh); **ils ont ri** they laughed
si *conj.,* if; *as an adv.,* so
le stylo *n.,* the pen
terminé *past part. of* **terminer** (to end)
voici here is, here are; **voilà** there is, there are (used when pointing out)
vu *past part. of* **voir** (to see); **elle a vu un homme** she saw a man

Exercises

Review the story and vocabulary before starting these exercises.

I.   Answer the following questions in complete sentences. They are based on the story in this unit.

1.   A quelle heure est-ce qu'ils ont quitté la maison pour aller à l'opéra? _____

_____

2.   A quelle heure sont-ils arrivés à l'opéra? _____

_____

3.   A quelle heure est-ce qu'ils ont pris leurs places? _____

_____

4.   A quelle heure la représentation a-t-elle commencé? _____

_____

II.   **Oui ou Non?**

1.   Hier soir la famille Paquet est allée à l'opéra.   _____

2.   Ils ont vu la représentation de *Carmen*.   _____

3.   Madame Paquet est allée parler avec quelques dames.   _____

4.   Monsieur Paquet est allé boire un jus d'orange.   _____

5.   Janine a l'autographe de Philippe Jirard.   _____

III. Fill in the blank lines with the past participle. Refer to the story if you have to. The answers are there!

   1. Hier soir la famille Paquet est _____ à l'opéra.

   2. Ils ont _____ la représentation de *Faust*.

   3. Ils ont _____ la maison à sept heures et demie.

   4. Ils sont _____ à l'opéra à huit heures.

   5. Ils sont _____ dans le théâtre.

   6. Ils ont _____ leurs places.

   7. Madame Paquet est _____ parler avec quelques dames.

   8. Monsieur Paquet est _____ faire un appel sur son téléphone portable.

   9. Pierre est _____ acheter du chocolat.

  10. Janine est _____ boire un jus d'orange.

IV. **Word Search.** Find the past participles *in French* in this puzzle and circle them.

A	L	L	É	T	F	U	M	É	L
P	A	R	L	É	A	L	A	B	U
P	R	I	S	D	I	T	N	T	O
R	Q	U	I	T	T	É	U	R	I
U	R	É	P	O	N	D	U	F	T

1.	allé	6.	parlé
2.	bu	7.	pris
3.	dit	8.	quitté
4.	fait	9.	répondu
5.	lu	10.	ri

Structures de la Langue

The Passé Composé (past indefinite *or* compound past)

A. Verbs conjugated with avoir

	1st Conjugation	2nd Conjugation	3rd Conjugation
	-ER	**-IR**	**-RE**
INFINITIVES ———⟶	**danser** *to dance*	**finir** *to finish*	**vendre** *to sell*
	I danced, *or* I have danced, *or* I did dance; you danced, etc.	I finished, *or* I have finished, *or* I did finish; you finished; etc.	I sold, *or* I have sold, *or* I did sell; you sold, etc.
SINGULAR			
1. **j'** (I)	**ai dansé**	**ai fini**	**ai vendu**
2. **tu** (you—*familiar only*)	**as dansé**	**as fini**	**as vendu**
3. **il** } (he *or* it) **elle** } (she *or* it)	**a dansé**	**a fini**	**a vendu**
PLURAL			
1. **nous** (we)	**avons dansé**	**avons fini**	**avons vendu**
2. **vous** (you)	**avez dansé**	**avez fini**	**avez vendu**
3. **ils** } (they) **elles** }	**ont dansé**	**ont fini**	**ont vendu**

Rules and observations:

1. To form the passé composé of verbs conjugated with **avoir**, use the present indicative of **avoir** plus the past participle of the verb. All verbs are conjugated with **avoir** except *all reflexive verbs and the 17 verbs listed in section C of this lesson.*

2. To form the past participle of a regular **-er** verb, drop the **-er** ending and add **é**.

3. To form the past participle of a regular **-ir** verb, drop the **-ir** ending and add **i**.

4. To form the past participle of a regular **-re** verb, drop the **-re** ending and add **u**.

5. The passé composé is used to express an action that was completed in the past. It is used in conversation and in informal writing.

6. The passé composé can be translated into English in three different ways, as noted on page 168.

7. To form the negative, place **n'** in front of the present indicative of **avoir**, which in the passé composé is called the auxiliary or helping verb. Then put **pas** after it:

1st Conjugation	2nd Conjugation	3rd Conjugation
je **n'ai pas** dansé	je **n'ai pas** fini	je **n'ai pas** vendu
tu **n'as pas** dansé	tu **n'as pas** fini	tu **n'as pas** vendu
il (*or*) elle **n'a pas** dansé	il (*or*) elle **n'a pas** fini	il (*or*) elle **n'a pas** vendu
nous **n'avons pas** dansé	nous **n'avons pas** fini	nous **n'avons pas** vendu
vous **n'avez pas** dansé	vous **n'avez pas** fini	vous **n'avez pas** vendu
ils (*or*) elles **n'ont pas** dansé	ils (*or*) elles **n'ont pas** fini	ils (*or*) elles **n'ont pas** vendu

8. To form the interrogative, use either (a) the **est-ce que** form in front of the subject, or (b) the inverted form, both of which you learned when you formed the present indicative tense:

(a) Est-ce que j'ai dansé?	(b) ai-je dansé?
Est-ce que tu as dansé?	as-tu dansé?
Est-ce qu'il a dansé?	a-t-il dansé?
Est-ce qu'elle a dansé?	a-t-elle dansé?
Est-ce que nous avons dansé?	avons-nous dansé?
Est-ce que vous avez dansé?	avez-vous dansé?
Est-ce qu'ils ont dansé?	ont-ils dansé?
Est-ce qu'elles ont dansé?	ont-elles dansé?

Note: In box (b) above, if you use the inverted form, you need to add **-t-** in the third person singular between the auxiliary verb and the subject pronoun. You already learned to do this when you used the inverted form in the present indicative tense.

9. To form the negative interrogative, use either (a) the **est-ce que** form in front of the subject in the negative form or (b) the inverted form in the negative.

(a) Est-ce que je n'ai pas dansé?	(b) n'ai-je pas dansé?
Est-ce que tu n'as pas dansé?	n'as-tu pas dansé?
Est-ce qu'il n'a pas dansé?	n'a-t-il pas dansé?
Est-ce qu'elle n'a pas dansé?	n'a-t-elle pas dansé?
Est-ce que nous n'avons pas dansé?	n'avons-nous pas dansé?
Est-ce que vous n'avez pas dansé?	n'avez-vous pas dansé?
Est-ce qu'ils n'ont pas dansé?	n'ont-ils pas dansé?
Est-ce qu'elles n'ont pas dansé?	n'ont-elles pas dansé?

Note: In boxes (a) and (b) above, it is very easy to form the negative interrogative of a verb in the passé composé. If you just drop, for a minute, the past participle *dansé*, what you have left is actually what you already learned: the negative interrogative of the present indicative tense of the verb **avoir**. See the summary at the end of Work Unit 11.

Exercises

Review the preceding material before starting these exercises.

I. Write the answers to the following in complete sentences.

A. Passé composé with **avoir** in the affirmative—answer in the affirmative.

Model:	**Avez-vous vendu la maison?**	**You answer:**	**Oui, j'ai vendu la maison.**
	(Did you sell the house?)		(Yes, I sold the house.)

1. Avez-vous vendu la voiture? _____

2. Avez-vous acheté la propriété? _____

3. Avez-vous fini les leçons? _____

4. Avez-vous réussi la vente de la propriété? _____

5. Avez-vous fermé les portes et les fenêtres? _____

B. Passé composé with **avoir** in the negative—answer in the negative.

Model:	**Janine a-t-elle dansé hier soir?**	**You answer:**	**Non, elle n'a pas dansé hier soir.**
	(Did Janine dance last evening?)		(No, she did not dance last evening.)

> Use a pronoun subject in your answer where a noun subject is given in the question.

1. Janine a-t-elle chanté hier soir? _____

2. Robert a-t-il choisi une jolie cravate? _____

3. As-tu mangé l'éclair? _____

4. Janine et Pierre ont-ils étudié les leçons? _____

5. Avons-nous fini le travail? _____

C. Passé composé with **avoir** in the interrogative—change to the interrogative in the inverted form.

Model:	**Janine a parlé à Madame Richy.**	**You ask:**	**Janine a-t-elle parlé à Madame Richy?**
	(Janine talked to Mrs. Richy.)		(Did Janine talk to Mrs. Richy?)

1. Pierre a vu Madame Richy. _____

2. Hélène a choisi une jolie robe. _____

3. Coco a mangé le gâteau. _____

Coco a mangé le gâteau.

4. Suzanne et Georges ont navigué sur Internet. _____

5. Marie et Betty ont voyagé en France. _____

D. Passé composé with **avoir** in the interrogative—change to the interrogative with **est-ce que**.

Model:	**Madame Banluc a chanté hier soir.**	**You ask:**	**Est-ce que Madame Banluc a chanté hier soir?**
	(Mrs. Banluc sang last evening.)		(Did Mrs. Banluc sing last evening?)

1. Madame Paquet a acheté un beau chapeau. _____

2. Pierre a perdu sa montre. _____

3. Monsieur Paquet a fait un appel sur son téléphone portable. _____

4. Paul a mangé du chocolat. _____

5. Janine a bu un jus d'orange. _____

E. Passé composé with **avoir** in the negative interrogative—change into the negative interrogative using the inverted form only.

Model:	Madame Paquet n'a pas acheté un beau chapeau. (Mrs. Paquet did not buy a beautiful hat.)	**You ask:**	Madame Paquet n'a-t-elle pas acheté un beau chapeau? (Didn't Mrs. Paquet buy a beautiful hat?)

1. Madame Richy n'a pas acheté une automobile. _____

    _____

2. Monsieur Richy n'a pas voyagé aux États-Unis. _____

    _____

3. Madame et Monsieur Armstrong n'ont pas aimé le dessert. _____

    _____

4. Mathilde n'a pas entendu la musique. _____

    _____

5. Joseph n'a pas choisi une jolie cravate. _____

    _____

F. Passé composé with **avoir** in the negative interrogative—change into the negative interrogative using the **est-ce que** form only.

Model:	Suzanne n'a pas fini le livre. (Suzanne did not finish the book.)	**You ask:**	Est-ce que Suzanne n'a pas fini le livre? (Didn't Suzanne finish the book?)

1. Robert n'a pas dansé hier soir. _____

2. Joséphine n'a pas chanté ce matin. _____

3. Guy et Michel n'ont pas fini leurs leçons. _____

4. Françoise et Simone n'ont pas entendu la musique. _____

    _____

5. Charles n'a pas perdu son ami. _____

II. Match the following.

1. She drank some milk.	_____ Il a vendu sa voiture.
2. They heard a big noise.	_____ Elles ont fini le travail.
3. She played in the park.	_____ Il a fermé la fenêtre.
4. She worked yesterday.	_____ Ils ont oublié de venir.
5. They lost their dog.	_____ Il a expliqué la leçon.
6. He explained the lesson.	_____ Elle a joué dans le parc.
7. He sold his car.	_____ Elles ont perdu leur chien.
8. He closed the window.	_____ Ils ont entendu un grand bruit.
9. They forgot to come.	_____ Elle a bu du lait.
10. They finished the work.	_____ Elle a travaillé hier.

III. Change the infinitive in parentheses to the past participle.

> **Model: (voir) Ils ont _____**   **You write on the blank line: vu** (saw)
> **la représentation de *Carmen*.**
> (They _____ the performance of *Carmen*.)

1. (aimer)   Ils ont _____ la représentation de *Carmen*.

2. (quitter)   Ils ont _____ la maison à sept heures et demie.

3. (prendre)   Ils ont _____ leurs places à huit heures et quart.

4. (commencer)   La représentation a _____ à huit heures et demie.

5. (parler)   Madame Paquet a _____ avec les dames.

6. (parler)   Monsieur Paquet a _____ au téléphone.

7. (manger)   Pierre a _____ son chocolat.

8. (boire)   Janine a _____ son jus d'orange.

9. (voir)   Elle a _____ un homme.

10. (dire)   Elle a _____ . —Oh! Monsieur! Votre autographe!

IV. Give the three English translations for each of the following French verb forms in the passé composé. Refer to the chart in section **A. Verbs conjugated with avoir.**

1. J'ai dansé.   _____   _____   _____

2. Vous avez fini.   _____   _____   _____

3. Nous avons vendu.   _____   _____   _____

V. For each of the following verbs in the passé composé, write the correct form of **avoir** (i.e., the present indicative tense of **avoir**).

1. J'_____ joué.   7. Vous _____ perdu.

2. Tu _____ pleuré.   8. Ils _____ répondu.

3. Il _____ fini.   9. J' _____ étudié.

4. Elle _____ choisi.   10. Il _____ parlé.

5. Janine _____ chanté.   11. Robert _____ travaillé.

6. Nous _____ dansé.   12. Marie et Bob _____ dîné.

B. Verbs conjugated with **être**

MASCULINE SUBJECTS		FEMININE SUBJECTS	
Singular	Plural	Singular	Plural
je suis allé	nous sommes allé**s**	je suis allé**e**	nous sommes allé**es**
tu es allé	vous êtes allé**(s)**	tu es allé**e**	vous êtes allé**e(s)**
il est allé	ils sont allé**s**	elle est allé**e**	elles sont allé**es**
English equivalents: I went, *or* I have gone, *or* I did go; you went, *or* you have gone, *or* you did go; etc.			

Rules and observations:

1. To form the *passé composé* of verbs conjugated with **être**, use the present indicative of **être** plus the past participle of the verb. All reflexive verbs are conjugated with **être** as are the 17 verbs in the chart in section **C**.

2. The past participle of a verb conjugated with **être** agrees in gender (*i.e.*, whether masculine or feminine) and number (*i.e.,* whether singular or plural) with the subject, as shown in the box. The past participle of a verb conjugated with **être**, therefore, is like an adjective because it describes the subject in some way.

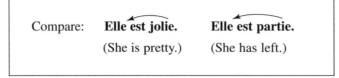

> Compare: **Elle est jolie.**   **Elle est partie.**
>
> (She is pretty.)   (She has left.)

3. To form the negative, interrogative, and negative interrogative, do the same as you did for verbs conjugated with **avoir** in the passé composé. The word order is the same. See the summary at the end of Work Unit 11.

C. The 17 verbs conjugated with **être***

1. **aller**   to go

2. **arriver**   to arrive

3. ***descendre**   to go down, come down

    Elle est descendue vite.
    She came down quickly.

    BUT: *Elle a descendu la valise.*
            She brought down the suitcase.

4. **devenir**   to become

5. **entrer**   to enter, go in, come in

6. ***monter**   to go up, come up

    Elle est montée lentement.
    She went up slowly.

BUT: *Elle a monté l'escalier.*
        She went up the stairs.

7. **mourir**   to die

8. **naître**   to be born

9. **partir**   to leave

10. ***passer**   to go by, pass by

    Elle est passée chez moi.
    She came by my house.

    BUT: *Elle m'a passé le sel.*
            She passed me the salt.

    AND: *Elle a passé un examen.*
            She took an exam.

*Some of these verbs, as noted above, are conjugated with **avoir** if the verb is used in a transitive sense and has a direct object.*

11.	***rentrer** to go in again, to return (home)	15.	***sortir** to go out

Elle est rentrée tôt.
She returned home early.

BUT: *Elle a rentré le chat dans la maison.*
        She brought (took) the cat into the house.

12. **rester**   to remain, stay

13. **retourner**   to return, go back

14. **revenir**   to come back

Elle est sortie hier soir.
She went out last night.

BUT: *Elle a sorti son mouchoir.*
        She took out her handkerchief.

16. **tomber**   to fall

17. **venir**   to come

*Some of these verbs, as noted on page 174, are conjugated with **avoir** if the verb is used in a transitive sense and has a direct object.*

D. Some irregular past participles

1.	**apprendre** *to learn*	appris	16.	**naître** *to be born*	né
2.	**avoir** *to have*	eu	17.	**ouvrir** *to open*	ouvert
3.	**boire** *to drink*	bu	18.	**paraître** *to appear, seem*	paru
4.	**comprendre** *to understand*	compris	19.	**permettre** *to permit*	permis
5.	**couvrir** *to cover*	couvert	20.	**pouvoir** *to be able, can*	pu
6.	**croire** *to believe*	cru	21.	**prendre** *to take*	pris
7.	**devenir** *to become*	devenu	22.	**promettre** *to promise*	promis
8.	**devoir** *to owe, have to, should*	dû	23.	**recevoir** *to receive*	reçu
9.	**dire** *to say, tell*	dit	24.	**revenir** *to come back*	revenu
10.	**écrire** *to write*	écrit	25.	**rire** *to laugh*	ri
11.	**être** *to be*	été	26.	**savoir** *to know*	su
12.	**faire** *to do, make*	fait	27.	**tenir** *to hold*	tenu
13.	**lire** *to read*	lu	28.	**venir** *to come*	venu
14.	**mettre** *to put, place*	mis	29.	**voir** *to see*	vu
15.	**mourir** *to die*	mort	30.	**vouloir** *to want*	voulu

Exercises

Review the preceding material before starting these exercises.

I. Write the answers to the following in complete sentences.

A. Passé composé with **être** in the affirmative—answer the questions in the affirmative.

Drill on **aller**

REMEMBER TO WATCH FOR AN AGREEMENT OF THE PAST PARTICIPLE WITH THE SUBJECT IN THE PASSÉ COMPOSÉ WHEN THE VERB IS CONJUGATED WITH **être**!

Model: **Madame Paquet est-elle allée à l'opéra?**
(Did Mrs. Paquet go to the opera?)

You answer: **Oui, Madame Paquet est allée à l'opéra.**
(Yes, Mrs. Paquet went to the opera.)

1. Janine est-elle allée au cinéma? _____

2. Monique est-elle allée à l'école? _____

3. Robert est-il allé au théâtre? _____

4. Pierre et Raymond sont-ils allés au parc? _____

5. Anne et Béatrice sont-elles allées au Canada? _____

6. Jacques et Jeanne sont-ils allés à l'aéroport? _____

7. Monsieur et Madame Beaupuy sont-ils allés aux États-Unis? _____

8. La mère est-elle allée dans le garage? _____

9. Le père est-il allé dans la cuisine? _____

10. La jeune fille est-elle allée à la pharmacie? _____

B. Passé composé with **être** in the negative—answer the questions in the negative.

Model:	**Janine est-elle arrivée à l'opéra à huit heures et demie?**	**You answer:**	**Non, elle n'est pas arrivée à l'opéra à huit heures et demie.**

> Use a pronoun subject in your answer where a noun subject is given in the question.

1. Madame Paquet est-elle arrivée à l'opéra à huit heures et demie? _____

    _____

2. Est-ce qu'ils sont entrés dans le théâtre à huit heures? _____

    _____

3. Monsieur et Madame Paquet sont-ils partis de bonne heure? _____

    _____

4. Est-ce qu'il est resté à la maison? _____

5. Simone est-elle sortie ce soir? _____

C. Passé composé with **être** in the interrogative—change to the interrogative in the inverted form.

Model:	**Monique est tombée dans la rue.**	**You ask:**	**Monique est-elle tombée dans la rue?**

1. Yolande est venue ce soir. _____

2. François est retourné à midi. _____

3. Les garçons sont restés dans l'école. _____

4. Les jeunes filles sont descendues vite. _____

5. Monsieur et Madame Paquet sont rentrés à minuit. _____

    _____

D. Passé composé with **être** in the interrogative—change to the interrogative with **est-ce-que**.

Model:	**Madame Banluc est née à la Martinique.**	**You ask:**	**Est-ce que Madame Banluc est née à la Martinique?**

1. John James Audubon est né aux Cayes à Haïti. _____

    _____

2. Napoléon Bonaparte est mort à Sainte-Hélène. _____

    _____

3. Marie-Antoinette est née à Vienne. _____

4. Jacques Chirac est devenu président de la République Française en 1995. _____

    _____

5. Joséphine est née à la Martinique. _____

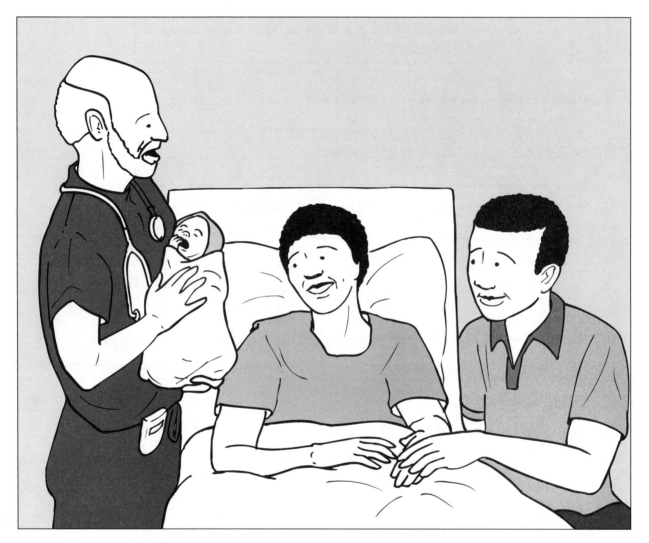

Joséphine est née à la Martinique.

6. Marie-Antoinette est morte à Paris. _____

7. Joséphine est devenue impératrice en 1804. _____

    _____

E. Passé composé with **être** in the negative interrogative—change the following negative sentences into the negative interrogative using the inverted form only.

Model:	**Tu n'es pas sorti hier soir.**	**You ask:**	**N'es-tu pas sorti hier soir?**
	(You did not go out last evening.)		(Didn't you go out last evening?)

1. Tu n'es pas resté à la maison. _____

2. Elle n'est pas tombée dans le jardin. _____

3. Il n'est pas parti ce matin. _____

4. Vous n'êtes pas arrivé à dix heures. _____

5. Elles ne sont pas allées à l'école aujourd'hui. _____

_____

II. Match the following.

1. She has left. _____ Il a bu du vin.

2. They have read some books. _____ Elle est partie.

3. They died. _____ Ils ont lu des livres.

4. He drank some wine. _____ Elles sont mortes.

5. We went into the living room. _____ Vous avez appris la leçon.

6. You went to the restaurant. _____ Nous sommes entrés dans le salon.

7. He has had an accident. _____ Tu es allée au restaurant.

8. She has been sick. _____ Vous êtes devenu médecin.

9. You became a doctor. _____ Il a eu un accident.

10. You learned the lesson. _____ Elle a été malade.

III. Give the three English translations for each of the following French verb forms in the passé composé. Refer to the chart in section **B. Verbs conjugated with être.**

1. Je suis allé au cinéma. _____ _____ _____

2. Elle est partie. _____ _____ _____

3. Nous sommes arrivés. _____ _____ _____

IV. For each of the following verbs in the passé composé write the correct form of **être**.

1. Je _____ allé.	5. Jean _____ sorti.	9. Elles _____ allées.
2. Tu _____ venu.	6. Nous _____ entrés.	10. Je _____ descendu.
3. Il _____ arrivé.	7. Vous _____ tombé.	11. Michel _____ rentré.
4. Elle _____ partie.	8. Ils _____ montés.	12. Elle _____ morte.

V. Un acrostiche. Finish writing the past participle for each of the following verbs.

1. lire

2. avoir

3. prendre

4. arriver

5. rire

6. tenir

8. croire

10. promettre

11. entrer

12. pouvoir

13. aller

14. savoir

15. sortir

16. être

```
 1 L  |
 2 E  |
 3 P  |  |  |
 4 A  |  |  |  |
 5 R  |
 6 T  |  |  |
 7 I  |
 8 C  |  |
 9 I  |
10 P  |  |  |  |  |
11 E  |  |  |  |
12 P  |
13 A  |  |
14 S  |
15 S  |  |
16 É  |  |
```

VI. For each of the following verbs in the passé composé write the correct form of either **avoir** or **être**, depending on which is required.

1. Suzanne _____ parlé.

2. Il _____ monté.

3. Elle _____ sortie.

4. Elle _____ compris.

5. Nous _____ arrivés.

6. Vous _____ dit.

7. Elles _____ lu.

8. Tu _____ fait.

9. Robert _____ resté.

10. Ils _____ ri.

11. Je _____ allé.

12. Madame Paquet _____ bu.

VII. Identify the following past particles by writing the infinitive form. These past participles are all irregular.

Model: dit You write: **dire**

1. appris _____
2. devenu _____
3. eu _____
4. couvert _____
5. cru _____
6. compris _____
7. permis _____
8. reçu _____
9. promis _____
10. voulu _____

11. dû _____
12. vu _____
13. dit _____
14. venu _____
15. écrit _____
16. été _____
17. bu _____
18. fait _____
19. tenu _____
20. lu _____

21. ouvert _____
22. mis _____
23. su _____
24. mort _____
25. ri _____
26. né _____
27. revenu _____
28. paru _____
29. pu _____
30. pris _____

VIII. Write the past participle for each of the following verbs. Some are regular, some are irregular.

Model: vendre You write: **vendu**

1. avoir _____
2. danser _____
3. faire _____
4. finir _____
5. savoir _____
6. lire _____

7. apprendre _____
8. défendre _____
9. choisir _____
10. aller _____
11. sortir _____
12. saisir _____

13. aider _____
14. bâtir _____
15. jouer _____
16. voir _____
17. danser _____
18. vendre _____

IX. Some verbs in French are conjugated with **avoir** to form the passé composé and some verbs are conjugated with **être**. For each of the following verbs write on the blank line either **avoir** or **être**, depending on which is required to form the passé composé.

Models: aller You write: **être**
parler You write: **avoir**

1. rester _____
2. danser _____
3. finir _____
4. vendre _____
5. arriver _____
6. entrer _____
7. aimer _____

8. chanter _____
9. mourir _____
10. donner _____
11. dire _____
12. naître _____
13. aller _____
14. étudier _____

15. partir _____
16. chercher _____
17. retourner _____
18. choisir _____
19. avoir _____
20. être _____
21. venir _____

X. Change from the passé composé to the present indicative tense.

> **Model:** **Il a bu du lait.**   **You write:** **Il boit du lait.**
>   (He drank milk.)   (He is drinking milk.)

1. Il a lu un bon livre. _____

2. J'ai vendu la voiture. _____

3. Elle est allée à l'opéra. _____

4. Nous avons écrit des lettres. _____

5. Vous êtes arrivé tôt. _____

XI. Change from the present indicative tense to the passé composé.

> **Model:** **Monsieur Paquet a une belle**   **You write:** **Monsieur Paquet a eu une belle**
>   **voiture grise.**   **voiture grise.**
>   (Mr. Paquet has a beautiful gray car.)   (Mr. Paquet had a beautiful gray car.)

1. Madame Paquet a un beau chapeau rouge. _____

2. Janine boit un jus d'orange. _____

3. Pierre mange du chocolat. _____

4. Monique va au cinéma. _____

5. Jeanne et Joséphine entrent dans le théâtre. _____

XII. Fill in the ending of the past participle with the appropriate agreement, if needed. If none is needed, write a dash (—). Refer to the story at the beginning of this unit if you have to. The answers are there!

> **Model:** **La famille Paquet est**   **Fill in the ending of the past participle if an**
>   **allé_____ à l'opéra.**   **agreement is needed:**   **é or s**
>   (The Paquet family went to the opera.)

1. La famille Paquet est allé_____ à l'opéra.

2. Monsieur Paquet est retourné_____ à sa place.

3. Madame Paquet est retourné_____ à sa place.

4. Janine est retourné_____ à sa place.

5. Ils sont arrivé_____ à l'opéra à huit heures.

6. Ils sont entré_____ dans le théâtre.

7. Pierre est retourné_____ à sa place.

XIII. On the blank line, write the appropriate past participle of the verb in parentheses. Refer to the story at the beginning of this unit if you have to. The answers are there!

> **Model: (aller)   La famille Paquet est _____   Write on the blank line: allée**
> **à l'opéra.**

1. (aller)   La famille Paquet est _____ à l'opéra.

2. (arriver)   Ils sont _____ à l'opéra à huit heures.

3. (entrer)   Ils sont _____ dans le théâtre.

4. (aller)   Madame Paquet est _____ parler avec quelques dames.

5. (aller)   Monsieur Paquet est _____ faire un appel sur son téléphone portable.

6. (aller)   Pierre est _____ acheter du chocolat.

7. (aller)   Janine est _____ boire un jus d'orange.

8. (retourner)   Madame Paquet est _____ à sa place.

9. (retourner)   Monsieur Paquet est _____ à sa place.

10. (retourner)   Janine est _____ à sa place.

XIV. French Opera.   Proficiency in Speaking and Writing.

Situation: Last night you went to the Opera House in Paris. You saw the opera *Pelléas et Mélisande*, music composed by Claude Debussy. Say aloud at least three statements in French using the **passé composé** tense. You may use your own ideas and words, those used in the story at the beginning of this lesson, and/or the following: **Hier soir, je suis allé(e) à l'Opéra; J'ai vu l'opéra *Pelléas et Mélisande*; Pendant l'entracte, j'ai bu un jus d'orange et j'ai mangé du chocolat.** Write what you said on the following lines:

_____

_____

_____

The Opera House, Paris.

XV. Socializing.   Proficiency in Speaking and Writing.

Situation: Look at the picture at the beginning of this lesson. During an evening with members of her family at the Opera House in Paris, Janine talked to a gentleman during intermission. In at least three sentences in the **passé composé**, tell us what happened in that scene.

You may use your own ideas and words, those used in the story, and/or the following: **Hier soir, Janine est allée à l'Opéra. Elle a vu la représentation de *Faust*. Pendant l'entracte, elle a parlé avec un homme. Elle a donné son programme et son stylo à l'homme pour son autographe.**

Write what you said here:

1. _____

2. _____

3. _____

XVI. Folklore Basque.   Proficiency in Speaking and Writing.

Situation: Look at the picture on the following page of the young men dressed in costume doing the saber dance. Basque is located in southwest France.

In at least three sentences, tell us what the young men are doing, what they are wearing (**porter**/*to wear*), and something about their berets (**les bérets**). Include your own ideas and words.

1. _____

2. _____

3. _____

Folklore Basque. La Danse des Sabres.

WORK UNIT 13

Direct Object Pronouns, including *en*

A chacun son goût

Let's see how the family stew turns out!
Here's a recipe in French for a stew. Try making it yourself. It's fun!

RAGOÛT DE MOUTON
À L'IRLANDAISE (IRISH STEW)

Pour 6 personnes   cuisson: 2 heures, 35 min.

1500 grammes de mouton coupé en morceaux
3 grosses pommes de terre
300 grammes d'oignons
sel, poivre, blanc de céleri, et 3 gousses d'ail
3 cuillères à soupe de farine blanche

1. Disposez dans une cocotte:

    (a) une couche d'oignons hachés
    (b) une grosse pomme de terre coupée en lamelles
    (c) un tiers des morceaux de mouton
    (d) du sel, du poivre
    (e) une gousse d'ail haché (si vous désirez)

2. Répétez en disposant une deuxième couche d'oignons hachés, une grosse pomme de terre coupée en lamelles, un tiers des morceaux de mouton, du sel, du poivre, une gousse d'ail haché.

3. Répétez en disposant une troisième couche d'oignons hachés, une grosse pomme de terre coupée en lamelles, un tiers des morceaux de mouton, du sel, du poivre, une gousse d'ail haché.

4. Ajoutez une tasse et demie d'eau chaude.

5. Faites bouillir pendant 5 min.

6. Laissez cuire doucement, à couvert, pendant 1 heure 30 min.

7. Après une heure et demie, si le mélange est épais, ajoutez un peu d'eau chaude. Maintenant, mettez dans la cocotte le céleri coupé en petits morceaux.

8. Laissez cuire doucement pendant 1 heure.

9. Maintenant, ajoutez 3 cuillères à soupe de farine blanche, lentement, pendant que vous remuez le mélange.

10. Bonne chance! Ne le brûlez pas!

Ce soir Madame Paquet a préparé le dîner. Pierre a servi le dîner pour la famille et les voisins, Monsieur et Madame Richy. Il a servi un ragoût de mouton à l'irlandaise. La recette pour le ragoût est sur la page d'en face.

Pierre:	Voici le ragoût! Je vais le servir maintenant. A table, s'il vous plaît!
	(Tout le monde va s'asseoir à table: Monsieur et Madame Paquet, Janine, Pierre, Monsieur et Madame Richy.)
Janine:	Oh! Il sent bon!
Monsieur Paquet:	Et comment! Il sent très bon. Moi, j'ai grand faim.
Madame Paquet:	Il est magnifique, n'est-ce pas? . . . Excusez-moi, je vais dans la cuisine. Vous pouvez commencer sans moi.
	(Madame Paquet se lève. Elle quitte la table pour aller dans la cuisine.)
Madame Richy:	Vraiment extraordinaire!
Monsieur Richy:	J'adore les ragoûts.
Madame Richy:	Moi aussi. Pierre, tu es un bon garçon!
Pierre:	Alors, qui va commencer?
Monsieur Paquet:	Après toi, Pierre. Tu peux commencer si tu veux.
Janine:	Vas-y, Pierre! Tu goûtes le premier.
Pierre:	Bon. Alors, je vais commencer . . . Maintenant, je goûte le ragoût . . .
Janine:	Je vais le goûter aussi . . . Oh! Oh! Il est brûlé! C'est dégoûtant. Je vais être malade. Il est brûlé! Goûtez-en!
	(Janine se lève et quitte la table.)
Pierre:	Oui. Il est brûlé. Janine a raison. Il est brûlé. Je ne l'aime pas. Je vais être malade aussi. Goûtez-en!
	(Pierre se lève et quitte la table.)
Monsieur Paquet:	Je vais le goûter aussi… Oui. Il est brûlé. Janine et Pierre ont raison. Je ne l'aime pas.
	(Monsieur Paquet se lève et quitte la table.)
Monsieur Richy:	Moi, je vais le goûter maintenant… Ce ragoût est délicieux! Il est bien cuit, comme le ragoût de ma mère. Bien cuit! Excellent… Chérie, pourqoi ne fais-tu pas un ragoût si bien cuit aussi?
Madame Richy:	Tu as raison, chéri. La prochaine fois je vais le faire trop cuire. Je vais le brûler pour toi et tu peux le manger seul. Tiens! Mange toute la cocotte!
	(Madame Richy se lève. Monsieur Richy reste seul à la table avec la cocotte de ragoût brûlé devant lui.)
	(Madame Paquet rentre dans la salle à manger avec le dessert.)
Madame Paquet:	Alors, est-ce que tout le monde aime mon ragoût? J'ai un dessert que j'ai fait aussi. Qui veut une crème brûlée? Goûtez-en!

Vocabulaire

à couvert covered

à table to (at) the table, come to the table!

l'ail *n.m.,* garlic; **une gousse d'ail** a clove of garlic

aime *v. form of* **aimer**; **Je ne l'aime pas!** I don't like it!

ajouter *v.,* to add

avoir faim *v.,* to be hungry; **avoir raison** to be right; **J'ai grand faim** I'm very hungry; **Janine et Pierre ont raison!** Janine and Pierre are right!

blanc *m.,* **blanche** *f., adj.,* white

bouillir *v.,* to boil

brûler *v.,* to burn; **brûlé** burned; **ne le brûlez pas!** don't burn it!

le céleri *n.,* celery; **le blanc de céleri** celery stalk

chacun *pron.,* each one; **à chacun son goût** to each his/her own (taste)

la chance *n.,* chance, luck; **bonne chance!** good luck!

chaud *m.,* **chaude** *f., adj.,* hot

la cocotte *n.,* the stewing pot; **toute la cocotte** the whole pot

comment *adv.,* how

connaît *v. form of* **connaître** to know (someone), to be acquainted with (someone); **Est-ce que Pierre connaît Madeleine?** Does Pierre know Madeleine? *(pres. indicative):* **je connais, tu connais, il (elle) connaît, nous connaissons, vous connaissez, ils (elles) connaissent**

la couche *n.,* layer

couper *v.,* to cut; **coupé** sliced

la crème brûlée crème brûlée (a custard dessert with caramelized sugar on top)

la cuillère *n.,* the spoon; **cuillère à soupe** soup spoon

cuire *v.,* to cook; **cuit** cooked; **cuisson** cooking time; **bien cuit** well done (cooked); **trop cuit** overdone (overcooked)

dégoûtant *adj.,* disgusting, revolting

devant *prep.,* in front of; **devant lui** in front of him

disposer *v.,* to dispose, to arrange; **en disposant** arranging

doucement *adv.,* gently (low flame)

en *partitive,* some; **goûtez-en!** taste some!

épais *m.,* **épaisse** *f., adj.,* thick

la faim *n.,* hunger; **avoir faim** to be hungry

faire bouillir *v.,* to boil; **faire trop cuire** to overcook

la farine *n.,* flour

goûter *v.,* to taste; **le goût** the taste; **Qui veut en goûter?** Who wants to taste some? **Goûtez-en!** Taste some!

le gramme *n.,* the gram (metric unit of measurement); 1 gram equals about .035 ounce; 500 grams equal about 1.1 lbs.; 300 grams equal about 10 oz.

gros *m.,* **grosse** *f., adj.,* big, fat, large

hacher *v.,* to chop (up); **haché** chopped

irlandais *m.,* **irlandaise** *f., adj.,* Irish; **à l'irlandaise** Irish style

le kilogramme *n.,* kilogram (1,000 grams; 1 kilo equals about 2.2 lbs.)

laisser *v.,* to let, to allow

la lamelle *n.* the thin slice

malade *adj.,* sick

le mélange *n.,* the mixture

mettez *v. form of* **mettre** (to put, to place)

le morceau *n.,* the piece, morsel

le mouton *n.,* the mutton

l'oignon *n. m.,* the onion

la page *n.,* the page; **page d'en face** opposite page

pendant *prep.,* during; **pendant que** *conj.,* while

peux *v. form of pouvoir*; **tu peux commencer** you can begin

le poivre *n.,* the pepper

la pomme de terre *n.,* the potato

prochain *m.,* **prochaine** *f., adj.,* next; **la prochaine fois** the next time

le ragoût *n.,* the stew

la raison *n.,* the reason; **avoir raison** to be right

la recette *n.,* the recipe

remuer *v.,* to stir

le sel *n.,* the salt

sent *v. form of* **sentir** (to smell, to feel); **il sent très bon!** it smells very good!

servir *v.,* to serve; **je vais le servir maintenant** I'm going to serve it now

seul *m.,* **seule** *f., adj.,* alone

tiens! *exclam.,* here!

un tiers one-third

vas-y! go to it!

veux *v. form of* **vouloir** (to want); **si tu veux** if you want

le voisin, la voisine *n.,* the neighbor

Exercises

Review the story and vocabulary before starting these exercises.

I. Answer the following questions in complete sentences. They are based on the story "A chacun son goût."

1. Qui a servi le dîner ce soir? _____

2. Pour qui a-t-il servi le dîner? _____

3. Qui commence à goûter le ragoût? _____

4. Qui aime le ragoût? _____

5. Pourquoi aime-t-il le ragoût? _____

6. Qui a fait le ragoût? _____

II. Answer the following questions in complete sentences. They are personal questions and require answers of your own.

1. Aimez-vous manger du ragoût? _____

2. Savez-vous faire un ragoût? _____

3. Aimez-vous le ragoût brûlé? _____

III. **Comment dit-on en français . . . ?** Find these statements in the story and write them in French.

1. And how! It smells very good. I'm very hungry. _____

   _____

2. Janine is right. It's burned. I don't like it. Taste some! _____

   _____

3. I'm going to taste it. _____

4. Mrs. Paquet comes back into the dining room with the dessert. _____

   _____

5. Does everybody like my stew? I have a dessert that I made also. Who wants a crème brûlée? Taste some!

   _____

   _____

Structures de la Langue

A. Direct object pronouns

	Singular			Plural
me or **m'**	me		**nous**	us
te or **t'**	you (familiar)		**vous**	you (sing. polite or plural)
le or **l'**	him, it ⎫		**les**	them (persons or things)
la or **l'**	her, it ⎭ person or thing			

Rules and observations:

1. A direct object **pronoun** takes the place of a direct object **noun**.

2. A direct object noun ordinarily comes after the verb, but a direct object pronoun is ordinarily placed *in front of* the verb.

3. The vowel **e** in **me**, **te**, **le** and the vowel **a** in **la** drop and an apostrophe is added if the verb right after it starts with a vowel or a silent *h*; e.g., **je l'aime**. (I like it.)

4. You might say that the direct object "receives" the action of the verb.

5. Study the direct object pronouns in the above box and the model sentences in the boxes below.

B. Direct object pronoun referring to a thing in the present indicative

The noun as direct object of the verb.	The pronoun in place of the noun.
(a) **Janine lit le poème.** *Janine is reading the poem.*	(a) **Janine le lit.** *Janine is reading it.*
(b) **Pierre lit la lettre.** *Pierre is reading the letter.*	(b) **Pierre la lit.** *Pierre is reading it.*
(c) **Janine apprend le poème.** *Janine is learning the poem.*	(c) **Janine l'apprend.** *Janine is learning it.*
(d) **Pierre écrit la lettre.** *Pierre is writing the letter.*	(d) **Pierre l'écrit.** *Pierre is writing it.*
(e) **Janine lit les poèmes.** *Janine is reading the poems.*	(e) **Janine les lit.** *Janine is reading them.*

Rules and observations:

1.   The direct object pronoun must agree in gender and number with the noun it is replacing. Gender means masculine or feminine. Number means singular or plural.

2.   Actually, what you do is drop the noun direct object. The definite article that remains becomes the pronoun direct object. Put it *in front of* the verb. If the verb starts with a vowel or a mute *h*, drop the **e** in **le** and the **a** in **la** and add an apostrophe.

(a)   From: **Janine lit le poème.**

      You get: **Janine le lit.**

                     Janine lit le poème.

(b)   From: **Pierre lit la lettre.**

      You get: **Pierre la lit.**

                     Pierre lit la lettre.

(c)   From: **Janine apprend le poème.**

      You get: **Janine l'apprend.**

                     Janine apprend le poème.

(d)   From: **Pierre écrit la lettre.**

      You get: **Pierre l'écrit.**

                     Pierre écrit la lettre.

(e)   From: **Janine lit les poèmes.**

      You get: **Janine les lit.**

                     Janine lit les poèmes.

C. Direct object pronoun referring to a person in the present indicative

Pierre	**me**	connaît		Pierre knows	*me.*
	te				*you. (familiar)*
	le				*him.*
	la				*her.*
	nous				*us.*
	vous				*you. (sing. polite or plural)*
	les				*them.*

Rules and observations:

1. Direct object pronouns, whether they refer to persons or things, are ordinarily placed *in front of* the verb.

2. If the verb is negative, put **ne** *in front of the direct object pronoun* and **pas** *after* the verb, as in the examples in this box.

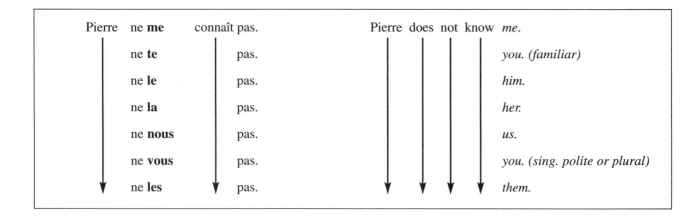

Pierre	ne **me**	connaît pas.	Pierre does not know	*me.*
	ne **te**	pas.		*you. (familiar)*
	ne **le**	pas.		*him.*
	ne **la**	pas.		*her.*
	ne **nous**	pas.		*us.*
	ne **vous**	pas.		*you. (sing. polite or plural)*
	ne **les**	pas.		*them.*

D. Direct object pronoun in the affirmative and negative command

Affirmative command.		Negative command.	
with noun direct object	with pronoun direct object	with noun direct object	with pronoun direct object
Apprenez le poème!	**Apprenez-le!**	N'apprenez pas le poème.	**Ne l'apprenez pas!**
Ecrivez la lettre!	**Ecrivez-la!**	N'écrivez pas la lettre.	**Ne l'écrivez pas!**
Etudiez les leçons!	**Etudiez-les!**	N'étudiez pas les leçons.	**Ne les étudiez pas!**

Rules and observations:

1. In the affirmative command, a direct object pronoun is placed *right after* the verb and joined with a hyphen.

2. In the negative command, a direct object pronoun is placed *in front of* the verb, where it ordinarily goes.

3. In the negative command, the **ne** is placed *in front of* the direct object pronoun and the **pas** *after* the verb.

E. Direct object pronoun as object of an infinitive

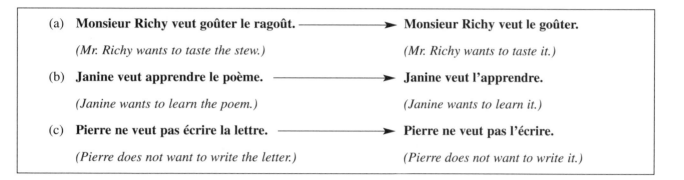

(a) **Monsieur Richy veut goûter le ragoût.** ⟶ **Monsieur Richy veut le goûter.**

   (Mr. Richy wants to taste the stew.)   *(Mr. Richy wants to taste it.)*

(b) **Janine veut apprendre le poème.** ⟶ **Janine veut l'apprendre.**

   (Janine wants to learn the poem.)   *(Janine wants to learn it.)*

(c) **Pierre ne veut pas écrire la lettre.** ⟶ **Pierre ne veut pas l'écrire.**

   (Pierre does not want to write the letter.)   *(Pierre does not want to write it.)*

Rules and observations:

1. A pronoun as object of an infinitive is placed *in front* of the infinitive.

2. In a negative statement with a pronoun as object of an infinitive, **ne** is placed in front of the verb and **pas** after it (as is usual) and the pronoun as object of the infinitive still remains in front of the infinitive.

3. The point is that the verb can be made negative and it has nothing to do with the logical position of the pronoun as object of an infinitive.

F. Direct object pronoun with a verb in the passé composé

The noun as direct object of the verb.	The pronoun in place of the noun.
(a) **Marie a préparé le dîner.**	(a) **Elle l'a préparé.**
(Mary prepared the dinner.)	*(She prepared it.)*
(b) **Robert a préparé la salade.**	(b) **Il l'a préparée.**
(Robert prepared the salad.)	*(He prepared it.)*
(c) **Jean a préparé les dîners.**	(c) **Il les a préparés.**
(John prepared the dinners.)	*(He prepared them.)*
(d) **Anne a préparé les salades.**	(d) **Elle les a préparées.**
(Anne prepared the salads.)	*(She prepared them.)*

Rules and observations:

1. The verb form **a préparé** is in the passé composé, third person, singular tense. Review how to form the passé composé in Work Unit 12.

2. You still put the direct object pronoun *in front of* the verb form (**a préparé**), just as you put it *in front of* the simple verb form in the present indicative. Review the position of the direct object pronoun in the present indicative in section **B**.

3.   There is one new thing to be learned here: the past participle (**préparé**) of the verb in the passé composé must agree in gender (masculine or feminine) and number (singular or plural) with the *preceding* direct object pronoun, if there is one.

4.   If the *preceding* direct object pronoun is **le** (masculine, singular), no agreement is required on the past participle.

5.   If the *preceding* direct object pronoun is **la** (feminine, singular), you must add **e** to the past participle.

6.   If the *preceding* direct object pronoun is **les** (masculine, plural), you must add **s** to the past participle.

7.   If the *preceding* direct object pronoun is **les** (feminine, plural), you must add **es** to the past participle.

8.   To sum it up: There must be an agreement in both gender and number in the past participle of a verb conjugated with **avoir** with the *preceding* direct object pronoun if there is one. No agreement if the direct object is a *noun* and it follows the verb. Compare the column on the right and the column on the left in the box on page 193.

9.   A reminder: When we conjugate a verb with **être**, there is an agreement between the past participle and the subject (e.g., **Janine est allée au théâtre**). Review sections **B** and **C** in Work Unit 12.

G. Meanings and positions of en as an object pronoun

(a)	Avez-vous **du café?**	Oui, j'**en** ai.
	(Have you *any coffee?*) (Have you *some coffee?*)	(Yes, I have *some* [*of it*].)
(b)	Buvez-vous **de l'eau?**	Oui, j'**en** bois.
	(Do you drink *any water?*)	(Yes, I drink *some*.)
(c)	Mangez-vous **de la glace?**	Oui, j'**en** mange.
	(Do you eat *any ice cream?*)	(Yes, I eat *some*.)
(d)	Mangez-vous **des pommes?**	Oui, j'**en** mange.
	(Do you eat *any apples?*)	(Yes, I eat *some*.)
(e)	Avez-vous **des soeurs?**	Oui, j'**en** ai deux.
	(Do you have *any sisters?*)	(Yes, I have two [*of them*].)
(f)	Vient-il **de Paris?**	Oui, il **en** vient.
	(Does he come *from Paris?*)	(Yes, he comes *from there*.)
(g)	Avez-vous peur **des serpents?**	Oui, j'**en** ai peur.
	(Are you afraid *of snakes?*)	(Yes, I'm afraid *of them*.)
(h)	Buvez **du café!**	Buvez-**en!**
	(Drink *some coffee!*)	(Drink *some!*)
(i)	Ne buvez pas **de café!**	N'**en** buvez pas!
	(Don't drink *any coffee!*)	(Don't drink *any* [*of it*]*!*)

Rules and observations:

1. The pronoun **en** has more than one translation in English, as you can see from the model sentences in the box.

2. **En** is used to replace a noun preceded by the preposition **de** or any combination of **de** (e.g., **du, de l', de la, des**).

3. **En** is used to refer to persons or things if the noun is used in a partitive sense.

4. **En** is used to refer to places and things but not to persons, if the noun is not used in a partitive sense. See (f) and (g) in section **G**.

5. In the affirmative imperative, **en** is placed *right after* the verb and joined with a hyphen. In the negative imperative, **en** is placed in front of the verb, where it is ordinarily placed, e.g., **Goûtez-en!** (Taste some!), **N'en goûtez pas!** (Don't taste any!)

Exercises

I. Change the following sentences by substituting a pronoun as object of the verb in place of the noun object. Rewrite the entire sentence.

Model: **Janine lit *le poème*.** (Janine is reading the poem.) **You write:** **Janine le lit.** (Janine is reading it.)

1. Pierre lit *la lettre.* _____

2. Janine écrit *la leçon.* _____

3. Michel apprend *l'espagnol.* _____

4. Christophe fait *les devoirs.* _____

5. Alexandre écoute *la musique.* _____

6. Yolande prononce *le mot.* _____

7. Théodore voit *l'hôtel.* _____

8. Monique dit *la phrase.* _____

9. Joséphine attend *l'autobus.* _____

10. Anne mange *les gâteaux.* _____

II. Answer the following questions in the affirmative, substituting a pronoun as object of the verb in place of the noun object. Also, substitute a pronoun in place of the noun subject. Rewrite the entire sentence.

Model: **Janine écrit-elle *la leçon*?** (Is Janine writing the lesson?) **You write:** **Oui, elle l'écrit.** (Yes, she is writing it.)

1. Monique dit-elle *la phrase?* _____

2. Joséphine attend-elle *l'autobus?* _____

3. Pierre lit-il *la lettre?* _____

4. Michel mange-t-il *les gâteaux?* _____

5. Yolande écoute-t-elle *la musique?* _____

III. Answer the following questions in the negative, substituting a pronoun as object of the verb in place of the noun object. Also, substitute a pronoun in place of the noun subject. Rewrite the entire sentence.

Model:	**Est-ce que Janine boit le jus d'orange?**	**You write:**	**Non, elle ne le boit pas.**
	(Is Janine drinking the orange juice?)		(No, she is not drinking it.)

1. Est-ce que Pierre mange la saucisse? _____

2. Est-ce que Joséphine prononce le mot? _____

3. Est-ce qu'Henri aime le saucisson? _____

4. Est-ce que Georges lit la lettre? _____

5. Est-ce que Georgette apporte les gâteaux? _____

IV. Answer the following questions in complete sentences in the affirmative, substituting a direct object pronoun for the noun object.

Model:	**Apprenez-vous le français maintenant?**	**You write:**	**Oui, je l'apprends maintenant.**
	(Are you learning French now?)		(Yes, I am learning it now.)

1. Comprenez-vous la leçon aujourd'hui? _____

2. Dites-vous toujours la vérité? _____

3. Faites-vous les devoirs maintenant? _____

4. Lisez-vous le journal tous les jours? _____

5. Ecrivez-vous la phrase en ce moment? _____

V. Answer the following questions in the affirmative in complete sentences, substituting a direct object pronoun for the noun object. Also, substitute a pronoun for the noun subject.

Model:	**Est-ce que Pierre connaît Madeleine?**	**You write:**	**Oui, il la connaît.**
	(Does Pierre know Madeleine?)		(Yes, he knows her.)

1. Est-ce que Janine connaît Monique? _____

2. Est-ce que Monique connaît Robert? _____

3. Est-ce que Robert connaît Pierre et Hélène? _____

4. Est-ce que Marie connaît Monsieur et Madame Paquet? _____

5. Est-ce qu'Henri connaît Anne et Françoise? _____

VI. Answer the following questions in the affirmative.

Model:	**Est-ce qu'elle vous voit?**	**You write:**	**Oui, elle me voit.**
	(Does she see you?)		(Yes, she sees me.)

1. Est-ce qu'elle vous connaît? _____

2. Est-ce qu'il te voit? _____

3. Est-ce qu'elle nous aime? _____

4. Est-ce qu'ils les attendent? _____

5. Est-ce qu'il l'adore? _____

VII. Answer the following questions in the affirmative.

Model:	**Est-ce que vous m'aimez bien?**	**You write:**	**Oui, je vous aime bien.**
	(Do you like me?)		(Yes, I like you.)

1. Est-ce que tu m'aimes bien? _____

2. Est-ce que vous l'aimez bien aussi? _____

3. Est-ce que tu l'aimes bien aussi? _____

4. Est-ce qu'il vous aime bien? _____

5. Est-ce qu'elle vous aime bien aussi? _____

VIII. Answer the following questions in the affirmative.

Model:	**Est-ce que vous m'aimez?**	**You write:**	**Oui, je vous aime.**
	(Do you love me?)		(Yes, I love you.)

1. Est-ce que tu m'aimes? _____

2. Est-ce qu'il vous aime? _____

3. Est-ce que vous l'aimez aussi? _____

4. Est-ce qu'il t'aime? _____

5. Est-ce qu'elle vous aime? _____

IX. For each statement write a response in the affirmative imperative. Use a pronoun object in place of the noun object. Review the imperative in Work Units 10 and 11.

Model:	**Je veux apprendre le poème!**	**You write:**	**Bon! Alors, apprenez-le!**
	(I want to learn the poem!)		(Good! Then learn it!)

1. Je veux écrire la lettre! _____

2. Je veux étudier les leçons! _____

3.   Je veux lire le livre! _____

4.   Je veux boire le lait! _____

5.   Je veux faire les devoirs! _____

X.   For each statement write a response in the negative imperative. Use a pronoun object in place of the noun object. Review the imperative in Work Units 10 and 11.

Model:	**Je ne veux pas apprendre le poème!**	**You write:**	**Bon! Alors, ne l'apprenez pas!**
	(I don't want to learn the poem!)		(Good! Then don't learn it!)

1.   Je ne veux pas écrire la lettre! _____

2.   Je ne veux pas étudier les leçons! _____

3.   Je ne veux pas lire le livre! _____

4.   Je ne veux pas boire le lait! _____

5.   Je ne veux pas faire les devoirs! _____

XI.   Change the following sentences by substituting a pronoun as object of the infinitive in place of the noun object. Rewrite the entire sentence.

Model:	**Janine veut lire *la lettre*.**	**You write:**	**Janine veut la lire.**
	(Janine wants to read the letter.)		(Janine wants to read it.)

1.   Pierre veut lire *le livre*. _____

2.   Madeleine veut apprendre *le poème*. _____

3.   Paul ne veut pas écrire *la lettre*. _____

4.   Philippe ne veut pas manger *la saucisse*. _____

5.   Gertrude ne veut pas apporter *les gâteaux*. _____

XII.   Answer the following questions in the affirmative, substituting **en** as a pronoun object of the verb in place of the words indicated.

Model:	**Avez-vous du café?**	**You write:**	**Oui, j'en ai.**
	(Do you have any coffee?)		(Yes, I have some.)

1.   Avez-vous *du lait?* _____

2.   Buvez-vous *de l'eau?* _____

3.   Mangez-vous *de la glace?* _____

4.   Mangez-vous *des pommes?* _____

5.   Avez-vous *des soeurs?* _____

As-tu du lait?

6. Avez-vous *des frères?* _____

7. Vient-il *de Paris?* _____

8. Avez-vous peur *des serpents?* _____

9. Mangez-vous *du rosbif?* _____

10. Buvez-vous *du café?* _____

XIII. Answer the following questions in the negative, substituting **en** as a pronoun object of the verb in place of the words indicated.

Model:	**Avez-vous *du vin?***	**You write:**	**Non, je n'en ai pas.**
	(Do you have any wine?)		(No, I don't have any.)

1. Avez-vous *du café?* _____

2. Avez-vous *de l'eau?* _____

3. Avez-vous *de la glace?* _____

4. Avez-vous *des gâteaux?* _____

5. Avez-vous *des frères?* _____

XIV. For each statement write a response in the affirmative imperative, substituting **en** in place of the words indicated. Review the imperative in Work Units 10 and 11.

Model: **Je veux boire *du café*!**	**You write:** **Bon! Alors, buvez-en!**
(I want to drink some coffee!)	(Good! Then drink some!)

1. Je veux boire *du lait!* _____

2. Je veux manger *du gâteau!* _____

3. Je veux écrire *des lettres!* _____

4. Je veux boire *de l'eau!* _____

5. Je veux manger *de la salade!* _____

XV. For each statement write a response in the negative imperative, substituting **en** in place of the words indicated. Review the imperative in Work Units 10 and 11.

Model: **Je ne veux pas boire *de café*!**	**You write:** **Bon! Alors, n'en buvez pas!**
(I don't want to drink any coffee!)	(Good! Then don't drink any!)

1. Je ne veux pas boire *de vin!* _____

2. Je ne veux pas manger *de gâteau!* _____

3. Je ne veux pas écrire *de lettres!* _____

XVI. Change the following sentences in the passé composé by substituting a pronoun as object of the verb in place of the noun object. Rewrite the entire sentence. Watch for agreement of the past participle with a preceding direct object pronoun.

Model: **Pierre a préparé *la leçon*.**	**You write:** **Pierre l'a préparée.**
(Pierre prepared the lesson.)	(Pierre prepared it.)

1. Madame Paquet a préparé *le dîner.* _____

2. Monsieur Richy a mangé *le ragoût.* _____

3. Pierre a servi *le dîner.* _____

4. Janine a préparé *les devoirs.* _____

5. Monsieur Paquet a préparé *les salades.* _____

XVII. Answer the following questions in the affirmative, substituting a pronoun as object of the verb in place of the noun object. Also, substitute a pronoun in place of the noun subject. Rewrite the entire sentence. Watch for agreement on the past participle!

Model: **Est-ce que Pierre a préparé *la salade*?**   **You write:** **Oui, il l'a préparée.**
       (Did Pierre prepare the salad?)   (Yes, he prepared it.)

1. Est-ce que Pierre a servi *le dîner?* _____

2. Est-ce que Madame Paquet a préparé *le dîner?* _____

3. Est-ce que Monsieur Richy a mangé *le ragoût?* _____

4. Est-ce que Janine a écrit *la lettre?* _____

5. Est-ce que Christophe a fait *les devoirs?* _____

XVIII. Answer the following questions in the negative, substituting a pronoun as object of the verb in place of the noun object. Also, substitute a pronoun in place of the noun subject. Rewrite the entire sentence. Watch for agreement of the past participle!

Model: **Est-ce que Pierre a préparé *le dîner*?**   **You write:** **Non, il ne l'a pas préparé.**
       (Did Pierre prepare the dinner?)   (No, he did not prepare it.)

1. Est-ce que Guy a préparé *la salade?* _____

2. Est-ce que Pierre a fait *le dîner?* _____

3. Est-ce que Janine a lu *le poème?* _____

4. Est-ce que Madame Richy a mangé *le ragoût?* _____

5. Est-ce que Robert a fait *les devoirs?* _____

XIX. Dinner Talk. Proficiency in Speaking, Reading, and Writing.

Situation: Monsieur and Madame Dufy are dinner guests at your home.

In this guided conversation, you are providing the needed French words on the blank lines. This gives you practice to say what someone else would say if you were in their place. You may use your own ideas and words or follow the suggested words under the blank lines. Later, write what you said on the lines.

Mme Dufy: **La salade est délicieuse. Qui l'a préparée?**

Janine: _____
                My brother Pierre prepared it.

M. Dufy: **Les pommes de terre sont vraiment excellentes. Qui les a préparées?**

Pierre: _____
                Me. I prepared them.

M. Paquet: **Janine, veux-tu un peu de salade?**

Janine: _____
                No, thank you, Dad. I don't want any [of it].

Mme Paquet:	**Tu n'en veux pas, Janine? Pourquoi?**
Janine:	_____
	*I already ate some [of it]./***J'en ai déjà mangé.**
Mme Dufy:	_____
	*I would like a cup of tea with the dessert, please. I don't drink any coffee./***J'aimerais une tasse de thé avec le dessert, s'il vous plaît. Je ne bois pas de café.**
Mme Paquet:	**Avec citron ou crème?/***With lemon or cream?*
Mme Dufy:	_____
	*Lemon, please, if there is any/***s'il y en a.**
Mme Paquet:	**Pierre, va dans la cuisine, s'il te plaît. Le citron est sur la table.**
Pierre:	_____
	*Yes, Mom. Right away./***Tout de suite.**

XX. Snack Time. Proficiency in Speaking, Reading, and Writing.

Situation: You and some friends are having afternoon snacks at your kitchen table.

In this guided conversation, you are providing the needed French words on the blank lines. This gives you practice to say what someone else would say. The familiar form *tu* is used in this conversation because the participants are all friends. You may use your own ideas and words or follow the suggested words under the blank lines. Later, write what you said on the lines.

Pierre:	**Raymond, passe-moi la pizza, s'il te plaît.**
Raymond:	_____
	*Okay, Here it is./***La voici.**
Pierre:	**Robert, tu n'en manges pas. Tu ne l'aimes pas?**
Robert:	_____
	No, I don't like it. Tell me, Pierre, did you do the biology assignments **(les devoirs de biologie)** *for tomorrow?*
Janine:	**Il ne les fait jamais.**
Pierre:	_____
	No. I didn't do them.
Janine:	**Pierre, passe-moi les hamburgers, s'il te plaît.**
Pierre:	**Les voici. Robert, tu n'aimes pas les hamburgers?**
Robert:	_____
	*No. I don't like them. I don't eat them. I don't like fast food/***la cuisine rapide.**
Monique:	**Qui a apporté les gâteaux?**
Pierre:	_____
	Janine brought them.
Monique:	**Robert, tu ne manges rien.**
Robert:	_____
	*I like cakes. I'm going to eat them all/***tous.**

XXI. Dining Out. Proficiency in Writing.

Situation: You are having something to eat and drink at a sidewalk café-restaurant while on your summer vacation in Paris.

Look at the picture on this page. On the lines under the picture, write at least three sentences. You may use your own ideas and words and/or the following suggested vocabulary: **manger**/*to eat*; **boire**/*to drink*; **parler**/*to talk*; **regarder**/*to look (at), to watch*; **la serveuse**/*the waitress*; **servir**/*to serve*; **les clients**/*the customers*; **il y a des personnes qui marchent sur le trottoir**/*there are people who are walking on the sidewalk*; **les petites tables rondes**/*the small round tables.*

1. _____

2. _____

3. _____

Indirect Object Pronouns, Including *y*

Prête à prêter

Janine lent her cell phone to a friend. Now she doesn't know where it is. Let's see how Janine finds her phone.

Qui a mon téléphone portable?

Ce matin, Janine a prêté son téléphone portable à son amie Suzanne. Suzanne avait besoin du portable pour téléphoner à son petit ami. Maintenant, Janine veut son téléphone portable pour téléphoner à sa mère. Elle va voir son amie Suzanne et elle lui dit:

Janine:	Suzanne, je t'ai prêté mon téléphone portable à neuf heures du matin. Il est maintenant trois heures de l'après-midi et il faut que je téléphone à ma mère. Veux-tu me rendre mon portable, s'il te plaît?
Suzanne:	Je ne l'ai pas, Janine. Je l'ai donné à Monique. Va la voir. Je lui ai donné le portable.
Janine:	Monique, j'ai prêté mon portable à Suzanne et elle m'a dit que tu l'as maintenant. Je lui ai donné mon portable ce matin.
Monique:	Je ne l'ai pas, Janine. Je l'ai prêté à Mimi. Va la voir. Je lui ai donné le portable.
	(Janine va voir Mimi.)
Janine:	Mimi, as-tu mon téléphone portable? Tu l'as, je sais. Je l'ai prêté à Suzanne, elle l'a donné à Monique, et Monique m'a dit que tu l'as maintenant.
Mimi:	Oh! Le portable! Quel portable? Le portable avec appareil photo numérique?
Janine:	Oui. C'est ça.
Mimi:	Non. Je ne l'ai pas. Je l'ai donné à Raymond. Va le voir. Je lui ai donné le portable.
	(Janine cherche Raymond. Elle ne le trouve pas. Janine va voir Paul, qui a un téléphone portable.)
Janine:	Paul, pourrais-tu me prêter ton portable?
Paul:	Pas de problème, Janine. Vas-y!
	(Janine prend le téléphone portable et elle compose son propre numéro de téléphone. C'est Raymond qui répond.)
Raymond:	Allô. Ici Raymond.
Janine:	Raymond, c'est Janine. Rends-moi mon téléphone portable!

Vocabulaire

l'ami *m.,* **l'amie** *f., n.,* the friend

l'appareil *m. n.* **photo numérique** digital camera

l'après-midi *m. n.,* afternoon; **de l'après-midi** in the afternoon (time)

le besoin *n.* need; **avoir besoin de (quelque chose)** to need (something)

écouter *v.,* to listen (to)

faut *v. form of* **falloir** to be necessary; **il faut que** it is necessary (that). This expression takes the subjunctive mood.

l' (**la** or **le** before vowel), *direct obj. pron.,* it

le, *direct obj. pron.,* it

les *direct obj. pron.,* them

lui *indirect obj. pron.,* to her, to him

le matin *n.,* morning; **du matin** in the morning (time)

me *indirect obj. pron.,* to me

mes *poss. adj. pl.,* my

le portable *n.* the cell phone (short for **le téléphone portable**); can also mean laptop computer

prêt, prête *adj. m. f.,* ready

prêté *past part. of* **prêter** *v.* to lend

propre *adj.,* own; **son propre numéro (de téléphone)** her own (phone) number

rendre *v.,* to return (something), to give back; **rends-moi...** Give me back...

reprendre *v.,* to take back, get back

ses *poss. adj. pl.,* his, her

s'il te plaît please *(fam. use);* **s'il vous plaît** *(polite use)*

te *indirect obj. pron.,* to you *(fam.)*

le téléphone portable cell phone

va la (le) voir go see her (him)

Vas-y! *v. form of* **aller** Go ahead!

Exercises

Review the story and vocabulary before starting these exercises.

I. Answer the following questions in complete sentences. They are all based on the dialogue in this unit, "Prête à prêter."

1. Qui a prêté son téléphone portable à Suzanne? _____

2. Pourquoi Janine veut-elle reprendre son téléphone portable? _____

3. Qui prête son téléphone portable à Janine? _____

II. **Comment dit-on en français…?** Refer to the dialogue in this unit if you have to.

1. She said to me that you have it now. _____

2. I don't have it. I gave it to Monique. Go see her. _____

3. I gave the cell phone to Mimi. Mimi gave it to Raymond. _____

4. I gave the cell phone to him. Go see him. _____

III. Unscramble the French words listed below and write them in the appropriate squares.

1. BLATEROP

2. ENDERR

3. RÊTEP

4. REST

5. ETROCUE

6. REPROP

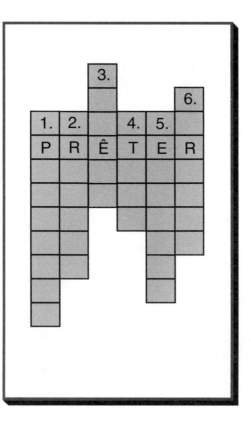

Structures de la Langue

A. Indirect object pronouns

	Singular			Plural	
me or **m'**	to me		**nous**	to us	
te or **t'**	to you *(familiar)*		**vous**	to you *(sing. polite or plural)*	
lui	to him, to her, to it		**leur**	to them	

Rules and observations:

1. An indirect object pronoun takes the place of an indirect object noun.

2. You might say that an indirect object "receives" the direct object because it is usually a matter of something "going" to someone (e.g., *to me, to you, to him, to her, to it, to us, to them*). Sometimes the *to* is not mentioned in English: *I am giving him the book*; what we really mean to say is, *I am giving the book to him*. Then, too, some verbs in French take an indirect object pronoun because the verb takes the preposition **à** (*to*); for example, **Je lui réponds** can be translated into English as *I am answering her (or) him*, or, *I am responding to her (or) to him*.

3. An indirect object pronoun is ordinarily placed *in front of* the verb.

4. Study the indirect object pronouns in the preceding box and the model sentences in the box below.

Pierre	**me**	donne le gâteau.	Pierre is giving the cake	*to me.*
	te			*to you.*
	lui			*to him.*
	lui			*to her.*
	lui			*to it.*
	nous			*to us.*
	vous			*to you.*
	leur			*to them.*

5. To make the verb negative, put **ne** *in front of the indirect object pronoun* and **pas** after the verb, as you did for the direct object pronouns:

Pierre ne me donne pas le gâteau.

(Peter is not giving the cake to me.)

6. In the affirmative imperative, do the same as you did for the direct object pronouns. The indirect object pronoun is put *right after* the verb and joined with a hyphen:

> **Donnez-lui le gâteau!**   *(Give the cake to him/her.)*

7. In the affirmative imperative, **me** changes to **moi** when it is tacked on to the verb and joined with a hyphen:

> **Donnez-moi le gâteau!**   *(Give me the cake!)*

8. In the negative imperative, do the same as you did for the direct object pronouns. Put the indirect object pronoun *in front of* the verb, where it ordinarily goes:

> **Ne me donnez pas le gâteau!**   *(Don't give me the cake!)*
> **Ne lui donnez pas le gâteau!**   *(Don't give her/him the cake!)*

9. If the indirect object pronoun is the object of an infinitive, do the same as you did for the direct object pronouns. Put the indirect object pronoun *in front of* the infinitive:

> **Janine veut leur parler.**   *(Janine wants to talk to them.)*

10. Remember that there is *no agreement* between the past participle of a verb conjugated with **avoir** in the passé composé if there is an indirect object. However, *an agreement* (both in gender and in number) is *required if there is a preceding direct object.* Compare:

> **Je lui ai donné les disques.**   **Je les ai donnés à Mimi.**
> (I *gave* the records *to her.*)   (I *gave them* to Mimi.)

B. Y is an indirect object form that is used to refer to places or to things. It ordinarily replaces a noun preceded by the preposition à, dans, or sur:

> (a) Allez-vous **à la bibliothèque**?   Oui, j'**y** vais.
>   (Are you going *to the library?*)   (Yes, I'm going *there.*)
>
> (b) Les gants sont-ils **dans le tiroir**?   Oui, ils **y** sont.
>   (Are the gloves *in the drawer*?)   (Yes, they are *there.*)
>
> (c) Est-ce que le chapeau est **sur la commode**?   Oui, il **y** est.
>   (Is the hat *on the dresser*?)   (Yes, it is *there.*)
>
> (d) Aimez-vous aller **au cinéma**?   Oui, j'aime **y** aller.
>   (Do you like going *to the movies*?)   (Yes, I like going *there.*)

Exercises

Review the preceding material before starting these exercises.

I. Change the following sentences by substituting an indirect object pronoun in place of the nouns. Put the indirect object pronoun in its proper position. Rewrite the entire sentence.

Model: **Pierre donne le gâteau *à Janine*.**   **You write:** **Pierre lui donne le gâteau.**

1. Janine donne le journal *à Pierre*. _____

2. Madeleine donne le livre *à Mathilde*. _____

3. Gloria donne la fleur *à Hélène*. _____

4. Robert donne la balle *aux garçons*. _____

5. Monique donne les stylos *à Marie et à Henri*. _____

II. Answer the following questions in complete sentences, using an appropriate indirect object pronoun in place of the words in parentheses.

A. Model: **A qui parlez-vous? (à la jeune fille)**   **You write:** **Je lui parle.**

1. A qui parlez-vous? (à la femme) _____

2. A qui parlez-vous? (au garçon) _____

3. A qui parlez-vous? (à Madeleine) _____

4. A qui parlez-vous? (à l'ami) _____

5. A qui parlez-vous? (à Robert) _____

B. Model: **A qui donnez-vous les fleurs? (aux femmes)**   **You write:** **Je leur donne les fleurs.**

1. A qui donnez-vous les gâteaux? (aux garçons) _____

2. A qui donnez-vous les livres? (à Marie et à Robert) _____

3. A qui donnez-vous le ragoût brûlé? (aux chiens) _____

4. A qui donnez-vous les lettres? (à la mère et au père) _____

5. A qui donnez-vous le jus? (à Janine et à Pierre) _____

III. Answer the following questions in the affirmative using an indirect object pronoun in each answer.

Model: **Est-ce que vous me parlez?**   **You write:** **Oui, je vous parle.**

1. Est-ce que vous me parlez? _____

2. Est-ce que vous lui parlez? _____

3. Est-ce que vous nous parlez? _____

IV. For each statement write a response in the affirmative imperative. Use an indirect object pronoun in place of the words indicated.

> **Model: Je veux donner le ragoût *à Pierre*.**   You write: **Bon! Alors, donnez-lui le ragoût!**

1. Je veux donner le gâteau *à Marie*. _____

2. Je veux donner le parapluie *à la femme*. _____

3. Je veux donner le bonbon *à l'enfant*. _____

4. Je veux donner le jus de fruit *à Robert*. _____

5. Je veux donner le ragoût brûlé *à Monsieur Richy*. _____

V. For each statement write a response in the negative imperative. Use an indirect object pronoun in place of the words indicated.

> **Model: Je ne veux pas donner les**   You write: **Bon! Alors, ne leur donnez pas**
> **   bonbons *aux enfants*.**   **les bonbons!**

1. Je ne veux pas donner le chocolat *aux garçons*. _____

2. Je ne veux pas donner les devoirs *à la maîtresse*. _____

3. Je ne veux pas donner le billet *à Françoise*. _____

VI. For each statement write a response in the affirmative imperative. Use an indirect object pronoun in your response.

> **Model: Je veux vous parler.**   You write: **Bon! Alors, parlez-moi!**

1. Je veux vous parler. _____

2. Je veux lui parler. _____

3. Je veux leur parler. _____

VII. For each statement write a response in the negative imperative. Use an indirect object pronoun in your response.

> **Model: Je ne veux pas vous parler.**   You write: **Bon! Alors, ne me parlez pas!**

1. Je ne veux pas vous parler! _____

2. Je ne veux pas lui parler! _____

3. Je ne veux pas leur parler! _____

VIII. Match the following.

1. He is giving the assignments to them.

2. She is giving him the hat.

3. She is giving you the juice.

4. She is giving me the cake.

5. He is giving you the book.

6. He is giving us the chocolate.

_____ Elle me donne le gâteau.

_____ Il te donne le livre.

_____ Elle lui donne le chapeau.

_____ Il nous donne le chocolat.

_____ Elle vous donne le jus.

_____ Il leur donne les devoirs.

IX. Answer the following questions in the affirmative using **y** in your answer to take the place of the words indicated.

Model: **Allez-vous *à la bibliothèque?***   **You write:** **Oui, j'y vais.**

1. Allez-vous *à la maison?* _____

2. Allez-vous *au cinéma?* _____

3. Allez-vous *à l'aéroport?* _____

X. The words in the following boxes are scrambled. Unscramble them to find a meaningful sentence. Write the sentence on the line.

Model:

donne	me	ragoût
Pierre	le	

You write: *Pierre me donne le ragoût.*

1.

lui	parlez	Bon!	Alors,

2.

leur	parler
veut	Janine

3.

donne	Elle
nous	le chocolat

1. _____

2. _____

3. _____

XI. **Providing and Obtaining Information. Proficiency in Speaking and Writing.**

Situation: You are talking to your friend Anne on the telephone. You are trying to obtain information about the whereabouts of the CDs (**les disques compacts**, *m. n.*) you let her borrow in September. She is providing you with some information.

You may use your own ideas and words or follow the suggested words under the blank lines. Say your words aloud; then write them on the lines.

Vous: _____

_____

Anne, I lent you my CDs in the month of September and today is December first.

Anne: **Oui, je sais. Je ne les ai pas.**

Vous: _____

You don't have them? Where are they?

Anne: **Je ne sais pas. Je les ai donnés à Suzanne. Va la voir.**

Vous: _____

*I can't go to see her. She is on vacation in Canada./***Elle est en vacances au Canada.**

Anne: **Oh! Je sais maintenant! Suzanne les a donnés à Jacqueline. Elle les a.**

Vous: _____

No. She does not have them. I talked to her yesterday.

Anne: **Qu'est-ce qu'elle t'a dit?/***What did she say to you?*

Vous: _____

*She told me that (***que***) you have them.*

Anne: **Elle t'a dit que je les ai? Impossible! Je ne les ai pas, je te dis.**

Vous: _____

*And I am telling you that I don't have them! Apparently my CDs are lost!/***Apparemment mes disques compacts sont perdus!** *Good-bye!*

Basic Sentence Word Order

Summary of word order of elements in a French declarative sentence in the **present tense.**

SUBJECT	ne	me	le	lui	y	en	VERB	pas
	n'	m'	la	leur				
		te	l'					
		t'	les					
		se						
		s'						
		nous						
		vous						

Models. Follow the words in the model sentences with the basic word order outlined above.

Affirmative

1. **Janine lit le poème.**
   (Janine is reading the poem.)

2. **Janine le lit.**
   (Janine is reading it.)

3. **Madame Coty me donne le ragoût.**
   (Mrs. Coty is giving me the stew.)

4. **Madame Coty me le donne.**
   (Mrs. Coty is giving it to me.)

Negative

1. **Janine ne lit pas le poème.**
   (Janine is not reading the poem.)

2. **Janine ne le lit pas.**
   (Janine is not reading it.)

3. **Madame Coty ne me donne pas le ragoût.**
   (Mrs. Coty is not giving me the stew.)

4. **Madame Coty ne me le donne pas.**
   (Mrs. Coty is not giving it to me.)

Summary of word order of elements in a French declarative sentence in the **passé composé.**

SUBJECT	ne	me	le	lui	y	en	VERB	pas	past participle
	n'	m'	la	leur			(Auxiliary		
		te	l'				verb		
		t'	les				**avoir** or		
		se					**être** in the		
		s'					present tense)		
		nous							
		vous							

Models. Follow the words in the model sentences with the basic word order outlined above.

Affirmative

1. **Rita a préparé le dîner.**
   (Rita prepared the dinner.)

2. **Rita l'a préparé.**
   (Rita prepared it.)

3. **Louis a préparé les salades.**
   (Louis prepared the salads.)

4. **Louis les a préparées.**
   (Louis prepared them.)

Negative

1. **Rita n'a pas préparé le dîner.**
   (Rita did not prepare the dinner.)

2. **Rita ne l'a pas préparé.**
   (Rita did not prepare it.)

3. **Louis n'a pas préparé les salades.**
   (Louis did not prepare the salads.)

4. **Louis ne les a pas préparées.**
   (Louis did not prepare them.)

5. **J'ai donné le livre à Robert.**
   (I gave the book to Robert.)

5. **Je n'ai pas donné le livre à Anne.**
   (I did not give the book to Anne.)

6. **Je le lui ai donné.**
   (I gave it to him.)

6. **Je ne le lui ai pas donné.**
   (I did not give it to her.)

7. **J'ai donné les roses aux enfants.**
   (I gave the roses to the children.)

7. **Je n'ai pas donné les roses aux enfants.**
   (I did not give the roses to the children.)

8. **Je les leur ai données.**
   (I gave them to them.)

8. **Je ne les leur ai pas données.**
   (I did not give them to them.)

Summary of word order of elements in a French **affirmative imperative** sentence.

VERB	le la l' les	moi m' toi t' nous vous	lui leur	y	en

Models. Compare these affirmative imperatives with those in the negative models that follow.

1. **Écrivez la lettre à Marie!**
   (Write the letter to Mary!)

4. **Répondez à la question!**
   (Respond to the question!)

2. **Écrivez-la!**
   (Write it!)

5. **Répondez-y!**
   (Respond to it!)

3. **Écrivez-la-lui!**
   (Write it to her!)

6. **Donnez m'en!**
   (Give me some [of it]!)

Summary of word order of elements in a French **negative imperative** sentence.

Ne N'	me m' te t' nous vous	le la l' les	lui leur	y	en	VERB	pas

Models. Compare these negative imperatives with those in the affirmative.

1. **N'écrivez pas la lettre à Marie!**
   (Don't write the letter to Mary!)

4. **Ne répondez pas à la question!**
   (Don't respond to the question!)

2. **Ne l'écrivez pas!**
   (Don't write it!)

5. **N'y répondez pas!**
   (Don't respond to it!)

3. **Ne la lui écrivez pas!**
   (Don't write it to her!)

6. **Ne me le donnez pas!**
   (Don't give it to me!)

Interrogative Pronouns

Quinze devinettes

Qui suis-je?
Who am I?

Qui suis-je?
Who am I?

Qui suis-je?
Who am I?

Que suis-je?
What am I?

Qu'est-ce que je suis?
What am I?

215

Have you ever guessed any riddles in English? In French? Here are fifteen riddles in French; some are easy, some are not so easy. The answers are upside down at the bottom of the page.

1. Je porte toujours un chapeau mais je n'ai pas de tête. Que suis-je?

2. Je vole comme un oiseau. Qu'est-ce que je suis?

3. J'ai un cou très, très long et je peux voir les autres animaux de très haut. Qui suis-je?

4. Je suis toujours au milieu de Paris. Que suis-je?

5. J'habite dans l'eau. J'ai des yeux mais je n'ai pas de paupières. Qui suis-je?

6. J'ai des jambes et j'ai des bras mais je n'ai pas de mains. Qu'est-ce que je suis?

7. Je vais, je viens, je sors, je retourne, sans quitter ma maison. Qui suis-je?

8. Je n'ai pas de pieds et de jambes. J'ai seulement deux aiguilles. Que suis-je?

9. Je suis un animal qui porte mes petits enfants dans ma poche. Qui suis-je?

10. Je suis jaune dedans et blanc dessus. Qu'est-ce que je suis?

11. Quand je quitte la maison, je ne sors jamais par la porte et jamais par la fenêtre. Je sors par la cheminée. Que suis-je?

12. J'entre le premier dans la maison. Qu'est-ce que je suis?

13. Je peux traverser une vitre sans la casser. Que suis-je?

14. Je suis le plus sale de la maison. Qu'est-ce que je suis?

15. Je suis utile pour surfer, mais ne me mets pas dans l'eau! Que suis-je?

15. un ordinateur		10. un oeuf		5. un poisson	
14. un balai		9. un kangourou		4. la lettre "r"	
13. la lumière		8. une horloge		3. une girafe	
12. une clef		7. une tortue		2. un avion	
11. la fumée		6. un fauteuil		1. un champignon	

Vocabulaire

l'aiguille *n. f.*, the needle, hand of a clock

l'animal *n. m.*, **les animaux** *pl.*, the animal, the animals

l'avion *n. m.*, the airplane

le balai *n.*, the broom

le bras *n.*, the arm

casser *v.*, to break; **sans la casser** without breaking it

le champignon *n.*, the mushroom

la cheminée *n.*, the chimney

la clef *n.*, the key

le cou *n.*, the neck

dedans *adv.*, inside

dessus *adv.*, on top, above

deviner *v.*, to guess; **une devinette** a riddle

le fauteuil *n.*, the armchair

la fenêtre *n.*, the window

la fumée *n.*, the smoke

la girafe *n.*, the giraffe

habite *v. form of* **habiter** (to live, reside, inhabit)

haut *adv.*, high

l'horloge *n. f.*, the clock

jamais *adv.*, ever; **ne ... jamais** never

la jambe *n.*, the leg

le kangourou *n.*, the kangaroo

le lait *n.*, the milk

la lumière *n.*, the light

la main *n.*, the hand

le milieu *n.*, the middle; **au milieu de** in the middle of

l'oeuf *n. m.*, the egg

la paupière *n.*, the eyelid

peux *v. form of* **pouvoir** (to be able, may, can); **je peux** I can

le pied *n.*, the foot

la poche *n.*, the pocket

le poisson *n.,* the fish
porte *v. form of* **porter** (to wear, carry)
que *interrog. pron.,* what
que suis-je? what am I?
qu'est-ce que je suis? what am I?
qui suis-je? who am I?
quitter *v.,* to leave; **sans quitter**
without leaving

sale *adj.,* dirty, soiled; **le plus sale
de la maison** the dirtiest in the
house
sors *v. form of* **sortir** (to go out); **je
sors** I go out; **je ne sors jamais** I
never go out
suis *v. form of* **être** (to be); **je suis** I
am

la tortue *n.,* the turtle
tourner *v.,* to turn, to turn sour
traverser *v.,* to cross, to go through
viens *v. form of* **venir** (to come); **je
viens** I come
la vitre *n.,* the windowpane (glass)

Exercises

Review the preceding material before starting these exercises.

I. Fill in the blank lines after each picture by writing the French word for it. Use the indefinite article. They are based on the riddles in this unit.

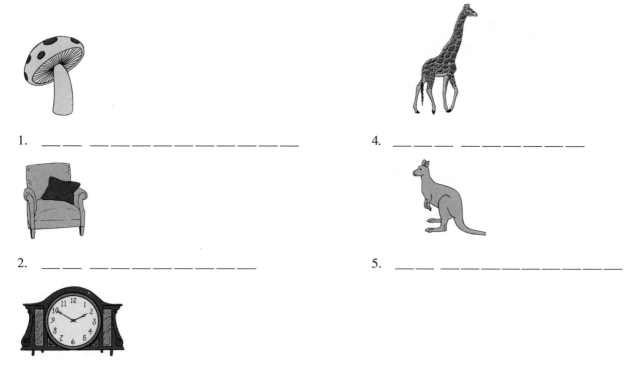

Model:

U N E   M A I S O N

1. __ __ __ __ __ __ __ __ __ __ __ __ __

4. __ __ __ __ __ __ __ __ __ __

2. __ __ __ __ __ __ __ __ __ __ __

5. __ __ __ __ __ __ __ __ __ __ __ __

3. __ __ __ __ __ __ __ __ __ __

II. Complete the following statements by writing the appropriate words in French. They are based on the fifteen riddles in this unit.

1. Je suis un kangourou. Je _____ mes petits enfants dans ma poche.

2. Je suis un poisson. J'ai des _____ , mais je _____ de paupières.

3. Je suis un balai et je _____ le plus sale de la maison.

4. Je suis un fauteuil. J'ai deux bras mais je _____ de mains.

5. Je suis une girafe. J'ai un cou très, très _____ et je _____ voir les autres animaux de très haut.

III. Fill in the squares by writing the French words across for the English words in the list.

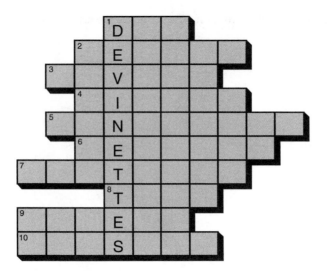

1. ten
2. I am
3. he sells
4. giraffe
5. kangaroo
6. window
7. armchair
8. very
9. I can
10. fish

Structures de la Langue

A. Interrogative pronouns

1. Qui

1. **Qui** parle?		1. *Who* is talking?	
2. **Qui** aimez-vous?		2. *Whom* do you love?	
3. **A qui** parlez-vous?		3. *To whom* are you talking?	
4. **De qui** parlez-vous?		4. *About whom* are you talking?	

Rules and observations:

1. **Qui** is used as a subject. See example 1 in the above box.

2. **Qui** is used as a direct object and translated into English as *whom*. See example 2 in the above box.

3. **Qui** is used as an object of a preposition. See example 3 in the box on page 218 (**qui** is the object of the preposition *à*).

4. In example 4 in the box on page 218, **qui** is used as the object of the preposition *de*.

5. The *i* in **qui** never drops. Note that **qui** can mean *who* or *whom*.

2. Que and **Qu'est-ce que**

1. **Que** mangez-vous?	1. *What* are you eating?
2. **Qu'est-ce que** vous mangez?	2. *What* are you eating?

Rules and observations:

1. **Que** is used as a direct object of a verb for things.

2. **Qu'est-ce que** can be used instead of **que** as direct object of a verb, but when you use it, keep the normal word order of what follows (i.e., subject plus verb). See example 2 in the above box.

3. The **e** in **que** drops if the word that follows begins with a vowel or silent *h* and an apostrophe replaces it.

Exercises

Review the preceding material before starting these exercises.

I. Match the following.

1. De qui parlez-vous?   _____ Who is talking?

2. Que dites-vous?   _____ Whom do you love?

3. Qui aimez-vous?   _____ Whom are you talking to?

4. Qu'est-ce que vous mangez?   _____ About whom are you talking?

5. A qui parlez-vous?   _____ What are you eating?

6. Qui parle?   _____ What are you saying?

II. Fill in the missing words with either **qui**, **que**, or **qu'est-ce que**, as required.

1. _____ parle?   6. _____ vous mangez?

2. _____ est à la porte?   7. _____ dites-vous?

3. A _____ parlez-vous?   8. _____ vous dites?

4. De _____ parlez-vous?   9. _____ arrive?

5. _____ mangez-vous?   10. _____ faites-vous?

III. Write the question in French that must have been asked for each of the following answers. In your question use **qui**, **que**, or **qu'est-ce que**, as indicated in parentheses.

Model: Robert parle. (qui)	**You write: Qui parle?**
(Robert is talking. [who])	(Who is talking?)

1. Monsieur Richy mange une pomme. (qui) _____

2. Je bois du lait. (que) _____

3. Monique parle à Roger. (qui) _____

4. Je dis la réponse. (qu'est-ce que) _____

5. Janine écrit une lettre. (qu'est-ce que) _____

6. J'ai lancé la balle. (qui) _____

7. Elle lit un livre. (que) _____

8. Je mange une orange. (qu'est-ce que) _____

9. Pierre a servi la salade. (qu'est-ce que) _____

10. Madame Paquet a fait le ragoût. (qui) _____

IV. Look who's talking to whom! Proficiency in Speaking and Writing.

Situation: You have been on the phone for about an hour. Your brother wants to call someone and he is pestering you by asking you one question after the next. You interrupt your telephone conversation every few seconds to answer his questions. You are acting the role of *Vous.*

After you have finished answering his questions, you may practice writing what you said on the lines. You may add your own words and ideas to expand this dialogue. Ask a friend to play the role of your brother/*ton frère.* Or, if you prefer, *ta soeur*/your sister.

Ton frère:	**Je veux téléphoner à mon ami.**
Vous:	_____
	Don't you see that **(que)** *I'm talking to someone* **(quelqu'un)**?
Ton frère:	**Oui, je vois que tu parles à quelqu'un. A qui parles-tu? Tu parles à Lily?**
Vous:	_____
	No. I'm not talking to her.
Ton frère:	**Tu ne lui parles pas?**
Vous:	_____
	_____
	I'm not talking to her at this moment/**en ce moment.** *I talked to her yesterday.*
Ton frère:	**À qui parles-tu? Tu parles à Janine et à Monique?**
Vous:	_____
	I'm not talking to them now. I talked to them this morning.
Ton frère:	**Dis-moi à qui tu parles.**
Vous:	_____
	I'm talking to you, to you!/**Je te parle, à toi!** *Go away!*/**Va-t'en!***

***Va-t'en** is the second person, singular, familiar form, the imperative of **s'en aller** to go away.

V. Appreciating French Art. Proficiency in Speaking and Writing.

Situation: You are at a museum admiring the painting ***Danseuse au repos****/Dancer Resting,* by Edgar Degas, a great French artist/**grand artiste français**. He studied painting in Paris at the **École des Beaux-Arts/**School of Fine Arts.

Look at the picture below and say aloud French words that come to mind. Then write them on the lines or use them in two or three sentences. You may use your own ideas and words and/or the following suggestions.

Je regarde le tableau de Degas/*I am looking at the painting by Degas*; **C'est une danseuse de ballet au repos/***It's a ballet dancer resting*; **Elle s'appelle Claudette/***Her name is Claudette*; **Elle est assise/***She is sitting*; **Elle a la main droite sur un genou/***She has her right hand on one knee*; **et la main gauche sur le pied/***and her left hand on her foot*; **le tutu qu'elle porte est joli/***the ballet skirt* (**tutu**) *that she is wearing is pretty*; **Elle se repose/***She is resting*; **C'est un tableau spendide/***It's a splendid painting.*

_____

_____

_____

Danseuse au repos by Degas. Courtesy of The Granger Collection.

Toulouse-Lautrec's Poster for the Moulin Rouge
Courtesy of The Granger Collection

Review Test: Work Units 11–15

I. How many French words can you find hidden in the word **MAISON**? Find at least eight.

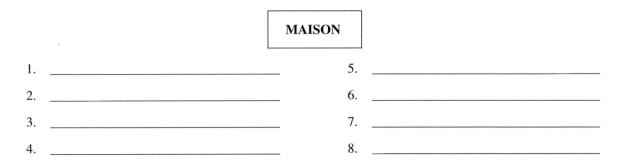

MAISON

1. _____   5. _____

2. _____   6. _____

3. _____   7. _____

4. _____   8. _____

II. Now, take the same French word, **MAISON**, scramble all the letters, and find another French word that has the same letters. Hint: It's a verb form in the imperative.

III. Five French words are hidden in this clock. Note that for most of the words, the first letter is the same as the last letter of the previous word. This clock has no hands because it's a "word clock"! Write the missing letters on the lines.

CLUES: From 12 to 4, give the French for the word "when."
From 4 to 5, give the French for the word "of" or "from."
From 5 to 7, give the French for the word "water."
From 7 to 8, give the indefinite article, masculine, singular.
From 8 to 11, give the French for the word "nine."

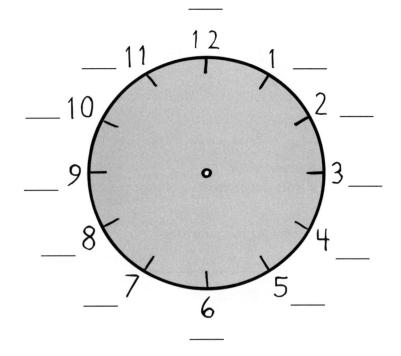

IV. Choose the verb form that would make sense in the statement or question.

1. Est-ce que vous _____ beaucoup de livres?
   (a) venez   (b) pouvez   (c) lisez   (d) partez

2. Les étudiants _____ -ils le français?
   (a) vendent   (b) apprennent   (c) ouvrent   (d) boivent

3. Janine aime beaucoup _____ du jus d'orange.
   (a) boire   (b) dire   (c) lire   (d) devoir

V. Choose the correct imperative form of the verb that would make sense in each statement.

1. _____ les livres sur la table, s'il vous plaît.
   (a) Buvez   (b) Mettez   (c) Soyez   (d) Venez

2. _____ la leçon pour demain, s'il vous plaît!
   (a) Faites   (b) Revenez   (c) Partez   (d) Buvez

3. _____ au cinéma ce soir!
   (a) Prenons   (b) Prêtons   (c) Allons   (d) Pouvons

4. _____ cette belle pâtisserie, s'il te plaît!
   (a) Mangez   (b) Mange   (c) Sois   (d) Bois

5. _____ ici à cinq heures, s'il vous plaît!
   (a) Soyez   (b) Sois   (c) Comprenez   (d) Entendez

VI. Choose the verb form that could replace the underlined verb and make sense in the statement.

1. Pour demain, <u>préparez</u>, les pages cinq à dix.
   (a) ayez   (b) soyez   (c) lisez   (d) partez

2. S'il vous plaît, Joseph, <u>ouvrez</u> la fenêtre.
   (a) apprenez   (b) fermez   (c) écrivez   (d) allez

3. Hier, <u>j'ai reçu</u> une lettre de mon ami.
   (a) j'ai lu   (b) j'ai écrit   (c) je suis allé   (d) je suis venu

4. Nous <u>avons fait</u> les devoirs à l'école.
   (a) avons parlé   (b) avons fini   (c) avez écrit   (d) ont lu

5. Mes parents <u>sont sortis</u> à huit heures ce soir.
   (a) avons ri   (b) ai parlé   (c) sont devenus   (d) sont partis

VII. Write the infinitive for each of the following past participles.

Model: vu		**You write: <u>voir</u>**

1. eu _____
2. été _____
3. fait _____
4. dit _____
5. lu _____
6. su _____
7. compris _____
8. mis _____
9. ri _____

VIII. For each of the following verbs in the passé composé, write the correct form of either **avoir** or **être** (whichever is required) in the present indicative.

> **Model:**   **Hier, Monsieur Dufy _____ allé au Canada.**   **You write: est**
> (Yesterday Mr. Dufy went to Canada.)

1. Les enfants _____ allés à l'école.

2. J' _____ mangé du chocolat.

3. Je _____ allé au cinéma hier soir.

4. Janine _____ chanté.

5. Robert _____ parti.

6. Claire _____ parlé avec les dames.

7. Pierre _____ bu un café.

8. Marie _____ sortie.

IX. In the second sentence, choose the correct direct object pronoun to take the place of the direct object noun stated in the first sentence.

1. Jacqueline lit le livre. Jacqueline _____ lit.
   (a) le   (b) la   (c) les   (d) l'

2. Robert écrit la lettre. Robert _____ écrit.
   (a) les   (b) la   (c) l'   (d) le

3. Odette apprend la leçon. Odette _____ apprend.
   (a) l'   (b) la   (c) le   (d) les

4. Je mange les gâteaux. Je _____ mange.
   (a) la   (b) le   (c) les   (d) l'

5. Tu fais la leçon. Tu _____ fais.
   (a) le   (b) l'   (c) les   (d) la

X. In the second sentence, choose the correct indirect object pronoun to take the place of the indirect object noun stated in the first sentence.

1. Ma mère donne l'argent à mon père. Elle _____ donne l'argent.
   (a) lui   (b) leur   (c) me   (d) vous

2. Madame Durand parle aux élèves. Elle _____ parle.
   (a) leur   (b) lui   (c) les   (d) la

3. Odette veut écrire à Jacques. Elle veut _____ écrire.
   (a) lui   (b) le   (c) leur   (d) l'

4. Robert pose une question à Marie. Il _____ pose une question.
   (a) le   (b) lui   (c) l'   (d) leur

5. L'élève répond au professeur. Il _____ répond.
   (a) lui   (b) le   (c) les   (d) leur

XI. On the blank line, write the interrogative pronoun in French for the English word under the line.

1. _____ parle?
    (who)

4. De _____ parle-t-il?
    (whom)

2. _____ aimez-vous?
    (whom)

5. _____ manges-tu?
    (what)

3. A _____ parlez-vous?
    (whom)

6. _____ dites-vous?
    (what)

XII. Proficiency in Reading.

Directions: In the following passage there are five numbered blank spaces. Each space represents a missing word. Four possible completions are provided for each. Only one of them is grammatically correct and makes sense in the context of the passage.

First, read the passage in its entirety to determine its general meaning. Then read it a second time. Choose the completion that makes the best sense and is grammatically correct, and write its letter in the space provided.

Hier soir, la famille Paquet est _____ au théâtre. Ils ont _____ une comédie.

1. A. allé
   B. allée
   C. allés
   D. allées

2. A. vu
   B. vue
   C. vus
   D. voir

Ils _____ quitté la maison à sept heures et demie et ils sont _____ au théâtre à

3. A. ont
   B. sont
   C. avons
   D. sommes

4. A. arrivé
   B. arrivés
   C. arrivée
   D. arrivées

huit heures. Ils _____ entrés dans le théâtre et ils ont pris leurs places à huit heures et quart.

5. A. ont
   B. sont
   C. avons
   D. sommes

XIII. Proficiency in Writing.

Directions: Of the following five situations, select four and write your statements on the lines below. For each situation, write at least three sentences.

Situation 1. Last night you went to the Opera House in Paris. You saw the opera *Pelléas et Mélisande*, music composed by Claude Debussy.

Situation 2. Look at the picture in Work Unit 12 of the young men dressed in white. Tell us what they are doing, what they are wearing, and something about their berets.

Situation 3. You are giving a party in your house. To entertain your friends, play three guessing games in French. After each one, ask: *What is it?* Then, give the answer.

Situation 4. Last week you were a dinner guest at the home of Monsieur et Madame Dufy. Tell us what you did (e.g., you ate, drank, talked, danced, sang).

Situation 5. You are talking on the telephone to your friend Anne. You are trying to obtain information about the whereabouts of the CDs you let her borrow in September.

Select four of the five situations described above and write your sentences on the following lines.

Situation 1

1. _____

2. _____

3. _____

Situation 2

1. _____

2. _____

3. _____

Situation 3

1. _____

2. _____

3. _____

Situation 4

1. _____

2. _____

3. _____

Situation 5

1. _____

2. _____

3. _____

Demonstrative Pronouns—*ceci, cela, ça*

Vrai ou faux?

Do you like answering true-false questions? Let's see how Mrs. Ravel's students make out.

—Madame, il est trois heures. La leçon est finie!

Madame Ravel est professeur de géographie. Elle pose des questions à la classe.

Madame Ravel:	Paris est la capitale de la France. Marie, ceci est vrai ou faux?
Marie:	Cela est vrai, madame.
Madame Ravel:	Bravo, Marie! Maintenant, Suzanne. Marseille est un port sur la Méditerranée. Suzanne, ceci est vrai ou faux?
Suzanne:	Cela est faux, madame.
Madame Ravel:	Non! Non! Non! Ceci est vrai: Marseille est un port sur la Méditerranée . . . Maintenant, Georges. La Seine est un fleuve. Georges, ceci est vrai ou faux?
Georges:	Cela est vrai, madame. La Seine est un fleuve.
Madame Ravel:	Bravo, Georges! C'est ça!

(La directrice de l'école entre dans la salle de classe.)

La Directrice:	Madame Ravel, on vous demande au téléphone dans mon bureau.
Madame Ravel:	Oh! Merci, madame. Je viens tout de suite.

(La directrice quitte la salle de classe.)

Madame Ravel:	Marie, tu es chargée de continuer la leçon. Viens ici devant la classe.

(Madame Ravel quitte la salle et Marie va devant la classe.)

Tous les élèves:	Paris est la capitale de la France. Ceci est vrai ou faux, Madame Marie? Oh, cela est vrai! Oh, bravo, Madame Marie! Tu as du génie! Quelle intelligence!

(Tous les élèves rient.)

(Robert lance un avion en papier contre l'horloge.)

Robert:	J'ai lancé un avion en papier contre l'horloge. Ceci est vrai ou faux, Madame Marie? Oh, cela est vrai! Oh, bravo, Madame Marie! Quel génie! Quelle intelligence!
Marie:	Silence! Silence! Robert, tu es insolent!
Robert:	Cela est vrai? Je suis insolent?? Oh! pardonnez-moi, Madame Marie!

(Madame Ravel rentre dans la salle de classe.)

Madame Ravel:	Bon! Merci, Marie. Tu peux t'asseoir. Nous allons continuer la leçon . . . Hélène, pose une question à Raymond.
Hélène:	Raymond, où se trouve la Grande Bretagne?
Raymond:	Près de la petite Bretagne!

(Tous les élèves rient.)

Madame Ravel:	Raymond, ta réponse est ridicule! . . . Suzanne, pose une question à Georges.
Suzanne:	Georges, qui habite le pôle nord?
Georges:	Un bonhomme de neige!

(Tous les élèves rient.)

Madame Ravel:	Georges, ta réponse est absurde!

Georges:	Peut-être le Père Noël? Ho! Ho! Ho!
	(Tous les élèves rient.)
Madame Ravel:	Ça suffit! . . . Soyons sérieux! Paulette, où est Nancy?
Paulette:	Elle est absente!
Madame Ravel:	Je ne parle pas de Nancy. Je parle de Nancy. Je parle de Nancy, la ville en France. Oh! Quelle classe!
Hélène:	Madame Ravel, j'ai une question à poser à Robert. Robert, où est Cadillac?
Robert:	Dans le garage de mon père!
	(Tous les élèves rient.)
Madame Ravel:	Oh! Quelle classe! Je deviens folle!
Robert:	Madame, il est trois heures. La leçon est finie! C'est vrai ou faux, madame?
Madame Ravel:	C'est superbe!

Vocabulaire

le bonhomme de neige *n.*, the snowman

le bureau *n.*, the office

ça *dem. pron.*, that (**ça** is short for **cela**)

ceci *dem. pron.*, this

cela *dem. pron.*, that

c'est ça! that's right!

contre *prep.*, against

demander *v.*, to ask (for); **on vous demande au téléphone** you're wanted on the phone

deviens *v. form of* **devenir** (to become); **je deviens folle!** I'm going crazy!

le directeur, la directrice *n.*, the director, the principal

faux *m.*, **fausse** *f.*, *adj.*, false

le fleuve *n.*, the river

le génie *n.*, genius

la Grande Bretagne *n.*, Great Britain

l'horloge *n.*, the clock

lancer *v.*, to throw, fling

la Méditerranée *n.*, the Mediterranean (Sea)

la neige *n.*, the snow; **un bonhomme de neige** a snowman

le nord *n.*, the north; **le pôle nord** the North Pole

le papier *n.*, paper

pardonner *v.*, to pardon, to forgive; **pardonnez-moi** forgive me

le Père Noël *n.*, Santa Claus

peut-être *adv.*, maybe, perhaps

poser une question to ask a question

près (de) *adv.*, near

quel génie! what genius! **quelle classe!** what a class!

rentrer *v.*, to return

la réponse *n.*, the answer; **ta réponse est ridicule!** your answer is ridiculous!

rient *v. form of* **rire** (to laugh); **tous les élèves rient** all the students laugh

sérieux *m.*, **sérieuse** *f.*, *adj.*, serious; **soyons sérieux!** let's be serious!

suffit *v. form of* **suffire** (to suffice, to be enough); **ça suffit** that's enough

trouver *v.*, to find: **se trouver** to be located

viens *v. form of* **venir** (to come); **je viens tout de suite** I'm coming right away; **viens ici!** come here!

vrai *m.*, **vraie** *f.*, *adj.*, true

Exercises

Review the story and vocabulary before starting these exercises.

I. **Vrai ou faux?** On the blank line write **vrai** if the statement is *true* or **faux** if the statement is *false*.

1. Paris est la capitale de la France. _____

2. Marseille est un port sur la Méditerranée. _____

3. La Seine est un flueve. _____

4. Madame Ravel est professeur de mathématiques. _____

5. La directrice de l'école n'entre pas dans la classe. _____

6. Suzanne est chargée de continuer la leçon. _____

7. Robert a lancé un avion en papier contre la fenêtre. _____

8. Il est trois heures, la leçon est finie, et Madame Ravel est heureuse. _____

II. Complete the following statements by writing the appropriate words.

1. Madame Ravel est _____ de _____ .

2. La capitale de la France est _____ .

3. Marseille est un _____ sur la Méditerranée.

4. La Seine est un _____ .

5. La directrice de l'école entre _____ la salle de _____ .

6. Madame Ravel, on vous demande _____ téléphone dans mon _____ .

7. Marie, tu es chargée de _____ la _____ .

8. J'ai une question à _____ à Robert.

III. Answer the following questions in complete sentences.

1. Qui est Madame Ravel? _____

2. Qui entre dans la salle de classe? _____

3. Quand Madame Ravel quitte la salle, où va-t-elle?_____

   _____

4. Qui a lancé un avion en papier contre l'horloge? _____

   _____

5. A quelle heure est-ce que la leçon finit? _____

   _____

Structures de la Langue

A. Demonstrative pronouns: **ceci, cela, ça**

1. **Ceci** est vrai.	1. *This* is true.
2. **Cela** est faux.	2. *That* is false.
3. C'est **ça**!	3. *That's* right!
4. Je fais **cela**.	4. I do *that*.
5. Je fais **ceci**.	5. I do *this*.

Rules and observations:

1. Ça is a contraction of **cela**.

2. **Ceci** and **cela** are demonstrative pronouns in a neuter sense. They usually refer to a general or indefinite concept, to an idea or to a statement. As pronouns, they do not refer to any particular masculine or feminine noun.

3. **Ceci** or **cela** can be used as the subject of a sentence. See examples 1 and 2 in the preceding box. They can also be used as the direct object of a verb. See examples 4 and 5 in the above box. They can also be used as the object of a preposition. **Elle parle toujours de cela.** (She always talks about that.)

Exercises

Review the preceding material before doing these exercises.

I. Match the following.

1. Je fais ceci.   _____ This is true.

2. C'est ça.   _____ That is true.

3. Je fais cela.   _____ That's right.

4. Cela est vrai.   _____ I do this.

5. Ceci est vrai.   _____ I do that.

II. Answer the following questions in French, using **Oui** in your answer and a complete statement.

Model: **Cela est vrai?**	**You write:** **Oui, cela est vrai.**
(Is that true?)	(Yes, that is true.)

1. Cela est faux? _____

2. Ceci est vrai? _____

3. C'est ça? _____

III. Find the following demonstrative pronouns in the puzzle and circle them.

1. ceci

2. cela

3. ça

```
E   C   E   L
C   E   I   C
E   C   A   E
I   I   Ç   L
L   C   A   A
```

IV. **Vrai ou Faux? Proficiency in Speaking and Writing.**

Read the situation below and respond in spoken French. Later, you may write your responses for intensive practice.

Situation: You are in French class. Each student has to make one statement in French followed by **Cela est vrai?** *(Is that true?)* and **Cela est faux?** *(Is that false?)* It's your turn. Make at least three statements and then ask if that's true or false. You may use any or all of the following: **être, capitale de la France, la Seine, un fleuve, Marseille, un port, la Méditerranée, les Alpes, en France.** You may use the **passé composé** tense or the present, or both.

V. **Sports. Proficiency in Reading.**

Situation: Look at the picture below and read the statements. After each statement, write on the line **C'est vrai** if the statement is true or **C'est faux** if the statement is false.

1. Les deux garçons jouent au football.

   _____

2. Le ballon est près des pieds des deux joueurs.

   _____

3. Derrière les deux garçons il y a des arbres.

   _____

4. Les deux joueurs sont en shorts.

   _____

5. Les deux garçons jouent sous la pluie.

   _____

VI. Shopping. Proficiency in Speaking and Writing.

Situation: You have been invited to a birthday party and you are looking for the perfect present for Annie, one of your relatives.

Look at the picture below. Find the French words in the advertisement for the English words, say them aloud, and write them on the lines.

1. two little girls _____
2. summer dresses _____
3. like tee shirts _____

4. easy to wear _____
5. the skirt and sleeves _____
6. the flowers _____

Or, you may want to make two short statements in spoken French, using the words in the picture and your own ideas and words. Then write them on the lines.

7. _____

8. _____

A l'heure des petites filles en fleurs
Des petites robes d'été pratiques
comme des tee-shirts, faciles à porter, et très romantiques.

ROBE coton.
haut style "Tee-shirt".
jupe et manches
toile écrue imprimée
"fleurs".
Coloris écru/rose
ou écru/bleu.
Du 18 mois au 8 ans.
Le 4 ans.

AUX TROIS QUARTIERS

boulevard de la Madeleine
ouvert tous les jours d 9 h 45 à 18 h 30
4 parkings gratuits
Madeleine, Concorde
Garages de Paris, Malesherbes

Reprinted with permission of AUX TROIS QUARTIERS, Paris.

Disjunctive Pronouns

R. S. V. P.

Monsieur and Madame Paquet received an invitation for dinner at the home of some neighbors. Are they in for a big surprise!

—Nous sommes très heureux de vous voir.

Monsieur et Madame Paquet ont reçu une invitation à dîner chez leurs voisins, Monsieur et Madame Berger. Voici l'invitation:

Madame Berger
vous invite à dîner
vendredi, 15 avril, à 20 h.
R.S.V.P.   21, rue des Jardins Paris

Madame Paquet:	Eh bien, François, est-ce que nous y allons ou est-ce que nous n'y allons pas? Il faut répondre à l'invitation.
Monsieur Paquet:	Claire, tu sais que je ne veux pas aller chez eux parce que je ne les aime pas. Lui et elle sont des snobs.
Madame Paquet:	Tu as raison. Quand je l'ai vue au supermarché hier, elle m'a parlé, mais elle m'a regardée d'un air supérieur.
Monsieur Paquet:	D'ailleurs, ils sont ennuyeux.
Madame Paquet:	Oui. Ils m'ennuient aussi. Mais tu sais que si nous refusons l'invitation, tout est fini entre eux et nous.
Monsieur Paquet:	Il faut accepter pour rester amis avec eux.

Claire accepte l'invitation. Quand ils arrivent pour dîner chez les Berger, ils entrent dans le salon. Ils voient d'autres voisins chez eux. Tout le monde crie: Surprise! Surprise!

—Nous sommes très heureux de vous voir. Ce dîner est en votre honneur, leur dit Madame Berger.

—Pour nous?! En notre honneur?! s'exclament Claire et François.

—Oui, répond Monsieur Berger.

—Mais pourquoi? Qu'est-ce que nous avons fait? leur demande Claire.

—Parce que vous êtes bons! Et vous êtes aimables et gentils! répond Madame Berger.

—Merci, merci, disent les Paquet.

Tout le monde a mangé, bu, chanté, et dansé jusqu'à minuit. Claire et François Paquet sont rentrés contents chez eux.

Quand ils arrivent chez eux, Monsieur Paquet dit à sa femme:

—Tu sais, Claire, j'ai toujours dit que les Berger étaient aimables et gentils. Je les aime beaucoup.

—Moi aussi, j'ai toujours dit cela, François.

Vocabulaire

d'ailleurs *adv.,* besides
aimable *adj.,* likable
chez *prep.,* at (to) the home (place) of; **chez eux** at their house; **chez moi** at my house; **chez leurs voisins** at the home of their neighbors; **chez les Berger** at the Bergers
ennuient *v. form of* **ennuyer** (to bore, annoy); **ils m'ennuient** they bore me; **ennuyeux** *adj. m. pl.,* boring

entre *prep.,* between; **entre eux et nous** between them and us
eux *disj. pron.,* them; **avec eux** with them
faut *v. form of* **falloir**; **il faut** it is necessary
gentil *m.,* **gentille** *f., adj.,* nice, kind
h. *abbrev. for* **heures**; **20 h.** is 8 o'clock in the evening
l'honneur *n. m.,* honor

leur dit Madame Berger Mrs. Berger says to them
pour *prep.,* for, in order (to)
R.S.V.P. please reply (**R**épondez, **s'il** **v**ous **pl**aît)
reçu *past part. of* **recevoir** (to receive); **ils ont reçu** they received
refusons *v. form of* **refuser** (to refuse); **si nous refusons** if we refuse
rester *v.,* to remain, to stay

Note: **étaient** verb form of **être**, were

Exercises

Review the story and vocabulary before starting these exercises.

I. Complete the dialogue in French between Mr. and Mrs. Paquet. They are deciding whether or not to accept a dinner invitation. Refer to the story if you have to.

Madame Paquet: Eh bien, François, est-ce que nous acceptons l'invitation à dîner chez les Berger?

Monsieur Paquet: _____

Madame Paquet: Pourquoi?

Monsieur Paquet: _____

Madame Paquet: Oui. Tu as raison. Ils m'ennuient aussi.

Monsieur Paquet: _____

II. Complete the following statements by writing the appropriate words from among these:

(a) à l'invitation   (b) chez eux   (c) je ne les aime pas   (d) entre eux et nous   (e) vous voir

1.   Si nous refusons l'invitation, tout est fini _____

2.   Nous sommes très heureux de_____

3.   Ils voient d'autres voisins _____

4.   Je ne veux pas y aller parce que _____

5.   Il faut répondre _____

III. Choose the correct answer based on the story in this unit.

1.   M. et Mme Paquet ont reçu
     (a) un balai.   (b) une voiture.   (c) un ami.   (d) une invitation.   _____

2.   M. Paquet ne veut pas aller chez les Berger parce qu'
     (a) il est malade.   (b) il est heureux.   (c) il est aimable.   (d) il ne les aime pas.   _____

3.   M. et Mme Berger sont très heureux
     (a) de recevoir les Paquet.   (b) d'aller dîner.   (c) d'accepter l'invitation.
     (d) d'aller au supermarché.   _____

Structures de la Langue

A. Disjunctive pronouns (also known as stressed pronouns or tonic pronouns)

Singular		Plural	
moi	me *or* I	**nous**	us *or* we
toi	you (*familiar*)	**vous**	you (*formal singular or plural*)
soi	oneself	**eux**	them, they (*masculine*)
lui	him *or* he	**elles**	them, they (*feminine*)
elle	her *or* she		

Rules and observations:

1. The disjunctive pronoun is used when it is the object of a preposition:
   Elle parle avec moi. (She is talking with me.)
   Nous allons chez eux. (We are going to their house.)

2. The disjunctive pronoun is used in a compound subject:
   Lui et elle sont intelligents. (He and she are intelligent.)

3. The disjunctive pronoun is used in a compound object:
   Je vous connais—toi et lui. (I know you—you and him.)

4. You may use **à** with a disjunctive pronoun to express possession only if the verb is **être** and if the subject is a noun, personal pronoun, or a demonstrative pronoun:
   Ce livre est à moi. (This book is mine.)
   Ces livres sont à elles. (These books are theirs.)
   Ces livres sont à eux. (These books are theirs.)

5. The disjunctive pronoun **moi** is used instead of **me** in the affirmative imperative when it is tacked on to the verb and joined with a hyphen; example:
   Excusez-moi. (Excuse me.)

6. A disjunctive pronoun is also known as a *stressed* or a *tonic* pronoun.

Exercises

Review the preceding material before starting these exercises.

I. On the blank line write the disjunctive pronoun that expresses possession as needed, according to what is given in English in parentheses.

   Model: Les livres sont à _____ (mine).   **You write: moi**
   (The books are _____ mine.)   (me)

1. Le parapluie est à _____ (mine).

2. Les balles sont à _____ (his).

3. L'orange est à _____ (hers).

4. La maison est à _____ (ours).

5. La voiture est à _____ (yours, *pl.*).

6. Les gâteaux sont à _____ (theirs, *m.*).

II. On the blank line write in French the proper disjunctive pronoun for the English given in parentheses.

Model:	**(me) Elle parle avec _____ .**	**You write:**	**Elle parle avec moi.**
	(She is talking with _____ .)		(She is talking with me.)

Elle parle avec moi.

1. (him)   Je suis allée au cinéma avec _____ .

2. (me)   Il va partir sans _____ .

3. (he)   Madeleine et _____ sont intelligents.

4. (she)   Marie et _____ écrivent les leçons.

5. (us)   Le ragoût est pour _____ .

6. (you, *formal singular*)   Elle va partir avec _____ .

7. (you, *familiar singular*)   Nous allons sortir avec _____ .

8. (them, *masculine*)   Ce courriel est pour _____ .

9. (them, *feminine*)   Ces petits fours sont pour _____ .

10. (he and I)   _____ nous allons au cinéma.

III. Fill in the missing pronouns. They are not all disjunctive!

Monsieur Paquet annonce: J'ai les billets pour le théâtre. Ces quatre billets sont pour _____ . Ce
(us)

billet est pour _____ , ce billet est pour _____ , Claire; et ces deux billets sont pour
              (me)   (you)

_____ deux, Janine et Pierre. Prenez- _____ .
    (you)   (them)

Madame Paquet dit: François, ne _____ donne pas les billets. Je préfère _____ mettre dans
                              (to them)   (them)

ma poche.

Monsieur Paquet répond: Non, Claire, ne _____ mets pas dans ta poche. Je veux _____
                                      (them)   (them)

garder sur _____ .
            (me)

Janine demande: Papa, est-ce que nous allons au théâtre ce soir?

Monsieur Paquet répond: Oui, nous _____ allons ce soir.
                                    (there)

IV.   An Invitation to Dinner. Proficiency in Speaking and Writing.

Situation: Monsieur et Madame Dufy have received an invitation for dinner at the home of their neighbors, Monsieur et Madame Coty.

In this conversation, you are playing the role of *Mme Dufy*. You and *M. Dufy* are deciding whether or not to accept the invitation. You may use your own words or follow the suggestions under the lines. Then, write what you said on the lines. Later, you may switch roles with a friend.

Mme Dufy: _____

Well, are we going there or aren't we going there?

M. Dufy: **Tu sais que je ne veux pas aller chez eux. Lui et elle sont des snobs.**

Mme Dufy: _____

When I saw her at the supermarket yesterday, she talked to me and I talked to her.

M. Dufy: **Ils m'ennuient.**

Mme Dufy: _____

They bore me too. But if we refuse their invitation, everything is finished between them and us. You know that.

M. Dufy: **Pour rester amis avec eux, il faut accepter l'invitation.**

Mme Dufy: _____

That is true. You're right.

V. Appreciating French Art. Proficiency in Speaking and Writing.

Situation: You are at a museum admiring the painting *Le Balcon*/*The Balcony* by Édouard Manet, a great French artist/**grand artiste français.**

Look at the picture below and say aloud French words that come to mind. Then write them on the lines or use them in two or three sentences. You may use your own ideas and words and/or the following suggestions.

J'admire le tableau de Manet/*I am admiring the painting by Manet*; **C'est** *Le Balcon*/*it's* The Balcony; **Qui est le monsieur?**/*Who is the gentleman?* **Je ne sais pas**/*I don't know.* **Est-il le mari de la dame à droite ou la dame à gauche?**/*Is he the husband of the lady on the right or the lady on the left?* **Les deux dames sont belles et le monsieur est beau**/*The two ladies are beautiful and the gentleman is handsome.* **Quel beau tableau!**/*What a beautiful painting!*

_____

_____

_____

Manet—*Le Balcon*

VI. Expressing Love on Mother's Day. Proficiency in Speaking and Writing.

Situation: Next Sunday is Mother's Day. In the space provided, write your own card and give it to your mother or to some friend or relative who has been like a mother to you. Before you start, take a few minutes to gather your thoughts, jot down a few words in French that you will use, then say them aloud.

You may also use the following: **à la plus sympa de toutes les mamans**/*to the nicest of all Moms*; **de tout coeur**/*with all my heart*; **Je te souhaite une joyeuse Fête des Mères**/*I wish you a Happy Mother's Day*; **Je t'aime**/*I love you*; **Chez nous, j'ai appris la valeur de l'amour depuis mon enfance**/*In our home, I learned the value of love since childhood.*

Sur le pont d'Avignon

Sur le pont d'Avignon

On y danse, on y danse

Sur le pont d'Avignon

On y danse tout en rond

Adjectives

Tour d'écrou

Janine and her brother Pierre have nothing to do. They get into mischief when Pierre persuades her to look under the hood of their father's car. In this scene Pierre does something foolish despite his sister's objections.

Non! Non! Es-tu fou?

Quelle voiture! La famille Paquet a une belle voiture grise qui ne leur donne jamais de problèmes. Même les gross-es voitures neuves ne sont pas meilleures que la voiture de la famille Paquet.

Aujourd'hui Pierre fait quelque chose de bête. Il regarde dans le moteur de la voiture de leur père.

Pierre: Janine, donne-moi le tournevis.

Janine: Pourquoi? Que vas-tu faire, Pierre?

Pierre: Je vais régler le moteur. Je te dis, donne-moi le tournevis.

Janine: Quel tournevis? Il y en a beaucoup.

Pierre: Le plus petit.

Janine: Mais, que vas-tu faire, Pierre?

Pierre: Je vais engager le tournevis dans cette vis et je vais tourner.

Janine: Non! Non! Non!

Pierre: Maintenant je tourne le tournevis . . . là . . . là . . . là . . . J'enlève la vis et l'écrou. Ils ne sont pas utiles. Maintenant je les mets dans la poubelle.

Janine: Non! Es-tu fou?

Pierre: C'est fait.

Quand Monsieur Paquet veut aller faire des courses dans sa voiture, il va au garage, il monte dans sa voiture, et il tourne la clef pour mettre le moteur en marche. Il entend du bruit et le moteur ne marche pas.

Il appelle la station-service et le garagiste arrive; il emporte la voiture de Monsieur Paquet au garage de service.

Le lendemain, le garagiste téléphone à Monsieur Paquet et lui dit: Le montant à payer est de 200 euros, monsieur. Voilà le problème: Il manque une vis dans le moteur.

Vocabulaire

appeler *v.*, to call
beau *m.*, **belle** *f.*, *adj.*, beautiful
bête *adj. m. f.*, foolish, dumb
le bruit *n.*, the noise
c'est fait it's done
la couleur *n.*, the color: **de quelle couleur est . . .** what color is . . .
l'écrou *n. m.*, nut that fits on a screw or bolt
emporter *v.*, to take (carry) away
engager *v.*, to engage, to put (machinery) in gear
enlever *v.*, to remove, to take off
entendre *v.*, to hear
faire des courses to do (go) shopping
fou *m.*, **folle** *f.*, *adj.*, crazy
le garagiste *n.*, the garage mechanic
gris *m.*, **grise** *f.*, *adj.*, gray

il y a there is, there are; **il y en a beaucoup** there are many (of them)
là *adv.*, there
le lendemain *n.*, the following day
manquer *v.*, to miss, to be missing, to be lacking something; **il manque une vis dans le moteur** a screw is missing in the motor
marcher *v.*, to walk, to run (a motor or apparatus); **mettre en marche** to put into operation
meilleur *m.*, **meilleure** *f.*, *adj.*, better
même *adv.*, even
le montant *n.*, total amount (of an account)
monter *v.*, to climb, to mount, to get into
le moteur *n.*, the motor, the engine
neuf *m.*, **neuve** *f.*, *adj.*, new

petit *m.*, **petite** *f.*, *adj.*, small; **plus petit, plus petite** smaller; **le plus petit, la plus petite** the smallest
la poubelle *n.*, the garbage can
que *conj.*, than, that; *pron.*, what
quel *m.*, **quelle** *f.*, *interrog. adj.*, what, which; **quel tournevis?** which screwdriver? **quelle voiture!** what a car!
qui *pron.*, which, who
régler *v.*, to adjust, to tune (engine)
le tour *n.*, the turn; **tour d'écrou** turn of the nut
le tournevis *n.*, the screwdriver
utile *adj.*, useful
la vis *n.*, the screw
la voiture *n.*, the car, automobile

Exercises

Review the story and vocabulary before starting these exercises.

I.   Answer the following questions in complete sentences. They are based on the story "Tour d'écrou."

1.   Qui a une belle voiture grise? _____

2.   Est-ce que les grosses voitures neuves sont meilleures que la voiture de Monsieur Paquet?_____

     _____

3.   Pourquoi Pierre veut-il le tournevis? _____

4.   Où est-ce que Pierre met la vis et l'écrou?_____

II.   Answer the following questions in complete sentences. They are personal questions and require answers of your own.

1.   Est-ce que votre famille a une voiture?_____

2.   Allez-vous faire des courses dans la voiture de votre famille?_____

     _____

3.   De quelle couleur est la voiture de votre famille?_____

III.   **Oui ou Non?**

1.   La voiture de la famille Paquet est belle.   _____

2.   Peirre fait quelque chose de bête.   _____

3.   Janine met le tournevis dans le moteur.   _____

4.   Pierre met la vis et l'écrou dans la poubelle.   _____

Structures de la Langue

A.   Agreement and position of descriptive adjectives

Masculine	Feminine
un chapeau **gris**	une voiture **grise** (gray)
des chapeaux **gris**	des voitures **grises**
un passage **étroit**	une rue **étroite** (narrow)
des passages **étroits**	des rues **étroites**
un homme **libre**	une femme **libre** (free)
des hommes **libres**	des femmes **libres**

Rules and observations:

1. Most descriptive adjectives *follow* the noun in French.

2. Here are some common adjectives that normally *precede* the noun: **autre, beau, bon, chaque, gros, jeune, joli, long, mauvais, petit, plusieurs, vieux,** and **grand** (exception: **un homme grand,** a tall man; **un grand homme,** a great man).

3. Adjectives must agree in gender and number with the nouns they modify.

B. Formation of masculine descriptive adjectives in the plural

1. To form the plural of a masculine singular adjective, ordinarly add **s**.

2. If a masculine singular adjective ends in **s**, it remains the same in the plural: **gris**.

3. If a masculine singular adjective ends in **x**, it remains the same in the plural: **dangereux**.

4. If a masculine singular adjective ends in **al**, it ordinarily changes to **aux** in the plural: **loyal, loyaux**.

C. Formation of regular feminine descriptive adjectives

1. To form the feminine singular of an adjective, ordinarily add **e** to the masculine singular, e.g., **gris, grise**.

2. If the masculine singular adjective ends in **e**, the feminine singular is the same, e.g., **libre**.

3. To form the feminine plural of an adjective, ordinarily add **s**, e.g., **grises**.

D. Formation of irregular feminine descriptive adjectives

Masculine		Feminine	
Singular	*Plural*	*Singular*	*Plural*
neuf	**neufs**	**neuve**	**neuves**
furieux	**furieux**	**furieuse**	**furieuses**
dernier	**derniers**	**dernière**	**dernières**
ancien	**anciens**	**ancienne**	**anciennes**
bon	**bons**	**bonne**	**bonnes**
cruel	**cruels**	**cruelle**	**cruelles**
muet	**muets**	**muette**	**muettes**

Rules and observations:

1. A masculine singular adjective that ends in **-f** changes to **-ve** to form the feminine singular: **neuf, neuve**.

2. A masculine singular adjective that ends in **-eux** changes to **-euse** to form the feminine singular: **furieux, furieuse**.

3. A masculine singular adjective that ends in **-ier** changes to **ière** to form the feminine singular: **dernier, dernière**.

4. Some adjectives double the final consonant in the masculine singular to form the feminine singular; then an **e** is added: **ancien, ancienne**.

E. Other irregular feminine forms of descriptive adjectives

Masculine		Feminine	
Singular	*Plural*	*Singular*	*Plural*
beau	beaux	belle	belles
frais	frais	fraîche	fraîches
sec	secs	sèche	sèches
gros	gros	grosse	grosses
long	longs	longue	longues
blanc	blancs	blanche	blanches
favori	favoris	favorite	favorites
public	publics	publique	publiques
doux	doux	douce	douces

Exercises

I. Answer the following questions in French, substituting the appropriate form of the descriptive adjective in parentheses for the one indicated. Use **non** in your answer, but write your sentence in the affirmative.

Model: **Avez-vous une voiture *grise*? (blanc)**   **You write: Non, j'ai une voiture blanche.**

1.   Avez-vous une maison blanche?   (gris) _____

2.   Avez-vous un bon ordinateur?   (mauvais) _____

3.   Avez-vous une grosse pomme?   (beau) _____

4.   Avez-vous une pêche fraîche?   (doux) _____

5.   Avez-vous un joli chapeau?   (vieux) _____

II. Answer the following questions in the affirmative in complete French sentences. In answer (a) use **oui**. In answer (b) use **aussi**. Write the appropriate form of the descriptive adjective in your answers. Use subject pronouns in your answers. Study the models.

Model: **(a) Est-ce que Monsieur Paquet est bon?**   **You answer: (a) Oui, il est bon.**
   (b) Et Madame Paquet?   **You answer: (b) Elle est bonne aussi.**

1.   (a) Est-ce que Janine est petite? _____

   (b) Et Pierre? _____

2.   (a) Est-ce que Monsieur Paquet est furieux? _____

   (b) Et Madame Paquet? _____

3. (a) Est-ce que Monique est gentille? _____

   (b) Et Pierre? _____

4. (a) Est-ce que Janine et Monique sont belles? _____

   (b) Et Pierre et Robert? _____

5. (a) Est-ce que la maison est neuve? _____

   (b) Et les voitures? _____

III. Answer the following questions in the negative in complete French sentences. In answer (a) use **non**. In answer (b) use **non plus**. Write the appropriate form of the descriptive adjective in your answers. Use subject pronouns in your answers. Study the models.

Model:	**(a) Est-ce que Madame Paquet est cruelle?**	**You answer:**	**(a) Non, elle n'est pas cruelle.**
	(b) Et Monsieur Paquet?	**You answer:**	**(b) Il n'est pas cruel non plus.**

1. (a) Est-ce que Madame Paquet est petite? _____

   (b) Et Monsieur Paquet? _____

2. (a) Est-ce que le professeur de français est mauvais? _____

   (b) Et le professeur d'espagnol? _____

3. (a) Est-ce que le maître d'italien est gros? _____

   (b) Et la maîtresse d'allemand? _____

4. (a) Est-ce que le petit garçon est muet? _____

   (b) Et la petite fille? _____

5. (a) Est-ce que les passages sont étroits? _____

   (b) Et les rues? _____

IV. Choose the form of the adjective that does not belong in the group.

Model:	**(a) beau**	**(b) sec**	**(c) gros**	**(d) longue**	_____d_____
1. (a) neuf	(b) ancien	(c) bon	(d) cruelle		_____
2. (a) muets	(b) cruels	(c) dernière	(d) beaux		_____
3. (a) neuve	(b) furieuse	(c) étroits	(d) bonne		_____
4. (a) belles	(b) grise	(c) fraîches	(d) blanches		_____
5. (a) beau	(b) longs	(c) sec	(d) blanc		_____

F. Possessive adjectives

Masculine			
Singular		*Plural*	
mon livre	my book	**mes livres**	my books
ton stylo	your pen	**tes stylos**	your pens
son ballon	his (her, its) balloon	**ses ballons**	his (her, its) balloons
notre parapluie	our umbrella	**nos parapluies**	our umbrellas
votre sandwich	your sandwich	**vos sandwichs**	your sandwiches
leur gâteau	their cake	**leurs gâteaux**	their cakes

Feminine			
Singular		*Plural*	
ma robe	my dress	**mes robes**	my dresses
ta jaquette	your jacket	**tes jaquettes**	your jackets
sa balle	his (her, its) ball	**ses balles**	his (her, its) balls
notre maison	our house	**nos maisons**	our houses
votre voiture	your car	**vos voitures**	your cars
leur soeur	their sister	**leurs soeurs**	their sisters

Rules and observations:

1. A possessive adjective agrees in gender and number *with the noun* it modifies, *not with the possessor.*

2. Some possessive adjectives do not agree with the gender of the noun *in the singular.* They are all the same, whether in front of a masculine or feminine singular noun: **notre**, **votre**, **leur**.

3. Some possessive adjectives do not agree with the gender of the noun *in the plural.* They are all the same, whether in front of a masculine or feminine plural noun: **mes**, **tes**, **ses**, **nos**, **vos**, **leurs**.

4. Be aware of the following possessive adjectives: **mon** or **ma**, **ton** or **ta**, **son** or **sa**.

5. In front of a *feminine singular noun* beginning with a vowel or silent *h*, use the masculine singular forms: **mon**, **ton**, **son**—instead of **ma**, **ta**, **sa**.

mon adresse	my address	**son** amie	his (or her) friend
ton opinion	your opinion	**mon** habitude	my habit (custom)

6. Since **son**, **sa**, and **ses** can mean *his* or *her*, you may add **à lui** or **à elle** to make the meaning clear.

sa maison à lui	his house	**son livre à elle**	her book
sa maison à elle	her house	**ses livres à lui**	his books
son livre à lui	his book	**ses livres à elle**	her books

7. If there is more than one noun, a possessive adjective must be used in front of each noun: **ma mère et mon père** (my mother and father).

8. Use the definite article instead of the possessive adjective when referring to parts of the body if it is clear who the possessor is.

J'ai de l'argent **dans la main.**　　　(I have some money *in my hand.*)

Exercises

Review the preceding material before starting these exercises.

I. Answer the following questions in the affirmative, using the appropriate form of the possessive adjective. Use **oui** in your answer.

Model:	**Aimes-tu ta robe grise?**	**You answer:**	**Oui, j'aime ma robe grise.**
	(Do you like your gray dress?)		(Yes, I like my gray dress.)

1. Aimes-tu ta petite voiture neuve? _____

2. Aimez-vous mon parapluie rouge? _____

3. Aimez-vous notre maison blanche? _____

4. Aimes-tu mon amie Monique? _____

5. Aimez-vous ton petit frère? _____

6. Aimes-tu ma jolie soeur? _____

7. Aimez-vous mes jaquettes? _____

8. Aimes-tu mes robes? _____

9. Aimez-vous leurs gâteaux? _____

10. Aimez-vous votre livre? _____

II. Answer the following questions in the affirmative, using the appropriate form of the possessive adjective. Use **oui** in your answer.

Model:	**Est-ce votre maison?**	**You answer:**	**Oui, c'est ma maison.**
	(Is it your house?)		(Yes, it is my house.)

1. Est-ce votre voiture? _____

2. Est-ce ton chapeau? _____

3. Est-ce son livre à lui? _____

4. Est-ce votre maîtresse de français? _____

5. Est-ce leur maison? _____

III. Answer the following questions in the affirmative, using the appropriate form of the possessive adjective. Use **oui** in your answer.

Model: **Ce sont vos livres?**	**You answer:** **Oui, ce sont mes livres.**
(Are they your books?)	(Yes, they are my books.)

1. Ce sont vos stylos? _____

2. Ce sont leurs crayons? _____

3. Ce sont tes gâteaux? _____

4. Ce sont mes pommes? _____

5. Ce sont nos pêches? _____

IV. Fill in the missing words, using the appropriate form of a possessive adjective so that the rest of the sentence and dialogue will make sense.

Madame Paquet: Bonjour, Madame Richy! Oh! Vous avez un joli chapeau! J'aime beaucoup _____ chapeau.

Madame Richy: Merci! J'ai aussi une nouvelle robe. Aimez-vous _____ nouvelle robe rouge?

Madame Paquet: Oui, j'aime beaucoup _____ nouveau chapeau et _____ nouvelle robe rouge. J'adore _____ vêtements!

Madame Richy: Mon mari a une nouvelle jaquette. J'aime beaucoup _____ nouvelle jaquette.

Madame Paquet: Et mon mari a un nouveau complet. J'aime beaucoup _____ nouveau complet.

Madame Richy: Alors, _____ maris ont de nouveaux vêtements. Nous aimons beaucoup _____ nouveaux vêtements.

V. Answer in a complete sentence, using the appropriate form of a possessive adjective. In your answer, use the noun given in parentheses.

Model: **Que mangez-vous? (pomme)**	**You answer:** **Je mange ma pomme.**
(What are you eating? [apple])	(I am eating my apple.)

1. Que mangez-vous? (pêche) _____

2. Que mange-t-il? (sandwich) _____

3. Que mangent-ils? (chocolat) _____

4. Que mangent-elles? (soupe) _____

5. Que mangez-vous? (petits fours) _____

VI. **Plans for Entertainment. Proficiency in Reading, Speaking, and Writing.**

Situation: Your friend Michelle is on the phone inviting you to go to the movies with her. Complete the conversation. First, express yourself in spoken French; then write your words on the lines. What you say and write in your role as *Vous* must coordinate with what Michelle is saying.

Michelle: **Il y a un bon film français au cinéma ce soir. Veux-tu y aller avec moi?**

1. *Vous:* _____
   Michelle: **C'est un film français qui a gagné un prix au Festival de Cannes.**

2. *Vous:* _____
   Michelle: **Tu veux demander à Jeanne et à Suzy de venir avec nous?**

3. *Vous:* _____
   Michelle: **Tu sais, le film commence à huit heures.**

4. *Vous:* _____
   Michelle: **Qu'est-ce que nous allons faire après le film?**

5. *Vous:* _____

VII. **Sports. Proficiency in Writing.**

Situation: Two boys and a coach are practicing soccer (**le football**).

Look at the picture and write at least three sentences about it. You may use your own ideas and words and/or the following suggestions: **Les trois personnes jouent au foot**/*The three people are playing soccer*; **Le jeune homme est l'entraîneur**/*The young man is the coach*; **C'est le gardien de but**/*He is the goalie*; **garder le but**/*to guard the goal*; **le filet**/*the net*; **envoyer le ballon au fond des filets**/*to send the ball into the back of the net*; **les deux garçons jouent**/*the two boys are playing*; **Un garçon a envoyé le ballon au fond des filets**/*One boy sent the ball into the back of the net*; **L'autre garçon est surpris!**/*The other boy is surprised!* **Ils se sont amusés**/*They had fun.*

1. _____

2. _____

3. _____

La Marseillaise—paroles en français

Allons enfants de la Patrie
Le jour de gloire est arrivé!
Contre nous de la tyrannie
L'étendard sanglant est levé
Entendez-vous dans nos campagnes
Mugir ces féroces soldats?
Ils viennent jusque dans vos bras.
Égorger vos fils, vos compagnes!

    Aux armes citoyens
    Formez vos bataillons
    Marchons, marchons
    Qu'un sang impur
    Abreuve nos sillons

Que veut cette horde d'esclaves
De traîtres, de rois conjurés?
Pour qui ces ignobles entraves
Ces fers dès longtemps préparés?
Français, pour nous, ah! quel outrage
Quels transports il doit exciter?
C'est nous qu'on ose méditer
De rendre à l'antique esclavage!

Quoi ces cohortes étrangères!
Feraient la loi dans nos foyers!
Quoi! ces phalanges mercenaires
Terrasseraient nos fils guerriers!
Grand Dieu! par des mains enchaînées
Nos fronts sous le joug se ploieraient
De vils despotes deviendraient
Les maîtres des destinées.

Tremblez, tyrans et vous perfides
L'opprobre de tous les partis
Tremblez! vos projets parricides
Vont enfin recevoir leurs prix!
Tout est soldat pour vous combattre
S'ils tombent, nos jeunes héros
La France en produit de nouveaux,
Contre vous tout prêts à se battre.

Français, en guerriers magnanimes
Portez ou retenez vos coups!
Épargnez ces tristes victimes
À regret s'armant contre nous
Mais ces despotes sanguinaires
Mais ces complices de Bouillé
Tous ces tigres qui, sans pitié
Déchirent le sein de leur mère!

Nous entrerons dans la carrière
Quand nos aînés n'y seront plus
Nous y trouverons leur poussière
Et la trace de leurs vertus
Bien moins jaloux de leur survivre
Que de partager leur cercueil
Nous aurons le sublime orgueil
De les venger ou de les suivre!

Amour sacré de la Patrie
Conduis, soutiens nos bras vengeurs
Liberté, Liberté chérie
Combats avec tes défenseurs!
Sous nos drapeaux, que la victoire
Accoure à tes mâles accents
Que tes ennemis expirants
Voient ton triomphe et notre gloire!

Château des Fines Roches, Provence, France

WORK UNIT 19

Adjectives (Continued)

Zodiaque

Let's see what Pierre's horoscope reveals for today. What does yours say?

Les Signes du Zodiaque.

Pierre lit le journal dans la cuisine. Il a la page de l'horoscope devant lui.

I   **Le Bélier** (Aries)

(21 mars–20 avril)

Vous êtes le meilleur juge de vos actions.

II   **Le Taureau** (Taurus)

(21 avril–21 mai)

Votre plus grande qualité, c'est votre patience. Attendez des nouvelles!

III   **Les Gémeaux** (Gemini)

(22 mai–21 juin)

La personne qui vous aime le plus attend un courriel de vous. Ecrivez-lui.

IV   **Le Cancer** (Cancer)

(22 juin–23 juillet)

Méfiez-vous des obstacles dangereux.

V   **Le Lion** (Leo)

(24 juillet–23 août)

Demain va être un jour parfait pour finir vos projets.

VI   **La Vierge** (Virgo)

(24 août–23 septembre)

Méfiez-vous des petites automobiles vertes.

VII   **La Balance** (Libra)

(24 septembre–23 octobre)

Quelle chance! Vous allez voir un grand changement.

VIII   **Le Scorpion** (Scorpio)

(24 octobre–22 novembre)

Vous avez un esprit inventif. Soyez prudent!

IX   **Le Sagittaire** (Sagittarius)

(23 novembre–21 décembre)

Votre plus grande qualité, c'est votre imagination.

X   **Le Capricorne** (Capricorn)

(22 décembre–20 janvier)

Ne sortez pas aujourd'hui. Restez dans votre maison. Il y a du danger dans les rues.

XI **Le Verseau** (Aquarius)

(21 janvier–19 février)

Il faut profiter du moment. Quelle semaine! Bonnes nouvelles!

XII **Les Poissons** (Pisces)

(20 février–20 mars)

N'allez pas à la plage aujourd'hui. Il y a un requin affamé dans l'eau.

Le téléphone sonne. Voici la conversation entre Pierre et Monique:

Monique: C'est toi, Pierre? Ici Monique.

Pierre: Oui, c'est moi. Comment vas-tu?

Monique: Ça va. Écoute, Pierre. Il y a une grande soirée chez moi ce soir. Nous allons danser et chanter. Ma mère a préparé un gâteau délicieux. Nous allons beaucoup nous amuser. Henri va venir, ainsi que Paul, Robert, Raymond, Suzanne, Hélène, ta soeur Janine, et d'autres amis. Veux-tu venir?

Pierre: Attends, Monique. Je vais regarder dans le journal. Je n'ai pas lu mon horoscope pour aujourd'hui.

Pierre regarde l'horoscope dans le journal. Il lit sous son signe du Zodiaque, Le Capricorne. Il retourne au téléphone.

Pierre: Monique, mon horoscope dit qu'il faut rester à la maison aujourd'hui parce qu'il y a du danger dans les rues.

Monique: Es-tu superstitieux? Tu es fou!

Pierre: Écoute. Je vais venir tout de même.

Plus tard, Pierre quitte la maison pour aller à la soirée chez Monique. Quand il traverse la rue, il voit un grand camion venant à toute vitesse. Pierre _____

_____

_____

(Note to the student: Write your own ending to this story in one or two sentences—in French, of course!)

Vocabulaire

affamé *adj.*, starved, famished

ainsi que *conj.*, as well as

amuser *v.*, to amuse; **s'amuser** *refl. v.*, to have a good time, to amuse oneself; **nous allons beaucoup nous amuser** we are going to have a very good time; **amusez-vous bien!** have a good time!

ça va *interj.*, I'm fine, it's fine, it's okay

le changement *n.*, the change, alteration

comment vas-tu? how are you?

un courriel *n.*, e-mail

écrivez *v. form of* **écrire**; **écrivez-lui** write to him/to her

fort *m.*, **forte** *f.*, *adj.*, strong: **votre qualité la plus forte** your strongest quality

ici *adv.*, here; **ici Monique** this is Monique here

intelligent *m.*, **intelligente** *f.*, *adj.*; **l'élève le plus intelligent de la classe** the most intelligent student in the class

inventif *m.*, **inventive** *f.*, *adj.*, inventive; **un esprit inventif** an inventive spirit

lit *v. form of* **lire**; **il lit** he is reading (he reads); **lu** *past part.*; **je n'ai pas lu** I haven't read

lui *disj. pron.*, him; **devant lui** in front of him; *as an indir. obj. pron.*, to him/to her

méfiez-vous *v. form (imperative) of* **se méfier** (to beware); **méfiez-vous des obstacles dangereux** beware of dangerous obstacles

meilleur *m.*, **meilleure** *f.*, *adj.*, better; **le meilleur, la meilleure** the best

même *adj.*, same; **tout de même** all the same, just the same

la **nouvelle** *n.*, (piece of) news;
  bonnes nouvelles good news
la **plage** *n.*, the beach
plus *adv.*, more; **le plus** the most
profiter *v.*, to profit, to take advantage (of); **il faut profiter du**
  moment you must take advantage
  of the moment

la **qualité** *n.*, the quality; **la qualité**
  la plus forte the strongest quality
le **requin** *n.*, the shark
le **signe** *n.*, the sign; **les signes du**
  Zodiaque the signs of the Zodiac
le **soir** *n.*, the evening; **ce soir** this
  evening, tonight; **une soirée** an
  evening party

sortez *v. form (imperative) of*
  sortir; **ne sortez pas** don't
  go out
soyez *v. form (imperative) of* **être**;
  soyez prudent! be prudent!

Exercises

Review the story and vocabulary before starting these exercises.

I. Complete the following statements by writing the appropriate words. They are all in the story. Refer to it if you have to.

1. Pierre _____ le journal dans la cuisine. Il a la page _____ devant _____ .

2. Vous êtes _____ juge de vos actions.

3. Votre qualité la _____ est la patience.

4. La personne qui vous aime _____ attend un courriel de vous.

5. Il faut profiter _____ . Quelle _____ ! Bonnes _____ !

II. Vrai our faux?

1. Pierre lit le journal dans le salon. _____

2. Pierre parle au téléphone avec Monique. _____

3. Il y a une grande soirée chez Monique. _____

4. Pierre reste dans la maison. _____

5. Quand Pierre traverse la rue, il voit un grand camion. _____

III. Unscramble the words to find a meaningful sentence. Write it on the blank line. Refer to the story in this unit if you have to.

1. Pierre / horoscope / son / lit. _____

2. Demain / parfait / jour / être / va / un. _____

3. Une / personne / aime / vous / beaucoup. _____

4. Il / a / y / requin / un / l'eau / dans. _____

5. Téléphone / sonne/ le. _____

Structures de la Langue

A. Forms of the interrogative adjective **Quel**

Masculine		Feminine	
Singular	*Plural*	*Singular*	*Plural*
quel *(what, which)*	**quels**	**quelle** *(what, which)*	**quelles**

Rules and observations:

1. The interrogative adjective **quel** agrees in gender and number with the noun it modifies.

2. Here are four examples to illustrate each form:

    1. **Quel livre** lisez-vous?   *Which (what) book are you reading?*

    2. **Quels fruits** aimez-vous?   *Which (what) fruits do you like?*

    3. **Quelle leçon** étudiez-vous?   *Which (what) lesson are you studying?*

    4. **Quelles phrases** écrivez-vous?   *Which (what) sentences are you writing?*

3. In exclamations, **quel** and **quelle** mean *what a . . . !*

Quel homme!

> **Quel** homme!   *What a man!*
>
> **Quelle** femme!   *What a woman!*
>
> **Quelle** semaine!   *What a week!*

4. When the verb **être** is used, the form of **quel** is not ordinarily in front of the noun it modifies:

    > **Quel** est votre nom?   *What is your name?*
    >
    > **Quelle** est votre adresse?   *What is your address?*

Exercises

Review the preceding material before starting these exercises.

I.   Write in French the questions that must have been asked.

Model:	**Il est dix heures et quart.**	**You write the question:**	**Quelle heure est-il?**
	(It is 10:15.)		(What time is it?)

1.   Mon nom est Pierre Paquet. _____

2.   Mon adresse est 17, rue de Rivoli. _____

3.   J'ai vingt ans.   _____

II.   Answer the following questions in complete sentences. They are personal questions and require answers of your own.

1.   Quel est votre nom? _____

2.   Quelle est votre adresse? _____

3.   Quel âge avez-vous?   _____

III.   Write the appropriate form of **quel** on the blank line.

1.   Vous lisez un livre! _____ livre lisez-vous?

2.   Vous écrivez des phrases! _____ phrases écrivez-vous?

3.   Vous aimez les fruits! _____ fruits aimez-vous?

4.   Vous étudiez une leçon! _____ leçon étudiez-vous?

IV. Match the following.

1.   Quel homme!   _____ What a car!

2.   Quelle femme!   _____ What a stew!

3.   Quel ragoût!   _____ What a man!

4.   Quel livre!   _____ What a book!

5.   Quelle voiture!   _____ What a woman!

V. Find the four different forms of **quel** and circle them.

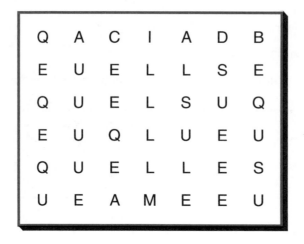

Q	A	C	I	A	D	B
E	U	E	L	L	S	E
Q	U	E	L	S	U	Q
E	U	Q	L	U	E	U
Q	U	E	L	L	E	S
U	E	A	M	E	E	U

B. Demonstrative adjectives

1.	**ce** garçon	1.	this (that) boy
2.	**cet** arbre	2.	this (that) tree
3.	**cet** homme	3.	this (that) man
4.	**cette** femme	4.	this (that) woman
5.	**cette** église	5.	this (that) church
6.	**ces** femmes	6.	these (those) women
7.	**ces** hommes	7.	these (those) men

Rules and observations:

1. **Ce** is used before a masculine singular noun that begins with a consonant. See example 1 in the above box.

2. **Cet** is used before a masculine singular noun that begins with a vowel or silent *h*. See examples 2 and 3 in the above box.

3. **Cette** is used before *all* feminine singular nouns.

4. **Ces** is used in front of *all* nouns in the plural.

5. These demonstrative adjectives can mean *this* or *that* in the singular, depending on the meaning intended. **Ces** can mean *these* or *those*.

6. If there is any doubt as to the meaning (*this, that, these, those*), just add **-ci** to the noun to give it the meaning of *this* or *these*. Actually, **-ci** is a shortening of *ici*, which means *here*. Add **-là** (which means *there*) to the noun to give it the meaning of *that* or *those*. Examples:

ce livre-ci	*this book*	**cette page-ci**	*this page*
ce livre-là	*that book*	**cette page-là**	*that page*
ces livres-ci	*these books*	**ces pages-ci**	*these pages*
ces livres-là	*those books*	**ces pages-là**	*those pages*

7. If there is more than one noun, a demonstrative adjective must be used in front of each noun; **cette dame et ce monsieur** (*this lady and gentleman*).

Exercises

Review the preceding material before starting these exercises.

I. Substitute the noun in parentheses for the noun in italics. Rewrite the sentence, using the appropriate form of the demonstrative adjective given.

Model:	**Je mange ce *fruit*. (pomme)**	**You write:**	**Je mange cette pomme.**
	(I am eating this fruit. [apple])		(I am eating this apple.)

A. Je mange cette *soupe*.

1. (pêche) _____

2. (gâteau) _____

3. (petits fours) _____

4. (ananas) _____

5. (tomate) _____

B. Etudiez-vous ce *vocabulaire*?

1. (leçon) _____

2. (livre) _____

3. (pages) _____

4. (phrases) _____

5. (poème) _____

C. Nous allons au ciméma avec ces *garçons*.

1. (jeunes filles) _____

2. (ami) _____

3. (amie) _____

4. (jeune homme) _____

5. (étudiants) _____

II. For each imperative that is given, write a response indicating that you are doing what you are told to do.

Model:	**Donnez-moi ce livre!**	**You write:**	**Bien! Je vous donne ce livre!**
	(Give me this book!)		(Good! I am giving you this book!)

1. Donnez-moi ce journal! _____

2. Donnez-lui cette pomme! _____

3. Donnez-leur ces pommes frites! _____

III. Change the demonstrative adjective and the noun, which are in italics, to the singular or plural, depending on what is given. Rewrite the sentence.

Model:	Je vais lire *ces livres* et *cette lettre*.	You write:	Je vais lire ce livre et ces lettres.
	(I am going to read these books and this letter.)		(I am going to read this book and these letters.)

1. Je vais manger *ces ananas* et *cette tomate*. _____

   _____

2. Je vais écrire *ces leçons* et *cette phrase*. _____

   _____

3. Je vais boire *ce vin* et *cette bière*. _____

4. Je vais envoyer *ces lettres*. _____

5. Je vais acheter *ces livres*. _____

C. Regular comparative and superlative adjectives

Adjective *(masc. and fem.)*	Comparative	Superlative
grand tall	**plus grand (que)** taller (than)	**le plus grand (de)** (the) tallest (in)
grande tall	**plus grande (que)** taller (than)	**la plus grande (de)** (the) tallest (in)
grand tall	**moins grand (que)** less tall (than)	**le moins grand (de)** (the) least tall (in)
grande tall	**moins grande (que)** less tall (than)	**la moins grande (de)** (the) least tall (in)
grand tall	**aussi grand (que)** as tall (as)	
grande tall	**aussi grande (que)** as tall (as)	
intelligent intelligent	**plus intelligent (que)** more intelligent (than)	**le plus intelligent (de)** (the) most intelligent (in)
intelligente intelligent	**plus intelligente (que)** more intelligent (than)	**la plus intelligente (de)** (the) most intelligent (in)
intelligent intelligent	**moins intelligent (que)** less intelligent (than)	**le moins intelligent (de)** (the) least intelligent (in)
intelligente intelligent	**moins intelligente (que)** less intelligent (than)	**la moins intelligente (de)** (the) least intelligent (in)
intelligent intelligent	**aussi intelligent (que)** as intelligent (as)	
intelligente intelligent	**aussi intelligente (que)** as intelligent (as)	

Rules and observations:

1. In making a comparison in English, we ordinarily add **-er** to the adjective (*tall, taller*) or we place *more* or *less* in front of the adjective (*more intelligent, less intelligent*). In French, we use **plus** or **moins** in front of the adjective. See the examples in the preceding box.

2. In order to express *as . . . as* in French, we use **aussi . . . que**.

3. The adjective must agree in gender and number with the noun it modifies. Example: Marie est plus **intelligente** que son frère. (Mary is more intelligent than her brother.)

4. In making a comparison, we use **que** in French to express *than*; we also use **que** in French to express *as*.

5. If the adjective is one that ordinarily is placed in front of the noun, then it remains in front of the noun when making a comparison. If the adjective is one that ordinarily is placed after the noun, then it remains after the noun when making a comparison. Examples:

    > **une jolie robe, une plus jolie robe, la plus jolie robe**
    > a pretty dress, a prettier dress, the prettiest dress

    > **une personne intelligente, une personne plus intelligente, la personne la plus intelligente**
    > an intelligent person, a more intelligent person, the most intelligent person

6. Note that **de** is used (and not **dans**) to express *in* when using the superlative.

D. Irregular comparative and superlative adjectives

Adjective (*masc.*)	Comparative	Superlative
bon, *good*	**meilleur**, *better*	**le meilleur**, *(the) best*
mauvais, *bad*	**plus mauvais**, *worse*	**le plus mauvais**, *(the) worst*
	pire, *worse*	**le pire**, *(the) worst*
petit, *small*	**plus petit**, *smaller (in size)*	**le plus petit**, *(the) smallest*
	moindre, *less (in importance)*	**le moindre**, *(the) least*

Rules and observations:

1. Actually, there are no rules that apply to these irregular adjectives of comparison. Just study them and make observations of your own.

2. Observe that **mauvais** and **petit** have regular and irregular comparisons.

Exercises

Review the preceding material before starting these exercises.

I. Answer the following questions in French, substituting the appropriate forms of the words in parentheses for the ones indicated. Use **non** in your answer, but write your sentence in the affirmative. Also, use a pronoun subject in place of the noun subject.

Model: **Est-ce que Paul est** *plus* **intelligent que son frère? (moins)** (Is Paul more intelligent than his brother? [less])

You write: **Non, il est moins intelligent que son frère.** (No, he is less intelligent than his brother.)

1. Est-ce que Pierre est *plus* grand que sa mère?   (moins) _____

   _____

2. Est-ce que Janine est *plus* grande que son père?   (moins) _____

   _____

3. Est-ce que Monique est *plus* intelligente que Janine?   (moins) _____

   _____

II. Answer the following questions in complete sentences. Use the noun in parentheses in your answer. Make all required changes in the forms of the adjectives.

Model: **Qui est plus grand que Robert? (Janine)** (Who is taller than Robert?)

You write: **Janine est plus grande que Robert.** (Janine is taller than Robert.)

1. Qui est plus grand que Janine?   (Madame Paquet) _____

   _____

2. Qui est moins grand que Pierre?   (Janine) _____

   _____

3. Qui est plus petit que Monique?   (Mathilde) _____

   _____

4. Qui est moins petit que Joseph?   (Suzanne) _____

   _____

5. Qui est aussi grand que Monsieur Paquet?   (Monsieur Richy) _____

   _____

6. Qui est aussi petit que Madame Banluc?   (Madame Paquet) _____

   _____

III. For each statement, write in French a response contradicting the statement. Begin your response with **Non, ce n'est pas vrai**. Then use the name in parentheses in your answer in place of the noun subject in the statement, which is in italics. Make all required changes in agreement.

| **Model:** | *Monique* **est la plus intelligente du cours d'anglais. (Joseph)** | **You write:** | **Non, ce n'est pas vrai. Joseph est le plus intelligent du cours d'anglais.** |

1. *Raymond* est le plus intelligent du cours de mathématiques. (Janine) _____

    _____

2. *Bob* est le plus grand du cours de français. (Suzanne) _____

    _____

Michelle est la moins grande de la famille.

3. *Michelle* est la moins grande de la famille. (Simon) _____

    _____

4. *Béatrice* est la plus belle du groupe. (Charles) _____

    _____

5. *Henri* est le plus petit. (Hélène) _____

    _____

IV. Answer the following questions in the affirmative in complete French sentences. In answer (a) use **oui** and write a complete sentence. In answer (b) write a complete answer and add **aussi**. Make the required changes in the adjectives.

Models:	(a) **Ce livre est-il plus long que les autres?**	You write:	(a) **Oui, ce livre est plus long que les autres.**
	(b) **Et cette lettre?**	You write:	(b) **Cette lettre est plus longue que les autres aussi.**

1. (a) Cette phrase est-elle moins facile que les autres? _____

    _____

    (b) Et ces questions? _____

2. (a) Ce poème est-il plus difficile que les autres? _____

    _____

    (b) Et cette leçon? _____

3. (a) Cette voiture est-elle plus belle que les autres? _____

    _____

    (b) Et ces maisons? _____

4. (a) Ce garçon est-il plus beau que les autres? _____

    _____

    (b) Et ces jeunes filles? _____

5. (a) Cette banane est-elle plus délicieuse que les autres? _____

    _____

    (b) Et ces gâteaux? _____

V. On the blank line write the French equivalent for the English words in parentheses.

1. (more)   Simone est _____ intelligente que sa soeur.

2. (tall)   Alain est aussi _____ que sa mère.

3. (as)   Monique est _____ petite que son père.

4. (prettier)   Anne est _____ que Suzanne.

5. (the least)   Michel est _____ grand.

VI.   Le Mot Mystère. (Mystery Word). In order to find the mystery word, you must first find and circle in the puzzle the French words given under it. The letters that remain in the puzzle are scrambled. Unscramble them to find **le mot mystère**.

E	M	A	R	C	H	E	E	T	R
N	V	Q	U	I	O	T	T	O	F
A	M	I	E	I	L	U	A	U	A
G	E	B	R	U	I	T	Y	R	I
R	M	Ê	M	E	I	P	N	N	R
I	D	A	N	S	À	L	O	E	E
S	P	A	Y	E	R	U	N	V	T
E	U	Q	U	E	L	S	E	I	S
P	O	U	B	E	L	L	E	S	O
B	E	A	U	C	O	U	P	N	

à	grise	poubelle
amie	il	quel
au	marche	qui
beaucoup	me	se
bruit	même	son
dans	non	tournevis
en	payer	tu
et	plus	y
faire		

VII.   Earning a Living. Proficiency in Speaking and Writing.

Ask a friend to act out the role of the customer in this dialogue. Later, you may switch roles. When you are satisfied with what you both said, write the conversation for practice.

Situation: You are a salesclerk in a UNISEX shop. A customer comes in to buy a few articles of clothing. Greet the customer by saying: **Bonjour! Vous désirez?** The customer wants to buy a few things, for example, a shirt, blouse, socks, necktie, and other items. After your opening statement, show the customer a few items and ask questions. You may use any or all of the following: **ce, cet, cette, ces, quel, quelle, quels, quelles; regarder, joli, meilleur, une soirée, aimer, préférer, plus joli(e) que, plus beau (belle) que, plus grand(e) que.**

VIII. Helping Others. Speaking and Writing Proficiency

Situation: You are the best student in your French class. A classmate is having problems with adjectives and needs your help. You are together at your kitchen table with your French books and some paper on which to practice.

You may use your own ideas and words and/or the suggestions under the lines. First, respond in spoken French; then write your words on the lines. Later, you may switch roles.

Ton ami (amie):   **Je ne comprends pas les adjectifs, les comparatifs, les superlatifs, et leur position. J'ai besoin de pratique/***I need practice.*

Toi: _____

*There's no problem/***Il n'y a pas de problème.** *Tell me, is Anne prettier than Monique?/***Dis-moi, est-ce qu'Anne est plus jolie que Monique?**

Ton ami (amie):   **Non. Anne n'est pas plus jolie que Monique. Monique est la plus jolie de la classe.**

Toi: _____

*Tell me, is my father taller than your father?/***Dis-moi, mon père est-il plus grand que ton père?**

Ton ami (amie):   **Non. Ton père n'est pas plus grand que mon père. Mais ta mère est plus grande que ma mère.**

Toi: _____

Who is the best student in our French class?

Ton ami (amie):   **C'est toi! Tu es le meilleur (la meilleure) étudiant(e) de notre classe de français.**

Toi: _____

*Me?!/***Moi?!** *You think that I am the best student in our French class?!/***Tu penses que je suis le meilleur (la meilleure) étudiant(e) de notre classe de français?!**

Ton ami (amie):   **Oui, oui. Je t'assure!**

Toi: _____

*Thank you! Now, let's eat some chocolate mousse/***Merci! Maintenant, mangeons de la mousse au chocolat.** *It's the best/***C'est la meilleure.**

IX. Appreciating French Sculpture. Proficiency in Writing.

Situation: Last year when you were in Paris, you visited **Le Musée Rodin** and were overwhelmed as you looked at Auguste Rodin's many sculptures, in particular, *Le Penseur/The Thinker*. This year you are visiting the Rodin Museum in Philadelphia where there are many bronze casts of his works.

Look at the photo below of *Le Penseur*. Write at least three sentences telling us your impressions. You may use your own ideas and words and/or any of the following: **C'est une oeuvre d'art magnifique**/*It's a magnificent work of art*. **Je pense que cette statue est la plus belle de toutes les oeuvres de Rodin**/*I think that this statue is the most beautiful of all the works of Rodin*. **C'est une grande joie de regarder cette statue**/*It's a great joy to look at this statue*.

1. _____

2. _____

3. _____

Le Penseur (The Thinker) by Auguste Rodin, French sculptor. A bronze cast of this magnificent statue is in front of Philosophy Hall on the Columbia University campus in New York City.

Adverbs and Tag Questions—*n'est-ce pas*?

La boîte de chocolats

Janine receives a phone call from a neighbor, Madame Bédier. She wants her to babysit with Renée, her five-year-old daughter, while she and her husband are at the movies. What do you suppose happens to the box of chocolates while they are out?

Donne-moi la boîte de chocolats!

C'est samedi. Janine n'a rien à faire. Elle est à la fenêtre dans sa chambre. Elle regarde les oiseaux sur les branches du pommier dans le jardin.

Le téléphone sonne.

—Janine! C'est pour toi, dit sa mère.

Janine quitte sa chambre et descend l'escalier.

—C'est Madame Bédier, dit sa mère. Elle va au cinéma ce soir avec son mari et elle a besoin de toi.

—Allô! J'écoute. Ici Janine . . . . Comment allez-vous, madame? . . . . Très bien, merci . . . . Je ne fais rien ce soir . . . . Vous allez au cinéma . . . Ah! Bon! . . . . D'accord . . . . Oui, je peux venir chez vous ce soir et rester avec Renée . . . . Oui, je sais . . . . Oh, elle a déjà cinq ans! . . . . Oui, elle est grande pour son âge . . . . Oui, je sais qu'elle est capricieuse . . . . Oui, je sais qu'elle parle plus vite que les autres enfants . . . . Oui, je sais qu'elle marche moins vite que les autres enfants . . . . Bon! . . . . D'accord! A six heures et demie . . . . A ce soir, madame.

A six heures vingt, Janine quitte la maison pour aller chez les Bédier qui habitent à côté de la maison des Paquet.

—Ah! Janine! s'exclame Madame Bédier. Philippe! C'est Janine! La meilleure gardienne d'enfants du voisinage! N'est-ce pas, Philippe?

Monsieur et Madame Bédier ont mis leurs chapeaux, manteaux, et gants. Avant de sortir, Madame Bédier dit:

—Renée, sois sage! A huit heures et demie tu vas te coucher, n'est-ce pas? Janine, tu sais où est la chambre de Renée, n'est-ce pas? La boîte de chocolats est là-bas sur la petite table ronde. Seulement un morceau pour Renée. Elle en a mangé trois aujourd'hui. Janine, tu peux en avoir deux morceaux si tu veux parce que tu es plus grande que Renée. Il y a une comédie à la télévision ce soir. Nous allons voir le film *La Lettre* au Bijou. A tout à l'heure!

Ils partent.

—Janine, je veux mon morceau de chocolat maintenant, dit Renée. J'aime mieux la cerise à la crème. Quel morceau est la cerise à la crème, Janine? demande Renée.

—Je ne sais pas! J'aime beaucoup les chocolats et mon favori est le nougat. Quel morceau est le nougat, Renée? demande Janine.

—Je ne sais pas! . . . . Ah! . . . . je sais comment savoir!

—Comment? demande Janine.

—Je vais écraser chaque morceau avec le doigt, répond Renée.

—Non! Renée! Non! Tu vas les abîmer! s'exclame Janine.

—Ça ne fait rien. Laisse-moi! crie Renée.

Renée arrache vigoureusement la boîte de chocolats des mains de Janine et elle commence à piquer chaque morceau avec son doigt.

—Voilà, Janine! Voilà la cerise à la crème pour moi et le nougat pour toi!

—Oh! Tous les morceaux de chocolat sont écrasés! Tout est abîmé! Qu'est-ce que je vais dire à tes parents? s'exclame Janine.

Renée quitte le salon avec la boîte de chocolats. Après quelques minutes, elle revient dans le salon et elle dit:

—Janine, ne t'inquiète pas. J'ai jeté la boîte de chocolats dans la poubelle avec les ordures! Maintenant, tu n'as pas besoin d'expliquer à mes parents.

—Ta mère a raison, lui dit Janine. Tu es vraiment capricieuse. Méchante! Va te coucher! Vite!

Trois heures plus tard, Monsieur et Madame Bédier rentrent à la maison. Madame entre dans le salon et dit:

—Janine, tu peux avoir toute la boîte de chocolats. Emporte la boîte avec toi. Bonsoir, et merci!

Vocabulaire

à tout à l'heure! see you in a little while!

abîmer *v.,* to spoil, to ruin

l'accord *n. m.,* the agreement; **d'accord** okay, agreed

allô *interj.,* hello (used when answering the telephone)

arracher *v.,* to pull away, to pull out

avant *prep.,* before; **avant de sortir** before going out

le besoin *n.,* the need; **avoir besoin de** to have need of, to need

la boîte *n.,* the box

bonsoir *salutation,* good evening

ça ne fait rien! that doesn't matter!

capricieux *m.,* **capricieuse** *f., adj.,* capricious, whimsical

la cerise *n.,* the cherry

chaque *adj.,* each

le côté *n.,* the side, **à côté de** next to

déjà *adv.,* already; **elle a déjà cinq ans!** she is already five years old!

descendre *v.,* to descend, to come (go) down

écraser *v.,* to crush

en *pron., partitive,* of them; **elle en a mangé trois!** she ate three (of them)

l'escalier *n. m.,* the staircase

le gant *n.,* the glove

le gardien, la gardienne *n.,* the guardian; **gardien (gardienne) d'enfants** babysitter

s'inquiéter *refl. v.,* to worry, to be upset; **ne t'inquiète pas!** don't worry!

jeter *v.,* to throw

laisse-moi! let me!

le manteau *n.,* the coat

méchant *m.,* **méchante** *f., adj.,* mean, nasty, naughty

mieux *adv.,* better; **j'aime mieux** I prefer, I like better

mignon *m.,* **mignonne** *f., adj.,* darling, cute

le morceau *n.,* piece; **les morceaux** *n. pl.,* pieces; **un morceau de chocolat** a piece of chocolate

l'oiseau *n. m.,* the bird

l'ordure *n. f.,* garbage, rubbish

la pièce *n.,* the piece

piquer *v.,* to poke, to puncture

le pommier *n.,* the apple tree

sois *v. form of* **être**; **sois sage!** be good!

va te coucher! go to bed! (*v. form of* **aller se coucher**)

le voisinage *n.,* the neighborhood

Exercises

Review the story and vocabulary before starting these exercises.

I. Oui or Non?

1. Janine est dans sa chambre; elle regarde les oiseaux sur les branches du pommier dans le jardin.   _____

2. Madame Bédier va au cinéma avec son mari et elle a besoin de Janine.   _____

3. Renée a dix ans.   _____

4. Janine écrase tous les morceaux de chocolat.   _____

5. Renée a mangé tous les chocolats.   _____

II. Choose the correct answer.

1. Janine est à la fenêtre dans

   (a) le salon.   (b) la cuisine.   (c) la salle de bains.   (d) sa chambre.   _____

2. Madame et Monsieur Bédier vont

   (a) au cinéma.   (b) à l'église.   (c) au théâtre.   (d) à l'opéra.   _____

3. Renée a jeté la boîte de chocolats

   (a) par la fenêtre.   (b) dans la rue.   (c) dans la poubelle.   (d) contre le mur.   _____

4. La boîte de chocolats est

   (a) dans le tiroir.   (b) sur la petite table ronde.   (c) dans la cuisine.
   (d) sous le lit.   _____

5. Renée est

   (a) très mignonne.   (b) très gentille.   (c) capricieuse.   (d) fatiguée.   _____

III.   Write in the missing words. Refer to the story if you have to.

1. Renée, à huit heures et demie tu vas _____ , n'est-ce pas!

2. J'ai _____ la boîte de chocolats dans la poubelle avec les ordures.

3. Janine, tu peux avoir _____ la boîte de chocolats!

4. Janine est la _____ gardienne d'enfants du voisinage.

5. Renée parle _____ vite que les autres enfants.

6. Renée marche _____ vite que les autres enfants.

Structures de la Langue

A. Position of an adverb

---

1. Janine aime **beaucoup** les chocolats.	(Janine likes chocolates *very much*.)
2. Madame Bédier a parlé **distinctement.**	(Mrs. Bédier spoke *distinctly*.)
3. Madame Bédier a **bien** parlé.	(Mrs. Bédier spoke *well*.)

Rules and observations:

1. An adverb is a word that describes a verb, an adjective, or another adverb.

2. In French, an adverb ordinarily *follows* the simple verb it modifies, as in the first model sentence in the above box.

3. If a verb is compound, as in the passé composé (model sentence 2), the adverb generally *follows* the past participle only if it is a long adverb. The adverb **distinctement** is long.

4. If a verb is compound, as in the passé composé (model sentence 3), *short common adverbs* (like **beaucoup**, **bien**, **déjà**, **encore**, **mal**, **mieux**, **souvent**, **toujours**) *must precede* the past participle.

B. Formation of some adverbs

1. Many adverbs are formed in French by adding the ending **-ment** to the *feminine singular* form of an adjective. This is similar to adding *-ly* to an adjective in English to form an adverb: *quick/quickly*.

seule/seulement	**furieuse/furieusement**
(alone/only)	(furious/furiously)

2. Ordinarily, adjectives that end in **-ant** are transformed into adverbs by dropping **-ant** and adding **-amment**.

constant/constamment   (constant/constantly)

3. Ordinarily, adjectives that end in **-ent** are transformed into adverbs by dropping **-ent** and adding **-emment**.

patient/patiemment   (patient/patiently)

C. Regular comparison of adverbs

Adverb	Comparative	Superlative
vite *(quickly)*	**plus vite (que)** *more quickly (than)* *faster (than)*	**le plus vite** *(the) most quickly* *(the) fastest*
	moins vite (que) *less quickly (than)*	**le moins vite** *(the) least quickly*
	aussi vite (que) *as quickly (as)* *as fast (as)*	

D. Tag question: n'est-ce pas?

The phrase *n'est-ce pas!* is tagged to a statement when the speaker expects the listener to agree. It can be translated into English in any number of ways: *isn't that right? isn't that so?* etc. The appropriate translation into English depends on the meaning of the statement in French.

Renée a cinq ans, **n'est-ce pas**?   (Renée is five years old, *isn't she*?)

Exercises

Review the preceding material before starting these exercises.

I. Change the following adjectives to adverbs.

Model: furieuse	**furieusement**

1. distincte _____

2. seule _____

3. courageuse _____

4. constant _____

5. patient _____

6. fière _____

II. Rewrite each sentence, adding the adverb in parentheses in its proper position.

Model: Madame Coty aime le café. (beaucoup)	**You write: Madame Coty aime beaucoup le café.**
(Mrs. Coty likes coffee. [very much])	(Mrs. Coty likes coffee very much.)

1. Monsieur Richy aime le ragoût brûlé. (beaucoup) _____

_____

2. Le professeur a parlé. (bien) _____

3. Janine a parlé. (constamment) _____

4. Elle est partie. (déjà) _____

5. Pierre a mangé. (beaucoup) _____

III. Write the French adverb for the English in italics.

Model: Pierre marche aussi *quickly* que son père.	**You write: vite**
(Pierre walks as *quickly* as his father.)	(quickly)

1. Janine parle aussi *well* que sa mère. _____

2. Joseph mange *more* vite que son frère. _____

3. Bob marche *as* lentement *as* son cousin. _____ _____

4. Raymond étudie *more* souvent *than* Michel. _____ _____

5. Mathilde parle *less* vite que sa soeur. _____

6. François travaille *the least* vite. _____

IV. Le Mot Mystère (Mystery Word). In order to find the *mystery word*, you must first find and circle in this puzzle the French words given under it. The letters that remain in the puzzle are scrambled. Unscramble them to find *le mot mystère.*

```
A  E  M  V  P  Y  G  R  I  S
U  N  O  O  L  A  L  L  E  R
T  F  I  I  U  A  L  A  C  A
O  J  N  T  S  A  U  S  S  I
M  O  S  U  G  A  R  Ç  O  N
O  L  P  R  R  F  E  M  M  E
B  I  E  E  A  N  E  P  A  S
I  R  T  B  N  N  L  U  I  E
L  I  I  O  D  L  U  N  D  I
E  L  T  N  O  P  É  R  A  S
```

à	garçon	moins petit
aller	gris	ne
aussi	il	opéras
automobile	joli	pas
bon	la	plus grand
en	lui	voiture
femme	lundi	y

V. Resolving a Quarrel. Proficiency in Writing.

Situation: You are babysitting in your neighbor's house next door. They have two children: Robert, who is five years old, and Debbie, who is seven. They are quarreling with each other about what to watch on TV. You do your best to settle the argument. They are behaving badly and it's your job to restore a pleasant atmosphere. In three sentences resolve the quarrel and restore order. You may use your own ideas or ideas suggested by the following: **avoir, être, sois (soyez) sage(s), avoir besoin de, capricieux, capricieuse, abîmer, laisse-moi! jeter, méchant(e), va te coucher! vite** *(quickly).*

After thinking about what you are going to say to the two children, write three sentences here:

1. _____

2. _____

3. _____

VI.   Expressing Love on Father's Day. Proficiency in Speaking and Writing.

Situation: Next Sunday is Father's Day. In the space provided, write your own card and give it to your father or to some friend or relative who has been like a father to you. Before you start, take a few minutes to gather your thoughts, jot down a few words in French that you will use, then say them aloud.

You may also use the following: **au plus sympa de tous les papas**/*to the nicest of all Dads*; **de tout coeur**/*with all my heart*; **Je te souhaite une joyeuse Fête des Pères**/*I wish you a Happy Father's Day*; **Je t'aime**/*I love you*; **Chez nous, j'ai appris la valeur de l'amour depuis mon enfance**/*In our home, I learned the value of love since childhood.*

Review Test: Work Units 16–20

I.   Complete this crossword puzzle (**mots-croisés**).

Verticalement

1. First person singular direct and indirect object pronoun.

3. Third person plural indirect object pronoun.

6. Preposition used with adverbs of quantity (e.g., *beaucoup, trop*).

7. Masculine plural demonstrative pronoun.

8. Masculine singular demonstrative pronoun.

9. Third person masculine singular direct object pronoun.

11. Pronoun that takes the place of the partitive and serves as a direct object.

Horizontalement

2. Feminine singular subject pronoun.

4. Pronoun commonly used in an interrogative sentence, as in *Est-ce qu'il . . . a?*

5. Third person singular indirect object pronoun.

8. Feminine singular demonstrative pronoun.

10. First person singular subject pronoun.

12. First person plural direct and indirect object pronoun.

II. Dans le potage (In the soup). In this word puzzle, find the verb form in the present indicative tense for each verb in the sentences below. When you find them, draw a line around each one. The verb form in the present tense of *faire* in the first statement is *faites*, and it has already been done to get you started. The words are written horizontally, vertically, diagonally, or backward.

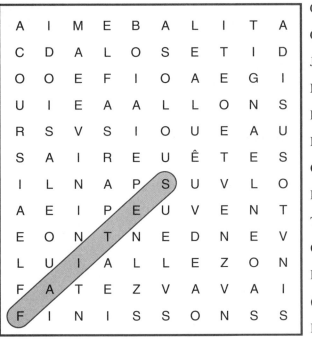

A	I	M	E	B	A	L	I	T	A
C	D	A	L	O	S	E	T	I	D
O	O	E	F	I	O	A	E	G	I
U	I	E	A	A	L	L	O	N	S
R	S	V	S	I	O	U	E	A	U
S	A	I	R	E	U	Ê	T	E	S
I	L	N	A	P	S	U	V	L	O
A	E	I	P	E	U	V	E	N	T
E	O	N	T	N	E	D	N	E	V
L	U	I	A	L	L	E	Z	O	N
F	A	T	E	Z	V	A	V	A	I
F	I	N	I	S	S	O	N	S	S

Que (faire)-vous ce soir?

Que me (dire)-vous?

J' (aimer) danser.

Moi, je (aller) chez moi.

Les garçons (avoir)-ils assez d'argent pour aller au cinéma?

Nous (aller) en France l'été prochain.

Quand (partir)-tu?

Et vous, (être)-vous heureux?

Tes parents (pouvoir)-ils venir avec nous?

Que (devoir)-tu faire maintenant?

Pourquoi (courir)-tu?

(Vendre)-ils leur maison?

Est-ce que nous (finir) le travail aujourd'hui?

III. Mots-croisés. This activity tests your knowledge of the **passé composé** tense. The missing words are the present tense of *avoir* or *être*, the correct form of the past participle, or a subject pronoun.

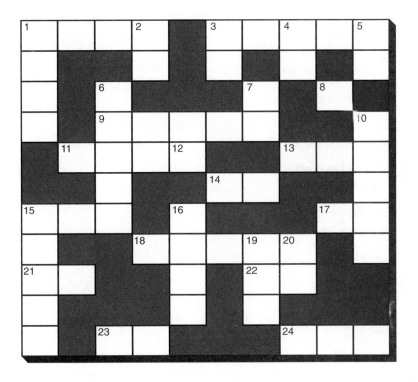

Horizontalement

1. *Hier, je _____ allé au cinéma.*

3. *Martine est _____ (aller) aux grands magasins.*

8. *Pierre _____ lu un livre.*

9. *Ils ont _____ (vouloir) partir.*

11. *_____ avez parlé assez.*

13. *La lettre? Je l'ai _____ (lire).*

14. *Pierre s'est _____ (taire).*

15. *J'ai _____ (mettre) du sucre dans le café.*

17. *J'ai _____ (devoir) (à l'envers)* partir.*

18. *Les lettres? Je les ai _____ (mettre) sur le bureau.*

21. *Nous avons bien _____ (rire).*

22. *Avez-vous _____ (savoir) la réponse?*

23. *Paul a-t- _____ compris?*

24. *Qu'a-t-elle _____ (dire)?*

**à l'envers*   backward

Verticalement

1. *Je _____ tombé en montant dans le bus.*

2. *J'ai _____ (savoir) la réponse.*

3. *Hier soir, j' _____ beaucoup mangé.*

4. *Ma camarade a _____ (lire) un livre intéressant.*

5. *Ce matin j'ai _____ (avoir) un petit accident.*

6. *Nous _____ pris le train.*

7. *Les enfants ont _____ (pouvoir) manger.*

10. *Nous avons _____ (vendre) la maison.*

12. *A-t-il _____ (savoir) (à l'envers)* répondre à la question?*

15. *Madame Durand est _____ (mourir) la semaine dernière.*

16. *Tu as _____ (finir) la leçon?*

19. *Jacqueline _____ restée à la maison.*

20. *Tu as _____ (savoir) cela, n'est-ce pas?*

**à l'envers*   backward

IV. Complete the paragraph about Colette, writing the appropriate form of the adjective. Make all required changes for agreement with the noun.

Colette occupe la _____ place dans la _____ salle de classe. Elle est une _____

              1. premier   2. grand   3. bon

amie de _____ le monde. Elle ne fait jamais de _____ choses. Elle prépare toujours

              4. tout   5. mauvais

_____ les leçons de français. Elle est une très _____ étudiante. Elle est toujours très

     6. tout   7. excellent

_____ . Elle porte une _____ jupe et une blouse _____ .

    8. studieux   9. joli   10. blanc

V. Change the following adjectives into adverbs using the *-ment* ending.

1. gentil _____

2. franc _____

3. affreux _____

4. amer _____

VI. Write at least ten common adverbs that do not end in *-ment*.

1. _____   3. _____   5. _____   7. _____   9. _____

2. _____   4. _____   6. _____   8. _____   10. _____

VII. In this dialogue, Yvette and you are talking about the exams in June and your summer vacation. Complete the conversation by choosing the appropriate French adverbs from the following: **bien, rapidement, déjà, toujours, aussi**.

Yvette: Es-tu prêt pour tes examens?

Vous: Oui, je suis _____ prêt pour mes examens.
                1.

Yvette: Demain j'ai encore un autre examen, et puis les vacances commencent.

Vous: Les jours de vacances vont passer _____ .
                        2.

Yvette: Nous avons passé l'été passé dans les montagnes.

Vous: Ma famille et moi allons _____ dans les montagnes.
                      3.

Yvette: En juillet nous allons faire un voyage en Australie.

Vous: Ma famille et moi _____ ! Nous allons à Melbourne!
                    4.

Yvette: Si tu me donnes ton adresse, je vais t'envoyer une carte postale de Sydney.

Vous: Mais je t'ai _____ donné mon adresse! L'as-tu perdue?
                5.

VIII. Proficiency in Reading.

Directions: In the following passage there are five numbered blank spaces. Each space represents a missing word. Four possible completions are provided for each. Only one of them is grammatically correct and makes sense in the context of the passage.

First, read the passage in its entirety to determine its general meaning. Then read it a second time. Choose the completion that makes the best sense and is grammatically correct, and write its letter in the space provided.

Monsieur et Madame Durand ont _____ une invitation à dîner chez leurs

         1. A. recevoir
            B. reçu
            C. reçoivent
            D. reçoit

voisins, Monsieur et Madame Debussy. Monsier et Madame Durand ont _____

         2. A. accepte
            B. acceptent
            C. accepté
            D. accepter

l'invitation. Quand ils _____ arrivés chez leurs amis, ils sont _____

   3. A. ont   4. A. entré
      B. sont   B. entrée
      C. a   C. entrées
      D. est   D. entrés

dans le foyer. Ils ont vu d'autres voisins chez _____ . Tout le monde a crié:

         5. A. eux
            B. elle
            C. lui
            D. leur

"Surprise! Surprise!"

IX. Proficiency in Writing.

Directions: Of the following ten situations, select eight and write your statements on the lines below. For each situation, write three short sentences.

Situation 1. You have been invited to a birthday party. You are in the department store *Le Bon Marché* in Paris looking for the perfect gift for Annie, one of your relatives. You are talking to a salesperson.

Situation 2. You received an invitation for dinner at the home of your neighbors, Monsieur et Madame Berty. You accepted. Tell us what you did there.

Situation 3. You are at **Le Musée du Louvre** in Paris. You are admiring a painting by Renoir, a great French artist. Tell us about it.

Situation 4. Last Sunday was **La Fête des Mères**. Instead of buying a Mother's Day card, you decided to make your own. What did you write on the card?

Situation 5. You have memorized the first few words of the French song, *Sur le Pont d'Avignon/On the Bridge of Avignon*. The song is in Work Unit 17. You want to ask a friend of yours who can play the piano to play it for you so you can sing the words. What would you say to your friend?

Situation 6. Your friend Michelle is on the phone inviting you to go to the movies with her. Before you accept, you would like to know the name of the film, where it is playing, if it is a love story, and at what time the show starts.

Situation 7. Yesterday you went to see a soccer game/**un match de football**. Tell us what happened.

Situation 8. You have memorized the first few lines of *La Marseillaise* by Rouget de Lisle. The song is in Work Unit 18. You want to ask a friend of yours who can play the piano to play it for you so you can sing the words. What would you say to your friend?

Situation 9. You are a salesperson in the department store *La Baie* in Montréal. A customer wants to buy a birthday present for a child but cannot make a decision. What would you say to the customer?

Situation 10. Last week you visited **Le Musée Rodin** in Paris. You were overwhelmed as you looked at Rodin's many sculptures. Tell us about it.

Select eight of the ten situations above and write your three short sentences here.

Situation 1

1. _____
2. _____
3. _____

Situation 2

1. _____
2. _____
3. _____

Situation 3

1. _____
2. _____
3. _____

Situation 4

1. _____
2. _____
3. _____

Situation 5

1. _____
2. _____
3. _____

Situation 6

1. _____
2. _____
3. _____

Situation 7

1. _____
2. _____
3. _____

Situation 8

1. _____
2. _____
3. _____

Situation 9

1. _____
2. _____
3. _____

Situation 10

1. _____
2. _____
3. _____

WORK UNIT 21

Negations and Other Structures of the Language

Manger pour vivre ou vivre pour manger?

Mrs. Paquet has been sick since yesterday. She has indigestion. What do you think of the doctor's advice? Would you do what he says or what she does?

Le Docteur: Il est ridicule de croire qu'il faut manger pour vivre.

Madame Paquet est malade depuis hier. Elle a mangé quelque chose qui lui a donné mal à l'estomac. Elle est souffrante dans son lit. Son mari a appelé le docteur pour lui donner un médicament. Le docteur va venir dans quelques minutes. Madame Paquet l'attend patiemment depuis vingt minutes.

Le docteur est arrivé. Il est dans la chambre de Madame Paquet depuis quinze minutes. Il l'examine. Monsieur Paquet est avec eux.

Monsieur Paquet: Dites-moi, docteur, faut-il appeler une ambulance pour transporter ma femme à l'hôpital?

Le Docteur: Non, monsieur. Il n'est pas nécessaire de la transporter à l'hôpital. Elle peut rester ici dans son lit. Elle n'est pas gravement malade. Les ambulances rendent grand service, mais dans ce cas votre femme peut rester où elle est.

J'insiste, chère madame. Prenez ce médicament et ne mangez rien.

Madame Paquet: Rien manger?!

Le Docteur: Absolument rien!

Madame Paquet: Pas même un oeuf à la coque?

Le Docteur: Pas même un oeuf à la coque!

Monsieur Paquet: Mais, docteur, soyez raisonnable.

Madame Paquet: Oui, docteur, soyez raisonnable? Rien à manger?

Le Docteur: Pendant au moins deux jours.

Madame Paquet: Je vais mourir de faim! Soyez raisonnable, docteur.

Le Docteur: Ju suis raisonnable, madame.

Madame Paquet: Pas même un petit morceau de pain grillé?

Le Docteur: Pas même un petit morceau de pain grillé!

Madame Paquet: . . . sans beurre . . . sans confiture . . . ?

Le Docteur: Pas de pain grillé, pas de beurre, pas de confiture. Rien. Il est ridicule de croire qu'il faut manger pour vivre. Rappelez-vous, madame, qu'une personne ne se nourrit pas seulement par le pain. Manger est mauvais pour la santé. Tout le monde mange mal. La chimie du corps ne peut pas tolérer les aliments modernes . . . Excusez-moi maintenant. Je dois partir parce que je vais dîner au Coq d'or: du poisson . . .

Madame Paquet: Du poisson! Ah!

Le Docteur: Un beau filet mignon . . .

Madame Paquet: Ah!

Le Docteur: Une belle salade . . .

Madame Paquet: Ah!

Le Docteur: Rappelez-vous, aussi, que quand j'ai pris le serment d'Hippocrate, j'ai promis de remplir mes devoirs.

Le docteur va à la porte.

Madame Paquet: Hippocrate ou hypocrite?! Docteur, n'oubliez pas le proverbe: "Dis-moi ce que tu manges et je te dirai ce que tu es!"

Le docteur sort.

Madame Paquet: François, y a-t-il quelque chose à manger dans le réfrigérateur? Et donne-moi mon médicament.

Vocabulaire

absolument *adv.*, absolutely

l'aliment *n. m.*, the food

la chimie *n.*, chemistry

Le Coq d'or Golden Rooster (name of a restaurant)

la coque *n.*, the shell (of an egg); **un oeuf à la coque** soft-boiled egg

depuis *adv., prep.*, since: **depuis quand** since when; **depuis combien de temps** since how long (a time); **Madame Paquet est malade depuis hier** Mrs. Paquet has been sick since yesterday

dîner *v.*, to dine, to have dinner

dis-moi ce que tu manges et je te dirai ce que tu es! tell me what you eat and I'll tell you what you are!

dois *v. form of* **devoir** (ought to, have to, must); **je dois** I have (to)

l'estomac *n. m.*, the stomach

griller *v.*, to grill, to toast; **grillé** toasted

Hippocrate *n. m.*, Hippocrates (ancient Greek physician)

le mal *n.*, pain, ache; **mal à l'estomac** stomach ache

malade *adj.*, sick, ill

manger *v.*, to eat

le médicament *n.*, medicine

moins *adv.*, less; **au moins** at least

le morceau *n.*, morsel, piece

mourir *v.*, to die

nourrir *v.*, to nourish; **se nourrir** *refl. v.*, to nourish oneself

l'oeuf *n. m.*, the egg

le pain *n.*, the bread; **pain grillé** toast

pas de pain no bread; **pas de beurre** no butter; **pas même** not even

patiemment *adv.*, patiently

pour *prep.*, for, in order (to)

prenez *v. form (imperative) of* **prendre**; **prenez** take

pris *past part. of* **prendre** (to take)

promis *past part. of* **promettre** (to promise)

quelque *adj.*, some; **quelques** a few; **quelque chose** something

rappelez-vous *v. form (imperative) of* **se rappeler** (to remember)

rendre service to perform a service

le serment *n.*, oath; **le serment d'Hippocrate** Hippocratic Oath (a code of medical ethics imposed by Hippocrates upon his students of medicine)

souffrir *v.*, to suffer; **souffrant** *m.*, **souffrante** *f., adj.*, sick

soyez *v. form (imperative) of* **être**; **soyez raisonnable!** be reasonable!

vivre *v.*, to live

Exercises

Review the story and vocabulary before starting these exercises.

I. Answer the following questions in complete sentences. They are based on the story in this unit.

1. Qui est malade? _____

2. Pourquoi est-elle malade? _____

3. Depuis quand est-elle malade? _____

4. Qui lui donne un médicament? _____

5. Pourquoi le docteur doit-il partir? _____

II. **Comment dit-on en français . . . ?** Write the French equivalent for the English given. Refer to the story in this unit if you have to.

1. Mrs. Paquet has been sick since yesterday. _____

2. Absolutely nothing! _____

3. Not even a soft-boiled egg! _____

4. Tell me what you eat and I'll tell you what you are! _____

   _____

5. Take this medicine and don't eat anything! _____

III. The words in the following boxes are scrambled. Unscramble them to find a **meaningful** sentence. Write the sentence in French on the line provided.

Model:

le	est
arrivé	docteur

You write: **Le docteur est arrivé.** (The doctor arrived.)

1.

le	est	n'
arrivé	docteur	pas

_____

2.

est	Madame Paquet	hier
depuis	malade	n'est-ce pas?

_____

3.

est	la	dans	quinze
chambre	il	depuis	minutes

_____

IV. Mots-croisés. (Crossword Puzzle). Give the French words for the English.

Verticalement

1. third person sing., pres. indicative of **devoir**

2. to call

5. butter

6. year

7. since

8. bed

Horizontalement

3. _____ à l'estomac

4. past part. of **pouvoir**

6. to wait

9. by

10. yesterday

11. past part. of **lire**

12. reflexive pronoun

Structures de la Langue

A. Negations: **ne . . . pas / ne . . . jamais / ne . . . rien**

Present Indicative	Passé Composé
1. Je **ne** fume **pas**. (I do not smoke.)	4. Je **n'**ai **pas** fumé. (I did not smoke.)
2. Je **ne** fume **jamais**. (I never smoke.)	5. Je **n'**ai **jamais** fumé. (I have never smoked.)
3. Elle **ne** mange **rien**. (She's eating nothing. or: She's not eating anything.)	6. Elle **n'**a **rien** mangé. (She has eaten nothing. or: She hasn't eaten anything.)

Rules and observations:

1. To make a sentence negative in the present indicative (as you already know from experience in previous work units), merely put **ne** in front of the verb and **pas** after it.

2. If you want to negate the verb by saying **never** in the present indicative, merely put **ne** in front of the verb and **jamais** after it.

3. If you want to negate a verb by saying **nothing** in the present indicative, merely put **ne** in front of the verb and **rien** after it.

4. In the passé composé, put **ne** in front of the auxiliary (or helping) verb and either **pas** or **jamais** or **rien** after it.

5. If the first letter of the verb is a vowel, drop the **e** in **ne** and add an apostrophe: **Je n'ai . . .**

B. Subordination with **quand, parce que,** and **que**

1. **Quand** j'ai faim, je mange.

   (*When* I'm hungry, I eat.)

2. Madame Paquet est dans son lit **parce qu'**elle est malade.

   (Mrs. Paquet is in her bed *because* she is sick.)

3. Je sais **que** vous **êtes** intelligent.

   (I know *that* you are intelligent.)

Rules and observations:

1. Each sentence in the preceding box contains two clauses: a main clause and a subordinate clause. In model sentence 1, the main clause is **je mange** and the subordinate clause is **quand j'ai faim**. As a main clause, **je mange** can stand alone. However, **quand j'ai faim** cannot stand alone; it is incomplete and subordinate to the main clause.

2. In model sentence 2, the main clause is **Madame Paquet est dans son lit** and the subordinate clause is **parce qu'elle est malade**. As a main clause, **Madame Paquet est dans son lit** can stand alone and make sense. However, **parce qu'elle est malade** cannot stand alone; it is incomplete and subordinate to the main clause. Of course, subordinate clauses are used frequently as fragmentary replies to questions or statements in conversation and informal writing. Nevertheless, a subordinate clause is not a complete sentence.

3. In model sentence 3, the main clause is **Je sais** and the subordinate clause is **que vous êtes intelligent**.

C. **Dans** and a duration of time

> Le docteur va venir **dans quelques minutes**.
>
> (The doctor is going to come *in a few minutes*.)

Rules and observations:

1. **Dans** and a duration of time indicates a definite time in the future when something will happen.

2. In the model sentence above, **dans quelques minutes** means *at the end of a few minutes.*

3. **Dans** and a duration of time can be at the beginning or the end of a sentence, but future time must be implied.

D. **En** and a duration of time

> **En une heure**, le docteur est venu.
>
> (*In one hour*, the doctor came.)

Rules and observations:

1. **En** and a duration of time indicates the completion of an action at any time *within* that period of time.

2. In the model sentence above, **en une heure** means *in* or *within* one hour; in other words, any time before the one hour is up. If that is what you mean, use **en** for *in.*

3. **En** and a duration of time must be at the beginning of a sentence if the action has already been completed (as a general rule).

E. **Depuis** and a duration of time

---

1.   **Depuis quand** Madame Paquet **est**-elle malade?

(*Since when has* Mrs. Paquet been sick?)

2.   Madame Paquet est malade **depuis hier**.

(Mrs. Paquet has been sick *since yesterday.*)

3.   **Depuis combien de temps** Mme Paquet **attend**-elle le docteur?

(*How long has* Mrs. Paquet *been waiting* for the doctor?)

4.   Madame Paquet **attend** le docteur **depuis vingt minutes**.

(Mrs. Paquet *has been waiting* for the doctor *for twenty minutes.*)

Rules and observations:

1.   In model sentence 1 in the above box, **depuis quand** is used in the question to express *since when*; in other words, at what point in the past. When you use this structure, you must use the present indicative tense of the verb.

2.   In model sentence 2, which is the answer to 1, **depuis hier** is used to express *since yesterday* and the verb is still in the present indicative tense. (Note the verb tense in English in the question and in the answer in both model sentences: *has been.*) In French, however, we use the simple present tense because the thought expressed in the verb still holds right *now* in the present.

3.   In model sentences 3 and 4, **depuis combien de temps** has a slightly different meaning. It asks: for how long. The answer to the question asked in this type of sentence structure usually requires a certain length of time to be stated (e.g., twenty minutes, three hours, a month, etc.). Note here, too, that in French we use the verb in the present tense because the action of the verb (in this case, *waiting*) is carried on right up to the present.

Exercises

I.   Answer the following questions in French in the negative using **ne . . . pas**.

Model:	**Fumez-vous?**	**You answer:**	**Non, je ne fume pas.**
	(Do you smoke?)		(No, I do not smoke.)

1.   Dansez-vous bien? _____

2.   Votre père chante-t-il souvent? _____

3.   Votre mère lit-elle beaucoup? _____

4.   Vos amis écrivent-ils bien? _____

5.   Fumes-tu? _____

II. Answer the following questions in the negative using **ne . . . jamais**.

Model: **Mangez-vous beaucoup?**   **You answer:** **Non, je ne mange jamais beaucoup.**
(Do you eat a lot?)   (No, I never eat a lot.)

1. Parlez-vous beaucoup? _____

2. Votre père boit-il beaucoup de lait? _____

3. Votre soeur travaille-t-elle beaucoup? _____

4. Ton ami étudie-t-il beaucoup? _____

5. Buvez-vous beaucoup d'eau? _____

III. Answer the following questions in the negative using **ne . . . rien**.

Model: **Est-ce que Madame Paquet**   **You answer:** **Non, Madame Paquet ne mange**
mange quelque chose? (Is Mrs. Paquet   **rien.** (No, Mrs. Paquet isn't
eating something?)   eating anything.)

1. Lucille mange-t-elle quelque chose? _____

2. Guy écrit-il quelque chose? _____

3. Lis-tu quelque chose? _____

4. Madame Paquet fait-elle quelque chose? _____

5. Étudiez-vous quelque chose? _____

IV. Answer the following questions in the negative, using the negation requested.

(A) Use **ne . . . rien** in your answers.

Model: **Avez-vous mangé quelque chose?**   **You answer:** **Non, je n'ai rien mangé.**
(Have you eaten something?)   (No, I haven't eaten anything.)

1. Avez-vous dit quelque chose? _____

2. Janine a-t-elle bu quelque chose? _____

3. Vos amis ont-ils étudié quelque chose? _____

4. Avez-vous lu quelque chose? _____

5. Avez-vous écrit quelque chose? _____

6. As-tu bu quelque chose? _____

7. Julie et Lucille ont-elles mangé quelque chose? _____

(B) Use **ne . . . jamais** in your answers.

Model: **Avez-vous jamais voyagé en France?**   **You answer:** **Non, je n'ai jamais voyagé en France.**
          (Have you ever traveled to France?)   (No, I have never traveled to France.)

> NOTE THAT SOME OF THESE VERBS IN THE PASSÉ
> COMPOSÉ ARE CONJUGATED WITH **AVOIR**, SOME
> WITH **ÊTRE**. BE CAREFUL!

1. Avez-vous jamais voyagé en Angleterre? _____

2. Êtes-vous jamais allé au Canada? _____

3. Avez-vous jamais vu un film français? _____

4. Juliette est-elle jamais allée à l'opéra? _____

5. Robert a-t-il jamais lu un journal français? _____

6. Monsieur et Madame Paquet sont-ils jamais allés en Espagne? _____

    _____

7. Lucille et Marie-Louise ont-elles jamais mangé un éclair? _____

    _____

V. The words in the following boxes are scrambled. Unscramble them to find a meaningful sentence. Write the sentence in French on the line provided.

Model:

sais	vous	que
êtes	intelligent	je

You write: **Je sais que vous êtes intelligent.** (I know you are intelligent.)

1.

êtes	malade	je
sais	vous	que

_____

2.

dans	est	lit	elle	est
son	Madame Paquet	parce qu'	malade	n'est-ce pas?

_____

3.

j'ai	je	faim
mange	quand	

_____

4.

venir	va	quelques
le docteur	minutes	dans

_____

5.

heure	le docteur	est
une	venu	en

_____

VI. Identify the following verb forms by giving the infinitive for each. They are all in the story in this unit.

Model: dis   **You write: dire**

1. est _____   4. attend _____

2. a _____   5. dites _____

3. va _____   6. prenez _____

VII. Answer the following questions in complete sentences. Use the French words in parentheses in your answers. Use a pronoun in place of the noun as subject.

Model: Depuis quand Madame Paquet   You answer: Elle est malade depuis hier.
est-elle malade? (hier)   (She has been sick since yesterday.)
(Since when has Mrs. Paquet been sick?)

1. Depuis quand Pierre est-il absent? (lundi) _____

2. Depuis combien de temps Madame Paquet attend-elle le docteur? (vingt minutes) _____

_____

3. Depuis combien de temps attendez-vous l'autobus? (dix minutes) _____

_____

4. Depuis quand travaillez-vous ici? (le premier avril) _____

_____

5. Depuis combien de temps lisez-vous ce livre? (une heure) _____

_____

6. Depuis quand lisez-vous ce livre? (ce matin) _____

_____

VIII. Answer the following questions in the affirmative in complete sentences.

Model:	**Faut-il manger pour vivre?**	**You answer:**	**Oui, il faut manger pour vivre.**
	(Is it necessary to eat in order to live?)		(Yes, it is necessary to eat in order to live.)

1. Faut-il boire pour vivre? _____

2. Faut-il étudier pour apprendre? _____

3. Faut-il parler français dans la classe de français? _____

_____

4. Faut-il parler espagnol dans la classe d'espagnol? _____

_____

5. Faut-il faire les devoirs pour apprendre? _____

_____

IX. **Planning Ahead. Proficiency in Speaking, Reading, and Writing.**

Situation: You and your friend Pierre are talking about your plans for the summer vacation.

Imagine a conversation between yourself and him. First, say the words aloud. Then write them on the lines. In order to say something sensible that would fit in this conversation, you must read Pierre's lines.

Pierre: **Dis-moi, est-ce que tu as l'intention de chercher du travail pour l'été prochain?**

1. *Vous:* _____

Pierre: **Où est-ce que tu vas travailler?**

2. *Vous:* _____

Pierre: **Tu as de la chance. Moi, je n'ai pas trouvé de travail.**

3. *Vous:* _____

Pierre: **Tu crois que je peux travailler avec toi?**

4. *Vous:* _____

Pierre: **Alors, je vais parler avec lui tout de suite.**

5. *Vous:* _____

X. Visiting a Friend in the Hospital. Proficiency in Speaking and Writing.

Situation: You are taking a summer course in conversational French at the **Alliance Française** institute in Paris. You are staying with a French family. Robert, a member of the family, broke a leg in a car accident. He is at the **Hôpital Américain**, located in Neuilly, about a twenty-minute ride by bus from **La Tour Eiffel**.

In this guided conversation, you are *Vous*. You may use your own ideas and words or those under the lines. After you make your statements, write them on the lines.

Vous: _____
Greet Robert and ask him how he is today.

Robert: **Salut! Je vais mieux aujourd'hui, merci.**

Vous: _____
Tell him you brought a box of chocolates.

Robert: **Tu as apporté une boîte de chocolats pour moi? C'est gentil. Merci. Ouvre la boîte. Mangeons-les!**

Vous: _____
*Tell me, Robert, how did you break your leg?/***Dis-moi, Robert, comment est-ce que tu t'es cassé la jambe?**

Robert: **J'ai eu un accident de voiture. Le chauffeur de l'autre voiture a brûlé un feu rouge/***I had a car accident. The driver of the other car ran a red traffic light.*

Vous: _____
*He ran a red traffic light?! What an idiot!/***Quel idiot!**

Robert: **La police est arrivée. J'ai été transporté** *(I was transported)* **à cet hôpital par ambulance.**

Vous: _____
These chocolates are delicious!

Robert: **Oui. Ces chocolats sont très délicieux. Où les as-tu achetés?**

Vous: _____
I bought them at **Chez Fauchon**, *behind the Madeleine Church.*

Robert: **L'Église de la Madeleine est très belle, n'est-ce pas?**

Vous: _____
Yes, it's a very beautiful church. Tell me, Robert, how long are you going to stay in the hospital?/
combien de temps vas-tu rester dans l'hôpital?

Robert: **Je vais rester ici deux semaines.**

Vous: _____
Who has come to see you?

Robert: **Jacques est venu. Colette est venue. Pierre et Claudette sont venus.**

Vous: _____
I'm leaving now. I'm going to come back tomorrow.

Robert: **D'accord. À demain!**

Vous: _____

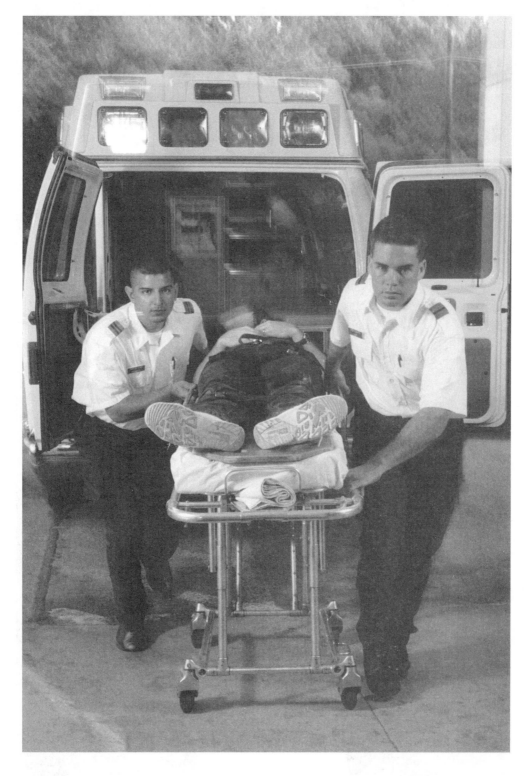

Orthographically Changing Verbs in the Present Indicative and Other Structures of the Language

Les secrets de votre main

Some people like to have their palms read. It can be fun—believe it or not.

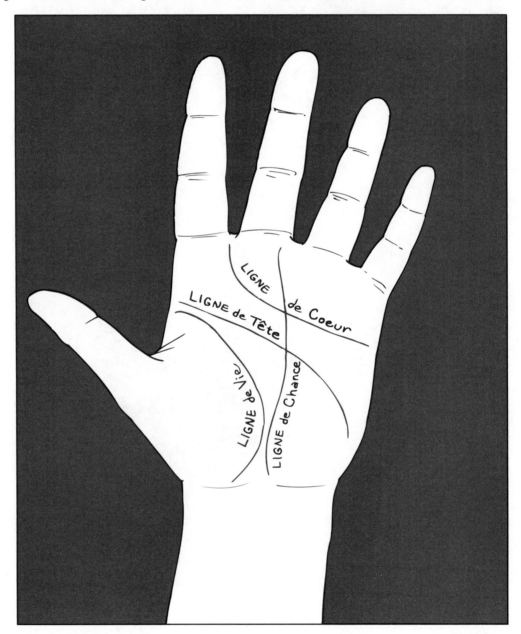

Les Secrets de votre main

Claire et François Paquet sont allés à la foire samedi. Là, ils se sont bien amusés. Ils ont vu des expositions, ils ont acheté des souvenirs, et ils sont entrés chez une chiromancienne pour se faire lire les lignes de la main.

—Tiens! François! Une chiromancienne! s'exclame Claire.

—Où? lui a demandé François.

—Là, devant nous. Ne vois-tu pas?

> Madame Sétou,
> chiromancienne,
>
> révèle les secrets de votre main.

—François, je vais me faire lire les lignes de la main. Toi aussi? lui a demandé Claire.

—Oui, je veux bien. Mais, tu sais que je n'y crois pas, dit François.

Ils entrent chez la chiromancienne.

—Est-ce que nous vous dérangeons, madame?

—Mais non, pas du tout! Entrez! Entrez! répond Madame Sétou.

—Je veux me faire lire les lignes de la main. Et mon mari aussi, dit Claire.

—Bon! répond la chiromancienne. Asseyez-vous et donnez-moi votre main.

Madame Sétou regarde fixement la main de Claire et elle commence à lire les lignes:

—Ah! Je vois dans votre ligne de chance que vous allez faire un voyage aux États-Unis avec un homme, s'exclame Madame Sétou.

—C'est curieux! dit Claire. Mon mari et moi, nous commençons à faire des préparations pour un autre voyage aux États-Unis.

—Maintenant, dit Madame Sétou, je regarde votre ligne de coeur. Je vois que vous êtes amoureuse d'un homme.

—C'est curieux! dit Claire. Vous avez raison. Je suis amoureuse de mon mari!

—Maintenant, monsieur, asseyez-vous et donnez-moi votre main, dit Madame Sétou.

François Paquet lui donne sa main.

—Ah! Je vois dans votre ligne de chance que vous allez faire un voyage aux États-Unis avec une femme, s'exclame Madame Sétou.

—C'est curieux! dit François. Ma femme et moi, nous commençons à faire des préparations pour un autre voyage aux États-Unis.

—Maintenant, dit Madame Sétou, je regarde votre ligne de coeur. Je vois que vous êtes amoureux d'une femme.

—C'est curieux! dit François. Vous avez raison. Je suis amoureux de ma femme! La main révèle tout, n'est-ce pas?

—Oui, monsieur, la main révèle les secrets de votre vie. Ça fait dix euros pour les révélations.

François lui paye les dix euros.

Dehors, Claire dit à François:

—Madame Sétou sait tout, n'est-ce pas?

—Oui, Madame Sétou sait tout, mais je n'ai rien appris de nouveau. Et toi?

—Moi non plus. Nous savons déjà que nous voyageons aux États-Unis et que nous sommes amoureux!

Vocabulaire

l'amour *n. m.,* love; **amoureux** *m.,*
  amoureuse *f. adj.,* in love; **nous**
  sommes amoureux we are in love
s'amuser *refl. v.,* to have a good
  time; **ils se sont bien amusés** they
  had a good time
appris *past part. of* **apprendre**; **je**
  n'ai rien appris de nouveau I
  didn't learn anything new
asseyez-vous *imperative of* **s'asseoir**
  (to sit down)
la chance *n.,* luck, fortune, chance
le chiromancien, la chiromancienne
  n., the palm reader
le coeur *n.,* the heart

crois *v. form of* **croire** (to believe);
  je n'y crois pas I don't believe
  in it
curieux *m.,* **curieuse** *f., adj.,* curious,
  odd
déranger *v.,* to disturb
donnez-moi la main give me your
  hand
fixement *adv.,* intently, fixedly
la foire *n.,* the fair
la ligne *n.,* the line; **se faire lire les**
  lignes de la main to have one's
  palm read (to have the lines of
  one's hand read)
pas du tout not at all

plus *adv.,* more; **non plus** neither;
  moi non plus me neither
révéler *v.,* to reveal
sais *v. form of* **savoir**; **tu sais** you
  know
veux *v. form of* **vouloir**; **veux-tu?** do
  you want to?; **je veux bien** I'd like
  to; **je veux me faire lire les lignes**
  de la main I want to have my
  palm read
vois *v. form of* **voir**; **ne vois-tu pas?**
  don't you see?
voyager *v.,* to travel
y *advl. pron.,* **je n'y crois pas** I
  don't believe *in it*

Exercises

Review the story and vocabulary before starting these exercises.

I. **Vrai ou faux?** On the blank line write **vrai** if the statement is true or **faux** if the statement is false.

1. Claire et François Paquet sont allés à une foire. _____

2. François refuse de se faire lire les lignes de la main. _____

3. Claire et François n'ont rien appris de nouveau chez la chiromancienne. _____

II. Write appropriate responses on the blank lines. The following is a conversation between Claire and François Paquet, who are about to have their palms read.

Claire:	Tiens! François! Une chiromancienne!
François:	_____
Claire:	Là, devant nous. Je vais me faire lire les lignes de la main. Veux-tu?
François:	_____
Claire:	Madame Sétou sait tout, n'est-ce pas?
François:	_____
Claire:	Je n'ai rien appris de nouveau. Et toi?
François:	_____

III. Write complete sentences using the cue words given below. Change the infinitives where necessary to either the present tense or the passé composé, whichever you prefer. Supply other words as needed.

Model: **Claire et François Paquet/ aller/ la foire.**
(Claire and François Paquet/ to go/ to the fair.)

You write: **Claire et François Paquet sont allés à la foire.**
(Claire and François Paquet went to the fair.)

or:

Claire et François Paquet vont à la foire.
(Claire and François Paquet are going to the fair.)

1. Joseph et Joséphine / aller / cinéma / samedi.

   _____

2. Ils / entrer / chez / chiromancienne.

   _____

3. Ils / ne / apprendre / rien / chez / chiromancienne.

   _____

4. François Paquet / lui / payer / euros / pour / révélations.

   _____

Structures de la Langue

A. Orthographically changing verbs in the present indicative

appeler (to call)	
Singular	*Plural*
j'appelle	nous appelons
tu appelles	vous appelez
il, elle, on appelle	ils, elles appellent

Rules and observations:

1. An orthographically changing verb is a verb that changes in spelling.

2. In the preceding box, **appeler** doubles the **l** in the three persons of the singular and in the third person plural. This is done because the stress falls on the syllable that contains the **l** when pronounced. The letter **l** does not double in the first and second persons of the plural because the stress is on the final syllable (**-ons** and **-ez**).

3. There are other verbs that double the consonant in the same persons as just described. For example: **jeter** (to throw) and **rappeler** (to recall, to call (someone) back).

---

employer (to use, employ)

Singular	*Plural*
j'emploie	nous employons
tu emploies	vous employez
il, elle, on emploie	ils, elles emploient

---

4. For verbs ending in **-oyer** or **-uyer**, you must change the **y** to **i** before a silent **e**, as noted in the preceding box.

5. Other verbs that end in **-oyer** or **-uyer** are **nettoyer** (to clean), **envoyer** (to send), **ennuyer** (to bore, to bother), **essuyer** (to wipe).

6. Verbs ending in **-ayer** may change the **y** to **i** or may keep the **y** before silent **e**. Two examples are **essayer** (to try, to try on) and **payer** (to pay, to pay for).

---

manger (to eat)

Singular	*Plural*
je mange	nous mangeons
tu manges	vous mangez
il, elle, on mange	ils, elles mangent

---

7. For verbs ending in **-ger**, add a silent **e** after **g** if the vowels **a** or **o** follow **g**. This is done in order to preserve the soft sound of **g** as it is pronounced in the infinitive. If a silent **e** were not inserted between **g** and **a** or **g** and **o**, the **g** would then have to be pronounced hard, as in the English word *go*.

8. Here are other verbs ending in **-ger** that are treated in the same way:

    arranger (to arrange); **changer** (to change); **corriger** (to correct); **déranger** (to disturb); **nager** (to swim); **obliger** (to oblige); **songer** (to think, to dream); **voyager** (to travel).

---

prononcer (to pronounce)

Singular	*Plural*
je prononce	nous prononçons
tu prononces	vous prononcez
il, elle, on prononce	ils, elles prononcent

---

9. For verbs ending in **-cer**, change **c** to **ç** before the vowels **a, o, u**. This is done in order to preserve the soft sound of **c** (like *s*) as it is pronounced in the infinitive. The little mark under the **c** (**ç**) is called *une cédille*. Actually, it is the lower half of the consonant *s* and indicates that **ç** should be pronounced as *s*.

10. Here are other verbs ending in **-cer** that are treated in the same way:

    annoncer (to announce); **avancer** (to advance); **commencer** (to begin); **effacer** (to efface, to erase); **lancer** (to hurl, to lance, to launch); **menacer** (to threaten, to menace); **placer** (to place, to put, to set); **remplacer** (to replace).

acheter (to buy)	
Singular	*Plural*
j'achète	nous achetons
tu achètes	vous achetez
il, elle, on achète	ils, elles achètent

11. If there is a silent **e** in the syllable just before the infinitive ending (as in ach**e**ter), it changes to **è** in a verb form—provided that the syllable right after it contains another silent **e**. Study the changes in spelling in the preceding box.

12. Other verbs that change in the same way are **lever** (to lift, to raise), **se lever** (to get up), and **enlever** (to remove, to take off).

Exercises

Review the preceding material before starting these exercises.

I. Answer the following questions in complete sentences (in French) in the affirmative. Substitute *nous* as the subject pronoun in place of "Et vous et votre soeur?" Also, substitute an object pronoun for the noun direct object, as shown in these two models:

Model:	**Bob arrange les fleurs.**	**You answer:**	**Nous les arrangeons aussi.**
	Et vous et votre soeur?		(We are arranging them too.)
	(Bob arranges the flowers.		
	And you and your sister?)		

Model:	**Simone efface le tableau.**	**You answer:**	**Nous l'effaçons aussi.**
	Et vous et votre soeur?		(We are erasing it too.)
	(Simone is erasing the board.		
	And you and your sister?)		

1. Hélène change la phrase. Et vous et votre soeur? _____

   _____

2. Yves corrige le devoir. Et vous et votre soeur? _____

   _____

3. Monique appelle les garçons. Et vous et votre soeur? _____

   _____

4. Guy emploie le dictionnaire. Et vous et votre soeur? _____

   _____

5. Lucille achète les roses. Et vous et votre soeur? _____

   _____

II. Do the same here as you did in the preceding exercise, substituting *nous* as the subject pronoun in place of "Et vous et votre frère?"

1.　Paulette lance la balle. Et vous et votre frère? _____

_____

2.　René avance les mains. Et vous et votre frère? _____

_____

3.　Renée lève les fenêtres. Et vous et votre frère? _____

_____

4.　Suzanne paye l'addition. Et vous et votre frère? _____

_____

5.　Charles mange les bananes. Et vous et votre frère? _____

_____

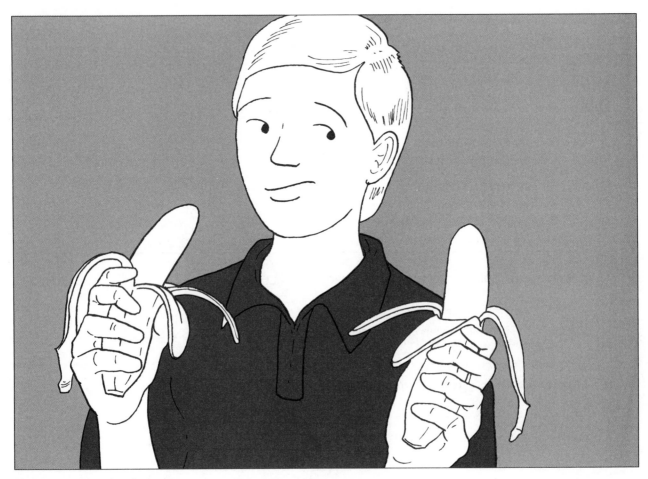

Charles mange les bananes.

III. Change to the passé composé.

Model:	**Claire et François Paquet vont à la foire.** (Claire and François Paquet are going to the fair.)	**You write:**	**Claire et François Paquet sont allés à la foire.** (Claire and François Paquet went to the fair.)

1. Janine et Monique vont au cinéma. _____

2. Nous voyageons aux États-Unis. _____

3. Madame Sétou regarde fixement la main de Madame Paquet. _____

_____

4. Madame Sétou révèle les secrets de votre main. _____

_____

5. Claire et François Paquet achètent des souvenirs. _____

_____

IV. Change to the present indicative.

Model:	**Nous avons mangé les pommes.** (We ate the apples.)	**You write:**	**Nous mangeons les pommes.** (We are eating the apples.)

1. Nous avons arrangé les fleurs. _____

2. Il a acheté une cravate. _____

3. Ils ont appelé la police. _____

4. Tu as employé le dictionnaire. _____

5. Nous avons prononcé le mot. _____

B. **Aller** in the present indicative with an infinitive

Je vais faire mes devoirs.	**Il va voir** ses amis.
(*I am going to do* my homework.)	(*He's going to see* his friends.)

Rule: It is customary to use **aller** in the present indicative with an infinitive form of a verb, as we do in English.

C. **Vouloir** in the present indicative with an infinitive

Elle **veut acheter** une nouvelle robe.

(She *wants to buy* a new dress.)

Monsieur Paquet **veut vendre** son auto.

(Mr. Paquet *wants to sell* his car.)

Rule: It is customary to use **vouloir** in the present indicative with an infinitive form of a verb, as we do in English.

D. The use of **il y a, y a-t-il . . .?**, **voici**, and **voilà**

(a) **Il ya a** un bon restaurant près d'ici.   (*There is* a good restaurant near here.)

(b) **Il y a** dix étudiants dans cette classe.   (*There are* ten students in this class.)

(c) J'ai vu Janine **il y a deux heures**.   (I saw Janine *two hours ago*.)

(d) **Y a-t-il** un arrêt d'autobus près d'ici?   (*Is there* a bus stop near here?)

(e) **Est-ce qu'il y a** des fruits sur la table?   (*Are there* fruits on the table?)

(f) **N'y a-t-il pas** de sel dans la soupe?   (*Isn't there* any salt in the soup?)

(g) Non, **il n'y a pas** de sel dans la soupe.   (No, *there isn't* any salt in the soup.)

(h) Je l'ai vue **il y a un an**.   (I saw her *a year ago*.)

(i) **Voici** ma mère et **voilà** mon père!   (*Here's* my mother and *there's* my father!)

(j) **Voici** un taxi et **voilà** un taxi!   (*Here is* a taxi and *there is* a taxi!)

(k) **Me voici!**   **Le voici!**   **Vous voilà!**   **Les voilà!**   **La voici!**

     (*Here I am!*)   (*Here he is!*   (*There you are!*)   (*There they are!*)   (*Here she is!*

                    Here it is!)   *Here it is!*)

Rules and observations:

1. **Il y a** is used simply to mention the existence of something that may or may not be known to the listener. It may be about people, things, or facts. Its equivalent in English is *there is* or *there are*.

2. **Il y a** also means *ago* when a length of time is stated right after it. See models (c) and (h) in the preceding box.

3. The interrogative form of **il y a** is given in models (d) and (e).

4. The negative form of **il y a** is given in model sentence (g).

5. The negative-interrogative form of **il y a** is given in model sentence (f). **Est-ce qu'il n'y a pas** is also a correct form.

6. **Voici** and **voilà** have a demonstrative characteristic. They are used to point out, to call attention to someone or something. They are based on **vois + ici (+ là)**. If you analyze the word, it actually means: *See (look) here! See (look) there!* See models (i) and (j).

7. If you regard **voici** or **voilà** as a "verb form" you will understand why the object pronoun is placed in front of it, as in the model sentences in (k).

Exercises

Review the preceding material before starting these exercises.

I. Answer the following questions in the affirmative in complete sentences.

Model: **Allez-vous faire vos devoirs?**	**You answer:** **Oui, je vais faire mes devoirs.**
(Are you going to do your homework?)	(Yes, I am going to do my homework.)

1. Allez-vous faire un voyage au Canada? _____

2. Va-t-elle écrire une lettre? _____

3. Est-ce qu'il va jouer dans le parc? _____

4. Vont-ils voyager en Angleterre? _____

5. Allons-nous répondre à la question? _____

II. Answer the following questions in the negative in complete sentences.

Model: **Voulez-vous acheter un nouveau chapeau?**	**You answer:** **Non, je ne veux pas acheter un nouveau chapeau.**
(Do you want to buy a new hat?)	(No, I do not want to buy a new hat.)

1. Voulez-vous acheter une nouvelle voiture? _____

    _____

2. Le professeur de français veut-il corriger les devoirs? _____

    _____

3. L'étudiant veut-il prononcer le mot? _____

4. Janine veut-elle employer le dictionnaire? _____

5. Monsieur Paquet veut-il fumer une cigarette? _____

III. Match the following.

1. There you are!   _____ Me voici!

2. Here she is!   _____ Vous voilà!

3. Here they are!   _____ Les voici!

4. Here I am!   _____ Le voilà!

5. There it is!   _____ La voici!

IV. Change to the negative.

Model:	**Il y a un bon restaurant près d'ici.**	**You write:**	**Il n'y a pas un bon restaurant près d'ici.**
	(There is a good restaurant near here.)		(There is not a good restaurant near here.)

1. Il y a un grand parc dans cette ville. _____

2. Y a-t-il un arrêt d'autobus ici? _____

3. Est-ce qu'il y a dix garçons dans la classe? _____

    _____

V. Answer the following questions in the affirmative in complete sentences, using French for the English in parentheses.

Model:	**Avez-vous vu Janine?** **(two hours ago)**	**You answer:**	**Oui, j'ai vu Janine il y a deux heures.**
	(Have you seen Janine?)		(Yes, I saw Janine two hours ago.)

1. Avez-vous lu *Le livre de mon ami* d'Anatole France? (three months ago) _____

    _____

2. A-t-il vu Pierre? (ten minutes ago) _____

3. Êtes-vous allé en Californie? (a year ago) _____

4. Sont-elles arrivées? (a half hour ago) _____

5. Est-elle partie? (an hour ago) _____

VI. **Joining the French Club. Proficiency in Speaking and Writing.**

Situation: You are the president of the French Club. Several new students are present at the first meeting and they are trying to decide whether or not to join the club. They want to know primarily what everybody does in the club. As president, you must tell them what you all do from time to time. Of course, you must use the first person plural of the verbs (the **nous** form) in the present tense. State at least six activities that all the members take part in, including yourself. You may use your own ideas or ideas suggested by the following: **appeler, employer, manger, corriger, arranger, commencer, danser, parler, voyager, il y a, à présent, avoir besoin de, effacer, placer**.

VII. Physical Activities. Proficiency in Speaking and Writing.

Situation: In your French Club students are looking at pictures in an album that one of the students brought to stimulate speaking in French.

Look at the photo below. Say aloud the French words you plan to write. Then answer the questions in complete sentences. Verbs you may want to use: **jouer**/*to play*; **s'amuser**/*to have fun*; **être debout**/*to be standing*; **être prêt à sauter**/*to be ready to jump*; **grimper sur un arbre abattu**/*to climb onto a felled (cut down, knocked down) tree.*

1. Combien d'enfants y a-t-il dans cette photo? _____

2. Où sont-ils? Dans un parc? _____

3. Qu'est-ce qu'ils font? _____

4. Que fait le petit garçon à gauche? _____

5. Que fait le garçon au milieu/*in the middle?* _____

6. Que fait le troisième garçon à droite? _____

VIII. Leisure.   Proficiency in Speaking and Writing.

Situation: A boy and a girl are riding their bicycles by the beach. They stop for a moment to rest. What do they say to each other?

Write two statements on the following lines.

Le garçon: _____

La jeune fille: _____

Prepositions and Infinitives and Other Structures of the Language

Le beau cadeau

In this story, the Paquet family is celebrating the wedding anniversary of Mr. and Mrs. Paquet. After a festive lunch, they attempt to play some music on their brand-new stereo that Mr. Paquet had bought as a present for his wife.

Papa! Papa! Attends! Attends!

C'est aujourd'hui samedi.

Monsieur Paquet est allé acheter une chaîne stéréo. C'est un cadeau pour sa femme à l'occasion de leur vingtième anniversaire de mariage. Madame Paquet est allée chez le coiffeur pour une nouvelle coiffure. Janine a préparé un grand déjeuner toute la matinée dans la cuisine, et Pierre est allé aux grands magasins acheter un petit cadeau pour sa mère de la part de lui et da sa soeur. Il est allé, aussi, chez un confiseur pour acheter une boîte de chocolats et chez un fleuriste pour acheter des fleurs.

Après un déjeuner délicieux, Monsieur Paquet dit:

—Et maintenant nouns allons écouter un peu de musique. Elle est belle, cette chaîne stéréo, n'est-ce pas?

Monsieur Paquet essaye d'allumer la chaîne stéréo, mais il n'y a pas de musique! Il n'y a pas de son! Il n'y a rien!

—Zut, alors! J'ai horreur de réparer les chaînes stéréo! dit-il.

—D'abord, le téléviseur il y a un an! Et maintenant, une nouvelle chaîne stéréo qui ne marche pas! Incroyable! Ces appareils gouvernent notre vie! s'exclame Madame Paquet. Monsieur Paquet va téléphoner au magasin où il a acheté la chaîne stéréo.

—Il faut appeler le magasin, dit-il.

A ce moment-là, Pierre s'exclame:

—Papa! Papa! Attends! Attends! Tu n'as pas branché la chaîne stéréo sur la prise de courant!

Vocabulaire

agréable *adj.,* pleasant

l'anniversaire *n. m.,* anniversary, birthday

brancher *v.,* to plug in, to connect (an electrical apparatus)

le cadeau *n.,* the gift, present

la chaîne *n.* **stéréo** stereo system

le coiffeur, la coiffeuse *n.,* the hairdresser; **une coiffure** *n.,* a hair style

le confiseur, la confiseuse *n.,* the confectioner, candy maker; **une confiserie** a candy story

d'abord *advl. phrase,* at first, first

essayer *v.,* to try

la fleur *n.,* the flower

le fleuriste, la fleuriste *n.,* the florist

gouverner *v.,* to govern, to rule, to direct

l'horreur *n. f.,* horror; **J'ai horreur de** + *inf.* I hate + *pres. part.*

le magasin *n.,* the store; **le grand magasin** the department store

le mariage *n.,* the marriage

le matin *n.,* the morning; **la matinée** the morning (long); **toute la matinée** all morning long

l'occasion *n. f.,* the occasion

la part *n.,* part, behalf; **de la part de lui** on his behalf

peu *adv.,* little

la prise *n.,* hold, grip; **une prise de courant** electric outlet (in the wall)

le son *n.,* the sound

Exercises

Review the story and vocabulary before starting these exercises.

I. Answer the following questions in complete sentences. They are all based on the story in this unit.

1. Où Monsieur Paquet est-il allé? _____

2. Qui a préparé un grand déjeuner? _____

3. Qui est allé chez le coiffeur? _____

4. Qui a acheté une boîte de chocolats? _____

5. Pourquoi la chaîne stéréo ne marche-t-elle pas d'abord? _____

_____

II. Oui ou Non?

1. Madame Paquet a acheté une chaîne stéréo.   _____

2. Pierre a acheté une boîte de chocolats chez un confiseur.   _____

3. Monsieur Paquet a horreur de réparer les chaînes stéréo.   _____

4. Monsieur Paquet va téléphoner au fleuriste.   _____

5. La chaîne stéréo ne marche pas d'abord parce que Monsieur Paquet n'a pas
    branché l'appareil sur la prise de courant.   _____

III. Write short sentences using the cue words in each group. They are all based on the story in this work unit. Use
the present indicative or the passé composé, whichever you prefer. Supply other words as needed.

1. Monsieur Paquet / acheter / chaîne stéréo.

    _____

2. Janine / préparer / déjeuner.

    _____

3. Pierre / aller / confiseur / chocolats.

    _____

Structure de la Langue

A. The use of **de** with an infinitive after certain idiomatic expressions

1. **avoir besoin de + inf.** (to need + inf.)	4. **avoir peur de + inf.** (to be afraid + inf.)
2. **avoir envie de + inf.** (to feel like + pres. part.)	5. **avoir raison de + inf.** (to be right + inf.)
3. **avoir horreur de + inf.** (to hate, to detest + pres. part. or inf.)	6. **avoir tort de + inf.** (to be wrong + inf.)

Models:

1. **J'ai besoin d'aller** chez le dentiste.   (*I need to go* to the dentist.)

2. **Tu as envie de dormir.**   (*You feel like sleeping.*)

3. **Il a horreur de réparer** les chaînes stéréo.   (*He hates repairing (to repair)* stereo systems.)

4. **Nouns avons peur de traverser** la mer.   (*We are afraid to cross* the sea.)

5. **Vous avez raison d'avoir** peur.   (*You are right to be* afraid.)

6. **Vous avez tort d'avoir** peur.   (*You are wrong to be* afraid.)

Rule: These idiomatic expressions take **de + infinitive form**. Note that in English we sometimes use a present participle (or gerund) instead of an infinitive, as in model sentences 2 and 3 in the box.

B. The use of **il est** + adjective + **de** + infinitive

1. **Il est agréable d'aller** à un bal.   (*It is pleasant to go (going)* to a dance.)

2. **Il est amusant d'aller** à un cirque.   (*It is fun to go (going)* to a circus.)

3. **Il est désagréable d'aller** chez le dentiste.   (*It is unpleasant to go (going)* to the dentist.)

4. **Il est impossible de lire** ce gros livre en une heure.   (*It is impossible to read* this thick book within an hour.)

5. **Il est intéressant d'aller** à un musée.   (*It is interesting to go (going)* to a museum.)

Rule: Use **Il est** (not **C'est**) + adjective + **de** + infinitive.

C. The use of **à** after certain verbs + infinitive

1. **J'apprends à lire** en français.   (*I am learning to read* in French.)

2. **Je commence à écrire** en français.   (*I am beginning to write* in French.)

3. **J'hésite à sortir** parce qu'il pleut.   (*I hesitate going (to go) out* because it's raining.)

Rule: In French, some verbs take **à** between the verb form and the infinitive. Study the above models.

D. The use of **pour, sans, avant de, au lieu de,** and **afin de** + infinitive

1. Il est parti **pour aller** voir ses amis.   (He left *to go* see his friends.)

2. Elle est sortie **sans dire** un mot.   (She went out *without saying* a word.)

3. Nous mangeons et buvons **pour vivre**.   (We eat and drink *(in order) to live*.)

4. Ils sont allés au cinéma **avant de finir** leurs devoirs.   (They went to the movies *before finishing* their homework.)

5. Elles sont sorties **au lieu de rester** à la maison.   (They went out *instead of staying* home.)

6. Il est revenu **afin de voir** ses amis.   (He came back *in order to* see his friends.)

Rule: The infinitive form of the verb is used *after* prepositions and prepositional phrases, except after **en**.

E. The use of no preposition after certain verbs + infinitive

1. **J'aime aller** au cinéma.   (*I like to go (going)* to the movies.)

2. **Tu aimes mieux aller** au théâtre.   (*You prefer to go (going)* to the theater.)

3. **Il déteste aller** chez le dentiste.   (*He hates to go (going)* to the dentist.)

4. **Elle veut aller** au Canada.   (*She wants to go* to Canada.)

5. **Nous pensons aller** en Angleterre.   (*We intend to go (going)* to England.)

6. **Vous pouvez aller** à l'opéra ce soir.   (*You can go* to the opera tonight.)

7. **Ils veulent aller** en Australie.   (*They want to go* to Australia.)

8. **Elles doivent aller** à la bibliothèque.   (*They have to go* to the library.)

ALSO MAKE A NOTE OF THE IMPERSONAL EXPRESSION **Il faut**, as in:

Il faut étudier pour apprendre. (*It is necessary to study* in order to learn.)

Rule: No preposition is needed between the verb form and the infinitive when you use the verbs that are listed above.

F. The use of **de** after certain verbs + infinitive

1. **J'ai oublié de fermer** la fenêtre.   (*I forgot to close* the window.)

2. **Je promets de venir** chez vous.   (*I promise to come* to your house.)

3. **Elle a refusé de sortir** hier soir.   (*She refused to go out* last night.)

4. **Je tâche de faire** mes devoirs.   (*I try to do* my homework.)

Rule: The preceding verbs require **de** + infinitive.

Exercises

Review the preceding material before starting these exercises.

I. Write the appropriate preposition in French, either **à** or **de**, on the blank line. If no preposition is needed, write a dash (—).

Model: Elle a oublié __de__ fermer la porte.

1. Tu as envie _____ jouer, n'est-ce pas?

2. Elle apprend _____ lire en espagnol.

3. J'aime _____ aller au cinéma.

4. Il a besoin _____ travailler.

5. Nous commençons _____ écrire en français.

6. Veux-tu _____ aller au Canada?

7. J'aime mieux _____ prendre du thé.

8. Elle hésite _____ fumer.

9. Vous avez raison _____ partir.

10. Nous avons tort _____ rester.

II. Answer the following questions in the affirmative in complete French sentences. In answer (a) use **oui**. In answer (b) use **aussi**. Study the models.

Models: (a) Avez-vous envie de sortir?
(Do you feel like going out?)

(b) Et Robert?

You answer: (a) Oui, j'ai envie de sortir.
(Yes, I feel like going out.)

(b) Il a envie de sortir aussi.
(He feels like going out too.)

> USE SUBJECT PRONOUNS IN YOUR ANSWERS.

1. (a) As-tu envie d'aller au cinéma? _____

   (b) Et tes amis? _____

2. (a) Madame Paquet a-t-elle besoin d'aller au supermarché? _____

   _____

   (b) Et Louise et Antoinette? _____

3. (a) Êtes-vous sorti sans dire un mot? _____

   (b) Et Joséphine? _____

4. (a) Apprenez-vous à lire en français? _____

   (b) Et Robert? _____

5. (a) Avez-vous horreur de manger dans un restaurant sale? _____

   _____

   (b) Et Michel et Marie? _____

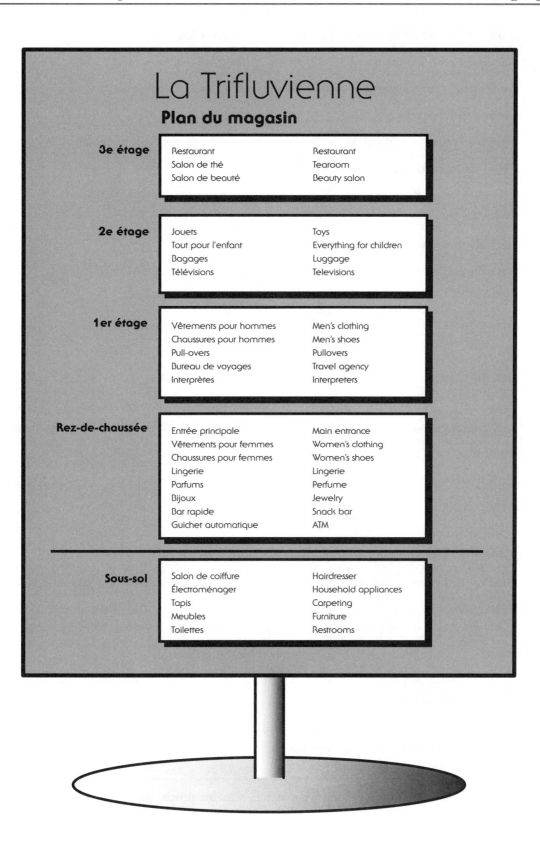

La Trifluvienne

Plan du magasin

3e étage

Restaurant	Restaurant
Salon de thé	Tearoom
Salon de beauté	Beauty salon

2e étage

Jouets	Toys
Tout pour l'enfant	Everything for children
Bagages	Luggage
Télévisions	Televisions

1er étage

Vêtements pour hommes	Men's clothing
Chaussures pour hommes	Men's shoes
Pull-overs	Pullovers
Bureau de voyages	Travel agency
Interprètes	Interpreters

Rez-de-chaussée

Entrée principale	Main entrance
Vêtements pour femmes	Women's clothing
Chaussures pour femmes	Women's shoes
Lingerie	Lingerie
Parfums	Perfume
Bijoux	Jewelry
Bar rapide	Snack bar
Guichet automatique	ATM

Sous-sol

Salon de coiffure	Hairdresser
Électroménager	Household appliances
Tapis	Carpeting
Meubles	Furniture
Toilettes	Restrooms

III. Choose the correct answer after studying the picture on the preceding page.

1. Un jouet est généralement pour

    (a) une dame.   (b) un monsieur.   (c) un enfant.   (d) un agent de police.   _____

2. Si vous avez faim, vous allez au

    (a) salon de coiffure.   (b) bureau de voyages.   (c) salon de beauté.   (d) restaurant.   _____

3. Si vous voulez prendre de la pâtisserie et du thé, vous allez

    (a) au salon de beauté.   (b) aux tapis.   (c) aux interprètes.   (d) au salon de thé.   _____

IV. Match the following after studying the picture on the preceding page.

1. everything for children   _____ chaussures pour femmes

2. carpeting   _____ bar rapide

3. women's shoes   _____ tout pour l'enfant

4. toys   _____ tapis

5. snack bar   _____ jouets

V. After studying the picture on the preceding page, choose the word that does not belong in the group.

1. (a) pull-overs   (b) chaussures   (c) vêtements   (d) parfums   _____

2. (a) interprètes   (b) bureau de voyages   (c) lingerie   (d) chaussures   _____

3. (a) tapis   (b) toilettes   (c) bar rapide   (d) électroménager   _____

VI.   Sports. Proficiency in Speaking, Reading, and Writing.

Situation: You and your friend Robert are talking about the basketball team at your school.

Imagine a conversation between yourself and him. First, say the words aloud. Then write them on the lines. In order to say something sensible that would fit in this conversation, you must read Robert's lines.

Robert: **Tu es allé au match de basket-ball hier soir?**

1. *Vous:*   _____

Robert: **Nous avons une bonne équipe, n'est-ce pas?**

2. *Vous:*   _____

Robert: **Albert est notre meilleur joueur.**

3. *Vous:*   _____

Robert: **Nous jouons notre dernier match la semaine prochaine.**

4. *Vous:*   _____

Robert: **Est-ce que tu vas venir?**

5. *Vous:*   _____

VII. Politics. Proficiency in Speaking and Writing.

Situation: You saw the photo here in a newspaper and you are saying a few words in French about it to a friend.

Look at the picture and jot down a few words you plan to use. First, say them aloud. Then write at least two sentences on the lines. You may use your own words and ideas and/or the following suggestions: **Monsieur Jacques Chirac, à gauche, est le président de la République Française**/*Mr. Jacques Chirac, on the left, is the president of the French Republic.* **Il a été élu en 1995**/*He was elected in 1995.* **L'homme à droite est Monsieur François Mitterrand, l'ancien président**/*The man on the right is Mr. François Mitterrand, the former president.* **Ils viennent de sortir du Palais de l'Élysée, célèbre résidence, à Paris**/*They have just come out of the Élysée Palace, the famous residence in Paris.*

1. _____

2. _____

VIII. Description. Proficiency in Speaking and Writing.

Situation: You are at a party. It's your turn to say a few words about a scene in a photo and to describe a person's appearance.

Look at the picture below. It is a snapshot of Anne-Marie and Pierre taken on their honeymoon in Paris ten years after they had graduated from high school. Do you remember how devoted they were to each other when they were classmates? Pierre protected her from embarrassment when he did not reveal to the teacher the secret note she had written to him. Read again the story in Work Unit 5 to refresh your memory.

Use your own words and ideas and/or any of the following suggestions: **passer la lune de miel à Paris**/*to spend the honeymoon in Paris.* **Anne-Marie et Pierre sont assis dans le parc**/*Anne-Marie and Pierre are sitting in the park.* **Elle lui parle**/*She is talking to him.* **Il écoute**/*He is listening.* **Comme elle est jolie!**/*How pretty she is!* **Elle a les cheveux bruns**/*She has brown hair.* **Pierre a les cheveux bruns**/*Pierre has brown hair.* **Comme il est beau!**/*How handsome he is!*

First, say aloud at least three statements about the scene. If they sound okay to you, then write them on the lines for practice.

1. _____

2. _____

3. _____

Review Test: Work Units 21–23

I. Write the following sentences in the negative.

| **Model:** **Je mange.** (I eat.) | **You write:** **Je ne mange pas.** (I do not eat.) |

1. Je prononce. _____

2. Madame Paquet est grande. _____

3. Nous allons au cinéma. _____

II. Read the following sentences and write either **quand**, **parce qu'**, or **que** on the line where they belong.

1. Je mange _____ j'ai faim.

2. Monsieur Bernard est dans son lit _____ il est malade.

3. Vous savez _____ mon professeur de français est très intelligent.

III. Write the missing word.

1. Depuis quand Madame Paquet est- _____ malade?

2. Madame est malade _____ hier.

3. Depuis combien de _____ Madame Paquet attend-elle le docteur?

4. Madame Paquet _____ le docteur depuis vingt minutes.

IV. Choose the verb form that is correct and makes sense in each statement.

1. Nous _____ pour vivre.

   (a) prononçons   (b) mangeons   (c) avancez   (d) obligent

2. Jeanne veut _____ une nouvelle robe rouge.

   (a) acheter   (b) achète   (c) effacer   (d) effaçons

V. Write the following sentences in French.

1. I have to go to the dentist. _____

2. You are right and I am wrong. _____

3. We are not afraid to cross the street. _____

4. I feel like sleeping. _____

5. It is interesting to go to a museum. _____

VI.   Match the following statements.

1.   I am learning to read in French.   _____ Noun mangeons et buvons pour vivre.

2.   I am beginning to write in French.   _____ Elle est partie pour aller voir ses amis.

3.   I hesitate going out because it's raining.   _____ J'apprends à lire en français.

4.   She left to go see her friends.   _____ J'hésite à sortir parce qu'il pleut.

5.   We eat and drink in order to live.   _____ Je commence à écrire en français.

VII.   Proficiency in Reading.

Directions: In the following passage there are ten numbered blank spaces. Each space represents a missing word. Four possible completions are provided for each. Only one of them is grammatically correct and makes sense in the context of the passage.

First, read the passage in its entirety to determine its general meaning. Then read it a second time. Choose the completion that makes the best sense and is grammatically correct. Write its letter in the space provided.

Madame Paquet est malade _____ hier. Elle _____ mangé quelque chose qui _____

1. A. de	2. A. est	3. A. la
B. d'	B. a	B. le
C. pour	C. va	C. lui
D. depuis	D. ai	D. leur

a donné mal à l'estomac. Elle est _____ dans son lit. Son mari a _____ le docteur pour

4. A. souffrant	5. A. appeler
B. souffrante	B. appelé
C. souffrants	C. appelée
D. souffrantes	D. appelés

lui _____ un médicament. Le docteur va _____ dans quelques minutes. Madame

6. A. donner	7. A. vient
B. donné	B. viens
C. donnée	C. venu
D. donnés	D. venir

Paquet _____ attend patiemment _____ vingt minutes.

8. A. le	9. A. depuis
B. l'	B. pour
C. lui	C. à
D. les	D. de

Ah! Le docteur vient d'arriver! Il est dans la chambre de Madame Paquet. Monsieur Paquet est

avec _____ .

10. A. ils
    B. les
    C. eux
    D. leur

VIII. Proficiency in Writing

Directions: Of the following eight situations, select six and write your statement on the lines on this and the next page. For each situation, write three short sentences.

Situation 1. You are talking to your friend Guy about your plans for the summer vacation.

Situation 2. You are taking a summer course in conversational French at the Alliance Française in Paris. You are staying with a French family. Robert, a member of the family, is in the hospital. He broke a leg in a car accident. He is at the Hôpital Américain in Neuilly, about a twenty-minute ride by bus from La Tour Eiffel. You are visiting him. What are you saying to him?

Situation 3. You are the president of the French Club. Several new students are present at the first meeting and they are trying to decide whether or not to join the club. They want to know what everybody does in the club. As president, you must tell them what you all do from time to time.

Situation 4. In your French Club students are looking at pictures in an album that one of the students brought to stimulate speaking in French. You are looking at a photo of three children in a park. What are they doing?

Situation 5. You are riding on a bicycle on a country road in France. In front of you is another cyclist with a young boy sitting behind him. The boy has turned his head and is looking at you. What is he saying to you? What are you saying to him?

Situation 6. You are talking to your friend Françoise about the basketball team at your school.

Situation 7. You recently saw a photo in a newspaper of Monsieur Jacques Chirac, the president of France, and Monsieur François Mitterrand, the former French president. They have just come out of the Palais de l'Élysée, the famous residence in Paris. Tell your friend Françoise about it.

Situation 8. Your friends Anne-Marie and Pierre are spending their honeymoon in Paris. Right now they are sitting on a bench enjoying the view of La Cathédrale Notre-Dame de Paris. Describe them to your friend Micheline.

Select six of the eight situations described above and write your three short sentences on the lines.

Situation 1

1. _____

2. _____

3. _____

Situation 2

1. _____

2. _____

3. _____

Situation 3

1. _____

2. _____

3. _____

Situation 4

1. _____

2. _____

3. _____

Situation 5

1. _____

2. _____

3. _____

Situation 6

1. _____

2. _____

3. _____

Situation 7

1. _____

2. _____

3. _____

Situation 8

1. _____

2. _____

3. _____

APPENDIX

French Idioms

Note: qqn stands for **quelqu'un**/someone; **qqch** stands for **quelque chose**/something

With ALLER

aller   to feel (health); **Comment allez-vous?**

aller à la rencontre de qqn   to go to meet someone

aller à pied   to walk, to go on foot

aller chercher   to go get

allons donc!   nonsense! come on, now!

With AVOIR

avoir…ans   to be…years old; **Quel âge avez-vous? J'ai dix-sept ans.**

avoir à + inf.   to have to, to be obliged to + inf.

avoir affaire à qqn   to deal with someone

avoir beau + inf.   to be useless + inf., to do something in vain; **Vous avez beau parler; je ne vous écoute pas** / You are talking in vain; I am not listening to you.

avoir besoin de   to need, to have need of

avoir bonne mine   to look well, to look good (persons)

avoir chaud   to be (feel) warm (persons)

avoir congé   to have a day off, a holiday

avoir de la chance   to be lucky

avoir envie de + inf.   to feel like, to have a desire to

avoir faim   to be (feel) hungry

avoir froid   to be (feel) cold (persons)

avoir hâte   to be in a hurry

avoir honte   to be ashamed of, to feel ashamed

avoir l'air + adj.   to seem, to appear, to look + adj.; **Vous avez l'air malade** / You look sick.

avoir l'air de + inf.   to appear + inf.; **Vous avez l'air d'être malade** / You appear to be sick.

avoir l'habitude de + inf.   to be accustomed to, to be in the habit of; **J'ai l'habitude de faire mes devoirs avant le dîner** / I'm in the habit of doing my homework before dinner.

avoir l'idée de + inf.   to have a notion + inf.

avoir l'intention de + inf.   to intend + inf.

avoir la bonté de + inf.   to have the kindness + inf.

avoir la parole   to have the floor (to speak)

avoir le temps de + inf.   to have (the) time + inf.

avoir lieu   to take place

avoir mal   to feel sick

avoir mal à + (place where it hurts)   to have a pain or ache in…; **J'ai mal à la jambe** / My leg hurts; **J'ai mal au dos** / My back hurts; **J'ai mal au cou** / I have a pain in my neck.

avoir mauvaise mine   to look ill, not to look well

avoir peine à + inf.   to have difficulty in + pres. part.

avoir peur de   to be afraid of

avoir raison   to be right (persons)

avoir soif   to be thirsty

avoir sommeil   to be sleepy

avoir tort   to be wrong (persons)

With ÊTRE

être à l'heure   to be on time

être à qqn   to belong to someone; **Ce livre est à moi** / This book belongs to me.

être à temps   to be in time

être au courant de   to be informed about

être bien   to be comfortable

être bien aise (de)   to be very glad, happy (to)

être d'accord avec   to agree with

être de retour   to be back

être en état de + inf.   to be able + inf.

être en retard   to be late, not to be on time

être en train de + inf.   to be in the act of + pres. part., to be in the process of, to be busy + pres. part.

être en vacances   to be on vacation

être enrhumé   to have a cold, to be sick with a cold

être le bienvenu (la bienvenue)   to be welcomed

être pressé(e)   to be in a hurry

être sur le point de + inf.   to be about + inf.

être temps de + inf.   to be time + inf.

Quelle heure est-il?   What time is it? **Il est une heure** / It is one o'clock; **Il est deux heures** / It is two o'clock.

y être   to be there, to understand it, to get it; **J'y suis!** / I get it! / I understand it!

il était une fois…   Once upon a time there was (there were)…

With FAIRE

Cela ne fait rien   That doesn't matter / That makes no difference.

Comment se fait-il?   How come?

en faire autant   to do the same, to do as much

faire + inf.   to have something done

faire à sa tête   to have one's way

faire attention (à)   to pay attention (to)

faire beau   to be pleasant, nice weather

faire bon accueil   to welcome

faire chaud   to be warm (weather)

faire de son mieux   to do one's best

faire des emplettes; faire des courses; faire du shopping   to do or to go shopping

faire des progrès   to make progress

faire du bien à qqn   to do good for someone; **Cela lui fera du bien** / That will do her (or him) some good.

faire face à   to oppose

faire faire qqch   to have something done or made; **Je me fais faire une robe** / I'm having a dress made (BY SOMEONE) for myself.

faire froid   to be cold (weather)

faire jour   to be daylight

faire la connaissance de qqn   to make the acquaintance of someone, to meet someone for the first time, to become acquainted with someone

faire la cuisine   to do the cooking

faire la queue   to line up, to get in line, to stand in line, to queue up

faire le ménage   to do housework

faire le tour de   to take a stroll, to go around

faire mal à qqn   to hurt, to harm someone

faire nuit   to be night(time)

faire part à qqn   to inform someone

faire part de qqch à qqn   to let someone know about something, to inform, to notify someone of something

faire partie de   to be a part of

faire peur à qqn   to frighten someone

faire plaisir à qqn   to please someone

faire savoir qqch à qqn   to inform someone of something

faire semblant de + inf.   to pretend + inf.

faire ses adieux   to say good-bye

faire son possible   to do one's best

faire un tour   to go for a stroll

faire un voyage   to take a trip

faire une partie de   to play a game of

faire une promenade   to take a walk

faire une promenade en voiture   to go for a drive

faire une question   to ask, to pose a question

faire une visite   to pay a visit

faire venir qqn   to have someone come; **Il a fait venir le docteur** / He had the doctor come.

Faites comme chez vous!   Make yourself at home!

Que faire?   What is to be done?

Quel temps fait-il?   What's the weather like?

Review of Basic Vocabulary by Topics

L'École (School)

le banc *n.,* the seat, the bench
la bibliothèque *n.,* the library
le bureau *n.,* the desk, the office
le cahier *n.,* the notebook
le calendrier *n.,* the calendar
le carnet *n.,* the small notebook
la carte *n.,* the map
la classe *n.,* the class; **la classe de français** French class
le congé *n.,* leave, permission; **jour de congé** day off (from school or work)
la cour *n.,* the playground, the courtyard
la craie *n.,* the chalk
le crayon *n.,* the pencil; **le crayon-feutre** felt-tip pen
les devoirs *n. m.,* homework assignments
la dictée *n.,* the dictation
le drapeau *n.,* the flag

l'école *n. f.,* the school
écrire *v.,* to write
l'élève *n. m. f.,* the pupil
l'encre *n. f.,* the ink
étudier *v.,* to study; **les études** *n. f. pl.,* the studies
l'étudiant *m.,* **l'étudiante** *f., n.,* the student
l'examen *n. m.,* the examination
l'exercice *n. m.,* the exercise
expliquer *v.,* to explain
la faute *n.,* the mistake
la leçon *n.,* the lesson; **leçon de français** French lesson
le livre *n.,* the book
le livret d'exercices *n.,* the workbook
le lycée *n.,* the high school
le maître *m.,* **la maîtresse** *f., n.,* the teacher
le papier *n.,* the paper; **une feuille de papier** a sheet of paper

passer *v.,* to pass; **passer un examen** to take an exam
poser *v.,* to pose; **poser une question** to ask a question
le professeur *m.,* **la professeur-dame, une femme professeur** *f., n.,* the professor
le pupitre *n.,* the desk (student's)
la règle *n.,* the rule, the ruler
répondre *v.,* to respond, to answer, to reply
la réponse *n.,* the answer
réussir *v.,* to succeed; **réussir à un examen** to pass an exam
la salle *n.,* the room; **la salle de classe** the classroom
le stylo *n.,* the pen
le tableau noir *n.,* the blackboard, the chalkboard
l'université *n. f.,* the university
le vocabulaire *n.,* the vocabulary

Les jours de la semaine, les mois de l'année, les saisons, et les jours de fête
(Days of the Week, Months of the Year, Seasons, and Holidays)

Les jours de la semaine

le dimanche, Sunday
le lundi, Monday
le mardi, Tuesday
le mercredi, Wednesday
le jeudi, Thursday
le vendredi, Friday
le samedi, Saturday

Les saisons

le printemps, spring
l'été *(m.),* summer
l'automne *(m.),* autumn, fall
l'hiver *(m.),* winter

Les mois de l'année

janvier, January
février, February
mars, March
avril, April
mai, May
juin, June
juillet, July
août, August
septembre, September
octobre, October
novembre, November
décembre, December

Les jours de fête

fêter *v.,* to celebrate a holiday;
   bonne fête! happy holiday!
l'anniversaire *m.,* anniversary,
   birthday; **bon anniversaire!**
   happy anniversary! *or* happy
   birthday!
le Jour de l'An, New Year's Day
Bonne année! Happy New Year!
les Pâques, Easter; **Joyeuses
   Pâques,** Happy Easter
la Pâque, Passover
le quatorze juillet (Bastille Day),
   July 14, French "Independence
   Day"
les grandes vacances, summer
   vacation
la Toussaint, All Saints' Day (le
   premier novembre)
le Noël, Christmas; **Joyeux Noël!**
   Merry Christmas!
à vous de même! the same to you!

Les légumes, les poissons, les viandes, les produits laitiers, les desserts, les fromages, et les boissons

(Vegetables, Fish, Meats, Dairy Products, Desserts, Cheeses, and Beverages)

Les légumes

l'aubergine *f.,* the eggplant
la carotte, the carrot
le champignon, the mushroom
les épinards *m.,* the spinach
les haricots verts *m.,* the string
  beans
le maïs, the corn
l'oignon *m.,* the onion
les petits pois *m.,* the peas
la pomme de terre, the potato

Les viandes

l'agneau *m.,* the lamb; **la côte
  d'agneau,** the lamb chop
le biftek, the steak
le jambon, the ham
le porc, the pork
le poulet, the chicken
le rosbif, the roast beef
le veau, the veal; **la côte de veau,**
  the veal chop

Les poissons

le maquereau, the mackerel
la morue, the cod
le saumon, the salmon
la sole, the sole
la truite, the trout

Les produits laitiers

le beurre, the butter
la crème, the cream
le fromage, the cheese
le lait, the milk
l'oeuf *m.,* the egg

Les desserts

le fruit, the fruit
le gâteau, the cake; **le gâteau sec,
  le biscuit,** the cookie
la glace, the ice cream
la pâtisserie, the pastry

Les fromages

le brie
le camembert
le gruyère
le petit suisse
le port-salut
le roquefort

Les boissons

la bière, the beer
le cacao, the cocoa
le café, the coffee
le chocolat chaud, the hot chocolate
le cidre, the cider
l'eau minérale *f.,* the mineral water
le jus, the juice; **le jus de tomate,**
  the tomato juice
le thé, the tea
le vin, the wine

Les animaux, les fleurs, les couleurs, les arbres, et les fruits
(Animals, Flowers, Colors, Trees, and Fruits)

Les animaux

l'âne *m.,* the donkey
le chat *m.,* **la chatte** *f.,* the cat
le cheval, the horse
le chien *m.,* **la chienne** *f.,* the dog
le cochon, the pig
le coq, the rooster
l'éléphant *m.,* the elephant
le lapin, the rabbit
le lion, the lion
l'oiseau *m.,* the bird
la poule, the hen
le poulet, the chicken
le renard, the fox
la souris, the mouse
le tigre, the tiger
la vache, the cow

Les fleurs

l'iris *m.,* the iris
le lilas, the lilac
le lis, the lily
la marguerite, the daisy
l'oeillet *m.,* the carnation
la rose, the rose
la tulipe, the tulip
la violette, the violet

Les couleurs

blanc, white
bleu, blue
brun, brown
gris, gray
jaune, yellow
noir, black
rouge, red
vert, green

Les arbres

le bananier, the banana tree
le cerisier, the cherry tree
le citronnier, the lemon tree
l'oranger *m.,* the orange tree
le palmier, the palm tree
le pêcher, the peach tree
le poirier, the pear tree
le pommier, the apple tree

Les fruits

la banane, the banana
la cerise, the cherry
le citron, the lemon; **citron vert,** lime
la fraise, the strawberry
la framboise, the raspberry
l'orange *f.,* the orange
le pamplemousse, the grapefruit
la pêche, the peach
la poire, the pear
la pomme, the apple
le raisin, the grape
la tomate, the tomato

Le corps humain, les vêtements, la toilette
(The Human Body, Clothing, Washing, and Dressing)

Le corps humain

la bouche, mouth
le bras, arm
les cheveux *m.,* hair
le cou, neck
les dents *f.,* teeth
le doigt, finger; **doigt de pied,**
    l'orteil *m.,* toe
l'épaule *f.,* shoulder
l'estomac *m.,* stomach
le genou, knee
la jambe, leg
la langue, tongue
les lèvres *f.,* lips
la main, hand
le menton, chin
le nez, nose
l'oeil *m.,* eye; **les yeux,** eyes
l'oreille *f.,* ear
la peau, skin
le pied, foot
la poitrine, chest
la tête, head
le visage, face

La toilette

se baigner *v.,* to bathe oneself
la baignoire *n.,* the bathtub
le bain *n.,* the bath

la brosse *n.,* the brush; **brosse à
    dents,** toothbrush
brosser *v.,* to brush; **se brosser les
    dents,** to brush one's teeth
la cuvette *n.,* the toilet bowl
le dentifrice *n.,* the toothpaste
le déodorant *n.,* deodorant
déshabiller *v.,* to undress; **se
    déshabiller,** to undress oneself
la douche *n.,* the shower; **prendre
    une douche,** to take a shower
enlever *v.,* to remove, to take off
le gant de toilette *n.,* the washcloth
la glace *n.,* the hand mirror
s'habiller *v.,* to dress oneself
le lavabo *n.,* the washroom,
    washstand
laver *v.,* to wash; **se laver,** to wash
    oneself
mettre *v.,* to put on
le miroir *n.,* the mirror
ôter *v.,* to take off, to remove
le peigne *n.,* the comb; **se peigner
    les cheveux,** to comb one's hair
porter *v.,* to wear
la salle de bains *n.,* the bathroom
le savon *n.,* the soap
la serviette *n.,* the towel
le shampooing *n.,* the shampoo

Les vêtements

le bas, stocking
le béret, beret
la blouse, blouse, smock
le blouson, jacket (often with zipper)
le chandail, sweater
le chapeau, hat
la chaussette, sock
la chaussure, shoe
la chemise, shirt
le collant, pantyhose
le complet, suit
le costume, suit
la cravate, necktie
l'écharpe *f.,* scarf
le gant, glove
le jean, jeans
la jupe, skirt
le maillot de bain, swimsuit
le manteau, coat
le pantalon, trousers, pants
la pantoufle, slipper
le pardessus, overcoat
la poche, pocket
le pullover, pullover or long-sleeved
    sweater
la robe, dress
le slip, underpants
le soulier, shoe
le soutien-gorge, bra
le veston, (suit) coat

La famille, la maison, les meubles
(Family, Home, Furniture)

La famille

le cousin, la cousine, cousin

l'enfant *m. f.,* child

l'époux *m.,* **l'épouse** *f.,* spouse (husband/wife)

la femme, wife

la fille, daughter

le fils, son

le frère, brother; **le beau-frère,** brother-in-law

la grand-mère, grandmother

le grand-père, grandfather

les grands-parents, grandparents

le mari, husband

la mère, la maman, mother; **la belle-mère,** mother-in-law

le neveu, nephew

la nièce, niece

l'oncle *m.,* uncle

le père, le papa, father; **le beau-père,** father-in-law

le petit-fils, grandson

la petite-fille, granddaughter

les petits-enfants, grandchildren

la soeur, sister; **la belle-soeur,** sister-in-law

la tante, aunt

La maison

la cave, the cellar

la chambre, the room; **chambre à coucher,** bedroom

la cheminée, the fireplace, chimney

la cuisine, the kitchen

l'escalier *m.,* the stairs, staircase

la fenêtre, the window

le mur, the wall

la pièce, the room

le plafond, the ceiling

le plancher, the floor

la porte, the door

la salle, the room; **la salle à manger,** the dining room; **la salle de bains,** bathroom

le salon, the living room

le toit, the roof

Les meubles

l'armoire *f.,* the wardrobe closet

le bureau, the desk

le canapé, the sofa, couch

la chaîne stéréo, stereo system

la chaise, the chair

la commode, the dresser, chest of drawers

la couchette, the bunk

l'évier *m.,* the kitchen sink

le fauteuil, the armchair

le four, the oven

la fournaise, the furnace

le fourneau, the kitchen stove, range

la lampe, the lamp

le lit, the bed

le piano, the piano

la table, the table

le tapis, the carpet

le téléphone, the telephone

le téléviseur, the television (set)

La ville, les bâtiments, les magasins, les divers modes de transport
(The City, Buildings, Stores, Various Means of Transportation)

La ville

l'avenue *f.,* the avenue
la boîte aux lettres, the mailbox
la bouche de métro, the subway entrance
le boulevard, the boulevard
le bruit, the noise
la chaussée, the road
défense d'afficher, post no bills
les feux *m.,* the traffic lights
le parc, the park
la pollution, the pollution
la rue, the street
le trottoir, the sidewalk
la voiture de police, the police car

Les bâtiments

la banque, the bank
la bibliothèque, the library
le bureau de poste, the post office
la cathédrale, the cathedral
la chapelle, the chapel
le château, the castle
le cinéma, the movie theatre
l'école *f.,* the school
l'église *f.,* the church
la gare, the railroad station

la grange, the barn
le gratte-ciel, the skyscraper
l'hôpital *m.,* the hospital
l'hôtel *m.,* the hotel
l'hôtel de ville, the city hall
la hutte *f.,* the hut, cabin
l'immeuble d'habitation, the apartment building
le musée, the museum
le palais, the palace
la synagogue, the synagogue
le temple, the temple
le théâtre, the theater
l'usine *f.,* the factory

Les divers modes de transport

l'autobus *m.,* the city bus
l'autocar *m.,* the interurban bus
l'automobile *f.,* the car
l'avion *m.,* the plane
le bateau, the boat
la bicyclette, the bicycle
le camion, the truck
le chemin de fer, the railroad
le métro, the subway
la moto, the motorcycle
le train, the train

le train à grande vitesse (le TGV), high-speed train
le transatlantique, the ocean liner
le vélo, the bike
la voiture, the car

Les magasins

la bijouterie, the jewelry shop
la blanchisserie, the laundry
la boucherie, the butcher shop
la boulangerie, the bakery (mostly for bread)
la boutique, the (small) shop
le bureau de tabac, the tobacco shop
le café, the café
la charcuterie, the pork store, delicatessen
la crémerie, the dairy store
l'épicerie *f.,* the grocery store
le grand magasin, the department store
la librairie, the bookstore
le magasin, the store
la pâtisserie, the pastry shop
la pharmacie, the drugstore
le supermarché, the supermarket

Les métiers et les professions, les langues, les pays, et les continents
(Trades and Professions, Languages, Countries, and Continents)

Les métiers et les professions

l'acteur *m.,* **l'actrice** *f.,* actor, actress

l'agent de police *m.,* police officer

l'auteur, author (of a book) *or* composer (of a song) *or* painter (of a picture)

l'avocat *m.,* **la femme-avocat** *f.,* lawyer

le bijoutier, la bijoutière, jeweler

le blanchisseur, la blanchisseuse, launderer

le boucher, la bouchère, butcher

le boulanger, la boulangère, baker

le charcutier, la charcutière, pork butcher

le chauffeur, driver, chauffeur

le coiffeur, la coiffeuse, hairdresser, barber

le, la dentiste, dentist

l'épicier, l'épicière, grocer

le facteur, letter carrier

le fermier, la fermière, farmer

le, la libraire, bookseller

le maître, la maîtresse, teacher

le marchand, la marchande, merchant

le médecin, la femme-médecin, doctor

le pâtissier, la pâtissière, pastry chef

le pharmacien, la pharmacienne, pharmacist

le professeur, la femme-professeur, professor

le sénateur, senator

le serveur, la serveuse, waiter, waitress

le tailleur, la tailleuse, tailor

le vendeur, la vendeuse, salesperson

Les langues (all are masculine)

allemand, German

anglais, English

chinois, Chinese

danois, Danish

espagnol, Spanish; **castillan,** Castilian (Spanish)

français, French

grec ancien, ancient Greek

grec moderne, modern Greek

hébreu, Hebrew

italien, Italian

japonais, Japanese

latin, Latin

norvégien, Norwegian

portugais, Portuguese

russe, Russian

suédois, Swedish

Les pays, les continents

l'Allemagne *f.,* Germany

l'Angleterre *f.,* England

l'Australie *f.,* Australia

la Belgique, Belgium

le Canada, Canada

la Chine, China

le Danemark, Denmark

l'Espagne *f.,* Spain

les États-Unis *m.,* United States

l'Europe *f.,* Europe

la France, France

la Grande-Bretagne, Great Britain

la Grèce, Greece

la Hollande, Holland

l'Irlande *f.,* Ireland

l'Israël *m.,* Israel

l'Italie *f.,* Italy

le Japon, Japan

le Luxembourg, Luxembourg

le Mexique, Mexico

la Norvège, Norway

la Pologne, Poland

le Portugal, Portugal

la Russie, Russia

la Suède, Sweden

la Suisse, Switzerland

La technologie
(Technology)

la banque de données, database
le billet électronique, electronic ticket, e-ticket
la boîte vocale, voice mail
le bouton de démarrage, power button
le bouton du pavé tactile, touch pad button
la calculatrice, calculator
la carte bancaire/la carte de crédit, credit card
la carte d'embarquement, boarding pass
le CD, CD
le cédérom, le CD-ROM, CD-ROM
le clavardage, chat (Internet)
clavarder, to chat (Internet)
le clavier, keyboard
le clavier d'identification personnelle, PIN pad
le commerce électronique, e-commerce
le contrôle de sécurité, security check (in airports, public buildings)
le courriel, e-mail
le courrier électronique, e-mail
le cybercafé, cybercafé
le disque dur, hard drive

le disque, compact CD
le disque DVD, DVD
l'écran *m.,* display screen (computer)
l'écran *m.* **plasma,** plasma screen, plasma display
l'écran *m.* **tactile,** touch screen
le fichier MP3, MP3
le guichet automatique (bancaire), ATM (automated teller machine)
l'Internet *m.,* Internet
l'iPod *m.,* iPod
le lecteur de CD, CD player
le lecteur de DVD, DVD player
le lecteur multimédia, multimedia player
la machine à rayons X, X-ray machine (in airports)
la messagerie, voice mail
naviguer (sur Internet), to navigate, to surf the Internet
le NIP (le numéro d'identification personnelle), PIN
l'ordinateur *m.,* computer
l'ordinateur *m.* **de bureau** *m.,* desktop computer
l'ordinateur *m.* **de poche,** PDA (personal digital assistant), handheld computer

l'ordinateur *m.* **portable,** laptop computer (A laptop computer may just be called "un portable." The same word is sometimes used for a cell phone.)
la pagette, pager
le pavé tactile, touch pad
le portable, cell phone **(le téléphone portable),** laptop computer **(l'ordinateur** *m.* **portable)**
le répondeur, answering machine
le sac de vol, carry-on bag
le salon de clavardage, chat room
la souris, mouse
surfer, to surf (the Internet)
télécopier, to fax
la télécopie, fax
le télécopieur, fax machine
le téléphone portable, cell phone (A cell phone may just be called "un portable." The same word is sometimes used for a laptop computer.)
le téléviseur à écran plasma, plasma screen television set
la touche d'appel, talk key
la touche de sélection, selection key

Definitions of Basic Grammatical Terms with Examples

Active voice

When we speak or write in the active voice, the subject of the verb performs the action. The action falls on the direct object.

Example:
Everyone loves Janine. / **Tout le monde aime Janine.**

The subject is *everyone*/**tout le monde.** The verb is *loves*/**aime.** The direct object is *Janine.*

Review **aimer** in the verb tables. See also *passive voice* in this list. Compare the preceding sentence with the example in the passive voice.

Adjective

An adjective is a word that modifies a noun or a pronoun. In grammar, to modify a word means to describe, limit, expand, or make the meaning particular. In French an adjective agrees in gender (masculine or feminine) and in number (singular or plural) with the noun or pronoun it modifies.

Examples:
This garden is beautiful. / **Ce jardin est beau.**
She is beautiful. / **Elle est belle.**

The adjective *beautiful*/**beau** modifies the noun *garden*/**jardin.** It is masculine singular because **le jardin** is masculine singular. The adjective *beautiful*/**belle** modifies the pronoun *She*/**Elle.** It is feminine singular because *she* is feminine singular.

Review **être** in the verb tables. Review adjectives in Work Units 18 and 19. In French there are different kinds of adjectives. *See also* comparative adjective, demonstrative adjective, descriptive adjective, interrogative adjective, limiting adjective, possessive adjective, superlative adjective.

Adverb

An adverb is a word that modifies a verb, an adjective, or another adverb. An adverb says something about how, when, where, to what extent, or in what way.

Examples:
Jane runs swiftly. / **Jeanne court rapidement.**
The adverb *swiftly*/**rapidement** modifies the verb *runs*/**court.** The adverb shows *how* she runs.

Jack is a very good friend. / **Jacques est un très bon ami.**
The adverb *very*/**très** modifies the adjective *good*/**bon.** The adverb shows *how good* a friend he is.

The boy is eating too fast now. / **Le garçon mange trop vite maintenant.**
The adverb *too*/**trop** modifies the adverb *fast*/**vite.** The adverb shows *to what extent* he is eating *fast.* The adverb *now*/**maintenant** tells us *when.*

The post office is there. / **Le bureau de poste est là.**
The adverb *there*/**là** modifies the verb *is*/**est.** It tells us *where* the post office is.

Mary writes carefully. / **Marie écrit soigneusement.**
The adverb *carefully*/**soigneusement** modifies the verb *writes*/**écrit**. It tells us *in what way* she writes.

Review adverbs in Work Unit 20. Review **courir, écrire, être, manger** in the verb tables.

Affirmative statement, negative statement

A statement in the affirmative is the opposite of a statement in the negative. To negate an affirmative statement is to make it negative.

Examples:
In the affirmative: I like chocolate ice cream. / **J'aime la glace au chocolat.**
In the negative: I do not like chocolate ice cream. / **Je n'aime pas la glace au chocolat.**

Review **aimer** in the verb tables.

Agreement of adjective with noun

Agreement is made on the adjective with the noun it modifies in gender (masculine or feminine) and number (singular or plural).

Examples:
a white house / **une maison blanche.** The adjective **blanche** is feminine singular because the noun **une maison** is feminine singular.
two white houses / **deux maisons blanches.** The adjective **blanches** is feminine plural because the noun **maisons** is feminine plural.

Review Work Unit 18.

Agreement of past participle of a reflexive verb with its reflexive pronoun

Agreement is made on the past participle of a reflexive verb with its reflexive pronoun in gender (masculine or feminine) and number (singular or plural) if that pronoun is the *direct object* of the verb. The agreement is determined by looking at the subject to see its gender and number, which is the same as its reflexive pronoun. If the reflexive pronoun is the *indirect object*, an agreement is *not* made.

Examples:
to wash oneself / **se laver**
She washed herself. / **Elle s'est lavée.**

There is a feminine agreement on the past participle **lavée** (added **e**) with the reflexive pronoun **se** (here, **s'**) because it serves as a direct object pronoun. What or whom did she wash? Herself, which is expressed in **se (s').**

But:

She washed her hair. / **Elle s'est lavé les cheveux.**
There is no feminine agreement on the past participle **lavé** here because the reflexive pronoun (**se**, here, **s'**) serves as an *indirect object*. The direct object is **les cheveux** and it is stated *after* the verb. What did she wash? She washed her hair *on herself (s').*

Review reflexive verbs in Work Unit 7. Review **se laver** and other reflexive verbs, in the verb tables. *See also* reflexive pronoun and reflexive verb.

Agreement of past participle with its preceding direct object

Agreement is made on the past participle with its direct object in gender (masculine or feminine) and number (singular or plural) when the verb is conjugated with **avoir** in the compound tenses. Agreement is made when the direct object, if there is one, *precedes* the verb.

Examples:
Where are the little cakes? Paul ate them. / **Où sont les petits gâteaux? Paul les a mangés.**

The verb **a mangés** is in the *passé composé*; **manger** is conjugated with **avoir**. There is a plural agreement on the past participle **mangés** (added **s**) because the *preceding* direct object *them*/**les** is masculine plural, referring to *les petits gâteaux,* which is masculine plural.

Who wrote the letters? Robert wrote them. / **Qui a écrit les lettres? Robert les a écrites.**

The verb **a écrites** is in the *passé composé*; **écrire** is conjugated with **avoir**. There is a feminine plural agreement on the past participle **écrites** (added **e** and **s**) because the *preceding* direct object *them*/**les** is feminine plural, referring to *les lettres,* which is feminine plural. A past participle functions as an adjective. An agreement in gender and number is *not* made with *an indirect object. See* indirect object noun, indirect object pronoun. Review the **passé composé** in Work Units 12 and 13. Review **écrire, être, manger** in the verb tables. *See also* direct object noun, direct object pronoun.

Agreement of past participle with the subject

Agreement is made on the past participle with the subject in gender (masculine or feminine) and number (singular or plural) when the verb is conjugated with **être** in the compound tenses.

Examples:
She went to Paris. / **Elle est allée à Paris.**

The verb **est allée** is in the *passé composé*; **aller** is conjugated with **être**. There is a feminine agreement on the past participle **allée** (added **e**) because the subject **elle** is feminine singular.

The boys have arrived. / **Les garçons sont arrivés.**

The verb **sont arrivés** is in the *passé composé*; **arriver** is conjugated with **être**. There is a plural agreement on the past participle **arrivés** (added **s**) because the subject **les garçons** is masculine plural. Review Work Unit 12 to find out about verbs conjugated with either **avoir** or **être** to form the **passé composé** tense. Review **aller** and **arriver** in the verb tables. *See also* past participle and subject.

Agreement of verb with its subject

A verb agrees in person (1st, 2nd, or 3rd) and in number (singular or plural) with its subject.

Examples:
Does he always tell the truth? / **Dit-il toujours la vérité?**

The verb **dit** (of **dire**) is third person singular because the subject **il**/*he* is third person singular.

Where are they going? / **Où vont-ils?**

The verb **vont** (of **aller**) is third person plural because the subject **ils**/*they* is third person plural. Review **aller** and **dire** in the verb tables. For subject pronouns in the singular and plural, review Work Unit 4.

Antecedent

An antecedent is a word to which a relative pronoun refers. It comes *before* the pronoun.

Examples:
The girl who is laughing over there is my sister. / **La jeune fille qui rit là-bas est ma soeur.**

The antecedent is *girl*/**la jeune fille.** The relative pronoun *who*/**qui** refers to the girl.

The car that I bought is expensive. / **La voiture que j'ai achetée est chère.**

The antecedent is *car*/**la voiture.** The relative pronoun *that*/**que** refers to the car. Note also that the past participle **achetée** is feminine singular because it refers to *la voiture* (fem. sing.), which precedes the verb. Review **acheter** and **rire** in the verb tables. *See also* relative pronoun.

Auxiliary verb

An auxiliary verb is a helping verb. In English grammar it is *to have.* In French grammar it is **avoir** (to have) or **être** (to be). An auxiliary verb is used to help form the **passé composé** tense.

Examples:
I have eaten. / **J'*ai* mangé.**
She has left. / **Elle *est* partie.**

Review Work Unit 12 to find out about verbs conjugated with either **avoir** or **être** as helping verbs to form the **passé composé.** Also, review **manger** and **partir** in the verb tables.

Cardinal number

A cardinal number is a number that expresses an amount, such as *one, two, three,* and so on. Review Work Unit 8. *See also* ordinal number.

Causative *faire*

In English grammar, a causative verb causes something to be done. In French grammar the idea is the same. The subject of the verb causes the action expressed in the verb to be carried out by someone else.

Examples:
Mrs. Roth makes her students work in French class. / **Madame Roth fait travailler ses élèves dans la classe de français.**
Mr. Reis is having a house built. / **Monsieur Reis fait construire une maison.**

Review **construire, faire,** and **travailler** in the verb tables.

Clause

A clause is a group of words that contains a subject and a predicate. A predicate may contain more than one word. A conjugated verb form is revealed in the predicate.

Example:
Mrs. Coty lives in a small apartment. / **Madame Coty demeure dans un petit appartement.**

The subject is *Mrs. Coty*/**Madame Coty**. The predicate is *lives in a small apartment*/**demeure dans un petit appartement.** The verb is *lives*/**demeure.**

See also dependent clause, independent clause, predicate.

Comparative adjective

When making a comparison between two persons or things, an adjective is used to express the degree of comparison in the following ways.

Examples:
Of the same degree of comparison: Raymond is *as tall as* his father. / **Raymond est *aussi grand que* son père.**

Of a lesser degree of comparison: Monique is *less intelligent than* her sister. / **Monique *est moins intelligente que* sa soeur.**

Of a higher degree of comparison: This apple is *more delicious than* that apple. / **Cette pomme-ci est *plus délicieuse que* cette pomme-là.**

Review comparative and superlative adjectives in Work Unit 19. *See also* superlative adjective.

Comparative adverb

An adverb is compared in the same way as an adjective is compared. *See* comparative adjective.

Examples:
Of the same degree of comparison: Mr. Bernard speaks *as fast as* Mr. Claude. / **Monsieur Bernard parle *aussi vite que* Monsieur Claude.**

Of a lesser degree of comparison: Alice studies *less seriously than* her sister. / **Alice étudie *moins sérieusement que* sa soeur.**

Of a higher degree of comparison: Albert works *more slowly than* his brother. / **Albert travaille *plus lentement que* son frère.**

Review comparative and superlative adverbs in Work Unit 20. Review **étudier, parler, travailler** in the verb tables. *See also* superlative adverb.

Complex sentence

A complex sentence contains one independent clause and one or more dependent clauses.

Examples:
One independent clause and one dependent clause: Jack is handsome but his brother isn't. / **Jacques est beau mais son frère ne l'est pas.**

The independent clause is *Jack is handsome*. It makes sense when it stands alone because it expresses a complete thought. The dependent clause is *but his brother isn't*. The dependent clause, which is introduced by the conjunction *but*, does not make complete sense when it stands alone because it *depends* on the thought expressed in the independent clause.

One independent clause and two dependent clauses: Mary gets good grades in school because she studies but her sister never studies. / **Marie reçoit de bonnes notes à l'école parce qu'elle étudie mais sa soeur n'étudie jamais.**

The independent clause is *Mary gets good grades in school*. It makes sense when it stands alone because it expresses a complete thought. The first dependent clause is *because she studies*. This dependent clause, which is introduced by the conjunction *because*, does not make complete sense when it stands alone because it *depends* on the thought expressed in the independent clause. The second dependent clause is *but her sister never studies*. That dependent clause, which is introduced by the conjunction *but*, does not make complete sense either when it stands alone because it *depends* on the thought expressed in the independent clause. Review **étudier** and **recevoir** in the verb tables. *See also* dependent clause, independent clause.

Compound sentence

A compound sentence contains two or more independent clauses.

> *Example:*
> Mrs. Dubois went to the supermarket, she bought some groceries, and then she returned home. / **Madame Dubois est allée au supermarché, elle a acheté des provisions, et puis elle est rentrée chez elle.**

This compound sentence contains three independent clauses. They are independent because they make sense when they stand alone. Review the **passé composé** in Work Unit 12. Review **acheter, aller, rentrer** in the verb tables. *See also* clause, independent clause.

Conjugation

The conjugation of a verb is the fixed order of all its forms showing their inflections (changes) in the three persons of the singular and the three persons of the plural in a particular tense.

In French there are three major types of regular verb conjugations:

> 1st conjugation type: regular verbs that end in **er,** for example, **donner.**
>
> 2nd conjugation type: regular verbs that end in **ir,** for example, **finir.**
>
> 3rd conjugation type: regular verbs that end in **re,** for example, **vendre.**

Review Work Units 4, 5, 6. Review also the verb tables for the conjugation of verbs used in this book.

Conjunction

A conjunction is a word that connects words or groups of words.

> *Examples:*
> and/**et,** or/**ou,** but/**mais**
> You *and* I are going downtown. / **Toi *et* moi, nous allons en ville.**
> You can stay home *or* you can come with us. / **Tu peux rester à la maison *ou* tu peux venir avec nous.**

Review **aller, pouvoir, rester, venir** in the verb tables.

Declarative sentence

A declarative sentence makes a statement.

> *Example:*
> I have finished the work. / **J'ai fini le travail.**

Review the **passé composé** in Work Unit 12. Review **finir** in the verb tables.

Definite article

The definite article in French has four forms and they all mean *the*.

> They are: **le, la, l', les,** as in:
> **le livre**/the book, **la maison**/the house, **l'école**/the school, **les enfants**/the children

Review Work Units 1, 2, 3. The definite articles are also used as direct object pronouns. *See* direct object pronoun.

Demonstrative adjective

A demonstrative adjective is an adjective that points out. It is placed in front of a noun.

> *Examples:*
> this book/**ce livre;** this hotel/**cet hôtel;** this child/**cet enfant;** this house/**cette maison;** these flowers/**ces fleurs**

Review Work Unit 19.

Demonstrative pronoun

A demonstrative pronoun is a pronoun that points out. It takes the place of a noun. It agrees in gender and number with the noun it replaces.

> *Examples:*
> I have two apples; do you prefer *this one* or *that one?* / **J'ai deux pommes; préférez-vous celle-ci ou celle-là?**
> Sorry, but I prefer *those.* / **Je regrette, mais je préfère celles-là.**
> Do you like the ones that are on the table? / **Aimez-vous celles qui sont sur la table?**

Review **aimer, avoir, être, préférer, regretter** in the verb tables. For demonstrative pronouns that are neuter, *see* neuter.

Dependent clause

A dependent clause is a group of words that contains a subject and a predicate. It does not express a complete thought when it stands alone. It is called *dependent* because it depends on the independent clause for a complete meaning. Subordinate clause is another term for dependent clause.

> *Example:*
> Mary is absent today because she is sick. / **Marie est absente aujourd'hui parce qu'elle est malade.**

The independent clause is *Mary is absent today.* The dependent clause is *because she is sick.* Review **être** in the verb tables. *See also* clause, independent clause.

Descriptive adjective

A descriptive adjective is an adjective that describes a person, place, or thing.

> *Examples:*
> a pretty girl/**une jolie jeune fille;** a handsome boy/**un beau garçon;** a small house/**une petite maison;** a big city/**une grande ville;** an expensive car/**une voiture chère.**

Review Work Unit 18. *See also* adjective.

Direct object noun

A direct object noun receives the action of the verb *directly*. That is why it is called a *direct* object, as opposed to an indirect object. A direct object noun is normally placed *after* the verb.

Examples:
I am writing a letter./**J'écris une lettre.**

The subject is *I*/**J' (Je).** The verb is *am writing*/**écris.** The direct object is the noun *letter*/**une lettre.**

I wrote a letter./**J'ai écrit une lettre.**

The subject is *I*/**J' (Je).** The verb is *wrote*/**ai écrit.** The direct object is the noun *letter*/**une lettre.**

Review Work Unit 13. Also, review **écrire** in the verb tables. *See also* direct object pronoun.

Direct object pronoun

A direct object pronoun receives the action of the verb *directly*. It takes the place of a direct object noun. In French a pronoun that is a direct object of a verb is ordinarily placed *in front of* the verb.

Example:
I am reading it [the letter]. / **Je *la* lis.**

A direct object pronoun is placed *after* the verb and joined with a hyphen *in the affirmative imperative.*

Example:
Write it [the letter] now. / **Écrivez-*la* maintenant.**

Review Work Unit 13. Also, review **écrire** and **lire** in the verb tables. The direct object pronouns are summed up here:

Person	Singular		Plural	
1st	**me (m')**	me	**nous**	us
2nd	**te (t')**	you *(fam.)*	**vous**	you *(sing. polite or pl.)*
3rd	**le (l')**	him, it (person or thing)	**les**	them (persons or things)
	la (l')	her, it (person or thing)		

See also imperative. Review the imperative (command) in Work Units 10 and 11. Also, review word order in a sentence in Work Unit 14.

Disjunctive pronoun

In French grammar a disjunctive pronoun is a pronoun that is stressed; in other words, emphasis is placed on it.

Examples:
I speak well; *he* does not speak well. / *Moi,* **je parle bien;** *lui,* **il ne parle pas bien.**
Talk to me. / **Parlez-*moi.***

A disjunctive pronoun is also object of a preposition.

Examples:
She is talking with me. / **Elle parle** *avec moi.*
I always think of you. / **Je pense toujours** *à toi.*

The disjunctive pronouns are summed up here:

Person	Singular		Plural	
1st	**moi**	me, I	**nous**	us, we
2nd	**toi**	you *(fam.)*	**vous**	you *(sing. polite or pl.)*
3rd	**soi** **lui** **elle**	oneself him, he her, she	**eux** **elles**	them, they *(m.)* them, they *(f.)*

Review **parler** and **penser** in the verb tables. Review Work Unit 17. Also review word order in a sentence in Work Unit 14.

Ending of a verb

In French grammar the ending of a verb form changes according to the person and number of the subject and the tense of the verb.

Example:
To form the present indicative tense of a regular **-er** type verb like **parler,** drop the **er** ending of the infinitive and add the following endings: **-e, -es, -e** for the first, second, and third persons of the singular; **-ons, -ez, -ent** for the first, second, and third persons of the plural.

You then get: **je parle, tu parles, il (elle, on) parle;**
nous parlons, vous parlez, ils (elles) parlent

Review Work Units 4, 5, 6. Review **parler** in the verb tables. *See also* stem of a verb.

Feminine

In French grammar the gender of a noun, pronoun, or adjective is feminine or masculine, not female or male.

Examples:

	Masculine				Feminine		
noun	**pronoun**	**adjective**		**noun**	**pronoun**	**adjective**	
le garçon *the boy*	**il** *he*	**grand** *tall*		**la femme** *the woman*	**elle** *she*	**grande** *tall*	
le livre *the book*	**il** *it*	**petit** *small*		**la voiture** *the car*	**elle** *it*	**petite** *small*	

See also gender.

Gender

In French and English grammar, gender means masculine or feminine.

Examples:
Masculine: the boy/**le garçon;** he, it/**il;** the rooster/**le coq;** the book/**le livre**
Feminine: the girl/**la jeune fille;** she, it/**elle;** the hen/**la poule;** the house/**la maison**

Gerund

In English grammar, a gerund is a word formed from a verb. It ends in *ing.* Actually, it is the present participle of a verb. But it is not used as a verb. It is used as a noun.

Example:
Seeing is believing. / **Voir c'est croire.**

However, in French grammar, the infinitive form of the verb is used, as in the preceding example, when the verb is used as a noun. In French, *seeing is believing* is expressed as *to see is to believe.*

The French gerund is also a word formed from a verb. It ends in ***ant.*** It is also the present participle of a verb. As a gerund, it is normally preceded by the preposition **en.**

Example:
En partant, il a fait ses excuses. / While leaving, he made his excuses.

Review **faire** and **partir** in the verb tables. *See also* present participle.

Imperative

The imperative is a mood, not a tense. It is used to express a command. In French it is used in the second person of the singular **(tu),** the second person of the plural **(vous),** and in the first person of the plural **(nous).** Review the imperative (command) with examples in Work Units 10 and 11. *See also* person (1st, 2nd, 3rd).

Indefinite article

In English the indefinite articles are *a, an*, as in *a book, an apple.* They are indefinite because they do not refer to any definite or particular noun.

In French there are two indefinite articles in the singular: one in the masculine form **(un)** and one in the feminine form **(une).**

Examples:
Masculine singular: **un livre/***a book*
Feminine singular: **une pomme/***an apple*

In French they both change to **des** in the plural.

Examples:
I have a brother. / **J'ai un frère;** I have brothers. / **J'ai des frères.**
I have a sister. / **J'ai une soeur;** I have sisters. / **J'ai des soeurs.**
I have an apple. / **J'ai une pomme;** I have apples. / **J'ai des pommes.**

Review Work Units 1, 2, 3. Review **avoir** in the verb tables. *See also* definite article.

Indefinite pronoun

An indefinite pronoun is a pronoun that does not refer to any definite or particular noun.

Examples:
something/**quelque chose;** someone, somebody/**quelqu'un, quelqu'une;** one, "they"/**on** (3rd pers., sing.), as in **On ne sait jamais**/One never knows; **On dit qu'il va neiger/**They say it's going to snow; each one/**chacun, chacune;** anything/**n'importe quoi.**

Independent clause

An independent clause is a group of words that contains a subject and a predicate. It expresses a complete thought when it stands alone.

Example:
The cat is sleeping under the bed. / **Le chat dort sous le lit.**

Review **dormir** in the verb tables. *See also* clause, dependent clause, predicate.

Indicative mood

The indicative mood is used in sentences that make a statement or ask a question. The indicative mood is used most of the time when we speak or write in English or French.

Examples:
I am going home now. / **Je vais chez moi maintenant.**
Where are you going? / **Où allez-vous?**

Review **aller** in the verb tables.

Indirect object noun

An indirect object noun receives the action of the verb *indirectly*.

Example:
I am writing a letter to Mary *or* I am writing Mary a letter. / **J'écris une lettre à Marie.**

The subject is *I*/**Je.** The verb is *am writing*/**écris.** The direct object noun is *a letter*/**une lettre.** The indirect object noun is *to Mary*/**à Marie.** An agreement is not made with an indirect object noun. Review Work Unit 14. *See also* indirect object pronoun, direct object noun, direct object pronoun.

Indirect object pronoun

An indirect object pronoun takes the place of an indirect object noun. It receives the action of the verb *indirectly*. In French a pronoun that is the indirect object of a verb is ordinarily placed *in front of* the verb.

Example:
I am writing a letter to her *or* I am writing her a letter. / **Je lui écris une lettre.**

The indirect object pronoun is *(to) her*/**lui.**

An agreement is not made with an indirect object pronoun. An indirect object pronoun is placed *after* the verb and joined with a hyphen *in the affirmative imperative.*

Example:
Write to her now./**Écris-lui maintenant.**

The indirect object pronouns are summed up here:

Person	Singular		Plural	
1st	**me (m')**	to me	**nous**	to us
2nd	**te (t')**	to you *(fam.)*	**vous**	to you *(sing. polite or pl.)*
3rd	**lui**	to him, to her	**leur**	to them

Review Work Unit 14. Also review the imperative (command) in Work Units 10 and 11. *See also* indirect object noun.

Infinitive

An infinitive is a verb form. In English, it is normally stated with the preposition *to,* as in *to talk, to finish, to sell.* In French, the infinitive form of a verb consists of three major types: those of the first conjugation that end in **-er,** those of the second conjugation that end in **-ir,** and those of the third conjugation that end in **-re.**

Examples:
parler/*to talk, to speak*; **finir**/*to finish*; **vendre**/*to sell*

Review these verbs in the verb tables.

Interjection

An interjection is a word that expresses emotion, a feeling of joy, of sadness, an exclamation of surprise, and other exclamations consisting of one or two words.

Examples:
Ah!/**Ah!**   Oh!/**Oh!**   Darn it!/**Zut!**   Whew!/**Ouf!**   My God!/**Mon Dieu!**

Interrogative adjective

An interrogative adjective is an adjective used in a question. It agrees in gender and number with the noun it modifies.

Examples:
What book do you want? / *Quel* **livre désirez-vous?**
What time is it? / *Quelle* **heure est-il?**

Review Work Unit 19. Also, review **désirer** and **être** in the verb tables.

Interrogative adverb

An interrogative adverb is an adverb that introduces a question. As an adverb, it modifies the verb.

Examples:
How are you? / *Comment* **allez-vous?**
How much does this book cost? / *Combien* **coûte ce livre?**
When are you leaving? / *Quand* **partez-vous?**

Review **aller, coûter, partir** in the verb tables.

Interrogative pronoun

An interrogative pronoun is a pronoun that asks a question. There are interrogative pronouns that refer to persons and those that refer to things.

Examples:
Who is on the phone? / *Qui* **est à l'appareil?**
What are you saying? / *Que* **dites-vous?** or *Qu'est-ce que* **vous dites?**

Review Work Unit 15. Also, review **dire, être** in the verb tables.

Interrogative sentence

An interrogative sentence asks a question.

Example:
What are you doing? / **Que faites-vous?** or **Qu'est-ce que vous faites?**

Review Work Unit 15. Also, review **faire** in the verb tables.

Intransitive verb

An intransitive verb is a verb that does not take a direct object.

Example:
The professor is talking too fast. / **Le professeur parle trop rapidement.**

An intransitive verb takes an indirect object.

Example:
The professor is talking to us. / **Le professeur nous parle.**

Review **parler** in the verb tables. *See also* indirect object pronoun and transitive verb.

Irregular verb

An irregular verb is a verb that does not follow a fixed pattern in its conjugation in the various verb tenses.

Examples of basic irregular verbs in French:
aller/to go   **avoir**/to have   **être**/to be   **faire**/to do, to make

Review irregular verbs in the present indicative tense and the imperative (command) in Work Unit 11. Review the verb tables. *See also* conjugation, regular verb.

Limiting adjective

A limiting adjective is an adjective that limits a quantity.

Example:
three tickets/**trois billets**

Review numbers in Work Unit 8.

Main clause

Main clause is another term for independent clause. *See* independent clause.

Masculine

In French grammar the gender of a noun, pronoun, or adjective is masculine or feminine, not male or female. For examples, *see* gender.

Mood of verbs

Some grammarians use the term *the mode* instead of *the mood* of a verb. Either term means *the manner or way* a verb is expressed. In English and in French grammar, a verb expresses an action or state of being in the following three moods (modes, *ways*): the indicative mood, the imperative mood, and the subjunctive mood. In French grammar, there is also the infinitive mood when the whole infinitive is used, e.g., **voir, croire,** as in **Voir c'est croire**/*Seeing is believing (to see is to believe).* Most of the time in English and French, we speak and write in the indicative mood.

Negative statement, affirmative statement

See affirmative statement, negative statement

Neuter

A word that is neuter is neither masculine nor feminine. Common neuter demonstrative pronouns are **ce (c')**/*it,* **ceci**/*this,* **cela**/*that,* **ça**/*that.* They are invariable, which means they do not change in gender and number.

> *Examples:*
> It's not true/**Ce n'est pas vrai;** it is true/**c'est vrai;** this is true/**ceci est vrai;** that is true/**cela est vrai;** what is that?/**qu'est-ce que c'est que ça?**

For demonstrative pronouns that are not neuter, *see* demonstrative pronoun.

There is also the neuter pronoun **le,** as in **Je le crois** / I believe it; **Je le pense** / I think so.

Review Work Unit 16.

Noun

A noun is a word that names a person, animal, place, thing, condition or state, or quality.

> *Examples:*
> the man/**l'homme,** the woman/**la femme,** the horse/**le cheval,** the house/**la maison,**
> the book/**le livre,** happiness/**le bonheur,** excellence/**l'excellence** *(fem.)*

In French the noun **le nom** is the word for name and noun. Review Work Units 1, 2, 3.

Number

In English and French grammar, number means singular or plural.

Examples:

Masc. sing.:	the boy/**le garçon**; the arm/**le bras**; the eye/**l'oeil**
Masc. pl.:	the boys/**les garçons**; the arms/**les bras**; the eyes/**les yeux**
Fem. sing.:	the girl/**la jeune fille**; the house/**la maison**; the hen/**la poule**
Fem. pl.:	the girls/**les jeunes filles**; the houses/**les maisons**; the hens/**les poules**

Ordinal number

An ordinal number expresses position in a series, such as *first, second, third,* and so on. In English and French grammar we talk about first person, second person, third person singular or plural regarding subjects and verbs. Review the ordinal numbers in Work Unit 8. *See also* cardinal number, and person (1st, 2nd, 3rd).

Orthographical changes in verb forms

An orthographical change in a verb form is a change in spelling.

Examples:

The second letter **c** in the verb **commencer**/*to begin* changes to **ç** if the letter after it is **a, o,** or **u,** as in ***nous commençons***/*we begin.* The reason for this spelling change is to preserve the sound of **s** as it is pronounced in the infinitive form **commencer.**

Ordinarily, when **a, o,** or **u** follow the letter **c,** the **c** is pronounced as in the sound of **k.** The mark under the letter **ç** is called **une cédille**/*cedilla.* Some linguists say it is the lower part of the letter **s** and it tells you to pronounce **ç** as an **s** sound. Other linguists say that the letter **ç** was borrowed from the Greek alphabet, which represents the sound of **s.**

The verb **s'appeler**/*to call oneself, to be named* contains a single **l.** When a verb form is stressed on the syllable containing one **l,** it doubles, as in **je m'appelle...**/*I call myself..., my name is...*

Review orthographically changing verbs in Work Unit 22.

Partitive

In French grammar the partitive denotes a *part* of a whole. In English we express the partitive by saying *some* or *any* in front of the noun. In French we use the following partitive forms in front of the noun:

Masculine singular: **du** or **de l'**   *Feminine singular:* **de la** or **de l'**

Masculine or feminine plural: **des**

Examples:
I have some coffee. / **J'ai du café.**
Bring me some water, please. / **Apportez-moi de l'eau, s'il vous plaît.**
Is there any meat? / **Y a-t-il de la viande?**
Do you have any candies? / **Avez-vous des bonbons?**

In the negative, these partitive forms change to **de** or **d':**
I don't have any coffee. / **Je n'ai pas de café.**
I don't want any water. / **Je ne veux pas d'eau.**
There isn't any meat. / **Il n'y a pas de viande.**
No, I don't have any candies. / **Non, je n'ai pas de bonbons.**

Review the partitive in Work Unit 3.

Passé composé

The name of a commonly used past tense is the **passé composé.** It is defined with examples in French and English in Work Units 12, 13, 14.

Passive voice

When we speak or write in the active voice and change to the passive voice, the direct object becomes the subject, the subject becomes the object of a preposition, and the verb becomes *to be* plus the past participle of the active verb. The past participle functions as an adjective.

Example:
Janine is loved by everyone. / **Janine est aimée de tout le monde.**

The subject is *Janine.* The verb is *is*/**est.** The object of the preposition *by*/**de** is *everyone*/**tout le monde.** *See also* active voice. Compare the preceding sentence with the example in the active voice.

Past indefinite tense

In French this tense is the **passé composé.** Review it in Work Units 12, 13, 14.

Past participle

A past participle is derived from a verb. It is used to form the compound tenses, for example, the **passé composé.** Its auxiliary verb in English is *to have.* In French, the auxiliary verb is **avoir**/*to have* or **être**/*to be.* It is part of the verb tense.

Examples:
with **avoir** as the auxiliary verb: **Elle a mangé.**/She has eaten. The subject is **elle**/*she.* The verb is **a mangé**/*has eaten.* The tense of the verb is the **passé composé.** The auxiliary verb is **a**/*has.* The past participle is **mangé**/*eaten.*

with **être** as the auxiliary verb: **Elle est arrivée.**/She has arrived. The verb is **est arrivée**/*has arrived.* The tense of the verb is the **passé composé.** The auxiliary verb is **est**/*has.* The past participle is **arrivée**/*arrived.*

Review Work Unit 12 for the regular formation of a past participle and a list of commonly used irregular past participles. In Work Unit 12 you can also find out about which verbs are conjugated with either **avoir** or **être** to form the **passé composé.**

Person (1st, 2nd, 3rd)

Verb forms in a particular tense are learned systematically according to person (1st, 2nd, 3rd) and number (singular, plural).

Example, showing the present indicative tense of the verb **aller**/to go:

Singular		Plural	
1st person:	**je vais**	1st person:	**nous allons**
2nd person:	**tu vas**	2nd person:	**vous allez**
3rd person:	**il, elle va**	3rd person:	**ils, elles vont**

Personal pronoun

A personal pronoun refers to a person. Review the personal subject pronouns in Work Unit 4. For examples of other types of pronouns, *see also* demonstrative pronoun, direct object pronoun, disjunctive pronoun, indefinite pronoun, indirect object pronoun, interrogative pronoun, reflexive pronoun, relative pronoun.

Plural

Plural means more than one. *See also* person (1st, 2nd, 3rd), and singular.

Possessive adjective

A possessive adjective is an adjective that is placed in front of a noun to show possession. In French their forms change in gender (masculine or feminine) and number (singular or plural) to agree with the noun they modify.

Examples:
my book/**mon livre**   my books/**mes livres**
my dress/**ma robe**   my dresses/**mes robes**

Review them all in Work Unit 18.

Predicate

The predicate is that part of the sentence that tells us something about the subject. The main word of the predicate is the verb.

Example:
The tourists are waiting for the tour bus. / **Les touristes attendent l'autocar.**

The subject is *the tourists*/**les touristes.** The predicate is *are waiting for the tour bus*/**attendent l'autocar.** The verb is *are waiting*/**attendent.** The direct object is *the tour bus*/**l'autocar.** Review **attendre** in the verb tables.

Preposition

A preposition is a word that establishes a rapport between words.

Examples: with, in, on, at, between
with me/*avec* **moi**   *in* the drawer/*dans* **le tiroir**   *on* the table/*sur* **la table**
at six o'clock/*à* **six heures**   *between* him and her/*entre* **lui et elle**

Review prepositions in Work Unit 23.

Present indicative tense

This is a commonly used tense. It is defined with examples in French and English in Work Units 4, 5, 6.

Present participle

A present participle is derived from a verb form. In French it is regularly formed like this: Take the **nous** form of the present indicative tense of the verb you have in mind, then drop the ending **ons** and add **ant.** In English a present participle ends in *ing*.

Examples:

Infinitive	Present Indicative **nous** form	Present participle
chanter to sing	**nous chantons** we sing	**chantant** singing
finir to finish	**nous finissons** we finish	**finissant** finishing
vendre to sell	**nous vendons** we sell	**vendant** selling

Review these three verbs in the verb tables. Regular and irregular present participles are given in the verb tables also.

Pronoun

A pronoun is a word that takes the place of a noun.

Examples:

l'homme/il	**la femme/**elle	**l'arbre/**il	**la voiture/**elle
the man/*he*	the woman/*she*	the tree/*it*	the car/*it*

For examples of other kinds of pronouns, *see also* demonstrative pronoun, direct object pronoun, disjunctive pronoun, indefinite pronoun, indirect object pronoun, interrogative pronoun, reflexive pronoun, relative pronoun.

Reflexive pronoun and reflexive verb

In English a reflexive pronoun is a personal pronoun that contains *self* or *selves*. In French and English a reflexive pronoun is used with a verb that is called reflexive because the action of the verb falls on the reflexive pronoun.

In French, as in English, there is a required set of reflexive pronouns for a reflexive verb.

Examples:
se laver/to wash oneself   **Je me lave. /** I wash myself.
se blesser/to hurt oneself   **Elle s'est blessée. /** She hurt herself.

In French a reflexive verb is conjugated with **être** to form a compound tense. The French term for a reflexive verb is **un verbe pronominal** because a pronoun goes with the verb.

Review the reflexive verbs **s'appeler, se blesser, se laver,** and **se lever** in the verb tables. Review reflexive verbs in Work Units 7 and 10. *See also* agreement of past participle of a reflexive verb with its reflexive pronoun.

Regular verb

A regular verb is a verb that is conjugated in the various tenses according to a fixed pattern. For examples, review regular **er, ir,** and **re** verbs in the present indicative tense in Work Units 4, 5, 6. *See also* conjugation, irregular verb.

Relative pronoun

A relative pronoun is a pronoun that refers to its antecedent.

Example:
The girl who is laughing over there is my sister. **/ La jeune fille qui rit là-bas est ma soeur.** The antecedent is *girl/***la jeune fille.** The relative pronoun *who/***qui** refers to the girl.

Review **rire** in the verb tables. *See also* antecedent.

Sentence

A sentence is a group of words that contains a subject and a predicate. The verb is contained in the predicate. A sentence expresses a complete thought.

Example:
The train leaves from the North Station at two o'clock in the afternoon. / **Le train part de la Gare du Nord à deux heures de l'après-midi.**

The subject is *train*/**le train.** The predicate is *leaves from the North Station at two o'clock in the afternoon*/**part de la Gare du Nord à deux heures de l'après-midi.** The verb is *leaves*/**part**.

Review **partir** in the verb tables. *See also* complex sentence, compound sentence, simple sentence.

Simple sentence

A simple sentence is a sentence that contains one subject and one predicate. The verb is the core of the predicate. The verb is the most important word in a sentence because it tells us what the subject is doing.

Example:
Mary is eating an apple from her garden. / **Marie mange une pomme de son jardin.**

The subject is *Mary*/**Marie.** The predicate is *is eating an apple from her garden*/**mange une pomme de son jardin.** The verb is *is eating*/**mange.** The direct object is *an apple*/**une pomme.** *From her garden*/**de son jardin** is an adverbial phrase. It tells you where the apple came from.

Review **manger** in the verb tables. *See also* complex sentence, compound sentence.

Singular

Singular means one. *See also* person (1st, 2nd, 3rd), and plural.

Stem of a verb

The stem of a verb is what is left after we drop the ending of its infinitive form. It is added to the required endings of a regular verb in a particular verb tense.

Examples:

Infinitive	Ending of infinitive	Stem
donner/to give	**er**	**donn**
choisir/to choose	**ir**	**chois**
vendre/to sell	**re**	**vend**

Review Work Units 4, 5, 6. Review **choisir, donner, vendre** in the verb tables. *See also* ending of a verb.

Subject

A subject is that part of a sentence that is related to its verb. The verb says something about the subject.

Examples:
Mary and Catherine are beautiful. / **Marie et Catherine sont belles.**
Peter and Paul are handsome. / **Pierre et Paul sont beaux.**

Subjunctive mood

The subjunctive mood of a verb is used in specific cases, e.g., after certain verbs expressing a wish, doubt, emotion, fear, joy, uncertainty, an indefinite expression, an indefinite antecedent, certain conjunctions, and others, for example, in the imperative mood of **avoir** and **être.** Review the present subjunctive in the imperative mood of **avoir** and **être** in Work Unit 11. *See also* mood of verbs.

Subordinate clause

Subordinate clause is another term for dependent clause. *See* dependent clause.

Superlative adjective

A superlative adjective is an adjective that expresses the highest degree when making a comparison of more than two persons or things.

Examples:

	Adjective	Comparative	Superlative
(masc.)	**bon**/good	**meilleur**/better	**le meilleur**/(the) best
(fem.)	**bonne**/good	**meilleure**/better	**la meilleure**/(the) best
(masc.)	**mauvais**/bad	**plus mauvais**/worse	**le plus mauvais**/(the) worst
(fem.)	**mauvaise**/bad	**plus mauvaise**/worse	**la plus mauvaise**/(the) worst

Review Work Unit 19. *See also* comparative adjective.

Superlative adverb

A superlative adverb is an adverb that expresses the highest degree when making a comparison of more than two persons or things.

Example:

Adverb	Comparative	Superlative
vite/quickly	**plus vite**/more quickly	**le plus vite**/most quickly
	moins vite/less quickly	**le moins vite**/least quickly

Review Work Unit 20. *See also* comparative adverb.

Tense of verb

In English and French grammar, tense means time. The tense of the verb indicates the time of the action or state of being. The three major segments of time are past, present, and future. Review the verb tables.

Transitive verb

A transitive verb is a verb that takes a direct object.

> *Example:*
> I am closing the window. / **Je ferme la fenêtre.**

The subject is *I*/**Je.** The verb is *am closing*/**ferme.** The direct object is *the window*/**la fenêtre.** Review **fermer** in the verb tables. *See also* intransitive verb.

Verb

A verb is a word that expresses action or a state of being.

> *Examples:*

> *Action:* **Nous sommes allés au cinéma hier soir.** / We went to the movies last night. The verb is **sommes allés**/went.

> *State of being:* **La jeune fille est heureuse.** / The girl is happy.
> The verb is **est**/is.

Review **aller** and **être** in the verb tables.

French Verb Conjugation Tables

Regular and irregular verbs in these tables are presented alphabetically in Part A. Reflexive verbs are in Part B. They are arranged separately by the reflexive pronoun **se** or **s'** plus the verb so you can see them all in one place, in alphabetical order. In this way, you can make your own observations about their repeated patterns. All verbs given here are used in this book.

For the various translations into English of the **présent de l'indicatif,** review Work Unit 4.

For the translation into English of the **impératif** (imperative, command), of reflexive and nonreflexive verbs in the affirmative and negative, review Work Units 10 and 11.

For the various translations into English of the **passé composé,** review Work Unit 12.

In the **passé composé,** the vowel **e** in parentheses denotes a feminine agreement if required; **s** in parentheses denotes a plural agreement if required.

For orthographical (spelling) changes in verb forms, review Work Unit 22.

The abbreviation *pr. part.* denotes *present participle*; *past part.* denotes *past participle.* See these two terms in the section on Definitions of Basic Grammatical Terms with Examples.

In the Imperative (Command), the first verb form is 2nd pers., sing. **(tu);** the second verb form is 1st pers., pl. **(nous)**/let's...; the third verb form is 2nd pers., pl. or sing. **(vous).**

Examples:

In the Affirmative Imperative

danser/to dance	**finir**/to finish	**vendre**/to sell
danse/dance!	**finis**/finish!	**vends**/sell!
dansons/let's dance!	**finissons**/let's finish!	**vendons**/let's sell!
dansez/dance!	**finissez**/finish!	**vendez**/sell!

In the Negative Imperative

ne danse pas!	**ne finis pas!**	**ne vends pas!**
ne dansons pas!	**ne finissons pas!**	**ne vendons pas!**
ne dansez pas!	**ne finissez pas!**	**ne vendez pas!**

Part A

acheter/to buy, to purchase   *pr. part.* **achetant**   *past part.* **acheté**

Singular   *Plural*

PRESENT INDICATIVE   IMPERATIVE (AFFIRMATIVE)

j'achète   nous achetons   achète
tu achètes   vous achetez   achetons
il/elle achète   ils/elles achètent   achetez

PASSÉ COMPOSÉ   IMPERATIVE (NEGATIVE)

j'ai acheté   nous avons acheté   n'achète pas
tu as acheté   vous avez acheté   n'achetons pas
il/elle a acheté   ils/elles ont acheté   n'achetez pas

---

aimer/to like, to love   *pr. part.* **aimant**   *past part.* **aimé**

Singular   *Plural*

PRESENT INDICATIVE   IMPERATIVE (AFFIRMATIVE)

j'aime   nous aimons   aime
tu aimes   vous aimez   aimons
il/elle aime   ils/elles aiment   aimez

PASSÉ COMPOSÉ   IMPERATIVE (NEGATIVE)

j'ai aimé   nous avons aimé   n'aime pas
tu as aimé   vous avez aimé   n'aimons pas
il/elle a aimé   ils/elles ont aimé   n'aimez pas

In this book the conditional of **aimer** is used at times to express courtesy when asking for something:
j'aimerais…/I would like…

---

aller/to go   *pr. part.* **allant**   *past part.* **allé**

Singular   *Plural*

PRESENT INDICATIVE   IMPERATIVE (AFFIRMATIVE)

je vais   nous allons   va
tu vas   vous allez   allons
il/elle va   ils/elles vont   allez

PASSÉ COMPOSÉ   IMPERATIVE (NEGATIVE)

je suis allé(e)   nous sommes allé(e)s   ne va pas
tu es allé(e)   vous êtes allé(e)(s)   n'allons pas
il est allé   ils sont allés   n'allez pas
elle est allée   elles sont allées

annoncer/to announce   *pr. part.* **annonçant**   *past part.* **annoncé**

Singular   *Plural*

PRESENT INDICATIVE   IMPERATIVE (AFFIRMATIVE)

j'annonce   nous annonçons   annonce
tu annonces   vous annoncez   annonçons
il/elle annonce   ils/elles annoncent   annoncez

PASSÉ COMPOSÉ   IMPERATIVE (NEGATIVE)

j'ai annoncé   nous avons annoncé   n'annonce pas
tu as annoncé   vous avez annoncé   n'annonçons pas
il/elle a annoncé   ils/elles ont annoncé   n'annoncez pas

---

appeler/to call   *pr. part.* **appelant**   *past part.* **appelé**

Singular   *Plural*

PRESENT INDICATIVE   IMPERATIVE (AFFIRMATIVE)

j'appelle   nous appelons   appelle
tu appelles   vous appelez   appelons
il/elle appelle   ils/elles appellent   appelez

PASSÉ COMPOSÉ   IMPERATIVE (NEGATIVE)

j'ai appelé   nous avons appelé   n'appelle pas
tu as appelé   vous avez appelé   n'appelons pas
il/elle a appelé   ils/elles ont appelé   n'appelez pas

---

apporter/to bring   *pr. part.* **apportant**   *past part.* **apporté**

Singular   *Plural*

PRESENT INDICATIVE   IMPERATIVE (AFFIRMATIVE)

j'apporte   nous apportons   apporte
tu apportes   vous apportez   apportons
il/elle apporte   ils/elles apportent   apportez

PASSÉ COMPOSÉ   IMPERATIVE (NEGATIVE)

j'ai apporté   nous avons apporté   n'apporte pas
tu as apporté   vous avez apporté   n'apportons pas
il/elle a apporté   ils/elles ont apporté   n'apportez pas

apprendre/to learn   *pr. part.* **apprenant**   *past part.* **appris**

Singular   *Plural*

PRESENT INDICATIVE   IMPERATIVE (AFFIRMATIVE)

j'apprends   nous apprenons   apprends
tu apprends   vous apprenez   apprenons
il/elle apprend   ils/elles apprennent   apprenez

PASSÉ COMPOSÉ   IMPERATIVE (NEGATIVE)

j'ai appris   nous avons appris   n'apprends pas
tu as appris   vous avez appris   n'apprenons pas
il/elle a appris   ils/elles ont appris   n'apprenez pas

---

arriver/to arrive   *pr. part.* **arrivant**   *past part.* **arrivé**

Singular   *Plural*

PRESENT INDICATIVE   IMPERATIVE (AFFIRMATIVE)

j'arrive   nous arrivons   arrive
tu arrives   vous arrivez   arrivons
il/elle arrive   ils/elles arrivent   arrivez

PASSÉ COMPOSÉ   IMPERATIVE (NEGATIVE)

je suis arrivé(e)   nous sommes arrivé(e)s   n'arrive pas
tu es arrivé(e)   vous êtes arrivé(e)(s)   n'arrivons pas
il est arrivé   ils sont arrivés   n'arrivez pas
elle est arrivée   elles sont arrivées

---

attendre/to wait (for)   *pr. part.* **attendant**   *past part.* **attendu**

Singular   *Plural*

PRESENT INDICATIVE   IMPERATIVE (AFFIRMATIVE)

j'attends   nous attendons   attends
tu attends   vous attendez   attendons
il/elle attend   ils/elles attendent   attendez

PASSÉ COMPOSÉ   IMPERATIVE (NEGATIVE)

j'ai attendu   nous avons attendu   n'attends pas
tu as attendu   vous avez attendu   n'attendons pas
il/elle a attendu   ils/elles ont attendu   n'attendez pas

avoir/to have   *pr. part.* **ayant**   *past part.* **eu**

Singular   *Plural*

PRESENT INDICATIVE   IMPERATIVE (AFFIRMATIVE)

j'ai	nous avons	aie
tu as	vous avez	ayons
il/elle a	ils/elles ont	ayez

PASSÉ COMPOSÉ   IMPERATIVE (NEGATIVE)

j'ai eu	nous avons eu	n'aie pas
tu as eu	vous avez eu	n'ayons pas
il/elle a eu	ils/elles ont eu	n'ayez pas

---

boire/to drink   *pr. part.* **buvant**   *past part.* **bu**

Singular   *Plural*

PRESENT INDICATIVE   IMPERATIVE (AFFIRMATIVE)

je bois	nous buvons	bois
tu bois	vous buvez	buvons
il/elle boit	ils/elles boivent	buvez

PASSÉ COMPOSÉ   IMPERATIVE (NEGATIVE)

j'ai bu	nous avons bu	ne bois pas
tu as bu	vous avez bu	ne buvons pas
il/elle a bu	ils/elles ont bu	ne buvez pas

---

chanter/to sing   *pr. part.* **chantant**   *past part.* **chanté**

Singular   *Plural*

PRESENT INDICATIVE   IMPERATIVE (AFFIRMATIVE)

je chante	nous chantons	chante
tu chantes	vous chantez	chantons
il/elle chante	ils/elles chantent	chantez

PASSÉ COMPOSÉ   IMPERATIVE (NEGATIVE)

j'ai chanté	nous avons chanté	ne chante pas
tu as chanté	vous avez chanté	ne chantons pas
il/elle a chanté	ils/elles ont chanté	ne chantez pas

chercher/to look for, search *pr. part.* **cherchant** *past part.* **cherché**

Singular *Plural*

PRESENT INDICATIVE IMPERATIVE (AFFIRMATIVE)

je cherche	nous cherchons	cherche
tu cherches	vous cherchez	cherchons
il/elle cherche	ils/elles cherchent	cherchez

PASSÉ COMPOSÉ IMPERATIVE (NEGATIVE)

j'ai cherché	nous avons cherché	ne cherche pas
tu as cherché	vous avez cherché	ne cherchons pas
il/elle a cherché	ils/elles ont cherché	ne cherchez pas

---

choisir/to choose *pr. part.* **choisissant** *past part.* **choisi**

Singular *Plural*

PRESENT INDICATIVE IMPERATIVE (AFFIRMATIVE)

je choisis	nous choisissons	choisis
tu choisis	vous choisissez	choisissons
il/elle choisit	ils/elles choisissent	choisissez

PASSÉ COMPOSÉ IMPERATIVE (NEGATIVE)

j'ai choisi	nous avons choisi	ne choisis pas
tu as choisi	vous avez choisi	ne choisissons pas
il/elle a choisi	ils/elles ont choisi	ne choisissez pas

---

commencer/to begin, commence *pr. part.* **commençant** *past part.* **commencé**

Singular *Plural*

PRESENT INDICATIVE IMPERATIVE (AFFIRMATIVE)

je commence	nous commençons	commence
tu commences	vous commencez	commençons
il/elle commence	ils/elles commencent	commencez

PASSÉ COMPOSÉ IMPERATIVE (NEGATIVE)

j'ai commencé	nous avons commencé	ne commence pas
tu as commencé	vous avez commencé	ne commençons pas
il/elle a commencé	ils/elles ont commencé	ne commencez pas

comprendre/to understand   *pr. part.* **comprenant**   *past part.* **compris**

Singular   *Plural*

PRESENT INDICATIVE

je comprends	nous comprenons	
tu comprends	vous comprenez	
il/elle comprend	ils/elles comprennent	

IMPERATIVE (AFFIRMATIVE)

comprends
comprenons
comprenez

PASSÉ COMPOSÉ

j'ai compris	nous avons compris
tu as compris	vous avez compris
il/elle a compris	ils/elles ont compris

IMPERATIVE (NEGATIVE)

ne comprends pas
ne comprenons pas
ne comprenez pas

---

connaître/to know, be acquainted with   *pr. part.* **connaissant**   *past part.* **connu**

Singular   *Plural*

PRESENT INDICATIVE

je connais	nous connaissons
tu connais	vous connaissez
il/elle connaît	ils/elles connaissent

IMPERATIVE (AFFIRMATIVE)

connais
connaissons
connaissez

PASSÉ COMPOSÉ

j'ai connu	nous avons connu
tu as connu	vous avez connu
il/elle a connu	ils/elles ont connu

IMPERATIVE (NEGATIVE)

ne connais pas
ne connaissons pas
ne connaissez pas

---

construire/to construct, build   *pr. part.* **construisant**   *past part.* **construit**

Singular   *Plural*

PRESENT INDICATIVE

je construis	nous construisons
tu construis	vous construisez
il/elle construit	ils/elles construisent

IMPERATIVE (AFFIRMATIVE)

construis
construisons
construisez

PASSÉ COMPOSÉ

j'ai construit	nous avons construit
tu as construit	vous avez construit
il/elle a construit	ils/elles ont construit

IMPERATIVE (NEGATIVE)

ne construis pas
ne construisons pas
ne construisez pas

corriger/to correct   *pr. part.* **corrigeant**   *past part.* **corrigé**

Singular   *Plural*

PRESENT INDICATIVE   IMPERATIVE (AFFIRMATIVE)

je corrige	nous corrigeons	corrige
tu corriges	vous corrigez	corrigeons
il/elle corrige	ils/elles corrigent	corrigez

PASSÉ COMPOSÉ   IMPERATIVE (NEGATIVE)

j'ai corrigé	nous avons corrigé	ne corrige pas
tu as corrigé	vous avez corrigé	ne corrigeons pas
il/elle a corrigé	ils/elles ont corrigé	ne corrigez pas

---

courir/to run   *pr. part.* **courant**   *past part.* **couru**

Singular   *Plural*

PRESENT INDICATIVE   IMPERATIVE (AFFIRMATIVE)

je cours	nous courons	cours
tu cours	vous courez	courons
il/elle court	ils/elles courent	courez

PASSÉ COMPOSÉ   IMPERATIVE (NEGATIVE)

j'ai couru	nous avons couru	ne cours pas
tu as couru	vous avez couru	ne courons pas
il/elle a couru	ils/elles ont couru	ne courez pas

---

coûter/to cost   *pr. part.* **coûtant**   *past part.* **coûté**

Singular   *Plural*

PRESENT INDICATIVE   IMPERATIVE (AFFIRMATIVE)

il/elle coûte	ils/elles coûtent	[not used]

PASSÉ COMPOSÉ   IMPERATIVE (NEGATIVE)

il/elle a coûté	ils/elles ont coûté	[not used]

Note that this verb is generally regarded as impersonal. That is why it is not conjugated in all six persons here. It is used primarily in the third person singular (it) and plural (they).

couvrir/to cover   *pr. part.* **couvrant**   *past part.* **couvert**

Singular   *Plural*

PRESENT INDICATIVE   IMPERATIVE (AFFIRMATIVE)

je couvre	nous couvrons	couvre
tu couvres	vous couvrez	couvrons
il/elle couvre	ils/elles couvrent	couvrez

PASSÉ COMPOSÉ   IMPERATIVE (NEGATIVE)

j'ai couvert	nous avons couvert	ne couvre pas
tu as couvert	vous avez couvert	ne couvrons pas
il/elle a couvert	ils/elles ont couvert	ne couvrez pas

---

croire/to believe   *pr. part.* **croyant**   *past part.* **cru**

Singular   *Plural*

PRESENT INDICATIVE   IMPERATIVE (AFFIRMATIVE)

je crois	nous croyons	crois
tu crois	vous croyez	croyons
il/elle croit	ils/elles croient	croyez

PASSÉ COMPOSÉ   IMPERATIVE (NEGATIVE)

j'ai cru	nous avons cru	ne crois pas
tu as cru	vous avez cru	ne croyons pas
il/elle a cru	ils/elles ont cru	ne croyez pas

---

cuire/to cook   *pr. part.* **cuisant**   *past part.* **cuit**

Singular   *Plural*

PRESENT INDICATIVE   IMPERATIVE (AFFIRMATIVE)

je cuis	nous cuisons	cuis
tu cuis	vous cuisez	cuisons
il/elle cuit	ils/elles cuisent	cuisez

PASSÉ COMPOSÉ   IMPERATIVE (NEGATIVE)

j'ai cuit	nous avons cuit	ne cuis pas
tu as cuit	vous avez cuit	ne cuisons pas
il/elle a cuit	ils/elles ont cuit	ne cuisez pas

danser/to dance   *pr. part.* **dansant**   *past part.* **dansé**

Singular   *Plural*

PRESENT INDICATIVE		IMPERATIVE (AFFIRMATIVE)
je danse	nous dansons	danse
tu danses	vous dansez	dansons
il/elle danse	ils/elles dansent	dansez

PASSÉ COMPOSÉ		IMPERATIVE (NEGATIVE)
j'ai dansé	nous avons dansé	ne danse pas
tu as dansé	vous avez dansé	ne dansons pas
il/elle a dansé	ils/elles ont dansé	ne dansez pas

---

déjeuner/to lunch, have lunch, breakfast   *pr. part.* **déjeunant**   *past part.* **déjeuné**

Singular   *Plural*

PRESENT INDICATIVE		IMPERATIVE (AFFIRMATIVE)
je déjeune	nous déjeunons	déjeune
tu déjeunes	vous déjeunez	déjeunons
il/elle déjeune	ils/elles déjeunent	déjeunez

PASSÉ COMPOSÉ		IMPERATIVE (NEGATIVE)
j'ai déjeuné	nous avons déjeuné	ne déjeune pas
tu as déjeuné	vous avez déjeuné	ne déjeunons pas
il/elle a déjeuné	ils/elles ont déjeuné	ne déjeunez pas

---

demander/to ask (for), request   *pr. part.* **demandant**   *past part.* **demandé**

Singular   *Plural*

PRESENT INDICATIVE		IMPERATIVE (AFFIRMATIVE)
je demande	nous demandons	demande
tu demandes	vous demandez	demandons
il/elle demande	ils/elles demandent	demandez

PASSÉ COMPOSÉ		IMPERATIVE (NEGATIVE)
j'ai demandé	nous avons demandé	ne demande pas
tu as demandé	vous avez demandé	ne demandons pas
il/elle a demandé	ils/elles ont demandé	ne demandez pas

demeurer/to live (somewhere), reside   *pr. part.* **demeurant**   *past part.* **demeuré**

Singular   *Plural*

PRESENT INDICATIVE		IMPERATIVE (AFFIRMATIVE)
je demeure	nous demeurons	demeure
tu demeures	vous demeurez	demeurons
il/elle demeure	ils/elles demeurent	demeurez

PASSÉ COMPOSÉ		IMPERATIVE (NEGATIVE)
j'ai demeuré	nous avons demeuré	ne demeure pas
tu as demeuré	vous avez demeuré	ne demeurons pas
il/elle a demeuré	ils/elles ont demeuré	ne demeurez pas

---

descendre/to descend, go (bring) down   *pr. part.* **descendant**   *past part.* **descendu**

Singular   *Plural*

PRESENT INDICATIVE		IMPERATIVE (AFFIRMATIVE)
je descends	nous descendons	descends
tu descends	vous descendez	descendons
il/elle descend	ils/elles descendent	descendez

PASSÉ COMPOSÉ		IMPERATIVE (NEGATIVE)
je suis descendu(e)	nous sommes descendu(e)s	ne descends pas
tu es descendu(e)	vous êtes descendu(e)(s)	ne descendons pas
il est descendu	ils sont descendus	ne descendez pas
elle est descendue	elles sont descendues	

This verb is conjugated with **avoir** in the **passé composé** when it has a direct object.
Examples: **J'ai descendu l'escalier**/*I went down the stairs;* **J'ai descendu les valises**/*I brought down the suitcases.* But:
Elle est descendue vite/*She came down quickly.*

---

désirer/to desire   *pr. part.* **désirant**   *past part.* **désiré**

Singular   *Plural*

PRESENT INDICATIVE		IMPERATIVE (AFFIRMATIVE)
je désire	nous désirons	désire
tu désires	vous désirez	désirons
il/elle désire	ils/elles désirent	désirez

PASSÉ COMPOSÉ		IMPERATIVE (NEGATIVE)
j'ai désiré	nous avons désiré	ne désire pas
tu as désiré	vous avez désiré	ne désirons pas
il/elle a désiré	ils/elles ont désiré	ne désirez pas

devenir/to become   *pr. part.* **devenant**   *past part.* **devenu**

Singular   *Plural*

PRESENT INDICATIVE   IMPERATIVE (AFFIRMATIVE)

je deviens   nous devenons   deviens
tu deviens   vous devenez   devenons
il/elle devient   ils/elles deviennent   devenez

PASSÉ COMPOSÉ   IMPERATIVE (NEGATIVE)

je suis devenu(e)   nous sommes devenu(e)s   ne deviens pas
tu es devenu(e)   vous êtes devenu(e)(s)   ne devenons pas
il est devenu   ils sont devenus   ne devenez pas
elle est devenue   elles sont devenues

---

devoir/to have to, must, ought, owe, should   *pr. part.* **devant**   *past part.* **dû**

Singular   *Plural*

PRESENT INDICATIVE   IMPERATIVE (AFFIRMATIVE)

je dois   nous devons   dois
tu dois   vous devez   devons
il/elle doit   ils/elles doivent   devez

PASSÉ COMPOSÉ   IMPERATIVE (NEGATIVE)

j'ai dû   nous avons dû   ne dois pas
tu as dû   vous avez dû   ne devons pas
il/elle a dû   ils/elles ont dû   ne devez pas

---

dîner/to dine, have dinner   *pr. part.* **dînant**   *past part.* **dîné**

Singular   *Plural*

PRESENT INDICATIVE   IMPERATIVE (AFFIRMATIVE)

je dîne   nous dînons   dîne
tu dînes   vous dînez   dînons
il/elle dîne   ils/elles dînent   dînez

PASSÉ COMPOSÉ   IMPERATIVE (NEGATIVE)

j'ai dîné   nous avons dîné   ne dîne pas
tu as dîné   vous avez dîné   ne dînons pas
il/elle a dîné   ils/elles ont dîné   ne dînez pas

dire/to say, tell   *pr. part.* **disant**   *past part.* **dit**

Singular   *Plural*

PRESENT INDICATIVE   IMPERATIVE (AFFIRMATIVE)

je dis	nous disons	dis
tu dis	vous dites	disons
il/elle dit	ils/elles disent	dites

PASSÉ COMPOSÉ   IMPERATIVE (NEGATIVE)

j'ai dit	nous avons dit	ne dis pas
tu as dit	vous avez dit	ne disons pas
il/elle a dit	ils/elles ont dit	ne dites pas

---

donner/to give   *pr. part.* **donnant**   *past part.* **donné**

Singular   *Plural*

PRESENT INDICATIVE   IMPERATIVE (AFFIRMATIVE)

je donne	nous donnons	donne
tu donnes	vous donnez	donnons
il/elle donne	ils/elles donnent	donnez

PASSÉ COMPOSÉ   IMPERATIVE (NEGATIVE)

j'ai donné	nous avons donné	ne donne pas
tu as donné	vous avez donné	ne donnons pas
il/elle a donné	ils/elles ont donné	ne donnez pas

---

dormir/to sleep   *pr. part.* **dormant**   *past part.* **dormi**

Singular   *Plural*

PRESENT INDICATIVE   IMPERATIVE (AFFIRMATIVE)

je dors	nous dormons	dors
tu dors	vous dormez	dormons
il/elle dort	ils/elles dorment	dormez

PASSÉ COMPOSÉ   IMPERATIVE (NEGATIVE)

j'ai dormi	nous avons dormi	ne dors pas
tu as dormi	vous avez dormi	ne dormons pas
il/elle a dormi	ils/elles ont dormi	ne dormez pas

écouter/to listen (to) *pr. part.* **écoutant** *past part.* **écouté**

Singular *Plural*

PRESENT INDICATIVE

		IMPERATIVE (AFFIRMATIVE)

j'écoute nous écoutons écoute
tu écoutes vous écoutez écoutons
il/elle écoute ils/elles écoutent écoutez

PASSÉ COMPOSÉ IMPERATIVE (NEGATIVE)

j'ai écouté nous avons écouté n'écoute pas
tu as écouté vous avez écouté n'écoutons pas
il/elle a écouté ils/elles ont écouté n'écoutez pas

écrire/to write *pr. part.* **écrivant** *past part.* **écrit**

Singular *Plural*

PRESENT INDICATIVE IMPERATIVE (AFFIRMATIVE)

j'écris nous écrivons écris
tu écris vous écrivez écrivons
il/elle écrit ils/elles écrivent écrivez

PASSÉ COMPOSÉ IMPERATIVE (NEGATIVE)

j'ai écrit nous avons écrit n'écris pas
tu as écrit vous avez écrit n'écrivons pas
il/elle a écrit ils/elles ont écrit n'écrivez pas

---

effacer/to erase *pr. part.* **effaçant** *past part.* **effacé**

Singular *Plural*

PRESENT INDICATIVE IMPERATIVE (AFFIRMATIVE)

j'efface nous effaçons efface
tu effaces vous effacez effaçons
il/elle efface ils/elles effacent effacez

PASSÉ COMPOSÉ IMPERATIVE (NEGATIVE)

j'ai effacé nous avons effacé n'efface pas
tu as effacé vous avez effacé n'effaçons pas
il/elle a effacé ils/elles ont effacé n'effacez pas

employer/to use, employ   *pr. part.* **employant**   *past part.* **employé**

Singular   *Plural*

PRESENT INDICATIVE   IMPERATIVE (AFFIRMATIVE)

j'emploie	nous employons	emploie
tu emploies	vous employez	employons
il/elle emploie	ils/elles emploient	employez

PASSÉ COMPOSÉ   IMPERATIVE (NEGATIVE)

j'ai employé	nous avons employé	n'emploie pas
tu as employé	vous avez employé	n'employons pas
il/elle a employé	ils/elles ont employé	n'employez pas

Verbs ending in *-oyer* must change *y* to *i* before mute *e*.

---

ennuyer/to annoy, bore, weary   *pr. part.* **ennuyant**   *past part.* **ennuyé**

Singular   *Plural*

PRESENT INDICATIVE   IMPERATIVE (AFFIRMATIVE)

j'ennuie	nous ennuyons	ennuie
tu ennuies	vous ennuyez	ennuyons
il/elle ennuie	ils/elles ennuient	ennuyez

PASSÉ COMPOSÉ   IMPERATIVE (NEGATIVE)

j'ai ennuyé	nous avons ennuyé	n'ennuie pas
tu as ennuyé	vous avez ennuyé	n'ennuyons pas
il/elle a ennuyé	ils/elles ont ennuyé	n'ennuyez pas

Verbs ending in *-uyer* must change *y* to *i* before mute *e*.

---

entendre/to hear   *pr. part.* **entendant**   *past part.* **entendu**

Singular   *Plural*

PRESENT INDICATIVE   IMPERATIVE (AFFIRMATIVE)

j'entends	nous entendons	entends
tu entends	vous entendez	entendons
il/elle entend	ils/elles entendent	entendez

PASSÉ COMPOSÉ   IMPERATIVE (NEGATIVE)

j'ai entendu	nous avons entendu	n'entends pas
tu as entendu	vous avez entendu	n'entendons pas
il/elle a entendu	ils/elles ont entendu	n'entendez pas

entrer/to enter, come in, go in   *pr. part.* **entrant**   *past part.* **entré**

Singular   *Plural*

PRESENT INDICATIVE   IMPERATIVE (AFFIRMATIVE)

j'entre	nous entrons	entre
tu entres	vous entrez	entrons
il/elle entre	ils/elles entrent	entrez

PASSÉ COMPOSÉ   IMPERATIVE (NEGATIVE)

je suis entré(e)	nous sommes entré(e)s	n'entre pas
tu es entré(e)	vous êtes entré(e)(s)	n'entrons pas
il est entré	ils sont entrés	n'entrez pas
elle est entrée	elles sont entrées	

---

envoyer/to send   *pr. part.* **envoyant**   *past part.* **envoyé**

Singular   *Plural*

PRESENT INDICATIVE   IMPERATIVE (AFFIRMATIVE)

j'envoie	nous envoyons	envoie
tu envoies	vous envoyez	envoyons
il/elle envoie	ils/elles envoient	envoyez

PASSÉ COMPOSÉ   IMPERATIVE (NEGATIVE)

j'ai envoyé	nous avons envoyé	n'envoie pas
tu as envoyé	vous avez envoyé	n'envoyons pas
il/elle a envoyé	ils/elles ont envoyé	n'envoyez pas

Verbs ending in *-oyer* must change *y* to *i* before mute *e*.

---

espérer/to hope   *pr. part.* **espérant**   *past part.* **espéré**

Singular   *Plural*

PRESENT INDICATIVE   IMPERATIVE (AFFIRMATIVE)

j'espère	nous espérons	espère
tu espères	vous espérez	espérons
il/elle espère	ils/elles espèrent	espérez

PASSÉ COMPOSÉ   IMPERATIVE (NEGATIVE)

j'ai espéré	nous avons espéré	n'espère pas
tu as espéré	vous avez espéré	n'espérons pas
il/elle a espéré	ils/elles ont espéré	n'espérez pas

essayer/to try, try on   *pr. part.* **essayant**   *past part.* **essayé**

Singular   *Plural*

PRESENT INDICATIVE

		IMPERATIVE (AFFIRMATIVE)

j'essaye   nous essayons   essaye
tu essayes   vous essayez   essayons
il/elle essaye   ils/elles essayent   essayez

PASSÉ COMPOSÉ   IMPERATIVE (NEGATIVE)

j'ai essayé   nous avons essayé   n'essaye pas
tu as essayé   vous avez essayé   n'essayons pas
il/elle a essayé   ils/elles ont essayé   n'essayez pas

Verbs ending in *-ayer* may change *y* to *i* before mute *e* or may keep *y*.

---

essuyer/to wipe   *pr. part.* **essuyant**   *past part.* **essuyé**

Singular   *Plural*

PRESENT INDICATIVE   IMPERATIVE (AFFIRMATIVE)

j'essuie   nous essuyons   essuie
tu essuies   vous essuyez   essuyons
il/elle essuie   ils/elles essuient   essuyez

PASSÉ COMPOSÉ   IMPERATIVE (NEGATIVE)

j'ai essuyé   nous avons essuyé   n'essuie pas
tu as essuyé   vous avez essuyé   n'essuyons pas
il/elle a essuyé   ils/elles ont essuyé   n'essuyez pas

Verbs ending in *-uyer* must change *y* to *i* before mute *e*.

être/to be   *pr. part.* **étant**   *past part.* **été**

Singular   *Plural*

PRESENT INDICATIVE   IMPERATIVE (AFFIRMATIVE)

je suis   nous sommes   sois
tu es   vous êtes   soyons
il/elle est   ils/elles sont   soyez

PASSÉ COMPOSÉ   IMPERATIVE (NEGATIVE)

j'ai été   nous avons été   ne sois pas
tu as été   vous avez été   ne soyons pas
il/elle a été   ils/elles ont été   ne soyez pas

étudier/to study   *pr. part.* **étudiant**   *past part.* **étudié**

Singular   *Plural*

	PRESENT INDICATIVE		IMPERATIVE (AFFIRMATIVE)
j'étudie	**nous étudions**		**étudie**
tu étudies	**vous étudiez**		**étudions**
il/elle étudie	**ils/elles étudient**		**étudiez**

	PASSÉ COMPOSÉ		IMPERATIVE (NEGATIVE)
j'ai étudié	**nous avons étudié**		**n'étudie pas**
tu as étudié	**vous avez étudié**		**n'étudions pas**
il/elle a étudié	**ils/elles ont étudié**		**n'étudiez pas**

---

faire/to do, make   *pr. part.* **faisant**   *past part.* **fait**

Singular   *Plural*

	PRESENT INDICATIVE		IMPERATIVE (AFFIRMATIVE)
je fais	**nous faisons**		**fais**
tu fais	**vous faites**		**faisons**
il/elle fait	**ils/elles font**		**faites**

	PASSÉ COMPOSÉ		IMPERATIVE (NEGATIVE)
j'ai fait	**nous avons fait**		**ne fais pas**
tu as fait	**vous avez fait**		**ne faisons pas**
il/elle a fait	**ils/elles ont fait**		**ne faites pas**

---

falloir/to be necessary, need to, must   *pr. part.* [not in use]   *past part.* **fallu**

Singular

	PRESENT INDICATIVE	IMPERATIVE (AFFIRMATIVE)
il faut		[not in use]

	PASSÉ COMPOSÉ	IMPERATIVE (NEGATIVE)
il a fallu		[not in use]

This is an impersonal verb that is used in the third person singular. *Examples:* **Il faut manger et boire pour vivre**/*It is necessary to eat and drink in order to live;* **Il a fallu partir**/*It was necessary to leave.*

fermer/to close   *pr. part.* **fermant**   *past part.* **fermé**

Singular   *Plural*

PRESENT INDICATIVE   IMPERATIVE (AFFIRMATIVE)

je ferme   nous fermons   ferme
tu fermes   vous fermez   fermons
il/elle ferme   ils/elles ferment   fermez

PASSÉ COMPOSÉ   IMPERATIVE (NEGATIVE)

j'ai fermé   nous avons fermé   ne ferme pas
tu as fermé   vous avez fermé   ne fermons pas
il/elle a fermé   ils/elles ont fermé   ne fermez pas

---

finir/to finish   *pr. part.* **finissant**   *past part.* **fini**

Singular   *Plural*

PRESENT INDICATIVE   IMPERATIVE (AFFIRMATIVE)

je finis   nous finissons   finis
tu finis   vous finissez   finissons
il/elle finit   ils/elles finissent   finissez

PASSÉ COMPOSÉ   IMPERATIVE (NEGATIVE)

j'ai fini   nous avons fini   ne finis pas
tu as fini   vous avez fini   ne finissons pas
il/elle a fini   ils/elles ont fini   ne finissez pas

---

habiter/to live (somewhere), inhabit   *pr. part.* **habitant**   *past part.* **habité**

Singular   *Plural*

PRESENT INDICATIVE   IMPERATIVE (AFFIRMATIVE)

j'habite   nous habitons   habite
tu habites   vous habitez   habitons
il/elle habite   ils/elles habitent   habitez

PASSÉ COMPOSÉ   IMPERATIVE (NEGATIVE)

j'ai habité   nous avons habité   n'habite pas
tu as habité   vous avez habité   n'habitons pas
il/elle a habité   ils/elles ont habité   n'habitez pas

jeter/to throw   *pr. part.* **jetant**   *past part.* **jeté**

Singular   *Plural*

PRESENT INDICATIVE   IMPERATIVE (AFFIRMATIVE)

je jette	nous jetons	jette
tu jettes	vous jetez	jetons
il/elle jette	ils/elles jettent	jetez

PASSÉ COMPOSÉ   IMPERATIVE (NEGATIVE)

j'ai jeté	nous avons jeté	ne jette pas
tu as jeté	vous avez jeté	ne jetons pas
il/elle a jeté	ils/elles ont jeté	ne jetez pas

---

jouer/to play   *pr. part.* **jouant**   *past part.* **joué**

Singular   *Plural*

PRESENT INDICATIVE   IMPERATIVE (AFFIRMATIVE)

je joue	nous jouons	joue
tu joues	vous jouez	jouons
il/elle joue	ils/elles jouent	jouez

PASSÉ COMPOSÉ   IMPERATIVE (NEGATIVE)

j'ai joué	nous avons joué	ne joue pas
tu as joué	vous avez joué	ne jouons pas
il/elle a joué	ils/elles ont joué	ne jouez pas

---

lire/to read   *pr. part.* **lisant**   *past part.* **lu**

Singular   *Plural*

PRESENT INDICATIVE   IMPERATIVE (AFFIRMATIVE)

je lis	nous lisons	lis
tu lis	vous lisez	lisons
il/elle lit	ils/elles lisent	lisez

PASSÉ COMPOSÉ   IMPERATIVE (NEGATIVE)

j'ai lu	nous avons lu	ne lis pas
tu as lu	vous avez lu	ne lisons pas
il/elle a lu	ils/elles ont lu	ne lisez pas

manger/to eat   *pr. part.* **mangeant**   *past part.* **mangé**

Singular   *Plural*

PRESENT INDICATIVE   IMPERATIVE (AFFIRMATIVE)

je mange	nous mangeons	mange
tu manges	vous mangez	mangeons
il/elle mange	ils/elles mangent	mangez

PASSÉ COMPOSÉ   IMPERATIVE (NEGATIVE)

j'ai mangé	nous avons mangé	ne mange pas
tu as mangé	vous avez mangé	ne mangeons pas
il/elle a mangé	ils/elles ont mangé	ne mangez pas

---

mettre/to put, place   *pr. part.* **mettant**   *past part.* **mis**

Singular   *Plural*

PRESENT INDICATIVE   IMPERATIVE (AFFIRMATIVE)

je mets	nous mettons	mets
tu mets	vous mettez	mettons
il/elle met	ils/elles mettent	mettez

PASSÉ COMPOSÉ   IMPERATIVE (NEGATIVE)

j'ai mis	nous avons mis	ne mets pas
tu as mis	vous avez mis	ne mettons pas
il/elle a mis	ils/elles ont mis	ne mettez pas

---

monter/to go up, bring up   *pr. part.* **montant**   *past part.* **monté**

Singular   *Plural*

PRESENT INDICATIVE   IMPERATIVE (AFFIRMATIVE)

je monte	nous montons	monte
tu montes	vous montez	montons
il/elle monte	ils/elles montent	montez

PASSÉ COMPOSÉ   IMPERATIVE (NEGATIVE)

je suis monté(e)	nous sommes monté(e)s	ne monte pas
tu es monté(e)	vous êtes monté(e)(s)	ne montons pas
il est monté	ils sont montés	ne montez pas
elle est montée	elles sont montées	

This verb is conjugated with **avoir** in the **passé composé** when it has a direct object. *Examples:* **J'ai monté l'escalier**/*I went up the stairs;* **J'ai monté les valises**/*I brought up the suitcases.* But: **Elle est montée vite**/*She went up quickly.*

mourir/to die   *pr. part.* **mourant**   *past part.* **mort**

Singular   *Plural*

	PRESENT INDICATIVE	IMPERATIVE (AFFIRMATIVE)
je meurs	**nous mourons**	**meurs**
tu meurs	**vous mourez**	**mourons**
il/elle meurt	**ils/elles meurent**	**mourez**

	PASSÉ COMPOSÉ	IMPERATIVE (NEGATIVE)
je suis mort(e)	**nous sommes morte(e)s**	**ne meurs pas**
tu es mort(e)	**vous êtes mort(e)(s)**	**ne mourons pas**
il est mort	**ils sont morts**	**ne mourez pas**
elle est morte	**elles sont mortes**	

---

nager/to swim   *pr. part.* **nageant**   *past part.* **nagé**

Singular   *Plural*

	PRESENT INDICATIVE	IMPERATIVE (AFFIRMATIVE)
je nage	**nous nageons**	**nage**
tu nages	**vous nagez**	**nageons**
il/elle nage	**ils/elles nagent**	**nagez**

	PASSÉ COMPOSÉ	IMPERATIVE (NEGATIVE)
j'ai nagé	**nous avons nagé**	**ne nage pas**
tu as nagé	**vous avez nagé**	**ne nageons pas**
il/elle a nagé	**ils/elles ont nagé**	**ne nagez pas**

---

naître/to be born   *pr. part.* **naissant**   *past part.* **né**

Singular   *Plural*

	PRESENT INDICATIVE	IMPERATIVE (AFFIRMATIVE)
je nais	**nous naissons**	**nais**
tu nais	**vous naissez**	**naissons**
il/elle naît	**ils/elles naissent**	**naissez**

	PASSÉ COMPOSÉ	IMPERATIVE (NEGATIVE)
je suis né(e)	**nous sommes né(e)s**	**ne nais pas**
tu es né(e)	**vous êtes né(e)(s)**	**ne naissons pas**
il est né	**ils sont nés**	**ne naissez pas**
elle est née	**elles sont nées**	

neiger/to snow　　　　　*pr. part.* **neigeant**　　　　　*past part.* **neigé**

Singular

PRESENT INDICATIVE	IMPERATIVE (AFFIRMATIVE)
il neige	[not in use]

PASSÉ COMPOSÉ	IMPERATIVE (NEGATIVE)
il a neigé	[not in use]

This is an impersonal verb that is used in the third person singular with the subject pronoun **il**/it.

---

nettoyer/to clean　　　　　*pr. part.* **nettoyant**　　　　　*past part.* **nettoyé**

Singular　　　　　　　　　*Plural*

PRESENT INDICATIVE　　　　　　　　　　IMPERATIVE (AFFIRMATIVE)

je nettoie	**nous nettoyons**	**nettoie**
tu nettoies	**vous nettoyez**	**nettoyons**
il/elle nettoie	**ils/elles nettoient**	**nettoyez**

PASSÉ COMPOSÉ　　　　　　　　　　IMPERATIVE (NEGATIVE)

j'ai nettoyé	**nous avons nettoyé**	**ne nettoie pas**
tu as nettoyé	**vous avez nettoyé**	**ne nettoyons pas**
il/elle a nettoyé	**ils/elles ont nettoyé**	**ne nettoyez pas**

Verbs ending in *-oyer* must change *y* to *i* before mute *e*.

---

offrir/to offer　　　　　*pr. part.* **offrant**　　　　　*past part.* **offert**

Singular　　　　　　　　　*Plural*

PRESENT INDICATIVE　　　　　　　　　　IMPERATIVE (AFFIRMATIVE)

j'offre	**nous offrons**	**offre**
tu offres	**vous offrez**	**offrons**
il/elle offre	**ils/elles offrent**	**offrez**

PASSÉ COMPOSÉ　　　　　　　　　　IMPERATIVE (NEGATIVE)

j'ai offert	**nous avons offert**	**n'offre pas**
tu as offert	**vous avez offert**	**n'offrons pas**
il/elle a offert	**ils/elles ont offert**	**n'offrez pas**

oublier/to forget   *pr. part.* **oubliant**   *past part.* **oublié**

Singular   *Plural*

PRESENT INDICATIVE   IMPERATIVE (AFFIRMATIVE)

j'oublie   nous oublions   oublie
tu oublies   vous oubliez   oublions
il/elle oublie   ils/elles oublient   oubliez

PASSÉ COMPOSÉ   IMPERATIVE (NEGATIVE)

j'ai oublié   nous avons oublié   n'oublie pas
tu as oublié   vous avez oublié   n'oublions pas
il/elle a oublié   ils/elles ont oublié   n'oubliez pas

---

ouvrir/to open   *pr. part.* **ouvrant**   *past part.* **ouvert**

Singular   *Plural*

PRESENT INDICATIVE   IMPERATIVE (AFFIRMATIVE)

j'ouvre   nous ouvrons   ouvre
tu ouvres   vous ouvrez   ouvrons
il/elle ouvre   ils/elles ouvrent   ouvrez

PASSÉ COMPOSÉ   IMPERATIVE (NEGATIVE)

j'ai ouvert   nous avons ouvert   n'ouvre pas
tu as ouvert   vous avez ouvert   n'ouvrons pas
il/elle a ouvert   ils/elles ont ouvert   n'ouvrez pas

---

parler/to talk, speak   *pr. part.* **parlant**   *past part.* **parlé**

Singular   *Plural*

PRESENT INDICATIVE   IMPERATIVE (AFFIRMATIVE)

je parle   nous parlons   parle
tu parles   vous parlez   parlons
il/elle parle   ils/elles parlent   parlez

PASSÉ COMPOSÉ   IMPERATIVE (NEGATIVE)

j'ai parlé   nous avons parlé   ne parle pas
tu as parlé   vous avez parlé   ne parlons pas
il/elle a parlé   ils/elles ont parlé   ne parlez pas

partir/to leave, depart   *pr. part.* **partant**   *past part.* **parti**

Singular   *Plural*

PRESENT INDICATIVE   IMPERATIVE (AFFIRMATIVE)

je pars	nous partons	pars
tu pars	vous partez	partons
il/elle part	ils/elles partent	partez

PASSÉ COMPOSÉ   IMPERATIVE (NEGATIVE)

je suis parti(e)	nous sommes parti(e)s	ne pars pas
tu es parti(e)	vous êtes parti(e)(s)	ne partons pas
il est parti	ils sont partis	ne partez pas
elle est partie	elles sont parties	

---

passer/to pass, spend (time)   *pr. part.* **passant**   *past part.* **passé**

Singular   *Plural*

PRESENT INDICATIVE   IMPERATIVE (AFFIRMATIVE)

je passe	nous passons	passe
tu passes	vous passez	passons
il/elle passe	ils/elles passent	passez

PASSÉ COMPOSÉ   IMPERATIVE (NEGATIVE)

j'ai passé	nous avons passé	ne passe pas
tu as passé	vous avez passé	ne passons pas
il/elle a passé	ils/elles ont passé	ne passez pas

This verb is conjugated with **être** in the **passé composé** when it means *to pass by, go by:* **Elle est passée chez moi**/*She came by my house.* It is conjugated with **avoir** when it has a direct object: **Elle a passé un examen**/*She took an exam;* **Elle m'a passé le sel**/*She passed me the salt.*

---

payer/to pay (for)   *pr. part.* **payant**   *past part.* **payé**

Singular   *Plural*

PRESENT INDICATIVE   IMPERATIVE (AFFIRMATIVE)

je paye	nous payons	paye
tu payes	vous payez	payons
il/elle paye	ils/elles payent	payez

PASSÉ COMPOSÉ   IMPERATIVE (NEGATIVE)

j'ai payé	nous avons payé	ne paye pas
tu as payé	vous avez payé	ne payons pas
il/elle a payé	ils/elles ont payé	ne payez pas

Verbs ending in *-ayer* may change *y* to *i* before mute *e* or may keep *y*.

penser/to think   *pr. part.* **pensant**   *past part.* **pensé**

Singular   *Plural*

PRESENT INDICATIVE   IMPERATIVE (AFFIRMATIVE)

je pense   nous pensons   pense
tu penses   vous pensez   pensons
il/elle pense   ils/elles pensent   pensez

PASSÉ COMPOSÉ   IMPERATIVE (NEGATIVE)

j'ai pensé   nous avons pensé   ne pense pas
tu as pensé   vous avez pensé   ne pensons pas
il/elle a pensé   ils/elles ont pensé   ne pensez pas

---

perdre/to lose   *pr. part.* **perdant**   *past part.* **perdu**

Singular   *Plural*

PRESENT INDICATIVE   IMPERATIVE (AFFIRMATIVE)

je perds   nous perdons   perds
tu perds   vous perdez   perdons
il/elle perd   ils/elles perdent   perdez

PASSÉ COMPOSÉ   IMPERATIVE (NEGATIVE)

j'ai perdu   nous avons perdu   ne perds pas
tu as perdu   vous avez perdu   ne perdons pas
il/elle a perdu   ils/elles ont perdu   ne perdez pas

---

pleuvoir/to rain   *pr. part.* **pleuvant**   *past part.* **plu**

Singular

PRESENT INDICATIVE   IMPERATIVE (AFFIRMATIVE)

il pleut   [not in use]

PASSÉ COMPOSÉ   IMPERATIVE (NEGATIVE)

il a plu   [not in use]

This is an impersonal verb that is used in the third person singular with the subject pronoun **il**/it.

pouvoir/to be able, can   *pr. part.* **pouvant**   *past part.* **pu**

Singular   *Plural*

PRESENT INDICATIVE   IMPERATIVE (AFFIRMATIVE)

je peux *or* je puis	nous pouvons	[not in use]
tu peux	vous pouvez	
il/elle peut	ils/elles peuvent	

PASSÉ COMPOSÉ   IMPERATIVE (NEGATIVE)

j'ai pu	nous avons pu	[not in use]
tu as pu	vous avez pu	
il/elle a pu	ils/elles ont pu	

---

préférer/to prefer   *pr. part.* **préférant**   *past part.* **préféré**

Singular   *Plural*

PRESENT INDICATIVE   IMPERATIVE (AFFIRMATIVE)

je préfère	nous préférons	préfère
tu préfères	vous préférez	préférons
il/elle préfère	ils/elles préfèrent	préférez

PASSÉ COMPOSÉ   IMPERATIVE (NEGATIVE)

j'ai préféré	nous avons préféré	ne préfère pas
tu as préféré	vous avez préféré	ne préférons pas
il/elle a préféré	ils/elles ont préféré	ne préférez pas

---

prendre/to take   *pr. part.* **prenant**   *past part.* **pris**

Singular   *Plural*

PRESENT INDICATIVE   IMPERATIVE (AFFIRMATIVE)

je prends	nous prenons	prends
tu prends	vous prenez	prenons
il/elle prend	ils/elles prennent	prenez

PASSÉ COMPOSÉ   IMPERATIVE (NEGATIVE)

j'ai pris	nous avons pris	ne prends pas
tu as pris	vous avez pris	ne prenons pas
il/elle a pris	ils/elles ont pris	ne prenez pas

recevoir/to receive   *pr. part.* **recevant**   *past part.* **reçu**

Singular   *Plural*

PRESENT INDICATIVE

je reçois   nous recevons
tu reçois   vous recevez
il/elle reçoit   ils/elles reçoivent

PASSÉ COMPOSÉ

j'ai reçu   nous avons reçu
tu as reçu   vous avez reçu
il/elle a reçu   ils/elles ont reçu

IMPERATIVE (AFFIRMATIVE)

reçois
recevons
recevez

IMPERATIVE (NEGATIVE)

ne reçois pas
ne recevons pas
ne recevez pas

---

regarder/to look (at), watch   *pr. part.* **regardant**   *past part.* **regardé**

Singular   *Plural*

PRESENT INDICATIVE

je regarde   nous regardons
tu regardes   vous regardez
il/elle regarde   ils/elles regardent

PASSÉ COMPOSÉ

j'ai regardé   nous avons regardé
tu as regardé   vous avez regardé
il/elle a regardé   ils/elles ont regardé

IMPERATIVE (AFFIRMATIVE)

regarde
regardons
regardez

IMPERATIVE (NEGATIVE)

ne regarde pas
ne regardons pas
ne regardez pas

---

rendre/to give back, to return (something)   *pr. part.* **rendant**   *past part.* **rendu**

Singular   *Plural*

PRESENT INDICATIVE

je rends   nous rendons
tu rends   vous rendez
il/elle rend   ils/elles rendent

PASSÉ COMPOSÉ

j'ai rendu   nous avons rendu
tu as rendu   vous avez rendu
il/elle a rendu   ils/elles ont rendu

IMPERATIVE (AFFIRMATIVE)

rends
rendons
rendez

IMPERATIVE (NEGATIVE)

ne rends pas
ne rendons pas
ne rendez pas

rentrer/to go in again, return (home)   *pr. part.* **rentrant**   *past part.* **rentré**

Singular   *Plural*

<table>
<tr><td colspan="2" align="center">PRESENT INDICATIVE</td><td align="center">IMPERATIVE (AFFIRMATIVE)</td></tr>
<tr><td>je rentre</td><td>nous rentrons</td><td align="center">rentre</td></tr>
<tr><td>tu rentres</td><td>vous rentrez</td><td align="center">rentrons</td></tr>
<tr><td>il/elle rentre</td><td>ils/elles rentrent</td><td align="center">rentrez</td></tr>
<tr><td colspan="2" align="center">PASSÉ COMPOSÉ</td><td align="center">IMPERATIVE (NEGATIVE)</td></tr>
<tr><td>je suis rentré(e)</td><td>nous sommes rentré(e)s</td><td align="center">ne rentre pas</td></tr>
<tr><td>tu es rentré(e)</td><td>vous êtes rentré(e)(s)</td><td align="center">ne rentrons pas</td></tr>
<tr><td>il est rentré</td><td>ils sont rentrés</td><td align="center">ne rentrez pas</td></tr>
<tr><td>elle est rentrée</td><td>elles sont rentrées</td><td></td></tr>
</table>

This verb is conjugated with **avoir** when it has a direct object. *Example:* **Elle a rentré le chat dans la maison**/*She brought (took) the cat back into the house.* But: **Elle est rentrée tôt**/*She returned (has returned) home early.*

---

répondre/to answer, respond, reply   *pr. part.* **répondant**   *past part.* **répondu**

Singular   *Plural*

<table>
<tr><td colspan="2" align="center">PRESENT INDICATIVE</td><td align="center">IMPERATIVE (AFFIRMATIVE)</td></tr>
<tr><td>je réponds</td><td>nous répondons</td><td align="center">réponds</td></tr>
<tr><td>tu réponds</td><td>vous répondez</td><td align="center">répondons</td></tr>
<tr><td>il/elle répond</td><td>ils/elles répondent</td><td align="center">répondez</td></tr>
<tr><td colspan="2" align="center">PASSÉ COMPOSÉ</td><td align="center">IMPERATIVE (NEGATIVE)</td></tr>
<tr><td>j'ai répondu</td><td>nous avons répondu</td><td align="center">ne réponds pas</td></tr>
<tr><td>tu as répondu</td><td>vous avez répondu</td><td align="center">ne répondons pas</td></tr>
<tr><td>il/elle a répondu</td><td>ils/elles ont répondu</td><td align="center">ne répondez pas</td></tr>
</table>

---

rester/to remain, stay   *pr. part.* **restant**   *past part.* **resté**

Singular   *Plural*

<table>
<tr><td colspan="2" align="center">PRESENT INDICATIVE</td><td align="center">IMPERATIVE (AFFIRMATIVE)</td></tr>
<tr><td>je reste</td><td>nous restons</td><td align="center">reste</td></tr>
<tr><td>tu restes</td><td>vous restez</td><td align="center">restons</td></tr>
<tr><td>il/elle reste</td><td>ils/elles restent</td><td align="center">restez</td></tr>
<tr><td colspan="2" align="center">PASSÉ COMPOSÉ</td><td align="center">IMPERATIVE (NEGATIVE)</td></tr>
<tr><td>je suis resté(e)</td><td>nous sommes resté(e)s</td><td align="center">ne reste pas</td></tr>
<tr><td>tu es resté(e)</td><td>vous êtes resté(e)(s)</td><td align="center">ne restons pas</td></tr>
<tr><td>il est resté</td><td>ils sont restés</td><td align="center">ne restez pas</td></tr>
<tr><td>elle est restée</td><td>elles sont restées</td><td></td></tr>
</table>

Do not confuse this verb with **se reposer**/to rest.

retourner/to go back, return   *pr. part.* **retournant**   *past part.* **retourné**

Singular   *Plural*

PRESENT INDICATIVE   IMPERATIVE (AFFIRMATIVE)

je retourne	**nous retournons**	**retourne**
tu retournes	**vous retournez**	**retournons**
il/elle retourne	**ils/elles retournent**	**retournez**

PASSÉ COMPOSÉ   IMPERATIVE (NEGATIVE)

je suis retourné(e)	**nous sommes retourné(e)s**	**ne retourne pas**
tu es retourné(e)	**vous êtes retourné(e)(s)**	**ne retournons pas**
il est retourné	**ils sont retournés**	**ne retournez pas**
elle est retournée	**elles sont retournées**	

---

revenir/to come back, return   *pr. part.* **revenant**   *past part.* **revenu**

Singular   *Plural*

PRESENT INDICATIVE   IMPERATIVE (AFFIRMATIVE)

je reviens	**nous revenons**	**reviens**
tu reviens	**vous revenez**	**revenons**
il/elle revient	**ils/elles reviennent**	**revenez**

PASSÉ COMPOSÉ   IMPERATIVE (NEGATIVE)

je suis revenu(e)	**nous sommes revenu(e)s**	**ne reviens pas**
tu es revenu(e)	**vous êtes revenu(e)(s)**	**ne revenons pas**
il est revenu	**ils sont revenus**	**ne revenez pas**
elle est revenue	**elles sont revenues**	

---

rire/to laugh   *pr. part.* **riant**   *past part.* **ri**

Singular   *Plural*

PRESENT INDICATIVE   IMPERATIVE (AFFIRMATIVE)

je ris	**nous rions**	**ris**
tu ris	**vous riez**	**rions**
il/elle rit	**ils/elles rient**	**riez**

PASSÉ COMPOSÉ   IMPERATIVE (NEGATIVE)

j'ai ri	**nous avons ri**	**ne ris pas**
tu as ri	**vous avez ri**	**ne rions pas**
il/elle a ri	**ils/elles ont ri**	**ne riez pas**

savoir/to know (how), to know (a fact)   *pr. part.* **sachant**   *past part.* **su**

Singular   *Plural*

PRESENT INDICATIVE

Singular	Plural
je sais	nous savons
tu sais	vous savez
il/elle sait	ils/elles savent

IMPERATIVE (AFFIRMATIVE)

sache
sachons
sachez

PASSÉ COMPOSÉ

Singular	Plural
j'ai su	nous avons su
tu as su	vous avez su
il/elle a su	ils/elles ont su

IMPERATIVE (NEGATIVE)

ne sache pas
ne sachons pas
ne sachez pas

---

sentir/to smell, feel   *pr. part.* **sentant**   *past part.* **senti**

Singular   *Plural*

PRESENT INDICATIVE

Singular	Plural
je sens	nous sentons
tu sens	vous sentez
il/elle sent	ils/elles sentent

IMPERATIVE (AFFIRMATIVE)

sens
sentons
sentez

PASSÉ COMPOSÉ

Singular	Plural
j'ai senti	nous avons senti
tu as senti	vous avez senti
il/elle a senti	ils/elles ont senti

IMPERATIVE (NEGATIVE)

ne sens pas
ne sentons pas
ne sentez pas

---

servir/to serve   *pr. part.* **servant**   *past part.* **servi**

Singular   *Plural*

PRESENT INDICATIVE

Singular	Plural
je sers	nous servons
tu sers	vous servez
il/elle sert	ils/elles servent

IMPERATIVE (AFFIRMATIVE)

sers
servons
servez

PASSÉ COMPOSÉ

Singular	Plural
j'ai servi	nous avons servi
tu as servi	vous avez servi
il/elle a servi	ils/elles ont servi

IMPERATIVE (NEGATIVE)

ne sers pas
ne servons pas
ne servez pas

sortir/to go out, leave   *pr. part.* **sortant**   *past part.* **sorti**

Singular   *Plural*

PRESENT INDICATIVE		IMPERATIVE (AFFIRMATIVE)
je sors	**nous sortons**	**sors**
tu sors	**vous sortez**	**sortons**
il/elle sort	**ils/elles sortent**	**sortez**

PASSÉ COMPOSÉ		IMPERATIVE (NEGATIVE)
je suis sorti(e)	**nous sommes sorti(e)s**	**ne sors pas**
tu es sorti(e)	**vous êtes sorti(e)(s)**	**ne sortons pas**
il est sorti	**ils sont sortis**	**ne sortez pas**
elle est sortie	**elles sont sorties**	

This verb is conjugated with **avoir** in the **passé composé** when it has a direct object. *Example:* **Elle a sorti son mouchoir**/*She took out her handkerchief.* But: **Elle est sortie**/*She went out (She has gone out).*

---

souffrir/to suffer, endure   *pr. part.* **souffrant**   *past part.* **souffert**

Singular   *Plural*

PRESENT INDICATIVE		IMPERATIVE (AFFIRMATIVE)
je souffre	**nous souffrons**	**souffre**
tu souffres	**vous souffrez**	**souffrons**
il/elle souffre	**ils/elles souffrent**	**souffrez**

PASSÉ COMPOSÉ		IMPERATIVE (NEGATIVE)
j'ai souffert	**nous avons souffert**	**ne souffre pas**
tu as souffert	**vous avez souffert**	**ne souffrons pas**
il/elle a souffert	**ils/elles ont souffert**	**ne souffrez pas**

---

suffire/to suffice, be enough   *pr. part.* **suffisant**   *past part.* **suffi**

Singular

PRESENT INDICATIVE	IMPERATIVE (AFFIRMATIVE)
il suffit	[not in use]

PASSÉ COMPOSÉ	IMPERATIVE (NEGATIVE)
il a suffi	[not in use]

This verb is generally impersonal and is used frequently in the third person singular with the subject pronoun **il**/it. The subject **cela** may be used, as in **Cela suffit**/*That is enough.*

téléphoner/to telephone   *pr. part.* **téléphonant**   *past part.* **téléphoné**

Singular   *Plural*

PRESENT INDICATIVE   IMPERATIVE (AFFIRMATIVE)

je téléphone   nous téléphonons   téléphone
tu téléphones   vous téléphonez   téléphonons
il/elle téléphone   ils/elles téléphonent   téléphonez

PASSÉ COMPOSÉ   IMPERATIVE (NEGATIVE)

j'ai téléphoné   nous avons téléphoné   ne téléphone pas
tu as téléphoné   vous avez téléphoné   ne téléphonons pas
il/elle a téléphoné   ils/elles ont téléphoné   ne téléphonez pas

---

tenir/to hold   *pr. part.* **tenant**   *past part.* **tenu**

Singular   *Plural*

PRESENT INDICATIVE   IMPERATIVE (AFFIRMATIVE)

je tiens   nous tenons   tiens
tu tiens   vous tenez   tenons
il/elle tient   ils/elles tiennent   tenez

PASSÉ COMPOSÉ   IMPERATIVE (NEGATIVE)

j'ai tenu   nous avons tenu   ne tiens pas
tu as tenu   vous avez tenu   ne tenons pas
il/elle a tenu   ils/elles ont tenu   ne tenez pas

---

tomber/to fall   *pr. part.* **tombant**   *past part.* **tombé**

Singular   *Plural*

PRESENT INDICATIVE   IMPERATIVE (AFFIRMATIVE)

je tombe   nous tombons   tombe
tu tombes   vous tombez   tombons
il/elle tombe   ils/elles tombent   tombez

PASSÉ COMPOSÉ   IMPERATIVE (NEGATIVE)

je suis tombé(e)   nous sommes tombé(e)s   ne tombe pas
tu es tombé(e)   vous êtes tombé(e)(s)   ne tombons pas
il est tombé   ils sont tombés   ne tombez pas
elle est tombée   elles sont tombées

travailler/to work   *pr. part.* **travaillant**   *past part.* **travaillé**

Singular   *Plural*

PRESENT INDICATIVE   IMPERATIVE (AFFIRMATIVE)

je travaille	**nous travaillons**	**travaille**
tu travailles	**vous travaillez**	**travaillons**
il/elle travaille	**ils/elles travaillent**	**travaillez**

PASSÉ COMPOSÉ   IMPERATIVE (NEGATIVE)

j'ai travaillé	**nous avons travaillé**	**ne travaille pas**
tu as travaillé	**vous avez travaillé**	**ne travaillons pas**
il/elle a travaillé	**ils/elles ont travaillé**	**ne travaillez pas**

---

trouver/to find   *pr. part.* **trouvant**   *past part.* **trouvé**

Singular   *Plural*

PRESENT INDICATIVE   IMPERATIVE (AFFIRMATIVE)

je trouve	**nous trouvons**	**trouve**
tu trouves	**vous trouvez**	**trouvons**
il/elle trouve	**ils/elles trouvent**	**trouvez**

PASSÉ COMPOSÉ   IMPERATIVE (NEGATIVE)

j'ai trouvé	**nous avons trouvé**	**ne trouve pas**
tu as trouvé	**vous avez trouvé**	**ne trouvons pas**
il/elle a trouvé	**ils/elles ont trouvé**	**ne trouvez pas**

---

vendre/to sell   *pr. part.* **vendant**   *past part.* **vendu**

Singular   *Plural*

PRESENT INDICATIVE   IMPERATIVE (AFFIRMATIVE)

je vends	**nous vendons**	**vends**
tu vends	**vous vendez**	**vendons**
il/elle vend	**ils/elles vendent**	**vendez**

PASSÉ COMPOSÉ   IMPERATIVE (NEGATIVE)

j'ai vendu	**nous avons vendu**	**ne vends pas**
tu as vendu	**vous avez vendu**	**ne vendons pas**
il/elle a vendu	**ils/elles ont vendu**	**ne vendez pas**

venir/to come   *pr. part.* **venant**   *past part.* **venu**

Singular   *Plural*

    PRESENT INDICATIVE   IMPERATIVE (AFFIRMATIVE)

je viens	**nous venons**	**viens**
tu viens	**vous venez**	**venons**
il/elle vient	**ils/elles viennent**	**venez**

    PASSÉ COMPOSÉ   IMPERATIVE (NEGATIVE)

je suis venu(e)	**nous sommes venu(e)s**	**ne viens pas**
tu es venu(e)	**vous êtes venu(e)(s)**	**ne venons pas**
il est venu	**ils sont venus**	**ne venez pas**
elle est venue	**elles sont venues**	

---

vivre/to live   *pr. part.* **vivant**   *past part.* **vécu**

Singular   *Plural*

    PRESENT INDICATIVE   IMPERATIVE (AFFIRMATIVE)

je vis	**nous vivons**	**vis**
tu vis	**vous vivez**	**vivons**
il/elle vit	**ils/elles vivent**	**vivez**

    PASSÉ COMPOSÉ   IMPERATIVE (NEGATIVE)

j'ai vécu	**nous avons vécu**	**ne vis pas**
tu as vécu	**vous avez vécu**	**ne vivons pas**
il/elle a vécu	**ils/elles ont vécu**	**ne vivez pas**

---

voir/to see   *pr. part.* **voyant**   *past part.* **vu**

Singular   *Plural*

    PRESENT INDICATIVE   IMPERATIVE (AFFIRMATIVE)

je vois	**nous voyons**	**vois**
tu vois	**vous voyez**	**voyons**
il/elle voit	**ils/elles voient**	**voyez**

    PASSÉ COMPOSÉ   IMPERATIVE (NEGATIVE)

j'ai vu	**nous avons vu**	**ne vois pas**
tu as vu	**vous avez vu**	**ne voyons pas**
il/elle a vu	**ils/elles ont vu**	**ne voyez pas**

voler/to fly; to steal   *pr. part.* **volant**   *past part.* **volé**

Singular   *Plural*

PRESENT INDICATIVE		IMPERATIVE (AFFIRMATIVE)
je vole	nous volons	vole
tu voles	vous volez	volons
il/elle vole	ils/elles volent	volez

PASSÉ COMPOSÉ		IMPERATIVE (NEGATIVE)
j'ai volé	nous avons volé	ne vole pas
tu as volé	vous avez volé	ne volons pas
il/elle a volé	ils/elles ont volé	ne volez pas

---

vouloir/to want   *pr. part.* **voulant**   *past part.* **voulu**

Singular   *Plural*

PRESENT INDICATIVE		IMPERATIVE (AFFIRMATIVE)
je veux	nous voulons	veuille
tu veux	vous voulez	veuillons
il/elle veut	ils/elles veulent	veuillez

PASSÉ COMPOSÉ		IMPERATIVE (NEGATIVE)
j'ai voulu	nous avons voulu	ne veuille pas
tu as voulu	vous avez voulu	ne veuillons pas
il/elle a voulu	ils/elles ont voulu	ne veuillez pas

---

voyager/to travel   *pr. part.* **voyageant**   *past part.* **voyagé**

Singular   *Plural*

PRESENT INDICATIVE		IMPERATIVE (AFFIRMATIVE)
je voyage	nous voyageons	voyage
tu voyages	vous voyagez	voyageons
il/elle voyage	ils/elles voyagent	voyagez

PASSÉ COMPOSÉ		IMPERATIVE (NEGATIVE)
j'ai voyagé	nous avons voyagé	ne voyage pas
tu as voyagé	vous avez voyagé	ne voyageons pas
il/elle a voyagé	ils/elles ont voyagé	ne voyagez pas

Part B

This part contains only reflexive verbs. They are grouped here so you can make your own observations about the repeated patterns. All reflexive verbs are conjugated with **être** to form the **passé composé** tense.

---

s'amuser/to have a good time, have fun *pr. part.* **s'amusant** *past part.* **amusé**

Singular *Plural*

PRESENT INDICATIVE

		IMPERATIVE (AFFIRMATIVE)

je m'amuse nous nous amusons **amuse-toi**
tu t'amuses vous vous amusez **amusons-nous**
il/elle s'amuse ils/elles s'amusent **amusez-vous**

PASSÉ COMPOSÉ

IMPERATIVE (NEGATIVE)

je me suis amusé(e) nous nous sommes amusé(e)s **ne t'amuse pas**
tu t'es amusé(e) vous vous êtes amusé(e)(s) **ne nous amusons pas**
il s'est amusé ils se sont amusés **ne vous amusez pas**
elle s'est amusée elles se sont amusées

---

s'appeler/to be named, call oneself *pr. part.* **s'appelant** *past part.* **appelé**

Singular *Plural*

PRESENT INDICATIVE

IMPERATIVE (AFFIRMATIVE)

je m'appelle nous nous appelons **appelle-toi**
tu t'appelles vous vous appelez **appelons-nous**
il/elle s'appelle ils/elles s'appellent **appelez-vous**

PASSÉ COMPOSÉ

IMPERATIVE (NEGATIVE)

je me suis appelé(e) nous nous sommes appelé(e)s **ne t'appelle pas**
tu t'es appelé(e) vous vous êtes appelé(e)(s) **ne nous appelons pas**
il s'est appelé ils se sont appelés **ne vous appelez pas**
elle s'est appelée elles se sont appelées

---

s'asseoir/to sit down *pr. part.* **s'asseyant** *past part.* **assis**

Singular *Plural*

PRESENT INDICATIVE

IMPERATIVE (AFFIRMATIVE)

je m'assieds nous nous asseyons **assieds-toi**
tu t'assieds vous vous asseyez **asseyons-nous**
il/elle s'assied ils/elles s'asseyent **asseyez-vous**

PASSÉ COMPOSÉ

IMPERATIVE (NEGATIVE)

je me suis assis(e) nous nous sommes assis(es) **ne t'assieds pas**
tu t'es assis(e) vous vous êtes assis(e)(es) **ne nous asseyons pas**
il s'est assis ils se sont assis **ne vous asseyez pas**
elle s'est assise elles se sont assises

---

s'en aller/to go away   *pr. part.* **s'en allant**   *past part.* **en allé**

Singular   *Plural*

PRESENT INDICATIVE   IMPERATIVE (AFFIRMATIVE)

je m'en vais   nous nous en allons   va-t'en
tu t'en vas   vous vous en allez   allons-nous-en
il/elle s'en va   ils/elles s'en vont   allez-vous-en

PASSÉ COMPOSÉ   IMPERATIVE (NEGATIVE)

je m'en suis allé(e)   nous nous en sommes allé(e)s   ne t'en va pas
tu t'en es allé(e)   vous vous en êtes allé(e)(s)   ne nous en allons pas
il s'en est allé   ils s'en sont allés   ne vous en allez pas
elle s'en est allée   elles s'en sont allées

---

s'habiller/to dress (oneself)   *pr. part.* **s'habillant**   *past part.* **habillé**

Singular   *Plural*

PRESENT INDICATIVE   IMPERATIVE (AFFIRMATIVE)

je m'habille   nous nous habillons   habille-toi
tu t'habilles   vous vous habillez   habillons-nous
il/elle s'habille   ils/elles s'habillent   habillez-vous

PASSÉ COMPOSÉ   IMPERATIVE (NEGATIVE)

je me suis habillé(e)   nous nous sommes habillé(e)s   ne t'habille pas
tu t'es habillé(e)   vous vous êtes habillé(e)(s)   ne nous habillons pas
il s'est habillé   ils se sont habillés   ne vous habillez pas
elle s'est habillée   elles se sont habillées

---

se blesser/to hurt (injure) oneself   *pr. part.* **se blessant**   *past part.* **blessé**

Singular   *Plural*

PRESENT INDICATIVE   IMPERATIVE (AFFIRMATIVE)

je me blesse   nous nous blessons   blesse-toi
tu te blesses   vous vous blessez   blessons-nous
il/elle se blesse   ils/elles se blessent   blessez-vous

PASSÉ COMPOSÉ   IMPERATIVE (NEGATIVE)

je me suis blessé(e)   nous nous sommes blessé(e)s   ne te blesse pas
tu t'es blessé(e)   vous vous êtes blessé(e)(s)   ne nous blessons pas
il s'est blessé   ils se sont blessés   ne vous blessez pas
elle s'est blessée   elles se sont blessées

se coucher/to go to bed, to lie down   *pr. part.* **se couchant**   *past part.* **couché**

Singular   *Plural*

PRESENT INDICATIVE

je me couche	nous nous couchons	
tu te couches	vous vous couchez	
il/elle se couche	ils/elles se couchent	

IMPERATIVE (AFFIRMATIVE)

couche-toi
couchons-nous
couchez-vous

PASSÉ COMPOSÉ

je me suis couché(e)	nous nous sommes couché(e)s
tu t'es couché(e)	vous vous êtes couché(e)(s)
il s'est couché	ils se sont couchés
elle s'est couchée	elles se sont couchées

IMPERATIVE (NEGATIVE)

ne te couche pas
ne nous couchons pas
ne vous couchez pas

---

se dépêcher/to hurry   *pr. part.* **se dépêchant**   *past part.* **dépêché**

Singular   *Plural*

PRESENT INDICATIVE

je me dépêche	nous nous dépêchons
tu te dépêches	vous vous dépêchez
il/elle se dépêche	ils/elles se dépêchent

IMPERATIVE (AFFIRMATIVE)

dépêche-toi
dépêchons-nous
dépêchez-vous

PASSÉ COMPOSÉ

je me suis dépêché(e)	nous nous sommes dépêché(e)s
tu t'es dépêché(e)	vous vous êtes dépêché(e)(s)
il s'est dépêché	ils se sont dépêchés
elle s'est dépêchée	elles se sont dépêchées

IMPERATIVE (NEGATIVE)

ne te dépêche pas
ne nous dépêchons pas
ne vous dépêchez pas

---

se laver/to wash oneself   *pr. part.* **se lavant**   *past part.* **lavé**

Singular   *Plural*

PRESENT INDICATIVE

je me lave	nous nous lavons
tu te laves	vous vous lavez
il/elle se lave	ils/elles se lavent

IMPERATIVE (AFFIRMATIVE)

lave-toi
lavons-nous
lavez-vous

PASSÉ COMPOSÉ

je me suis lavé(e)	nous nous sommes lavé(e)s
tu t'es lavé(e)	vous vous êtes lavé(e)(s)
il s'est lavé	ils se sont lavés
elle s'est lavée	elles se sont lavées

IMPERATIVE (NEGATIVE)

ne te lave pas
ne nous lavons pas
ne vous lavez pas

se lever/to get up   *pr. part.* **se levant**   *past part.* **levé**

Singular   *Plural*

PRESENT INDICATIVE   IMPERATIVE (AFFIRMATIVE)

je me lève   nous nous levons   lève-toi
tu te lèves   vous vous levez   levons-nous
il/elle se lève   ils/elles se lèvent   levez-vous

PASSÉ COMPOSÉ   IMPERATIVE (NEGATIVE)

je me suis levé(e)   nous nous sommes levé(e)s   ne te lève pas
tu t'es levé(e)   vous vous êtes levé(e)(s)   ne nous levons pas
il s'est levé   ils se sont levés   ne vous levez pas
elle s'est levée   elles se sont levées

---

se reposer/to rest   *pr. part.* **se reposant**   *past part.* **reposé**

Singular   *Plural*

PRESENT INDICATIVE   IMPERATIVE (AFFIRMATIVE)

je me repose   nous nous reposons   repose-toi
tu te reposes   vous vous reposez   reposons-nous
il/elle se repose   ils/elles se reposent   reposez-vous

PASSÉ COMPOSÉ   IMPERATIVE (NEGATIVE)

je me suis reposé(e)   nous nous sommes reposé(e)s   ne te repose pas
tu t'es reposé(e)   vous vous êtes reposé(e)(s)   ne nous reposons pas
il s'est reposé   ils se sont reposés   ne vous reposez pas
elle s'est reposée   elles se sont reposées

---

se souvenir/to remember   *pr. part.* **se souvenant**   *past part.* **souvenu**

Singular   *Plural*

PRESENT INDICATIVE   IMPERATIVE (AFFIRMATIVE)

je me souviens   nous nous souvenons   souviens-toi
tu te souviens   vous vous souvenez   souvenons-nous
il/elle se souvient   ils/elles se souviennent   souvenez-vous

PASSÉ COMPOSÉ   IMPERATIVE (NEGATIVE)

je me suis souvenu(e)   nous nous sommes souvenu(e)s   ne te souviens pas
tu t'es souvenu(e)   vous vous êtes souvenu(e)(s)   ne nous souvenons pas
il s'est souvenu   ils se sont souvenus   ne vous souvenez pas
elle s'est souvenue   elles se sont souvenues

A

à *prep.* at, to; **à bientôt** see you soon; **à ce moment-là** at that moment; **à couvert** covered; **à tout à l'heure** see you in a little while

a *v. form of* **avoir**; **il, elle a**/he, she, it has; **a eu** *v. form, passé composé of* **avoir**

abîmer *v.* to spoil, to damage

accepté *past part. of* **accepter** (to accept)

achat *n. m.* purchase; **achète** *v. form of* **acheter** (to buy); **acheté** *past part.*

addition *n. f.* bill, check (tab)

adieu *n. m.* farewell, good-bye

Afrique *n. f.* Africa

agent de police *n. m.* police officer

agréable *adj.* pleasant

ai *v. form of* **avoir**; **j'ai**/I have; **je n'ai pas**/I don't have

aidé *past part. of* **aider** (to help)

ail *n. m.* garlic

aile *n. f.* wing

aime *v. form of* **aimer** (to love, to like); **aimé** *past part.*; **aimer bien** to like; **aimer mieux** to prefer, to like better

ainsi que *conj.* as well as, (just) as

ajoute, ajoutez *v. forms of* **ajouter** (to add)

aliment *n. m.* **alimentation** *n. f.* food, nourishmnent

allé *past part. of* **aller** (to go); **allez, allons** *v. forms of* **aller**; **allez-y!** go there! go to it! **allez!** go! **n'allez pas!** don't go! **allons!** let's go!

allemand *n. m.* German (language); **Allemagne** *n. f.* Germany

allô *interj.* hello (used when answering a telephone)

allumer *v.* to turn on, switch on (an apparatus), to light

alors *adv.* so, then, well

américain *n. m.* American (language); **l'Amérique** *n. f.* America

ami *n. m.* **amie** *n. f.* friend; **amitié** *n. f.* friendship

amour *n. m.* love; **amoureux, amoureuse** *adj. m. f.* in love; **amoureuse de** in love with; **nous sommes amoureux** we are in love

amusant, amusante *adj.* amusing, enjoyable; **amuser** *v.* to amuse; **s'amuser** *refl. v.* to have a good time, amuse oneself, enjoy oneself; **nous allons beaucoup nous amuser** we are going to have a very good time; **amusez-vous bien!** have a good time! **ils se sont bien amusés** they had a very good time

an *n. m.* **année** *n. f.* year

ananas *n. m.* pineapple

ancien *adj. m. s.* **ancienne** *adj. f. s.* ancient, old, former

anglais *n. m.* English (language)

Angleterre *n. f.* England

animaux *n. m. pl.* animals

anniversaire *n. m.* birthday, anniversary

annoncé *past part. of* **annoncer** (to announce)

août *n. m.* August

appareil *n. m.* apparatus (telephone)

appelé *past part. of* **appeler** (to call); **s'appeler** to be called, be named; **Comment vous appelez-vous?**/What is your name? **Je m'appelle Janine.**/My name is Janine.

apporte *v. form of* **apporter** (to bring); **apporté** *past part.*; **apporte!**/bring!

apprendre *v.* to learn; **appris** *past part.*; **Je n'ai rien appris de nouveau**/I didn't learn anything new

s'approcher (de) *refl. v.* to approach, come (go) near

après *prep.* after; **après-midi** *n. m.* afternoon; **l'après-midi** in the afternoon

arbre *n. m.* tree

arc-en-ciel *n. m.* rainbow

argent *n. m.* money

armoire *n. f.* closet, wardrobe

arracher *v.* to pull (away)

arrêt *n. m.* stop; **arrêt d'autobus** bus stop; **arrêté** *past part. of* **arrêter** (to arrest), **s'arrêter** (to stop)

arrivent *v. form of* **arriver** (to arrive); **arrivé** *past part.*

as *v. form of* **avoir** (to have); **tu as**/you have; **as-tu?**/do you have

s'assembler *refl. v.* to gather together

s'assied *v. form of* **s'asseoir** (to sit down); **assis** *past part.*; **assis(e)** *adj.* seated, sitting; **assieds-toi!**/sit down! **asseyez-vous!**/sit down!

assiette *n. f.* plate, dish

assister à *v.* to attend, be present at

assourdissant(e) *adj. m. (f.) s.* deafening (very loud)

attendre *v.* to wait (for), expect

attention *n. f.* **à** watch out for

attraper *v.* to catch

au (*combining of* **à + le**) at the, to the, in the, with; **au caissier**/at the cashier's; **au courant**/in the know; **au four**/in the oven; **au guichet**/at the ticket window; **au lit**/in bed; **au mois de**/in the month of; **au régime**/on a diet; **au revoir**/good-bye, until we meet again

aujourd'hui *adv.* today

aussi *adv.* also, too, as

auteur *n. m.* author, writer

autobus *n. m.* city bus; **autocar** *n. m.* interurban bus

automne *n. m.* autumn, fall

autour *adv.* around

autre(s) *adj., pron.* other(s), another; **l'autre** the other one; **un (une) autre** another one

aux (*combining of* **à + les**) to the, in the, at the, with; **aux États-Unis** to (in) the United States

avancer *v.* to advance

avant *prep.* before; **avant de sortir** before going out

avec *prep.* with; **avec eux** with them

avez *v. form of* **avoir** (to have); **vous avez** you have, you do have

avion *n. m.* airplane

avis *n. m.* opinion; **avisé** *adj.* shrewd, smart

avocat *n. m.* lawyer

avoir *v.* to have

avoué *n. m.* attorney, lawyer

B

bague *n. f.* ring

se baigner *v. refl.* to bathe oneself

bal *n. m.* dance

balai *n. m.* broom

balançoir *n. f.* swing, seesaw

balle *n. f.* ball, bullet

ballon *n. m.* ball, balloon, football

banc *n. m.* bench (seat)

banque *n. f.* **de données** database

bar *n. m.* **rapide** snack bar

barrière *n. f.* fence

bas *n. m.* stocking; *adj.* low; *adv.* low down; **les plus bas** the lowest

basse *adj. f.* low

bat *v. form of* **battre** (to beat)

bâti *past part. of* **bâtir** (to build); **bâtiment** *n. m.* building

bâton *n. m.* wand, stick, baton

beau *adj. m. s.* beautiful, handsome; **beaux** *pl.*

beaucoup (de) *adv.* much, a lot, many

beauté *n. f.* beauty

bébé *n. m.* baby

belge *adj.* Belgian; **Belgique** *n. f.* Belgium; **Il est belge, Elle est belge**/He (She) is Belgian

belle *adj. f. s.* beautiful

bercer *v.* to rock, lull

besoin *n. m.* need

bête *adj.* foolish, dumb; **bêtise** *n. f.* foolish thing, dumb thing

beurre *n. m.* butter

bibliothèque *n. f.* library

bien *adv.* well; **bien sûr** of course; **bientôt** *adv.* soon

bière *n. f.* beer

billet *n. m.* ticket

billet *n. m.* **électronique** electronic ticket, e-ticket

blanc *adj. m. s.* **blanche** *adj. f. s.* white

blé *n. m.* wheat

blesser *v.* to hurt, injure

bleu *n. m., adj. m. sing.* **bleus** *adj. m. pl.* blue

boire *v.* to drink

bois *n. m.* woods

boisson *n. m.* drink, beverage

boit *v. form of* **boire**

boîte *n. f.* tin can, box

boîte *n. f.* **vocale** voice mail

bon *adj. m. s.,* **bons** *pl.;* **bonne** *adj. f. s.,* **bonnes** *pl.* good

bon voyage! have a good trip! **bon retour!** have a good return trip!

bonbon *n. m.* candy

bonheur *n. m.* happiness

bonhomme *n. m.* **de neige** snowman

bonjour *n. m.* hello, good day, good morning, good afternoon

bonne *adj. f. s.* good; **bonne chance!** good luck! **de bonne heure** early; **bonnes nouvelles!** good news!

bonsoir *n. m.* good night, good evening

bouche *n. f.* mouth

boucher *n. m.* butcher; **boucherie** *n. f.* butcher shop

bouillir *v.* to boil

boulanger *n. m.* baker; **boulangerie** *n. f.* bakery

bouteille *n. f.* bottle

boutique *n. f.* boutique, small shop

bouton *n. m.* **de démarrage** power button

bouton *n. m.* **du pavé tactile** touch pad button

bras *n. m.* arm

brave *adj.* good, fine, honest (when **brave** follows a noun, it means *brave*: **c'est un homme brave** he's a brave man; **c'est une femme brave** she's a brave woman)

briller *v.* to shine

brosse *n. f.* brush

bruit *n. m.* noise

brûler *v.* to burn; **brûlé** burned

bu *past part. of* **boire**

buffet *n. m.* china closet, hutch, sideboard

bureau *n. m.* desk, office

but *n. m.* goal

C

ça *dem. pron.* that (**ça** is short for **cela**); **Ça ne fait rien!** That doesn't matter! **Ça va!** (I'm) fine!

caché *adj. m. s.* hidden

cadeau *n. m.* present, gift

café *n. m.* coffee, café (coffeehouse)

cahier *n. m.* notebook

caisse *n. f.* cash box (register); **caissier** *n. m.* **caissière** *n. f.* cashier

calculatrice *n. f.* calculator

camarade *n. m. f.* comrade, buddy, pal, mate

camembert *n. m.* camembert (name of a cheese)

camion *n. m.* truck; **camionneur** *n. m.* truck driver

campagne *n. f.* countryside

Canada *n. m.* Canada; **Il est canadien**/He is Canadian; **Elle est canadienne**/She is Canadian

canne *n. f.* cane

carte *n. f.* map, menu

carte *n. f.* **bancaire/la carte de crédit** credit card

carte *n. f.* **d'embarquement** boarding pass

cas *n. m.* case

casser *v.* to break; **sans la casser** without breaking it

cave *n. f.* cellar

CD *n. m.* CD

ce *dem. adj. m. s.* this, that; **ce n'est pas…** it isn't…; **ce que** *pron.* that which, what; **ce qui** *pron.* that which; **ce soir** tonight; **ce sont…** they are… or it's…

ceci *dem. pron.* this; **cela** *dem. pron.* that; **Cela n'a pas d'importance** That has no importance; That's not important.

cédérom *n. m.,* **le CD-ROM**
CD-ROM

céleri *n. m.* celery; **blanc de céleri**
celery stalk

cent *adj.* one hundred

cerise *n. f.* cherry

ces *dem. adj. m. f. pl.* these, those

cesse *n. f.* ceasing, stopping

c'est... he's... she's... it's... **c'est**
aujourd'hui le premier
décembre today is December 1st;
c'est ça! that's right! **c'est bien**
ça! that's quite right! **c'est fait!** it
is done! **c'est fini!** it's finished

cet *dem. adj. m. s.* **cette** *f. s.* this

chacun *pron.* each one; **chacune**
fem.

chaise *n. f.* chair

chambre *n. f.* room; **chambre à**
coucher bedroom

champ *n. m.* field

champignon *n. m.* mushroom

chance *m. f.* luck, chance, fortune

changement *n. m.* change

chanté *past part. of* **chanter** (to
sing); **chanteur** *n. m.,* **chanteuse**
n. f. singer

chapeau *n. m.* hat

chapelle *n. f.* chapel

chaque *adj.* each

charmante *adj. f.* charming

chasser *v.* to chase away, hunt

chat *n. m.,* **chatte** *n. f.* cat

château *n. m.* castle

chaud, chaude *adj. m. f.* hot

chaussettes *n. f.* socks; **chaussure** *n.*
f. shoe

cheminée *n. f.* chimney

chemise *n. f.* shirt

cher, chère *adj. m. s., f. s.* dear; **cher**
adj., adv. expensive; **chéri, chérie**
n. m. f. darling, honey

cherché *past part. of* **chercher** to
look (for), search (for), get

cheval *n. m.* horse

cheveux *n. m. pl.* hair

chez *prep.* at (to) the home (place)
of; **chez moi** at my house; **chez le**
dentiste to (at) the dentist's; **chez**
le coiffeur to (at) the hairdresser's,

barber's; **chez le médecin** to (at)
the doctor's; **chez vous** to (at)
your house (place)

chien *n. m.* dog

choisi *part part. of* **choisir** (to
choose, select)

choisit, choisissez *v. forms of*
choisir; il choisit he chooses;
choisissez! choose!

chose *n. f.* thing

chuchoter *v.* to whisper

ciel *n. m.* sky

cigale *n. f.* cicada

cinéma *n. m.* movies

cinq *adj.* five; **cinquième** fifth;
cinquante fifty

clair *adj. m. s.* clear

clavardage *n. m.* chat (Internet)

clavarder *v.* to chat (Internet)

clavier *n. m.* keyboard

clavier *n. m.* **d'identification**
personnelle PIN pad

clef *n. f.* key

client *n. m.* customer

cloche *n. f.* bell

coeur *n. m.* heart

coiffeur *n. m.* hairdresser, barber;
coiffe *n. f.* headdress; **coiffure** *n. f.*
hairstyle; **se coiffer** *v. refl.* to
comb one's hair, style one's hair

coin *n. m.* corner

combien *adv.* how many, how much

comme *adv.* like, as; **comme il faut**
as it should be, proper and correct

commencé *past part. of* **commencer**
(to begin, commence)

comment *adv.* how

commerce *n. m.* **électronique**
e-commerce

commode *n. f.* dresser

comprendre *v.* to understand;
compris *past part.* understood

confiture *n. f.* jam, perserves

congé *see* **jour de congé**

connaissez-vous...? *v. form of*
connaître (to know someone, be
acquainted with); do you know...?
Est-ce que Pierre connaît
Robert? Does Pierre know Robert?
(*pres. indicative;* **je connais, tu**

connais, il (elle) connaît, nous
connaissons, vous connaissez, ils
(elles) connaissent)

conte *n. m.* story, tale

contraire *n. m., adj.* contrary,
opposite

contre *prep.* against

contrôle *n. m.* **de sécurité** security
check (travel)

contrôleur *n. m.* ticket taker, train
conductor

cordiaux *adj. m. pl.* cordial

corps *n. m.* body

corriger *v.* to correct

côté *n. m.* side; **à côté de** next to

cou *n. m.* neck

couché *adj.* lying down; **se coucher**
v. to go to bed

couleur *n. f.* color; **de quelle**
couleur est...? what color is...?

couloir *n. m.* hallway, corridor

se couper *v. refl.* to cut oneself

courent, court *v. forms of* **courir**
(to run)

courriel *n. m.* e-mail

courrier *n. m.* **électronique** e-mail

cours *n. m.* course; **cours de**
français French course

court, courte *adj. m. s., f. s.* short

couteau *n. m.* knife

coûter *v.* to cost

couvert *past part. of* **couvrir** (to
cover)

craie *n. f.* chalk

cravate *n. f.* necktie

crayon *n. m.* pencil

crémeux *adj. m.* creamy

crie, crient *v. forms of* **crier** (to
shout, to cry out)

crois *v. form of* **croire** (to believe);
je n'y crois pas. I don't believe
in it.

croix n. f. cross

cru *past part. of* **croire**

cuiller, cuillère *n. f.* spoon; **cuillère**
à soupe soup spoon

cuire *v.* to cook; **cuit** *past part.*

cuisine *n. f.* kitchen, cooking (food)

cuisson *n. f.* cooking (time)

cybercafé *n. m.* cybercafé

D

d' *prep.* (contraction of **de**)

d'abord *advl. expr.* at first, first

d'accord agreed, okay

d'ailleurs *adv.* besides

dame *n. f.* lady

dangereux *adj. m.* **dangereuse** *adj. f.* dangerous

dans *prep.* in

dansé *past part. of* **danser** (to dance); **danseur** *n. m.,* **danseuse** *n. f.* dancer

davantage *adj.* more

de *prep.* of, from, with; **de bonne heure** *adv.* early

de quelle couleur est... what color is...

de rien you're welcome

debout *adv.* standing

décembre *n. m.* December

déchirer *v.* to tear

décision *n. f.* decision

décréter *v.* to decree, to enact, to give an executive order

dedans *adv.* inside

défendre *v.* to defend, forbid; **défendu,** *past part.*

dégoûtant *adj. m. s.* disgusting, revolting

dehors *adv.* outside

déjà *adv.* already

déjeuner *v.* to have lunch, to eat lunch, to lunch; *n. m.* lunch; **le petit déjeuner** breakfast

délicieux *adj. m. s. pl.,* **délicieuse** *adj. f. s.* delicious

demain *adv.* tomorrow

demander *v.* to ask (for); **demandé** *past part.*

demeurer *v.* to live, reside, inhabit, stay, remain

demi *m.,* **demie** *f., adj.* half

d'en face opposite

dent *n. f.* tooth

se dépêcher *refl. v.* to hurry

depuis *adv., prep.* since

déranger *v.* to disturb

dernier *m.,* **dernière** *f., adj.* last; **la dernière mise** the last bid

derrière *adv., prep.* behind

descendre *v.* to go down, come down; **descendu** *past part.*

désir *n. m.* desire; **désirer** *v.* to desire

désobéir *v.* to disobey

dessert *n. m.* dessert

dessus *adv.* on top, above

détail *n. m.* detail

détective *n. m.* detective

détester *v.* to detest, to hate

deux *n. m., adj.* two; **tous les deux** both

deuxième *n. m. f., adj.* second

devant *prep.* before, in front of

devenir *v.* to become; **devenu** *past part.*

deviens, devient *v. forms of* **devenir; je deviens folle! je deviens fou!** I'm going crazy!

devinette *n. f.* riddle

devoir *v.* to owe, ought to, must, have to

devoirs *n. m. pl.* homework, assignments, duties

dictionnaire *n. m.,* dictionary

Dieu *n. m.* God

difficile *adj. m. f.* difficult

diligent *adj. m.* diligent, industrious

dîné *past part. of* **dîner**

dîner *v.* to dine, to have dinner; *n. m.* dinner

dire *v.* to say, to tell; **dire des histoires** to tell stories, make up stories, fibs

directeur *n. m.,* **directrice** *n. f.* director, principal

dis, disent *v. forms of* **dire; je dis** I say; **tu dis** you say; **ils, elles disent** they say; **dis-moi** tell me

disposer *v.* to dispose, arrange, prepare

disque *n. m.* record, disc, recording

disque *n. m.* **compact** CD

disque *n. m.* **dur** hard drive

disque *n. m.* **DVD** DVD

distinctement *adv.* distinctly

dit *v. form of* **dire; il/elle dit** he/she says, tells; *also past part. of* **dire**

dites-moi tell me; **dites-nous** tell us

divers *adj.* diverse, different

dix *n. m., adj.* ten

docteur *n. m.* doctor

dodo *n. m.* sleep; **fais dodo** go to sleep (child's language)

doigt *n. m.* finger

dois, doit, doivent *v. forms of* **devoir; je dois** I have to; **il/elle doit** he/she has to; **ils/elles doivent** they have to

domestique *adj.* domestic; **domestiqué** *adj.* domesticated

donne *v. form of* **donner; donne!** give! **donne-moi/donnez-moi** give me; **donné** *past part. of* **donner**

donner *v.* to give

dormir *v.* to sleep; **dors** *v. form of* **dormir**

dos *n. m.* back

dossier *n. m.* brief, file of papers

douane *n. f.* customs (duty or tax on imported goods)

douce *adj. f.* sweet, soft

doucement *adv.* softly, sweetly, gently (low flame)

douche *n. f.* shower

doute *n. m.* doubt; **sans doute** undoubtedly, without a doubt

doux *adj. m.* sweet, soft

drapeau *n. m.* flag

droite *n. f.* right (as opposed to left); **à droite, à la droite** to (on) the right

drôle *adj. m. f.* funny, droll

dû *past part. of* **devoir**

de (*contraction of* **de** + **le**)

E

eau *n. f.* water

échapper *v.* to escape, to get away; **le chapeau échappé** the hat that got away

éclair *n. m.* eclair

éclairant *pres. part. of* **éclairer** illuminating

éclairer *v.* to illuminate, to light up

école *n. f.* school

écouter *v.* to listen (to)

écran *n. m.* display screen (computer)

écran *n. m.* **plasma** plasma screen, plasma display

écran *n. m.* **tactile** touch screen

écraser *v.* to crush

écrire *v.* to write

écrit, écrivent, écrivez *v. forms of* **écrire**

écrivain *n. m.* writer, author

effacer *v.* to erase

église *n. f.* church

eh bien! *exclam.* well now!

élève *n. m. f.* pupil, student

elle *per. pron. f.* she, her, it; **elles** *per. pron. f. pl.* they, them; **avec elles** with them

embarras *n. m.* embarrassment, hindrance, fuss, distress

émission *n. f.* TV program, show

emplette *n. f.* purchase

employer *v.* to use, to employ

emporter *v.* to take along, to take (carry) away

en *prep.* in, into, on, while; *as pron.,* some (of it, of them), of them; *see* Work Unit 13

en arrivant on (upon) arriving; **en courant** running; **en disposant** arranging; **en forme** in good shape; **en tenue d'exercice** in a gym suit; **en ville** downtown, into town

enchère *n. f.* bid, bidding

encore *adv.* again; **encore une fois** once more, yet, still

endroit *n. m.* place

enfant *n. m. f.* child

enfin *adv.* finally, at last, in short

engager *v.* to apply to, to put into gear

enlever *v.* to remove, to take off

ennuyer *v.* to annoy, to bore; **ennuyeux** annoying, boring

enseignement *n. m.* teaching, instruction

enseigner *v.* to teach

ensemble *adv.* together

ensuite *adv.* then, after, next

entendre *v.* to hear; **entendu** *past part.*

entracte *n. m.* intermission

entraîneur *n. m.* coach, sports instructor

entre *prep.* between; **entre eux et nous** between them and us

entrer (dans) *v.* to enter, to go (into), to come in; **entré** *past part.;* **entrée** *n. f.* entrance

envoyer *v.* to send

épais *adj.* thick

épaule *n. f.* shoulder

épicerie *n. f.* grocery store; **épicier** *m.* **épicière** *f.,* grocer

épingle *n. f.* pin

épouse *n. f.* wife; **époux** *n. m.* husband

équipe *n. f.* team

érection *n. f.* construction, erection

erreur *n. f.* error, mistake

es *v. form of* **être; tu es** you are (*familiar use*); **es-tu…?** are you…?

espagnol *n. m.* Spanish

espérer *v.* to hope

esprit *n. m.* spirit

essayer *v.* to try

essence *n. f.* gasoline

est *v. form of* **être; il/elle est** he/she/it is

est-ce…? is it…?

estomac *n. m.* stomach

et *conj.* and

étage *n. m.* floor (of a building designated by number)

étais *v. form of* **être** (imperfect indicative); **j'étais** I was

États-Unis *n. m. pl.* United States; **aux États-Unis** in (to) the United States

été *n. m.* summer; *also past part. of* **être** (been); **j'ai été** I was, I have been

éteindre *v.* to extinguish, to snuff out

êtes *v. form of* **être; vous êtes** you are

être *v.* to be

êtroit *adj. m. s.* narrow

étudiant *n. m.* **étudiante** *n. f.,* student

étudié *past part. of* **étudier**

étudier *v.* to study

eu *past part. of* **avoir; j'ai eu** I had, I have had

euro *n. m.* euro

eux *disj. pron. m. pl.* them

éviter *v.* to avoid

exactement *adv.* exactly

examiner *v.* to examine

exclamer, s'exclamer *v., refl. v.* to exclaim

excuser *v.* to excuse

expliquer *v.* to explain

exposition *n. f.* exhibit

extraordinaire *adj. m. f. s.* extraordinary, unusual

extrêmement *adv.* extremely

F

fable *n. f.* fable

fâché *adj.* angry; **se fâcher** *refl. v.* to get angry

facile *adj.* easy; **facilement** *adv.* easily

façon *n. f.* way; **de façon à** so as to

facteur *n. m.* mail carrier

faible *adj.* weak

faim *n. f.* hunger; **avoir faim** to be hungry; **j'ai faim** I'm hungry

faire *v.* to do, to make; **faire bouillir** to boil; **faire connaissance** to meet, to become acquainted with; **faire de la gymnastique** to do gymnastics, to do exercises; **faire la toilette** to wash and dress oneself; **se faire lire les lignes de la main** to have one's palm read, to have the lines of one's hand read; **se faire mal** to hurt oneself; **faire réparer** to have repaired; **faire trop cuire** to overcook; **faire visite** to visit, to pay a visit

fais, fait, faites *v. forms of* **faire; fais dodo** go to sleep (child's language); **il/elle fait** he/she/it does (makes); **c'est fait** it's done, it's finished; **fait** *past part. of* **faire; elle a fait la leçon** she did (has done) the lesson; **faites le travail!** do the work! **faites bouillir l'eau, s'il vous plaît!** boil the water, please!

famille *n. f.* family

farine *n. f.* flour

fatigué *m.* **fatiguée** *f., adj.* tired

faut *v. form of* **falloir** (to be necessary, must); **il faut** it is necessary, you must, you have to, one must, we must, we have to, etc. (This is an impersonal verb and the subject is always **il**); **faut-il?** is it necessary?

faute *n. f.* mistake, error

fauteuil *n. m.* armchair

faux *adj.* false

favori *m.* favorite *f., adj.* favorite

femme *n. f.* woman, wife

fenêtre *n. f.* window

ferme *n. f.* farm

fermé *past part. of* **fermer** (to close)

fête *n. f.* holiday, feast, birthday

feu *n. m.* fire, traffic light

feuille *n. f.* leaf; **feuille de papier** sheet of paper

fichier *n. m.* **MP3** MP3

figure *n. f.* face

filer *v.* to go (away) quickly (*used familiarly*); **filez!** go away! beat it!

filet *n. m.* net

fille *n. f.* daughter; **une jeune fille** a girl

film *n. m.* film, movie

fils *n. m.* son

fin *n. f.* end

fini *m.,* **finie** *f. adj.* finished; **fini** *past part. of* **finir** (to finish)

finis, finissent, finissons, finit *v. forms of* **finir; finissons!** let's finish!

fixement *adv.* intently, fixedly

fleur *n. f.* flower; **fleuriste** *n. m. f.* florist

fleuve *n. m.* river

foire *n. f.* fair (as at a county or state fair)

fois *n. f.* time; **une fois** one time, once; **deux fois** two times, twice, etc.; **mille fois** a thousand times; **la prochaine fois** the next time

folle *adj. f. s.* crazy; **fou** *adj. m. s.*

font *v. form of* **faire**

football *n. m.* soccer (in the United States)

forme *n. f.* form, shape

formidable *adj.* terrific

fort *m.* **forte** *f., adj.* strong; **votre qualité la plus forte** your strongest quality; **le (la) plus fort (forte)** the strongest

fou *adj. m. s.* crazy

four *n. m.* oven

fourchette *n. f.* fork

fourmi *n. f.* ant

foyer *n. m.* hearth, home

frais *m. s. pl.,* **fraîche** *f. s. adj.* fresh; **il fait frais** it's cool

fraise *n. f.* strawberry

franc *n. m.* franc (former French unit of money)

français *n. m.* French (language); **Il est français**/He is French; **Elle est française**/She is French; **Je parle français**/I speak French

France *n. f.* France

fréquence *n. f.* frequency

frère *n. m.* brother

froid *n. m., adj.,* **froide** *f., adj.* cold

fromage *n. m.* cheese

fumé *past part. of* **fumer** (to smoke); **la fumée** the smoke

furieux *m. s. pl.,* **furieuse** *adj. f. s.* furious

G

gagner *v.* to win

galant *m.,* **galante** *f., adj.* gallant

gant *n. m.* glove

garagiste *n. m.* auto mechanic

garçon *n. m.* boy; **garçon (de restaurant);** (Nowadays, a customer addresses a waiter as *Monsieur*, not *garçon*; address a waitress as *Mademoiselle* or *Madame*)

garder *v.* to guard, keep

gardien *n. m.* guard; **un gardien (une gardienne) d'enfants** babysitter; **un gardien (une gardienne) de but** goalie

gare *n. f.* station (bus, train, etc.)

gâteau *n. m.* cake

gauche *n. f.* left (as opposed to *right*); **à gauche** on (to) the left

généralement *adv.* generally

généreux *adj., m. s. pl.* generous

génie *n. m.* genius

genou *n. m.* knee

gentil *adj., m. s.,* **gentille** *adj., f. s.* nice, kind

géographie *n. f.* geography

gilet *n. m.* vest

girafe *n. f.* giraffe

glace *n. f.* ice, ice cream, mirror; **glacé** *adj., m. s.,* **glacée** *adj., f. s.* glazed, frosted

gousse *n. f.* clove; **une gousse d'ail** clove of garlic

goût *n. m.* taste, flavor; **goûter** *v.* to taste; **goûtez-en!** taste some!

gouverner *v.* to govern

grain *n. m.* grain

gramme *n. m.* gram; 1 gram = about .035 ounce; 500 grams = about 1.1 lbs.

grand *adj., m. s.,* **grande** *adj., f. s.* great, big, large, tall; **grand faim (J'ai grand faim** I'm very hungry); **grand magasin** *n. m.* department store; **grand prix** *n. m.* grand prize

Grand Bretagne *n. f.* Great Britain

grande salle *n. f.* auditorium

grange *n. f.* barn

grave *adj., m. f.* grave, serious; **gravement** *adv.* seriously, gravely

grillé *adj., m. s.,* **grillée** *adj., f. s.* toasted, grilled

gris *adj., m. s. pl.,* **grise** *adj., f. s.* gray

gros *adj., m. s. pl.,* **grosse** *adj., f. s.* big huge, large, fat

groupe *n. m.* group

guérir *v.* to cure

gueule *n. f.* mouth (of an animal)

guichet *n. m.* ticket window

guichet *n. m.* **automatique (bancaire)** ATM (automated teller machine)

gymnase *n. m.* gymnasium, gym; **gymnastique** *n. f.* gymnastics

H

habillement *n. m.* clothing; **s'habiller** *refl. v.* to get dressed, to dress

habit *n. m.* clothing, attire (habit, *i.e.,* robe and hood of a monk)

habitant *n. m.* inhabitant

habite *v. form of* **habiter** (to live, to reside, to inhabit)

halte! *interj.* halt! stop!

haut *adv.* high, tall, **à haute voix** in a loud voice; **un chapeau haut-de-forme** top hat

herbe *n. f.* grass

heure *n. f.* hour; **heureux, heureuse** *adj., m. f.* happy

hideux *adj. m. s. pl.* hideous

hier *adv.* yesterday

histoire *n. f.* story, history

hiver *n. m.* winter; **en hiver** in winter

homme *n. m.* man

honneur *n. m.* honor

honte *n. f.* shame, disgrace

hôpital *n. m.* hospital

horizontalement *adv.* horizontally

horloge *n. f.* clock

horreur *n. f.* horror

hôtel *n. m.* hotel

huile *n. f.* oil

huit *adj.* eight

humain, humaine *adj.* human

humble *adj.* humble

hutte *n. f.* hut

I

ici *adv.* here; **ici Monique** this is Monique here

idée *n. f.* idea

identifier v. to identify

il *pron.* he *or* it; **il faut** it is necessary; **il y a** there is *or* there are; **il y en a beaucoup** there are many of them; **il n'y a pas (de)…** there isn't *or* aren't (any)… **il y a un an** a year ago

ils *pron. m.* they

image *n. f.* picture

immédiatement *adv.* immediately

immeuble *n. m.* building

incertain, incertaine *adj.* uncertain

incroyable *adj.* unbelievable

inquiet, inquiète *adj.* upset

s'inquiéter *refl. v.* to worry, to be upset; **ne t'inquiète pas!** don't worry!

insister *v.* to insist

insolent, insolente *adj., m. f.* insolent

intelligent, intelligente *adj., m. f.* intelligent; **l'élève le (la) plus intelligent (intelligente) de la classe** the most intelligent student in the class

intéressant, intéressante *adj., m. f.* interesting

Internet *n. m.* Internet

interroger *v.* to interrogate, to question

inventif, inventive *adj., m. f.* inventive

invitation *n. f.* invitation

inviter *v.* to invite

iPod *n. m.* iPod

irlandais, irlandaise *adj., m. f.* Irish

italien, italienne *adj., m. f.* Italian

J

j' (je) *per. pron.* I; **j'ai** I have; **j'ai grand faim** I'm very hungry; **j'ai seize ans** I'm sixteen years old

jamais *adv.* never, ever

jambe *n. f.* leg

jambon *n. m.* ham

jaquette *n. f.* jacket

jardin *n. m.* garden

jaune *n. m.* yellow

je *per. pron.* I; **je n'ai rien à faire** I have nothing to do; **je ne fais rien ce soir** I'm not doing anything tonight

jeter *v.* to throw

jeune *adj. m. f. s.* young; **jeune fille** *n. f.* girl

jeunesse *n. f.* youth

joli *adj. m. s.*, **jolie** *adj. f. s.* pretty

jouer *v.* to play; **joué** *past part.*

jouet *n. m.* toy

joueur *n. m.,* **joueuse** *n. f.* player

jour *n. m.* day; **jour de congé** day off (no school, no work); **Jour de la Bastille** Bastille Day (**le 14 juillet**)

journal *n. m.* newspaper

journée *n. f.* day; **toute la journée** all day long

joyeux, joyeuse *adj.* joyous, happy

juge *n. m.* judge

juillet *n. m.* July

jupe *n. f.* skirt

jus *n. m.* juice

jusque *prep.* until; **jusqu'à, jusqu'aux** until, up to; **jusqu'au printemps** until spring

juste *adj.* accurate, correct, exact

K

kangourou *n. m.* kangaroo

kilogramme *n. m.* kilogram; **1 kilogramme** = about 2.2 lbs.

kilomètre *n. m.* kilometer; **1 kilomètre** = about 0.621 mile

L

l' (le, la) *def. art. m. f.* the; *also, dir. obj. pron.* **Je la vois** (I see her *or* I see it.)

là *adv.* there; **là-bas** *adv.* over there

laideur *n. f.* ugliness

laisser *v.* to let, allow, leave (something behind); **laisse-moi!** let me!

lait *n. m.* milk

lamelle *n. f.* thin slice

lampe *n. f.* lamp

lancer *v.* to throw

langue *n. f.* language, tongue

lapin *n. m.* rabbit

large *n. m.* width, breadth; *adj.* wide

laver *v.* to wash; **se laver** *refl. v.* to wash oneself

le *def. art. m. s.* the; *also, dir. obj. pron.* **Je le vois** (I see him *or* I see it.)

leçon *n. f.* lesson

lecteur *n. m.* **de CD** CD player

lecteur *n. m.* **de DVD** DVD player

lecteur *n. m.* **multimédia** multimedia player

légume *n. m.* vegetable

lendemain *adv.* following day, next day

lentement *adv.* slowly

les *def. art. m. or f. pl.* the; *also, dir. obj. pron.* **Je les vois** (I see them.)

lettre *n. f.* letter

leur *indir. obj. pron.* (to) them; *also, poss. adj.* their; **Je leur parle** (I'm talking to them.); **J'aime leur voiture** (I like their car); **J'aime leurs amis** (I like their friends.)

lever *v.* to raise, life; **se lever** *refl. v.* to get up; **elle lève la main** (she raises her hand); **levez-vous!** get up! **lève-toi!** get up!

libéré *adj. m.* **libérée** *adj. f.,* liberated

liberté *n. f.* liberty

lieu *n. m.* place

ligne *n. f.* line

lire *v.* to read

lis, lit *v. forms of* **lire**

lit *n. m.* bed; **au lit** in bed

livre *n. m.* book; *n. f.,* pound

loi *n. f.* law

loin *adv.* far

long *adj. m. s.,* **longue** *adj. f. s.* long

Louisiane *n. f.* Louisiana

lu *past part. of* **lire**; **Je n'ai pas lu le livre.** (I haven't read the book/I didn't read the book.)

lui *indir. obj. pron.* (to) him, (to) her; *also, disj. pron.* him; **avec lui** with him; **avec elle** with her

lumière *n. f.* light

lunaire *adj.* lunar

lune *n. f.* moon

lunettes *n. f. pl.* eyeglasses

lustre *n. m.* chandelier

M

m' (me) *refl. pron., dir. and indir. obj. pron.* myself, me, to me

ma *poss. adj. f. sing.* my (**ma maison**)

machine *n. f.* **à rayons X** X-ray machine (in airports)

madame *n. f.* (*pl.* **mesdames**) Mrs., madam

mademoiselle *n. f.* (pl. **mesdemoiselles**) Miss

magasin *n. m.* store; **grand magasin** department store

magazine *n. m.* magazine

magicien *n. m.* **magicienne** *n. f.* magician

magnifique *adj.* magnificent, wonderful

maillot *n. m.* **de bain** swimsuit

main *n. f.* hand

maintenant *adv.* now

mais *conj.* but; **mais non!** of course not! why, no! **mais oui!** of course!

maison *n. f.* house

maître *n. m.,* **maîtresse** *n. f.* teacher

mal *n. m.* pain, harm; *adv.* badly, poorly; **se faire mal** to hurt oneself

malade *adj.* sick, ill

malheur *n. m.* unhappiness, misfortune

malheureux *adj. m.,* **malheureuse** *adj. f.* unhappy

malle *n. f.* trunk (luggage)

maman *m. f.* mama, mom

manche *n. f.* sleeve; **La Manche** English Channel

manger *v.* to eat; **mangeant** *pres. part.* **en mangeant** while eating

manquer *v.* to miss, be missing (lacking)

manteau *n. m.* coat

marchand *n. m.* **marchande** *n. f.* merchant

marchandise *n. f.* merchandise, goods

marché *n. m.* market; **le marché aux puces** flea market

marcher *v.* to walk; to work, run (an apparatus or machine)

mari *n. m.* husband; **le mariage** marriage

match *n. m.* game, match (sport)

mathématiques *n. f. pl.* mathematics

matin *n. m.* morning; **le matin** in the morning

matinée *n. f.* morning (all morning long); early afternoon theater performance

mauvais *adj. m.,* **mauvaise** *adj. f.* bad

me *refl. pron., dir. and indir. obj. pron.* myself, me, to me

méchant *adj. m.,* **méchante** *adj. f.* mean, nasty

mécontent *adj. m.* **mécontente** *adj. f.* unhappy, discontent, malcontent

médecin *n. m.* doctor

médicament *n. m.* medicine

Méditerranée *n. f.* Mediterranean (Sea)

se méfier *refl. v.* to beware; **méfiez-vous de...** beware of...

meilleur, meilleure *adj.* better; **le meilleur, la meilleure** the best

mélange *n. m.* mixture

même *adj.* same, self; **moi-même** myself; **la même chose** the same thing; **tout de même** all the same, just the same; **pas même** not even

ménagère *n. f.* housewife

mensonge *n. m.* lie, untruth, falsehood

merci *n. m.* thanks, thank you

mère *n. f.* mother

merveilleux, merveilleuse *adj., m. f.* marvelous, wonderful

mes *poss. adj. pl.* my (**mes livres**)

mesdames *n. f. pl.* ladies

mesdemoiselles *n. f. pl.* young ladies, Misses

messagerie *n. f.* voice mail

messieurs *n. m. pl.* gentlemen

mesure *n. f.* measure

met *v. form of* **mettre; elle met** she puts

métal *n. m.* metal

métier *n. m.* trade, occupation

métro, (métropolitain) *n. m.* subway

mettez *v. form of* **mettre** *v.* to put (on), place, wear; **mettre en marche** to put into operation, to start (a machine, apparatus)

meuble(s) *n. m.* furniture

midi *n. m.* noon; **le Midi** southern France

mieux *adv.* better; **j'aime mieux** I prefer, I like better

mignon, mignonne *adj., m. f.* darling, cute

milieu *n. m.* middle; **au milieu de** in the middle of

mille *adj.* thousand

minéral, minérale *adj., m. f.* mineral

minuit *n. m.* midnight

mis *past part. of* **mettre** (to put on); **ils ont mis…** they put on…

misérable *adj., m. or f.* miserable

mode *n. m.* method, mode, kind

modeste *adj.* modest

moi *stressed per. pron.* me (**avec moi**)

moine *n. m.* monk

moins *adv.* less; **le moins, la moins…** the least; **au moins** at least; *see also idioms with* **au** in Part III, Unit 1

mois *n. m.* month; **au mois de** in the month of

mon *poss. adj. m. sing.* my (**mon livre**)

monde *n. m.* world, **tout le monde** everybody

monsieur *n. m.* sir, gentleman, Mr., mister

monstrueux, monstrueuse *adj., m. f.* monstrous

montant *n. m.* amount, sum

monté *past part. of* **monter** (to get in, go up, come up)

montre *n. f.* watch (wrist)

montrer *v.* to show

se moquer de *v. refl.* to make fun of

morceau *n. m.* piece, morsel

mort *past part. of* **mourir** (to die)

mot *n. m.* word; **un petit mot** a note

moteur *n. m.* motor

mouche *n. f.* fly (insect)

mouchoir *n. m.* handkerchief

mourir *v.* to die

mouton *n. m.* mutton

mouvement *n. m.* action, movement

muet, muette *adj.* mute

mur *n. m.* wall

musée *n. m.* museum

musique *n. f.* music

N

nager *v.* to swim

naissance *n. f.* birth; **l'anniversaire** (*n. m.*) **de naissance** birthday

naître *v.* to be born

nappe *n. f.* tablecloth

naturellement *adv.* naturally

naviguer (sur Internet) *v.* to navigate, to surf the Internet

né *past part. of* **naître**

ne mangez rien don't eat anything

ne pas + *inf.* not to; **de ne pas révéler** not to reveal

nécessaire *adj.* necessary

neige *n. f.* snow; **neiger** *v.* to snow

n'est-ce pas? isn't that so? isn't it? *see* Work Unit 20

nettoyer *v.* to clean

neuf *adj.* nine; **neuf, neuve** *adj., m. f.* new

neveu *n. m.* nephew

nez *n. m.* nose

NIP *n. m.* (**le numéro d'identification personnelle**) PIN

Noël *n. m.* Christmas

noir, noire *adj.* black

nom *n. m.* name

nombre *n. m.* number; **nombreux, nombreuse** *adj., m. f.* numerous

non *adv.* no; **non plus** neither; **moi non plus** me neither

notre *poss. adj.* our; *pl.,* **nos (nos livres)**

nourriture *n. f.* nourishment, food

nous *per. pron.* we, us

nouveau, nouveaux *adj.* new; **Je n'ai rien appris de nouveau**/I didn't learn anything new; **un nouveau livre** (a new book)

nouvel, nouvelle *adj.* new; **un nouvel étudiant, une nouvelle étudiante**/a new student

Nouvelle-Orléans *n. f.* New Orleans

nouvelles *n. f. pl.* news; **bonnes nouvelles!** good news!

nuage *n. m.* cloud;

nuageux, nuageuse *adj.* cloudy

nuire *v.* to harm, hurt

O

obéir *v.* to obey

objet *n. m.* object, article

obscur, obscure *adj.* dark, obscure

observer *v.* to observe

occasion *n. f.* occasion

oeil *n. m.* eye; **yeux** *pl.*

oeuf *n. m.* egg; **oeuf à la coque** soft-boiled egg

oeuvre *n. f.* work; **une oeuvre d'art** a work of art

offre *v. form of* **offrir** (to offer); *past part.* **offert**

oignon *n. m.* onion

oiseau *n. m.* bird; **oiseaux** *pl.*

on *indef. per. pron.* one, people, you, someone, they; **On vous demande au téléphone**/You're wanted on the phone.

oncle *n. m.* uncle

ont *v. form of* **avoir** (to have); **ils (elles) ont** they have, they do have

opéra *n. m.* opera

orage *n. m.* storm

ordinateur *n. m.* computer

ordinateur *n. m.* **de bureau** *m.* desktop computer

ordinateur *n. m.* **de poche** PDA (personal digital assistant), handheld computer

ordinateur *n. m.* **portable** laptop computer (A laptop computer may just be called "un portable." The same word is sometimes used for a cell phone.)

ordures *n. f. pl.* garbage

oreille *n. f.* ear

ou *conj.* or; **où** *adv.* where

oublié *past part. of* **oublier** (to forget)

oui *adv.* yes

ouvert, ouverte *adj., m. f.* open; *also past part. of* **ouvrir** (to open)

ouvre *v. form of* **ouvrir; elle ouvre** she opens

P

page *n. f.* page

pagette *n. f.* pager

pain *n. m.* bread; **pain grillé** toast

paisible *adj.* peaceful

paix *n. f.* peace

palme *n. f.* palm branch

palmier *n. m.* palm tree

pamplemousse *n. m.* grapefruit

panier *n. m.* basket

papa *n. m.* papa, daddy, dad

papier *n. m.* paper; **une feuille de paper** a sheet of paper

par *prep.* by, through; **par terre** on the floor, on the ground

paraître *v.* to appear, seem

parapluie *n. m.* umbrella

parc *n. m.* park

parce que *conj.* because

par-dessous *adv.* underneath, below

par-dessus *adv.* over, above; **pardessus** *n. m.* coat, overcoat

parfait, parfaite *adj., m. f.* perfect

parle *v. form of* **parler** (to talk, to speak); **Qui parle?** Who is talking? **parlé** *past. part.*

part *n. f.* part, behalf; **de la part de lui**/on his behalf (from him)

part *v. form of* **partir** (to leave, to go away); **tout le monde part** everybody is leaving; **parti** *past part. of* **partir**

participe *n. m.* participle

partie *n. f.* part

partir *v.* to leave, to go away; **partons-nous?** are we leaving?

partout *adv.* everywhere

paru *past part. of* **paraître**

pas *adv.* not, none, no; **pas loin** not far; **pas du tout** not at all; **pas même** not even; *see also* **ne pas**; **Je n'ai pas de bananes**/I haven't any bananas, I don't have any bananas, I have no bananas

passage *n. m.* passage, passage way; **passage clouté** *n. m.* crosswalk

passé *n. m.* past; *also past part. of* **passer**

passe-moi le pain, passez-moi le beurre/pass me the bread, pass me the butter

passer *v.* to spend (time), to pass by, to go by

pâte *n. f.* dough, paste, "pasta" (macaroni, spaghetti, etc.)

patiemment *adv.* patiently

pâtisserie *n. f.* pastry, pastry shop

pâtissier, pâtissière *n. m. f.* pastry cook

patrie *n. f.* country (nation)

paupière *n. f.* eyelid

pauvre *adj.* poor

pavé *n. m.* **tactile** touch pad

payer *v.* to pay, to pay for; **payé** paid for

pays *n. m.* country (nation)

paysage *n. m.* countryside

peau *n. f.* skin

pêche *n. f.* peach

se peigner *v. refl.* to comb one's hair

peindre *v.* to paint; **peint** *past part.*

pendant *prep.* during; **pendant que** *conj.* while

perdre *v.* to lose; **perdu** *past part.*

père *n. m.* father; **Père Noël** *n. m.* Santa Claus

permettre *v.* to permit, to allow; **permis** *past part.*

personne *n. f.* person

petit, petite, petits, petites *adj.* small, little; **le plus petit, la plus petite, les plus petits, les plus petites** the smallest, the littlest; **le petit déjeuner** breakfast; **le petit four** little cake (usually square in shape with icing); **petits pois** *n. m. pl.* peas

peu *adv.* little, few, not much

peuple *n. m.* people (of a nation)

peur *n. f.* fear

peut *v. form of* **pouvoir**

peut-être *adv.* maybe, perhaps

peux *v. form of* **pouvoir**

pharmacie *n. f.* pharmacy, drugstore

pharmacien, pharmacienne *n.* pharmacist, druggist

photo *n. f.* photo

phrase *n. f.* sentence, phrase

pièce *n. f.* room, piece

pied *n. m.* foot

pinceau *n. m.* artist's brush

piquer *v.* to poke, puncture

piste *n. f.* track

pistolet *n. m.* pistol

placard *n. m.* closet

place *n. f.* place, seat, plaza

plafond *n. m.* ceiling

plage *n. f.* beach

plainte *n. f.* lamentation

plaire *v.* to please

plaisir *n. m.* pleasure

plaît *v. form of* **plaire; s'il vous plaît** please (if it is pleasing to you)

plat *n. m.* plate, dish

pleurer *v.* to cry, to weep

pleut *v. form of* **pleuvoir** (to rain); **il pleut** it's raining, it rains

pluie *n. f.* rain

plume *n. f.* feather

plus *adv.* more; **le plus, la plus, les plus** the most; **plus petit, plus petite** smaller; **plus tard** later; **ne...plus**/ no...longer, no...more

plusieurs *adv.* several

poche *n. f.* pocket

poème *n. m.* poem

poète, poétesse (femme poète) *n.* poet

poids *n. m.* weight

poire *n. f.* pear

pois *n. m.* pea; **les petits pois** peas

poisson *n. m.* fish

poivre *n. m.* pepper

pôle nord *n. m.* North Pole

pomme *n. f.* apple; **une pomme de terre** potato

pommes frites *n. f. pl.* French fries

pommier *n. m.* apple tree

porc *n. m.* pork

port *n. m.* port

portable *n. m.* cell phone (**le téléphone portable**), laptop computer (**l'ordinateur** *m.* **portable**)

porte *n. f.* door

porte *v. form of* **porter** (to wear, to carry)

poser *v.* to pose, to place; **poser une question** to ask a question

poubelle *n. f.* rubbish can

poulet *n. m.* chicken; **une poule** a hen

pour *prep.* for, in order (to)

pourquoi *adv.* why; **pourquoi pas?** why not?

pouvez, pouvons *v. forms of* **pouvoir** (can, to be able, may); **pu** *past part.*; **vous pouvez**/you can; **vous pouvez être**/you can be; **pouvez-vous?**/can you?

précéder *v.* to precede

préféré *past part. of* **préférer** (to prefer)

premier, première *adj., m. f.* first

prendre *v.* to take, to have (a meal); **Que prenez-vous pour le petit déjeuner?** What do you have for breakfast?

préparatoire *adj.* preparatory, preliminary

préparé *past part. of* **préparer** (to prepare); **se préparer** to prepare oneself

près (de) *adv.* near

présent *n. m.* present

presque *adv.* almost

prêt, prête *adj.* ready, prepared

prêté *past part. of* **prêter** (to lend)

prêtre, prêtresse *n.* priest, priestess

prier *v.* to beg, to request, to ask

printemps *n. m.* spring (season)

pris *past part. of* **prendre**

prise *n. f.* **de courant** electric outlet (wall)

prix *n. m.* price, prize; **le grand prix** the first prize

probablement *adv.* probably

prochain, prochaine *adj.* next; **la prochaine fois**/the next time

produits laitiers *n. m. pl.* dairy products

professeur, professeur-dame *n.* professor, teacher

profession *n. f.* profession

profiter *v.* to profit, to take advantage (of); **il faut profiter du moment**/you (one) must take advantage of the moment

programme *n. m.* program

projet *n. m.* project

se promener *v. refl.* to go for (to take) a walk, to stroll

promettre *v.* to promise; **promis** *past part.*

prononcer *v.* to pronounce

propriété *n. f.* property

proverbe *n. m.* proverb

pu *past part. of* **pouvoir**

public *n. m.* public; **public, publique** *adj.* public

puce *n. f.* flea; **le marché aux puces** flea market

puis *adv.* then

punit *v. form of* **punir** (to punish); **il punit**/he punishes

pupitre *n. m.* student's desk

Q

qualité *n. f.* quality; **la qualité la plus forte**/the strongest quality

quand *adv.* when

quatorze *adj.* fourteen

que *conj.* than, that; *interrog. pron.* what

quel *adj. m. s.* what, which; **quel sport?**/what (which) sport? **quel âge ont les enfants?**/how old are the children? what (a)…! what (an)…! **quel déjeuner!**/what a lunch! **quel embarras!**/what an embarrassment!

quelle *adj. f. s.* what, which; **quelle maison?**/what (which) house? what (a)…? what (an)…! **quelle classe!**/what a class! **quelle idée!**/what an idea! **Quelle heure est-il?**/What time is it? **Quelle est la date aujourd'hui?**/What's the date today? **De quelle couleur est…?** What color is…?

quelles *adj. f. pl.* what, which; **quelles maisons?**/what (which) houses? **quelles idées!**/what ideas!

quelque *adj.* some; **quelques** some, a few; **quelque chose**/something

quelquefois *adv.* sometimes

quels *adj. m. pl.* what, which; **quels livres?**/what (which) books?

qu'est-ce que c'est? what is it?

qu'est-ce que je suis? or **que suis-je?** what am I?

question *n. f.* question

qui *pron.,* who, whom, which, that; *in proverbs* he who/she who **Qui**

suis-je?/Who am I? **Avec qui sortez-vous?**/With whom are you going out? **Le livre qui est sur la table est à moi**/The book which (that) is on the table is mine.

quinze *adj.* fifteen; **j'ai quinze ans**/I am fifteen years old.

quitte, quittent *v. forms of* **quitter** (to leave); **quitté** *past part.*; **Elle a quitté la maison à huit heures**/She left the house at 8 o'clock.

quoi *pron.* what; **Quoi?**/What?! **Quoi de neuf?** What's new?

R

R.S.V.P. Répondez, s'il vous plaît/Reply, please.

raconter *v.* to tell, to relate

ragoût *n. m.* stew

raisin *n. m.* grape

raison *n. f.* reason; **avoir raison**/to be right; **Vous avez raison**/You are right; **Tu as raison**/You (*fam. sing.*) are right.

raisonnable *adj.* reasonable

rang *n. m.* rank, row

rapide *adj.* rapid; **rapidement** *adv.* rapidly, fast, quickly

se rappeler *v.* to remember, to recall

rare *adj.* rare; **rarement** *adv.* rarely

rayonner *v.* to radiate symmetrically

recette *n. f.* recipe

recevoir *v.* receive; **reçu** *past. part.*

refuser *v.* to refuse

regarder v. to look, to look at, to watch; **Regarde!**/Look! **Regardez!**/Look! **se regarder** (l'un à l'autre) *v.* to look at each other

régime *n. m.* diet

règle *n. f.* rule, ruler

regretter *v.* to regret, to be sorry

religieuse *n. f.* nun (sister); *adj.* religious

religieux *n. m.* monk, friar; *adj.* religious

rembourser *v.* to reimburse

remercier *v.* to thank; **Je vous remercie**/I thank you.

remplir *v.* to fill, fulfill

remuer *v.* to stir

rendez-vous *n. m.* appointment

rendre *v.* return (something), give back; **Rendez-moi mes disques**/ Give me back my (phono) records.

rendre visite à quelqu'un to visit someone

rentrer *v.* to go in again, to return (home)

réparer *v.* to repair

repas *n. m.* meal

répéter *v.* to repeat

répondeur *n. m.* answering machine

répondre *v.* to answer, to reply, to respond; **répondu**, *past part.*

résponse *n. f.* answer, response, reply

repos *n. f.* answer, response, reply

repos *n. m.* rest, repose (sleep); **au repos** at rest

se reposer *v. refl.* to rest

reprendre *v.* to take back, get back, to resume

représentation *n. f.* presentation, show, performance

requin *n. m.* shark

se ressembler *v. refl.* to resemble each other, to look alike

restaurant *n. m.* restaurant

reste *n. m.* rest, remainder

rester *v.* to remain, to stay; **resté** *past part.*; **restons-nous?** are we staying?

retard *n. m.* delay; **être en retard**/to be late

retentir *v.* to resound, to ring

retourner *v.* to return, to go back

réussir *v.* to succeed

réveille-matin *n. m.* alarm clock

révéler *v.* to reveal

revenir *v.* to return, to come back; **revenu**, *past part.*

rêver *v.* to dream

reviens, revient, reviennent *v. forms of* **revenir**

revoir *v.* to see again; **au revoir** good-bye

ri *past part. of* **rire**

riche *adj.* rich

ridicule *adj.* ridiculous

rien *indef. pron.* nothing; **ne...rien** nothing; **Je n'étudie rien**/I study nothing (I don't study anything); **de rien** you're welcome

rient, rira *v. forms of* **rire**; **Tous les élèves rient**/All the students laugh.

rire *v.* to laugh

risquer *v.* to risk

rit *v. form of* **rire**; **Il rit tout le temps**/He laughs all the time.

robe *n. f.* dress

rompre *v.* to break

rond, ronde *adj.* round; **ronde** *n. f.* round, roundelay

rosbif *n. m.* roast beef

rose *n. f.* rose

roue *n. f.* wheel

rouge *adj.* red

rougit *v. form of* **rougir** (to blush); **Pierre rougit**/Peter blushes.

route *n. f.* road

ruban *n. m.* ribbon

rue *n. f.* street

rumeur *n. f.* stir, stirring, muffled din, hum

S

s' *contraction of* **se**, *refl. pron.*

sa *poss. adj., f. sing.* his, her, its, one's; **sa voiture**/his (her, etc.) car

sac *n. m.* **de vol** carry-on bag

sagesse *n. f.* wisdom, discretion

sais *v. form of* **savoir**; **je sais**/I know, **tu sais**/you know, **vous savez**/you know; **je ne sais pas**/I don't know.

saisir *v.* to seize, to grasp

saison *n. f.* season

sait *v. form of* **savoir**; **elle (il, on), sait**/she (he, one) knows

sale *adj.* soiled, dirty; **le plus sale**/the dirtiest

salle *n. f.* (large) room; **une salle des ventes**/auction sales room; **une salle à manger**/dining room; **une salle de bains**/bathroom; **une salle de classe**/classroom; **une grande salle**/auditorium

salon *n. m.* living room

salon *n. m.* **de clavardage** chat room

samedi *n. m.* Saturday

sans *prep.* without; **sans doute**/ without doubt, undoubtedly; **sans la casser**/without breaking it

santé *n. f.* health

satisfaire *v.* to satisfy

saucisse *n. f.* sausage; **saucisson** *n. m.* bologna

sauter *v.* to jump, to leap

sauvage *adj.* wild, savage

savent, savez, savons *v. forms of* **savoir**

savoir *v.* to know (how), to find out; **savez-vous lire?**/do you know how to read?

scrupuleux, scrupuleuse *adj.* scrupulous

se *refl. pron.* himself, herself, oneself, themselves; (reflexive verbs are not alphabetized in this vocabulary under the refl. pron. **se**; they are alphabetized under the first letter of the verb, e.g., **se dépêcher** is listed under the **D**'s)

sec *adj. m. s.* dry; **sèche** *f.*

Seine *n. f.* Seine River (flows through Paris)

séjour *n. m.* stay, visit

sel *n. m.* salt

semaine *n. f.* week

sénateur *n. m.* senator

sent *v. form of* sentir (to smell); **Il sent bon!** It smells good!

sentiment *n. m.* feeling

serpent *n. m.* snake

service *n. m.* service

servir *v.* to serve; **se servir (de)** to serve oneself, to use

ses *poss. adj. pl.* his, her, its, one's; **(ses livres, ses parents)**

seul *adj. m. s.* alone, single

seulement *adv.* only

si *adv.* so; **si** *conj.* if

s'il te plaît please *(fam. use)*; **s'il vous plaît** *(polite use)*

silence *n. m.* silence

snob *n. m.* snob

soeur *n. f.* sister

soif *n. f.* thirst

soigneusement *adv.* carefully

soir *n. m.* evening; **ce soir** tonight; **le soir** in the evening

soirée *n. f.* evening party

sois *v. form of* **être; Sois sage!** Be good!

soixante *adj.* sixty

sol *n. m.* ground, soil

soldat *n. m.* soldier

soleil *n. m.* sun

sommeil *n. m.* slumber, sleep

sommes *v. form of* **être; nous sommes** we are

son *n. m.* sound

son *poss. adj. m. s.* his, her, its, one's; (**son livre**)

sonne *v. form of* **sonner** (to ring); **la cloche sonne** the bell rings

sont *v. form of* **être; ils, elles sont** they are

sors, sort *v. forms of* **sortir** (to go out, to leave); **Je sors** I go out/I do go out/I am going out; **Je ne sors jamais** I never go out.

sortez *v. form (imperative) of* **sortir; Ne sortez pas!** Don't go out!

sorti *past part. of* **sortir**

sortie *n. f.* exit

sortir *v.* to go out, to leave

souffrante *adj. f. s.* sick

souffrir *v.* to suffer

soulier *n. m.* shoe

soupe *n. f.* soup

sourire *n. m.* smile; *as a v.* to smile

souris *n. f.* mouse

sourit *v. form of* **sourire**

sous *prep.* under

souvent *adv.* often

soyez, soyons *v. forms of* **être** (*imperative*); **Soyez à l'heure!** Be on time! **Soyez prudent!** Be prudent! **Soyons sérieux!** Let's be serious!

spécial, spéciale *adj.* special

spectacle *n. m.* show (entertainment, e.g., movie, theater)

spectateur, spectatrice *n.* spectator (person in an audience)

splendide *adj.* splendid

sport *n. m.* sport

stade *n. m.* stadium

stupéfié(e) *adj.* stupefied, dumbfounded

stylo *n. m.* pen

su *past part. of* **savoir**

suffit *v. form of* **être; je suis**/I am; **je ne suis pas**/I am not

suisse *adj.* Swiss; **la Suisse** Switzerland

suit *v. form of* **suivre** (to follow); **Il suit la route**/He is following the route.

supermarché *n. m.* supermarket

superstitieux, superstitieuse *adj.* superstitious

sur *prep.* on, upon

sûr, sûre *adj.* sure, certain

sûrement *adv.* surely

surfer *v.* to surf (the Internet)

surtout *adv.* especially, above all

T

t' *contraction of* **te,** *refl. pron.*; (**Est-ce que tu t'appelles Janine?** Is your name Janine?)

ta *poss. adj., f. sing.* your (*fam. use*); **ta maison** your house

tableau *n. m.* chalkboard, picture, painting

tablier *n. m.* apron

tambour *n. m.* drum

tante *n. f.* aunt

tapis *n. m.* carpet, rug

tard *adv.* late; **plus tard** later

tarte *n. f.* tart

tasse *n. f.* cup; **une tasse de café** a cup of coffee; **une tasse à café** a coffee cup

te *refl. pron., dir. and indir. obj. pron. (fam.)* yourself, you, to you

tel, telle *adj.* such

télécopie *n. f.* fax

télécopier to fax

télécopieur *n. m.* fax machine

télégramme *n. m.* telegram

téléphone *n. m.* telephone; **au téléphone** to the telephone, on the telephone

téléphone *n. m.* **portable** cell phone (A cell phone may be called "un portable." The same word is sometimes used for a laptop computer.)

téléviseur *n. m.* television set (apparatus)

téléviseur *n. m.* **à écran plasma** plasma screen television set

télé *n. f.* TV; **la télévision** television; **à la télévision** on television

temps *n. m.* tense, time (duration), weather; **Quel temps fait-il?** What's the weather like? **Il a beaucoup de temps**/He has a lot of time.

tendrement *adv.* tenderly

tenir *v.* to hold

tenu *past part. of* **tenir**

tenue *n. f.* suit, attire; **en tenue d'exercice** in a gym suit

terminé *past part. of* **terminer** (to terminate, to end, to finish)

terrasse *n. f.* terrace; **une terasse de café** a sidewalk café

tes *poss. adj. pl (fam.)* your; (**tes livres**/your books)

tête *n. f.* head

théâtre *n. m.* theater

tiennent *v. form of* **tenir**

tiens! here! look!

tiens *v. form of* tenir

tiers one third

tigre *n. m.* tiger

tinte *v. form of* **tinter** (to ring, to toll)

tiroir *n. m.* drawer

toi *pron. (fam.)* you; **avec toi** with you; **toi que voilà...** you there...

toilette *n. f.* washing and dressing; **faire sa toilette** to groom oneself (wash and dress)

toit *n. m.* roof

tolérer *v.* to tolerate

tomate *n. f.* tomato

tombé *past part. of* **tomber** (to fall)

tombeau *n. m.* tombe, grave

ton *poss. adj. m. sing.* your (*fam. use*); (**ton stylo**/your pen)

tort *n. m.* wrong; **vous avez tort** you are wrong

tortue *n. f.* turtle

tôt *adv.* early

touche *n. f.* **d'appel** talk key

touche *n. f.* **de sélection** selection key

toujours *adv.* always, still

tour *n. m.* turn, tour; **un tour de force** trick

tourner *v.* to turn, to turn sour

tournevis *n. m.* screwdriver

tous *adj. m. pl.* all; **tous les deux** both; **toutes les deux** (*fem.*) both; **tous les élèves** all the pupils; **tous les élèves rient** all the pupils laugh; **tous les enfants** all the children; **tous les matins** every morning; **tous les soirs** every evening

tout *adj. pron., adv.* all, everything, every; **tout de même** just the same, all the same; **tout de suite** immediately; **tout d'un coup** all of a sudden; **Tout est bien qui finit bien!** All's well that ends well! **tout le monde** everybody; **tout l'été** all summer

toute, toutes *adj. f.* all; **toute la classe** the whole clase; **toutes les jeunes filles** all the girls; **toute la bôite de chocolats** the whole box of chocolates; **toute la cocotte!** the whole pot! **toute la journée** the whole day, all day long; **toute la matinée** all morning long, the whole morning

tranquille *adj.* calm, quiet, tranquil

tranquillement *adv.* calmly, peacefully, quietly

transporter *v.* to transport

travail *n. m.* work

travaille *past part. of* **travailler** (to work)

traverser *v.* to cross, to go through, to traverse; **à travers** through, across

très *adv.* very (*Note: never use* **très** *with* **beaucoup**)

tricolore *n. m. adj.* tricolor (French flag, consisting of three vertical bands of blue, white, red)

triompher *v.* to triumph

triste *adj. m. f.* sad, unhappy

trois *adj.* three; **troisième** *adj.* third

trop *adv.* too, too much, too many; **trop facile**/too easy; **il travaille trop**/he works too much; **il a trop d'argent**/he has too much money; **il fait trop de fautes**/he makes too many mistakes; (*Note: never say* **trop beaucoup**)

trottoir *n. m.* sidewalk

trouve *v. form of* **trouver** (to find); **il trouve**/he finds; **se trouver** to be located; **la bibliothèque se trouve près du parc**/the library is located near the park

tu *per. pron. fam.* you

tulipe *n. f.* tulip

U

un, une *adj.* one; *also, indef. art.* a, an; **j'ai un père**/I have a (one) father; **j'ai une mère**/I have a (one) mother; **j'ai un livre**/I have a (one) book; **j'ai une pomme**/I have an (one) apple

usine *n. f.* factory

usuel, usuelle *adj.* usual

utile *adj.* useful

V

va *v. form of* **aller; il, elle va**/he, she, it goes, does go, is going; **va te coucher!** go to bed! (*fam. use*)

vache *n. f.* cow

vais *v. form of* **aller; je vais**/I'm going, I do go, I go; **je vais me faire lire les lignes de la main**/ I'm going to have my palm read

valeur *n. f.* value

valise *n. f.* suitcase, valise

valoir *v.* to be worth

vanille *n. f.* vanilla; **j'aime la glace à la vanille**/I like vanilla ice cream

vas *v. form of* **aller; tu vas**/you go, you do go, you are going (*fam. use*); **comment vas-tu?**/how are you? (*fam. use*)

vase *n. m.* vase

vas-y! go to it!/go there!

vaut *v. form of* **valoir; il vaut mieux**/it is better

veau *n. m.* veal

vélo *n. m.* bike

venant *v. form of* **venir**

vend, vends, vendez, vendu *v. forms of* **vendre**

vendeur, vendeuse *n. m. f.* salesman, saleswoman

vendre *v.* to sell

vendu *past part. of* **vendre**

venez *v. form of* **venir** (to come)

vent *n. m.* wind

vente *n. f.* sale; **une vente aux enchères** auction

venu *past part. of* **venir**

vérité *n. f.* truth

vermisseau *n. m.* small worm

verra *v. form of* **voir; il, elle verra**/he, she will see

verre *n. m.* glass (drinking); **je bois un verre de lait**/I'm drinking a glass of milk

vers *prep.* toward

vert *n. m. adj.* green; **aimez-vous le vert?**/do you like green? **j'aime les petites automobiles vertes**/I like small green cars.

verticalement *adv.* vertically

veste *n. f.* vest (worn under a suit coat)

veston *n. m.* coat (of a suit)

vêtements *n. m. pl.* clothing

veut, veux *v. forms of* **vouloir** (to want); **je veux, tu veux, il** *ou* **elle** *ou* **on veut**/I want, you (*fam.*) want, he *or* she *or* it wants

viande *n. f.* meat

vie *n. f.* life

vieille *adj. f. s.* old; **une vieille dame**/an old lady; **vieux** *adj. m. s. pl.* old

viens, vient *v. forms of* **venir** (to come)

vigueur *n. f.* force

ville *n. f.* town, city

vin *n. m.* vine

vingt *adj.* twenty; **vingtième** twentieth

violence *n. f.* violence

vis *n. f.* screw

visage *n. m.* face

visite *n. f.* visit; **rendre visite à quelqu'un** to visit someone

visiter *v.* to visit

vite *adv.* quickly, fast

vitesse *n. f.* speed; **à toute vitesse** at full speed, quickly

vitre *n. f.* window (glass) pane

vive, vivent *v. forms of* **vivre** (to live); **Vive le quatorze juillet!**/Hurrah for July 14th! **Vive la France!**/Long live France! **Vive l'Amérique!**/Long live America!

vivra *v. form of* **vivre; il** *ou* **elle vivra**/ he *or* she will live

vivre *v.* to live

vocabulaire *n. m.* vocabulary

voici here is, here are; **voici les livres!**/here are the books! **voici Robert!**/Here's Robert!

voient *v. form of* **voir** (to see); **ils** *ou* **elles voient**/they see

voilà there is, there are; **voilà les livres!**/there are the books! **voilà Robert!**/There's Robert!

voir *v.* to see

voisin, voisine *n. m. f.* neighbor

voisinage *n. m.* neighborhood

voit *v. form of* **voir; il** *ou* **elle voit**/he *or* she sees, does see, is seeing

voiture *n. f.* car, automobile

voix *n. f.* voice; **à voix basse**/in a low voice, softly; **à haute voix**/in a loud voice

vol *n. m.* flight

voler *v.* to fly, to steal

vont *v. form of* **aller; ils** *ou* **elles vont**/they go, do go, are going

vos *poss. adj. pl.* your; **Voici vos livres!**/Here are your books!

votre *poss. adj. s.* your; **Voici votre livre!**Here's your book!

voudrais *v. form (conditional) of* **vouloir** (to want); **je voudrais une tasse de café**/I would like a cup of coffee

voulez *v. form of* **vouloir; Voulez-vous aller au cinéma avec moi?**/Do you want to go to the movies with me?

vouloir *v.* to want; **vouloir dire** to mean, to signify; **Que veut dire ce mot?**/What does this word mean?

voulu *past part. of* **vouloir**

vous *per. pron.* you; **vous deux**/you two

voyage *n. m.* trip; **faire un voyage** to take a trip

voyageons *v. form of* **voyager; nous voyageons**/we are travelling

voyager *v.* to travel

voyez-vous? do you see?

vrai *adj. m.,* **vraie** *f.* true, real

vraiment *adv.* really, truly

vu *past part. of* **voir** (to see); **Avez-vous vu Janine?**/Have you seen Janine?

Y

y *advl. pron., adv. of place* there; **il y a** there is, there are; **il y a vingt élèves dans cette classe**/there are 20 students in this class; **y a-t-il vingt étudiants dans cette classe?**/are there 20 students in this class? **il y a quelqu'un à la porte**/there is someone at the door.

yeux *n. m. pl.* eyes; **l'oeil** *n. m. s.* the eye

Z

zèbre *n. m.* zebra

zodiaque *n. m.* zodiac

zut *interj.* darn it!

English-French Vocabulary

A

a **un, une; un homme**/a man; **une femme**/a woman

above **au-dessus, en haut**

absolutely **absolument**

to accept **accepter**

accident **un accident**

acrostic **un acrostiche**

actor, actress **un acteur, une actrice**

to add **ajouter**

address **une adresse**

to adore **adorer**

to advance **avancer**

to affirm **affirmer**

after **après;** afternoon/**un après-midi;** in the afternoon/**l'après-midi**

again **encore, de nouveau**

age **un âge**

agreed **d'accord**

airplane **un avion**

airport **un aéroport;** air terminal/**une aérogare**

alarm clock **un réveille-matin**

all **tout, toute, toutes, tous;** all of a sudden/**tout d'un coup;** All's well that ends well/**Tout est bien qui finit bien;** all summer/**tout l'été;** all day long/**toute la journée;** all morning long/**toute la matinée;** all the girls/**toutes les jeunes filles;** all the boys/**tous les garçons**

to allow **permettre** (*past part.,* **permis**)

almost **presque**

already **déjà**

also **aussi**

always **toujours**

American (language) **l'américain** *n. m.;* He is American. She is American/**Il est américain, Elle est américaine**

to amuse **amuser;** to amuse oneself/**s'amuser**

amusing **amusant, amusante**

an **un, une; un tablier**/an apron; **une pomme**/an apple

ancient **ancien, ancienne**

and **et**

angry **fâché, fâchée;** to get angry/**se fâcher**

animal **un animal;** animals/**animaux**

to announce **annoncer**

to annoy **ennuyer**

annoying **ennuyant, ennuyante**

another **un autre, une autre**

answer **une réponse;** to answer/**répondre** (*past part.,* **répondu**)

answering machine **le répondeur**

ant **une fourmi**

apparatus **un appareil**

appetite **un appétit**

apple **une pomme**

apple tree **un pommier**

appointment **un rendez-vous**

to appreciate **apprécier**

to approach **s'approcher (de)**

arm **un bras**

armchair **un fauteuil**

around **autour;** he is traveling around the world/**il voyage autour du monde;** it is around two o'clock/**il est vers deux heures**

to arrange **arranger, disposer**

arrested **arrêté**

to arrive **arriver**

art **l'art,** *m.*

artist **l'artiste,** *m. f.*

as **comme**

as well as (just as) **ainsi que**

to ask (for) **demander**

to ask a question **poser une question**

aspirin **une aspirine**

to assert **affirmer**

assignments **les devoirs,** *m.*

astronomer **un astronome**

at **à**

at first **d'abord**

at last **enfin**

at that moment **à ce moment-là**

ATM (automated teller machine) **le guichet automatique (bancaire)**

to attend **assister à**

auditorium **une grande salle**

August **août,** *m.*

aunt **une tante**

author **un auteur, une femme auteur**

auto mechanic **un garagiste, une garagiste**

autograph **un autographe**

automobile **une automobile, une voiture**

autumn **l'automne,** *m.*

to avoid **éviter**

B

baby **un bébé**

babysitter **une gardienne d'enfants, un gardien d'enfants**

bad **mauvais, mauvaise**

badly **mal**

baker **un boulanger, une boulangère**

bakery **une boulangerie**

ball **une balle, un ballon**

balloon **un ballon**

banana **une banane**

barber **un coiffeur, une coiffeuse**

basket **un painer**

Bastille Day **Le Jour de la Bastille**

to bathe **baigner;** to bathe oneself **se baigner**

bathroom **une salle de bains**

baton **un bâton**

to be **être**

to be able **pouvoir** (*past part.,* **pu**)

to be born **naître** (*past part.,* **né**)

to be late **être en retard**

to be located **se trouver**

to be present at **assister à, être présent(e) à**

to be right **avoir raison**

to be sorry **regretter**

to beat **battre** (*past part.,* **battu**)

beautiful **beau, beaux, bel, belle, belles (un beau cadeau, de beaux cadeaux, un bel arbre, une belle femme, de belles femmes)** beauty **la beauté**

because **parce que**

to become **devenir**

bedroom **une chambre à coucher**

before **avant;** before going out/**avant de sortir**

to beg **prier**

to begin **commencer (à + inf.); je commence à travailler**/I'm beginning to work.

behind **derrière** (*in back of*)

Belgian **belge;** He is Belgian, She is Belgian/**Il est belge, Elle est belge**

Belgium **la Belgique**

to believe **croire** (*past part.,* **cru**)

below **par-dessous, au-dessous**

bench (seat) **un banc**

besides **d'ailleurs**

better *as an adj.,* **meilleur, meilleure;** *as an adv.,* **mieux;** the best **le meilleur, la meilleure, les meilleurs, les meilleures; cette pomme est meilleure**/this apple is better; **cette pomme est la meilleure**/this apple is the best; **Paul travaille mieux que Robert**/Paul works better than Robert.

between **entre; entre eux et nous**/between them and us

beverage **une boisson**

to beware **se méfier de; méfiez-vous des obstacles dangereux**/beware of dangerous obstacles

bid, bidding **une enchère**

bike **un vélo; une bicyclette**/a bicycle

bill **une addition**

bird **un oiseau**

birth **une naissance;** birthday/**un anniversaire de naissance**

black **noir, noire, noirs, noires**

blue **bleu, bleue, bleus, bleues**

boarding pass **la carte d'embarquement**

body **un corps**

to boil **bouillir, faire bouillir**

book **un livre**

to bore **ennuyer**

boring **ennuyant, ennuyante**

to be born **naître;** *past part.,* **né**

both **tous les deux, toutes les deux**

bottle **une bouteille**

boutique **une boutique**

box **une boîte**

boy **un garçon**

to break **briser, casser, rompre**

breakfast **le petit déjeuner**

to bring **apporter**

broom **un balai**

brother **un frère**

to brush **brosser, se brosser; je brosse le manteau**/I'm brushing the coat; **je me brosse les dents**/I brush my teeth

brush **une brosse**

to build **bâtir**

building **un bâtiment, un immeuble**

to burn **brûler**

bus **un autobus** (city bus); **un autocar** (interurban, long-distance bus)

but **mais**

butcher **un boucher, une bouchère**

butcher shop **une boucherie**

butter **le beurre**

to buy **acheter**

by **par**

C

cake **un gâteau, des gâteaux**

calculator **la calculatrice**

to call **appeler;** to be called, to be named **s'appeler; j'appelle le médecin**/I'm calling the doctor; **je m'appelle Janine, je m'appelle Pierre**/My name is Janine, my name is Peter.

can (may) **pouvoir; vous pouvez entrer**/you can (may) come in

Canada **le Canada**

Canadian *adj.* **canadien, canadienne;** *n.* **Canadien, Canadienne; un livre canadien**/a Canadian book; **Madame Dupont est canadienne**/Mrs. Dupont is Canadian.

candy **un bonbon**

capital **une capitale**

capricious **capricieux, capricieuse**

car **une voiture, une automobile**

carefully **soigneusement**

carpet **un tapis**

to carry **porter**

to carry away **emporter**

carry-on bag **le sac de vol**

cash box (register) **une caisse**

cashier **un caissier, une caissière**

castle **un château**

cat **un chat, une chatte**

to catch **attraper**

CD **le disque compact, le CD**

CD player **le lecteur de CD**

CD-ROM **le cédérom, le CD-ROM**

ceiling **un plafond**

to celebrate **célébrer**

cell phone **le téléphone portable** (A cell phone may be called "un portable." The same word is sometimes used for a laptop computer.)

cellar **une cave**

center **un centre**

certain **certain, certaine, sûr, sûre**

chair **une chaise**

chalk **une craie**

change **un changement**

chapel **une chapelle**

charming **charmant, charmante**

to chase, to chase away **chasser**

chat (Internet) **le clavardage**

to chat (Internet) **clavarder**

chat room **le salon de clavardage**

check (bill) **une addition**

cheese **un fromage**

cherry **une cerise**

chicken **un poulet**

child **un enfant, une enfant**

chimney **une cheminée**

chocolate **un chocolat**

to choose **choisir**

Christmas **le Noël;** Merry Christmas/**Joyeux Noël**

church **une église**

city **une ville**

class **une classe;** classroom/**une salle de classe;** a French class/**une classe de français**

to clean **nettoyer**

clear **clair, claire**

clock **une horloge;** alarm clock/**un réveille-matin**

to close **fermer**

closet **une armoire, un placard**

clothing **un vêtement, des vêtements**

cloud **un nuage;** cloudy/**nuageux, nuageuse;** a cloudy sky/**un ciel nuageux**

coat (overcoat) **un manteau, un pardessus**

coffee **le café**

cold **froid, froide;** the cold/**le froid; j'ai froid**/I'm cold, I feel cold; **il fait froid ici**/It's cold here.

color **la couleur;** what color is…/**de quelle couleur est…**

comb **un peigne;** to comb one's hair/**se peigner les cheveux**

to come **venir;** to come back/**revenir**

to come down **descendre**

to come in **entrer (dans)**

computer **l'ordinateur** *m.*

to confess **confesser**

contrary **contraire**

to cook **cuire, faire la cuisine**

to correct **corriger**

to cost **coûter**

country **un pays, une nation**

countryside **un paysage**

courageous **courageux, courageuse**

course **un cours;** a French course/**un cours de français**

cousin **un cousin, une cousine**

to cover **couvrir;** *past part.,* **couvert**

cow **une vache**

crazy **fou, fol, folle**

credit card **la carte bancaire/la carte de crédit**

cross **une croix;** to cross/**traverser**

cruel **cruel, cruelle**

to crush **écraser**

to cry **pleurer;** to cry out/**crier**

cup **une tasse;** a coffee cup/**une tasse à café;** a cup of coffee/**une tasse de café**

curious **curieux, curieuse**

customer **un client, une cliente**

to cut **couper;** to cut oneself/**se couper; j'ai coupé le pain**/I cut the bread; **je me suis coupé le doigt**/I cut my finger.

cut **mignon, mignonne,** *adj. m. f.*

cybercafé **le cybercafé**

D

dad, daddy **un papa**

dance **un bal;** to dance/**danser**

dancer **un danseur, une danseuse**

dangerous **dangereux, dangereuse**

dark **obscur, obscure**

darling **chéri, chérie**

darn it! **zut alors!**

database **la banque de données**

daughter **une fille**

day **un jour, une journée;** all day long/**toute la journée**

dear **cher, chère**

December **le décembre**

decision **une décision**

to defend **défendre**

delicious **délicieux, délicieuse**

department store **un grand magasin**

desire **un désir;** to desire/**désirer**

desk **un bureau;** desk (pupil's, student's)/**un pupitre**

desktop computer **l'ordinateur** *n.* de bureau *m.*

dessert **un dessert**

detail **un détail**

detective **un détective**

to detest **détester**

dictionary **un dictionnaire**

to die **mourir;** *past part.,* **mort**

diet **un régime;** on a diet/**au régime**

difficult **difficile**

to dine **dîner**

dining room **une salle à manger**

dinner **le dîner**

dirty **sale**

disk (record) **un disque**

disgusting **dégoûtant, dégoûtante**

dish **un plat, une assiette**

to disobey **désobéir (à)**

display screen (computer) **l'écran** *m.*

to dispose **disposer**

distinctly **distinctement**

to disturb **déranger**

to do **faire**

to do gymnastics **faire de la gymnastique**

doctor **un docteur, un médecin, une femme docteur, une femme médecin**

dog **un chien, une chienne**

door **une porte**

doubt **un doute;** to doubt/**douter, se douter**

dream **un rêve;** to dream/**rêver**

dress **une robe;** to dress/**s'habiller**

drink **une boisson;** to drink/**boire;** *past part.,* **bu**

drugstore **une pharmacie**

druggist **un pharmacien, une pharmacienne**

drum **un tambour**

dry **sec, sèche**

dumb **bête;** a dumb (stupid, foolish) thing/**une bêtise**

during **pendant**

DVD **le disque DVD**

DVD player **le lecteur de DVD**

E

each **chaque;** each one **chacun, chacune**

ear **une oreille**

early **de bonne heure, tôt**

easily **facilement**

easy **facile**

e-commerce **le commerce électronique**

to eat **manger**

egg **un oeuf;** soft-boiled egg/**un oeuf à la coque**

eight **huit**

electronic ticket, e-ticket **le billet électronique**

e-mail **le courriel, le courrier électronique**

to employ **employer**

to end **finir, terminer;** the end/**la fin**

English (language) **l'anglais,** *n. m.*
   He is English, She is English/**Il est anglais, Elle est anglaise**

English Channel **La Manche**

to enjoy oneself **s'amuser**

enjoyable **amusant, amusante**

to enter (in, into) **entrer (dans)**

entrance **une entrée**

to erase **effacer**

error **une faute, une erreur**

to escape **échapper, s'échapper**

euro **l'euro** *m.*

evening **le soir;** in the evening/**le soir;** this evening, tonight/**ce soir;** every evening/**tous les soirs**

evening party **une soirée**

everybody **tout le monde**

everything **tout, toutes les choses**

everywhere **partout**

exactly **exactement**

to examine **examiner**

to exclaim **exlamer, s'exclamer**

to excuse **excuser, s'excuser**

exhibit **une exposition**

to expect **attendre**

to explain **expliquer**

extraordinary **extraordinaire**

extremely **extrêmement**

eye **un oeil;** eyes/**les yeux**

eyeglasses **les lunettes,** *f.*

eyelid **la paupière**

F

face **le visage, la figure**

to fall **tomber**

false **faux, fausse**

family **la famille**

far **loin**

farewell **adieu**

farm **la ferme**

fast **vite, rapidement**

father **le père**

favorite **favori, favorite**

to fax **télécopier**

fax **la télécopie**

fax machine **le télécopieur**

fear **la peur;** to have fear, to be afraid/**avoir peur**

feast **la fête**

feel hungry **avoir faim**

fifteen **quinze**

to fill **remplir**

film **le film**

finally **enfin**

to find **trouver**

finger **le doigt**

to finish **finir, terminer**

fire **le feu**

first **premier, première;** at first/**d'abord**

fish **le poisson**

flag **le drapeau**

flea **la puce;** flea market/**le marché aux puces**

floor **le plancher;** floor (of a building designated by a number)/**un étage;** ground floor/**le rez de chaussée;** the first floor/**le premier étage**

florist **le, la fleuriste**

flour **la farine**

flower **la fleur**

fly (insect) **la mouche**

to fly **voler**

to follow **suivre**

food **la nourriture, l'aliment,** *m.,* **l'alimentation,** *f.*

foolish **bête;** a foolish thing/**une bêtise**

foot **le pied**

football **un ballon; jouer au football**/to play soccer

for **pour**

to forbid **défendre**

to forget **oublier**

fork **la fourchette**

fourteen **quatorze**

franc **un franc** (former French unit of money)

French (language) **le français;** He is French, She is French/**Il est français, Elle est française**

French fries **les pommes frites,** *f.*

fresh **frais, fraîche**

friend **un ami, une amie**

friendship **une amitié**

from **de**

to fulfill **remplir**

funny **drôle**

furious **furieux, furieuse**

furniture **le meuble**

G

game **le match**

garage **le garage**

garbage **les ordures,** *f.*

garden **le jardin**

garlic **l'ail,** *m.*

gasoline **l'essence,** *f.*

generally **généralement**

generous **généreux, généreuse**

genius **un génie**

gentleman **le monsieur; les messieurs,** *pl.*

geography **la géographie**

German (language) **l'allemand,** *m.*

to get angry **se fâcher**

to get away **échapper, s'échapper**

to get dressed **s'habiller**

girl **la jeune fille**

to give **donner**

to give back **rendre**

glass (drinking) **un verre**

glove **le gant**

to go **aller**

to go away **partir, s'en aller**

to go back **retourner**

to go by **passer**

to go down **descendre**

to go for a walk **se promener**

to go in (into) **entrer dans**

to go out **sortir**

to go through **traverser**

to go to bed **se coucher;** go to bed!/**va te coucher! allez vous coucher!**

goalie **le gardien de but, la gardienne de but**

God **le Dieu**

good **bon, bonne**

good afternoon, good day, good morning **bonjour**

good-bye **au revoir**

good evening, good night **bonsoir**

good luck **bonne chance**

grape **le raisin** (raisin/**le raisin sec**)

grapefruit **le pamplemousse**

Great Britain **la Grande Bretagne**

green **vert, verte**

grocer **un épicier, une épicière**

grocery store **une épicerie**

group **un groupe**

to guard **garder**

guard **un gardien, une gardienne**

H

hair **les cheveux,** *m.*

hairdresser **le coiffeur, la coiffeuse**

half **demi, demie**

ham **le jambon**

hand **la main**

handkerchief **le mouchoir**

handsome **bel, beau, beaux; un bel homme**/a handsome man

happiness **le bonheur**

happy **heureux, heureuse, joyeux, joyeuse**

hard drive **le disque dur**

to harm **nuire**

harm **le mal**

hat **le chapeau**

to hate **détester**

to have **avoir**

to have a good time **s'amuser; have a good time!/amusez-vous bien!**

have a good trip! **bon voyage!**

have a good return trip! **bon retour!**

to have a meal **prendre un repas**

to have dinner **dîner**

to have lunch **déjeuner**

to have to **devoir**

he **il**

head **la tête**

headdress **la coiffe**

health **la santé**

to hear **entendre**

heart **le coeur**

hello **bonjour; allô** (*used when answering the telephone*)

to help **aider**

her *as a poss. adj.,* **son, sa, ses** (**Alice a son livre**/Alice has her book; **Hélène lit sa leçon**/Helen is reading her lesson; **Marie a ses livres**/Mary has her books); *as a dir. obj. pron.,* **la** (**Voyez-vous Marie? Oui, je la vois**/Do you see Mary? Yes, I see her); *as obj. of a prep.,* **elle** (**avec elle**/with her); *as an indir. obj. pron.,* **lui**/to her (**Je lui donne le livre**/I'm giving [to] her the book)

here ici

here is, here are **voici** (**Voici Robert!**/Here's Robert!); (**Voici les livres!**/Here are the books!)

herself **se** (**Monique se lave**/Monique is washing herself)

to hide **cacher**

him *as a direct obj. pron.,* **le** (**Je le vois**/I see him); *as obj. of a prep.,* **lui** (**avec lui**/with him); *as an indir. obj. pron.,* **lui**/to him (**Je lui donne le livre**/I'm giving [to] him the book)

himself **se** (**Robert se lave**/Robert is washing himself

his **son, sa, ses** (**Robert a son livre**/Robert has his book; **Henri lit sa leçon**/Henry is reading his lesson; **Raymond a ses livres**/Raymond has his books)

to hold **tenir**

holiday **la fête**

homework **le devoir, les devoirs**

honor **l'honneur,** *m.*

to hope **espérer**

horse **le cheval**

hospital **l'hôpital,** *m.*

hot **chaud, chaude**

hotel **l'hôtel,** *m.*

hour **l'heure,** *f.*

house **la maison**

how **comment**

how many, how much **combien (de)**

human **humain, humaine**

hunger **la faim; to be hungry/avoir faim**

to hunt **chasser**

to hurry **se dépêcher**

to hurt **blesser, nuire; to hurt oneself/sa faire mal, se blesser**

husband **le mari, l'époux,** *m.*

I

ice **la glace**

ice cream **la glace;** vanilla ice cream/**la glace à la vanille;** chocolate ice cream/**la glace au chocolat**

idea **l'idée,** *f.*

if **si**

ill **malade**

to illuminate **éclairer**

immediately **tout de suite, immédiatement**

in **dans**

in front of **devant**

in love **amoureux, amoureuse;** in love with/**amoureux de, amoureuse de**

in order (to) **pour**

industrious **diligent, diligente, industrieux, industrieuse**

inhabit **demeurer, habiter**

to injure **blesser**

inside **dedans**

instruction **l'enseignement,** *m.*

intermission **l'entracte,** *m.*

Internet **l'Internet** *m.*

iPod **l'iPod** *m.*

Irish **irlandais, irlandaise;** Irish style/**à l'irlandaise**

isn't it? isn't that so? **n'est-ce pas?** *see also* Work Unit 20

it *per. pron. f., as subj.,* **elle** (**elle est ici**); *per. pron. m., as subj.,* **il** (**il est ici**); *as obj. of prep., m.,* **lui** (**avec lui**); *f.,* **elle** (**avec elle**); *dir. obj. pron. f.,* **la** (**Voyez-vous la maison? Oui, je la vois**); *dir. obj. pron. m.,* **le** (**Voyez-vous le garage? Oui, je le vois**)

it is necessary **il faut, il est nécessaire (de)**

it's (it is) **C'est...** (**C'est samedi**/It's Saturday)

its **son sa, ses,** *poss. adj.* (**Le petit chat a son jouet, sa nourriture, et ses rubans**/The little cat has its toy, its food, and its ribbons)

Italian (language) **l'italien,** *m.; as an adj.,* **italien, italienne**

J

jacket **la jaquette**

joyous **joyeux, joyeuse**

juice **le jus**

July **juillet,** *m.*

to jump **sauter**

just as **ainsi que**

K

kangaroo **le kangourou**

to keep **garder**

key **la clef**

keyboard **le clavier**

kilogram **le kilogramme** (1 kilogram equals about 2.2 lbs.)

kilometer **le kilomètre** (1 kilometer equals about 0.621 miles)

kind **gentil, gentille**

kitchen **la cuisine**

knee **le genou, les genoux**

knife **le couteau, les couteaux**

to know (how) **savoir; Savez-vous lire?**/Do you know how to read? **Savez-vous la leçon?**/Do you know the lesson?

to know (to be acquainted with) **connaître; Connaissez-vous Monique?**/Do you know Monique?/**Connaissez-vous Paris?**/Do you know Paris?

L

lady **la dame, les dames;** young lady/**la demoiselle;** *in direct address,* **mesdames, mesdemoiselles**

lamp **la lampe**

language **la langue**

laptop computer **l'ordinateur** *m.* **portable** (A laptop computer may just be called "un portable." The same word is sometimes used for a cell phone.)

last **dernier, dernière**

late **tard;** later/**plus tard;** to be late/**être en retard**

to laugh **rire;** *past part.,* **ri**

lawyer **un avocat, une (femme) avocate**

leaf **la feuille**

to leap **sauter**

to learn **apprendre**

to leave **partir, quitter, laisser; elle est partie**/she left; **j'ai quitté mes amis à six heures**/I left my friends at six o'clock; **j'ai laissé mon livre à l'école**/I left my book at school; **sortir** (to go out); **elle est sortie sans argent**/she went out without any money

left *(as opposed to right)* **gauche; à gauche**/on (to) the left

leg **la jambe**

to lend **prêter**

less **moins; au moins**/at least

lesson **la leçon**

let's go! **allons!**

letter **la lettre**

liberty **la liberté**

library **la bibliothèque**

life **la vie**

light **la lumière;** to light/**allumer, éclairer**

to like **aimer bien;** to like better/**aimer mieux, préférer**

line **la ligne**

to listen (to) **écouter;** to listen to music/**écouter la musique**

little (small) *adj.* **petit, petite, petits, petites**

little (not much) *adv.* **peu;** a little/**un peu;** a little sugar/**un peu de sucre**

to live **demeurer, vivre**

living room **le salon**

long *adj.* **long, longue, longs, longues**

to look (at) **regarder;** I'm looking at the sky/**Je regarde le ciel**

to look (for) **chercher;** I'm looking for the book/**Je cherche le livre**

to lose **perdre**

to love **aimer;** love/**l'amour** *n. m.*

low *adj.* **bas, basse, bas, basses**

luck **la chance;** you're lucky/**vous avez de la chance**

lunch, luncheon **le déjeuner;** to lunch, to have lunch/**déjeuner**

M

magazine **le magazine, la revue**

magnificent *adj.* **magnifique**

mail carrier **le facteur**

to make **faire**

to make fun of **se moquer de**

mama **la maman**

man **un homme**

many **beaucoup (de);** I have many friends/**J'ai beaucoup d'amis**

map **la carte**

marriage **le mariage**

mathematics **les mathématiques** *n. f.*

may (can) *v.* **pouvoir;** you may come in/**vous pouvez entrer**

maybe *adv.* **peut-être**

me *pron.* **me, moi** (when stressed); he knows me/**il me connaît;** she is talking to me/**elle me parle;** give me the book/**donnez-moi le livre**

meal **le repas**

to mean **vouloir dire;** What do you mean/**Que voulez-vous dire?**

meat **la viande**

medicine **le médicament**

to meet **rencontrer, faire connaissance, faire la connaissance de;** I met my friend at the movies/**J'ai recontré mon ami au cinéma;** Today I met a new student/**Aujourd'hui j'ai fait la connaissance d'une nouvelle étudiante**

menu **la carte**

merchant **le marchand, la marchande**

middle **le milieu;** in the middle of/**au milieu de**

midnight **le minuit**

milk **le lait**

mirror **une glace** (hand mirror); **un miroir** (wall mirror)

mistake **une erreur, une faute**

mister **monsieur**

mom **la maman**

money **l'argent** *n. m.*

month **le mois;** in the month of/**au mois de**

moon **la lune**

more **plus**

morning **le matin;** in the morning/**le matin;** I worked all morning/**J'ai travaillé toute la matinée;** every morning/**tous les matins**

mother **la mère**

motor **le moteur**

mouse **la souris**

mouth **la bouche**

movie (film) **le film;** movies (theater)/**le cinéma**

MP3 **le fichier MP3**

Mr. **Monsieur, M.**

Mrs. **Madame, Mme**

much **beaucoup (de)**

multimedia player **le lecteur multimédia**

museum **le musée**

mushroom **un champignon**

music **la musique**

must *v.* **devoir, falloir;** I must work now/**Je dois travailler maintenant;** One must be honest/**Il faut être honnête;** One must not lie/**Il ne faut pas mentir**

my *poss. adj.* **mon, ma, mes;** my book/**mon livre;** my room/**ma chambre;** my friends/**mes amis**

myself *pron.* **me, moi-même;** I wash myself/**Je me lave;** I did it myself/**Je l'ai fait moi-même**

N

name **le nom**

naturally *adv.* **naturellement**

to navigate (the Internet) **naviguer (sur Internet), surfer**

near *adv.* **près (de)**

necessary *adj.* **nécessaire;** it is necessary/**il est nécessaire**

neck **le cou**

necktie **la cravate**

need **le besoin;** to need/**avoir besoin (de);** I need a pen/**J'ai besoin d'un stylo**

neighbor **le voisin, la voisine**

neighborhood **le voisinage**

neither **ni...ni;** I have neither pen nor pencil/**Je n'ai ni stylo ni crayon**

nephew **le neveu**

net **le filet**

never *adj.* **jamais**

new *adj.* **nouveau, nouvel, nouvelle;** a new book/**un nouveau livre;** a new friend (boy)/**un nouvel ami;** a new friend (girl)/**une nouvelle amie;** a (brand) new suit/**un complet neuf;** a (brand) new dress/**une robe neuve**

New Orleans **la Nouvelle-Orléans**

news **la nouvelle, les nouvelles;** good news!/**bonnes nouvelles!**

newspaper **le journal**

next *adj.* **prochain, prochaine;** next time/**la prochaine fois**

next to **à côté de**

nice *adj.* **gentil, gentille**

nine *adj.* **neuf**

no *adv.* **non**

noise **le bruit**

noon **le midi**

nose **le nez, les nez**

not at all **pas du tout;** not far/**pas loin**

notebook **le cahier**

nourishment **la nourriture, l'aliment,** *m.,* **l'alimentation,** *f.*

now *adv.* **maintenant**

O

to obey **obéir (à);** I obey my mother and father/**J'obéis à ma mère et à mon père**

of *prep.* **de**

of course **bien sûr, mais oui;** of course not! **mais non!**

to offer **offrir**

office **le bureau**

often *adv.* **souvent**

okay **d'accord**

old *adj.* **ancien, ancienne, vieux, vieil, vieille**

on *prep.* **sur**

once **une fois;** once more/**encore une fois**

one *adj.* **un, une;** one book/**un livre;** one apple/**une pomme**

oneself *refl. pron.* **se;** One washes oneself here/**On se lave ici**

onion **un oignon**

only *adv.* **seulement, ne...que;** I have only two euros/**J'ai seulement deux euros; Je n'ai que deux euros**

to open **ouvrir**

opinion **un avis, une opinion**

opposite *adv.* **d'en face**

or *conj.* **ou**

orange **une orange**

other **autre;** the other/**l'autre;** another/**un autre, une autre**

ought to **devoir**

our *poss. adj.* **notre, nos;** our house/**notre maison;** our book/**notre livre;** our books/**nos livres**

outside *adv.* **dehors**

oven **un four**

over *adv.* **par-dessus;** over there/**là-bas**

overcoat **le pardessus**

to overcook **faire trop cuire**

to owe **devoir**

P

pager **la pagette**

pain **un mal**

to paint **peindre**

paper **le papier;** sheet of paper/**une feuille de papier;** newspaper/**le journal;** paper airplane/**un avion en papier**

park **le parc**

to pass (by) **passer**

past **le passé**

pastry **la pâtisserie;** pastry shop/**une pâtisserie;** pastry cook/**un pâtissier, une pâtissière**

patiently *adv.* **patiemment**

to pay a visit **faire visite**

to pay attention **faire attention**

to pay (for) **payer;** I paid for the book/**J'ai payé le livre**

PDA (personal digital assistant) **l'ordinateur** *m.* **de poche**

pea **le pois;** peas/**les petits pois**

peace **la paix**

peach **la pêche**

pear **la poire**

pen **le stylo**

pencil **le crayon**

pepper **le poivre**

perfect *adj.* **parfait, parfaite**

perhaps *adv.* **peut-être**

to permit **permettre**

person **une personne**

pharmacist **le pharmacien, la pharmacienne**

pharmacy **la pharmacie**

phonorecord **le disque**

picture **le tableau, une image**

piece **le morceau**

pin **une épingle**

PIN **le NIP (le numéro d'identification personnelle)**

PIN pad **le clavier d'identification personnelle**

pineapple **un ananas**

place **un endroit, un lieu**

to place **mettre**

plasma screen, plasma display **l'écran** *m.* **plasma**

plasma screen television set **le téléviseur à écran plasma**

plate **un plat, une assiette**

to play **jouer;** to play (a musical instrument); **jouer de;** to play the piano/**jouer du piano;** to play (a sport)/**jouer à;** to play tennis/**jouer au tennis**

player **un joueur, une joueuse**

pleasant *adj.* **agréable**

please **s'il vous plaît** (polite form); **s'il te plaît** (familiar form)

to please **plaire (à)**

pocket **la poche**

poem **le poème**

poet **un poète, une poétesse**

police officer **un agent de police**

poor *adj.* **pauvre**

postman **le facteur**

potato **une pomme de terre**

pound **une livre**

power button **le bouton de démarrage**

to prefer **préférer, aimer mieux**

to prepare **préparer;** to prepare oneself/**se préparer**

present (gift) **un cadeau;** the present (time)/**le présent**

pretty *adj.* **joli, jolie**

priest **un prêtre;** priestess/**une prêtresse**

principal (of a school) **un directeur, une directrice**

probably *adv.* **probablement**

to profit **profiter;** to take advantage of the moment/**profiter du moment**

promise **une promesse;** to

promise/**promettre**

to pull (away), to pull (out) **arracher**

to punish **punir**

pupil **un élève, une élève**

purchase **un achat, une emplette;** to purchase/**acheter**

to put **mettre;** to put on/**mettre**

Q

quality **la qualité**

quick *adj.* **rapide**

quickly *adv.* **vite, rapidement**

R

R.S.V.P. **R**épondez, **s**'il **v**ous **p**laît/Reply, please (please reply)

rabbit **le lapin**

rain **la pluie;** to rain/**pleuvoir;** it's raining/**il pleut**

rainbow **un arc-en-ciel**

to read **lire**

real *adj.* **vrai, vraie**

really *adv.* **vraiment**

to receive **recevoir**

record, recording **le disque**

red *adj.* **rouge**

to regret **regretter**

to relate **raconter;** to tell, to relate a story/**raconter une histoire**

religious *adj.* **religieux, religieuse**

to remain **rester, demeurer**

to remember **se rappeler, se souvenir (de)**

to remove **enlever**

to repair **réparer;** to have something repaired/**faire réparer quelque chose**

to repeat **répéter**

reply **la réponse;** to reply/**répondre (à)**

to request **demander, prier**

to reside **demeurer**

to respond **répondre (à)**

to return **retourner, revenir;** to return (home)/**rentrer;** to return something/**rendre quelque chose;** I returned the book to the library/ **J'ai rendu le livre à la bibliothèque**

to reveal **révéler**

ribbon **le ruban**

riddle **une devinette**

to be right **avoir raison;** Janine is right!/**Janine a raison!**

right (*as opposed to left*) **la droite;** on (to) the right/**à droite, à la droite**

to ring **sonner**

ring (*worn on finger*) **une bague**

river **un fleuve**

roast beef **le rosbif**

room **la chambre, la pièce**

to ruin **abîmer**

ruler **une règle**

to run **courir**

S

sad *adj.* **triste, malheureux, malheureuse**

salt **le sel**

same *adj.* **même;** all the same, just the same/**tout de même**

Santa Claus **le Père Noël**

to satisfy **satisfaire**

to say **dire**

school **une école**

season **la saison**

seat **la place;** seated/**assis, assise**

second **une seconde;** Wait a second, please/**Attendez une seconde, s'il vous plaît;** *adj.,* **deuxième, second(e);** February is the second month of the year/**Février est le deuxième mois de l'année;** the Second Empire/**le Second Empire**

security check (travel) **le contrôle de sécurité**

to see **voir;** to see again/**revoir;** see you in a little while!/**à tout à l'heure!** see you soon/**à bientôt**

to seize **saisir**

selection key **la touche de sélection**

to send **envoyer**

sentence **la phrase**

serious *adj.* **sérieux, sérieuse, sérieux, sérieuses;** seriously/**sérieusement** several *adj.* **plusieurs**

shame **la honte**

shark **un requin**

she *per. pron. f.* **elle**

to shine **briller**

shirt **la chemise**

shoe **la chaussure, le soulier**

shoo! shoo! **Ch! Ch!**

shop (small) **une boutique**

short *adj.* **court, courte**

shoulder **une épaule**

to shout **crier**

to show **montrer**

shower **une douche**; to take a shower/**prendre une douche**

sick *adj.* **malade, souffrant, souffrante**

sidewalk **le trottoir**

since **depuis**

to sing **chanter**

singer **un chanteur, une chanteuse**

sister **une sœur**

to sit down **s'asseoir**; sit down! **assieds-toi!** *or* **asseyez-vous!** (polite form)

sixty *adj.* **soixante**

skin **la peau**

skirt **la jupe**

sky **le ciel**

to sleep **dormir**

sleeve **une manche**

slow *adj.* **lent, lente**

slowly **lentement**

small *adj.* **petit, petite**

to smell **sentir**

smoke **la fumée**; to smoke/**fumer**

snack bar **un bar rapide**

snow **la neige**; to snow/**neiger**; it is snowing!/**il neige!**

snowman **un bonhomme de neige**

so *adv.* **alors**; so as to/**de façon à**

soccer (in the United States) **le football**

socks **les chaussettes,** *n. f.*

soft *adj.* **doux, douce, doux, douces**

soiled *adj.* **sale**

some (*partitive*) **de l', de la, du, des**; I drink some water/**Je bois de l'eau**; I eat some meat/**Je mange de la viande**; I drink some milk/**Je bois du lait**; I eat some potatoes/**Je mange des pommes de terre**; some (of it, of them) **en**; I am eating some/**J'en mange**; see also pp. 46–47

something *indef. pron.* **quelque chose**

sometimes *adv.* **quelquefois**

son **le fils** (pronouce as *feess*)

soon *adv.* **bientôt**

to be sorry **regretter**

soup **la soupe, le potage**

Spain **l'Espagne,** *n. f.*

Spanish (language) **l'espagnol** *n. m.*

to speak **parler**

speed **la vitesse**; at full speed, quickly/**à toute vitesse**

to spend (time) **passer**; I am spending one week in Paris/**Je passe une semaine à Paris**

spirit **l'esprit,** *n. m.*

to spoil **abîmer**

spoon **une cuiller, une cuillère**

spring (season of the year) **le printemps**

standing *adv.* **debout**

station (bus, train, *etc.*) **une gare**

to stay **demeurer, rester**

to steal **voler**

still *adv.* **toujours, encore**

stocking **le bas**

stomach **l'estomac,** *n. m.*

to stop **arrêter**; to stop (oneself) **s'arrêter**; I am stopping the bus/**J'arrête l'autobus**; I'm stopping to take the bus/**Je m'arrête pour prendre l'autobus**

store **le magasin**; department store/**le grand magasin**

storm **un orage**

story **un conte, une histoire**

strawberry **la fraise**

street **la rue**

strong *adj.* **fort, forte**; the strongest/**le plus fort, la plus forte**; your strongest quality/**votre qualité la plus forte**

student **un étudiant, une étudiante, un élève, une élève**

to study **étudier**

subway **le métro** (short for **métropolitain**)

to succeed **réussir (à)**

suit **le complet, le costume**

suitcase **la valise**

summer **l'été,** *n. m.*

sun **le soleil**

supermarket **le supermarché**

sure *adj.* **sûr, sûre, certain, certaine**

to surf (the Internet) **surfer, naviguer**

sweet *adj.* **doux, douce**

to swim **nager**

swimsuit **un maillot de bain**

to swing, to sway **se balancer**; a swing/**une balançoire**

Switzerland **la Suisse**

T

table **la table**

tablecloth **la nappe**

to take **prendre**; to take a walk/**faire une promenade, se promener**; to take advantage of/**profiter (de)**; to take along; to take away/**emporter**; to take off, to remove/**enlever**

to talk **parler**

talk key **la touche d'appel**

taste **le goût**; to taste/**goûter**; taste some!/**goûtez-en!**

to teach **enseigner**

teacher **un maître, une maîtresse, un professeur, une femme professeur**

team **une équipe**

to tear **déchirer**

television **la télévision, la télé, la TV, la T.V.**; on television/**à la télévision**; television set/**le téléviseur**

to tell **dire**

ten *adj.* **dix**

tense (verb) **le temps**; present indicative/**le présent de l'indicatif**

to terminate **terminer, finir**

terrific *adj.* **formidable**

than *conj.* **que;** She is taller than her sister/**Elle est plus grande que sa soeur**

to **thank remercier;** thank you/**Je vous remercie** *or* **merci**

that I know *that* you are right/**Je sais que vous avez raison;** The book *that* is on the table is mine/**Le livre** *qui* **est sur la table est à moi;** that book/**ce livre-là;** that tree/**cet arbre-là;** that lady/**cette dame-là;** *That* is not important/ *Cela* **n'est pas important**

that's right! c'est ça!

the *def. art.* **l', le, la, les;** the tree/**l'arbre;** the man/**l'homme;** the boy/**le garçon;** the girl/**la jeune fille;** the children/**les enfants**

theater le théâtre

their *poss. adj.* **leur, leurs;** their house/**leur maison;** their houses/**leurs maisons**

them *dir. obj. pron.* **les;** I like them/**Je les aime;** *as obj. of a prep.*, for them/**pour elles** (*fem.*), for them/**pour eux** (*masc.*)

themselves *refl. pron.* **se;** They wash themselves every morning/**Ils se lavent tous les matins**

then *adv.* **puis, alors**

there *adv. of place; advl. pron.* **y; Janine va à l'école**/Janine is going to school; She is going there/**Elle y va; Où est Janine?**/ Where is Janine? She's there/**Elle est là;** there is, there are/**il y a;** There is a fly in the soup/**Il y a une mouche dans la soupe;** There are many flowers in the garden/**Il y a beaucoup de fleurs dans le jardin;** there isn't, there aren't/**il n'y a pas;** There's Paul!/**Voilà Paul!**

these *dem. adj.* **ces;** these boys/**ces garçons;** these girls/**ces jeunes filles**

they *per. pron.* **ils, elles**

thick *adj.* **épais, épaisse**

thing une chose

third *adj.* **troisième**

thirst la soif; to be thirsty/**avoir soif;** I'm thirsty/**J'ai soif**

this *dem. adj.* **ce, cet, cette;** this boy/**ce garçon;** this tree/**cet arbre;** this girl/**cette jeune fille;** *dem. pron.* **ceci;** this is true/**ceci est vrai**

those *dem. adj.* **ces;** those boys/**ces garçons-là;** those girls/**ces jeunes filles-là**

three *adj.* **trois**

through *prep.* **par, à travers**

to **throw jeter, lancer**

ticket le billet

time (hour, time of day) **l'heure,** *n. f.*; What time is it?/**Quelle heure est-il?**

time (duration) **le temps;** Paul spent a lot of time in France/**Paul a passé beaucoup de temps en France**

time (different instances) **la fois;** one time, once/**une fois;** two times, twice/**deux fois;** many times/ **beaucoup de fois;** next time/**la prochaine fois**

tired *adj.* **fatigué, fatiguée**

to *prep.* **à**

toast le pain grillé

today *adv.* **aujourd'hui**

together *adv.* **ensemble**

tomato la tomate

tomorrow *adv.* **demain**

tongue la langue

tonight ce soir

too aussi, trop (de); Robert is coming too/**Robert vient aussi;** Janine works too much/**Janine travaille trop;** There is too much noise here/**Il y a trop de bruit ici;** There are too many people here/**Il y a trop de personnes ici**

tooth la dent

touch pad le pavé tactile

touch pad button le bouton du pavé tactile

touch screen l'écran *m.* **tactile**

town la ville

toy le jouet

traffic light le feu; red traffic light/**le feu rouge;** green traffic light/**le feu vert**

tree un arbre

trip un voyage; to take a trip/**faire un voyage**

truck le camion; truck driver/**le camionneur**

true *adj.* **vrai, vraie**

truly *adv.* **vraiment**

to **try essayer (de)**

to **turn on** (light) **allumer**

twentieth *adj.* **vingtième**

twenty *adj.* **vingt**

two *adj.* **deux**

U

umbrella le parapluie

unbelievable *adj.* **incroyable**

uncle un oncle

under *prep.* **sous;** underneath/ **dessous, par-dessous, en dessous**

to **understand comprendre**

undoubtedly *adv.* **sans doute**

unhappy *adj.* **malheureux, malheureuse, triste**

United States les États-Unis; to the United States/**aux États-Unis**

until *prep.* **jusque;** until spring/**jusqu'au printemps**

unusual *adj.* **extraordinaire**

upset *adj.* **inquiet, inquiète**

us *per. pron.* **nous;** for us/**pour nous**

to **use employer**

useful *adj.* **utile**

useless *adj.* **inutile**

V

vase un vase

vegetable un légume

very *adv.* **très**

vest un gilet

to **visit faire visite, visiter;** to visit someone/**rendre visite à quelqu'un**

voice une voix; in a loud voice/**à haute voix;** in a low voice, softly/**à voix basse**

voice mail la boîte vocale, la messagerie

W

to wait (for) **attendre**

waiter **un garçon (de café, de restaurant)**; (Nowadays, a customer addresses a waiter as *Monsieur*, not *garçon*)

to walk **marcher, aller à pied**

wall **un mur**

to want **vouloir**

to wash **laver**; I washed the car/**J'ai lavé la voiture**; to wash oneself/**se laver**; I washed myself/**Je me suis lavé(e)**

to wash and get dressed **faire la toilette**

to watch **regarder**; to watch television/**regarder la télévision**

water **l'eau**, *n. f.*

way **la façon**; I like your way of talking/**J'aime votre façon de parler**

we *per. pron.* **nous**; We like French/**Nous aimons le français**

weak *adj.* **faible**

to wear **porter**

weather **le temps**; What's the weather like today?/**Quel temps fait-il aujourd'hui?**

week **la semaine**

to weep **pleurer**

well *adv.* **bien**; She works well with her sister/**Elle travaille bien avec sa soeur**

what *What* are you saying?/*Que* **dites-vous?** *What* am I?/*Que* **suis-je?** *or* **Qu'est-ce qu** *je suis?* *What* you are saying is right/*Ce que* **vous dites est juste**; *What* is on the table is mine/*Ce qui* **est sur la table est à moi**; *what* book?/*quel* **livre?** *what* books?/*quels* **livres?** *what* house?/*quelle* **maison?** *what* houses?/*quelles* **maisons?** *What* time is it?/*Quelle* **heure est-il?** *What?!/*Quoi?!** *What* is it?/*Qu'est-ce que* **c'est?** *What's* new?/ **Quoi de neuf?** *What* is the date today?/*Quelle* **est la date aujourd'hui?** *What* day is it today?/*Quel* **jour est-ce aujourd'hui?** *What* color is your house?/**De** *quelle* **couleur est votre maison?**

wheel **la roue**

when *adv.* **quand**

where *adv.* **où**

which *pron.* The book *which* is on the table is mine/**Le livre** *qui* **est sur la table est à moi**; *as an adj.*, **quel, quelle, quels, quelles**; which boy?/**quel garçon?** which books?/**quels livres?** which girl?/**quelle jeune fille?** which colors?/**quelles couleurs?**

while *conj.* **pendant que**

white *adj.* **blanc, blanche**

who *pron.* **qui**; Who are you?/**Qui êtes-vous?**

whom *pron.* **qui, que**; Whom do you see?/**Qui voyez-vous?** with whom/**avec qui** The boy whom you see over there is my brother/**Le garçon que vous voyez là-bas est mon frère**

why **pourquoi**; why not?/**pourquoi pas?**

wife **une femme, une épouse**

to win **gagner**

wind **le vent**; It is windy/**Il fait du vent**

window **une fenêtre**

wine **le vin**

wing **une aile**

winter **l'hiver**, *n. m.*; in winter/**en hiver**

with *prep.* **avec**

without *prep.* **sans**

woman **la femme**

wonderful *adj.* **magnifique, merveilleux, merveilleuse**

woods **le bois, les bois**

word **le mot**; **la parole** (the spoken word)

work **le travail, l'oeuvre**, *n. f.;* a work of art/**une oeuvre d'art**

to work **travailler**

world **le monde**

to worry **s'inquiéter**; Don't worry!/**Ne vous inquiétez pas!** *or* **Ne t'inquiète pas!**

to write **écrire**

writer **un écrivain, une femme écrivain**

wrong **un tort**; to be wrong/**avoir tort**; You are wrong/**Vous avez tort**

X

X-ray machine (in airports) **la machine à rayons X**

Y

year **un an, une année**

yellow *adj.* **jaune**

yes *adv.* **oui**

yesterday *adv.* **hier**

you *pron.* Where are you going?/**Où vas-tu? Où allez-vous?** with you/**avec toi, avec vous**; I am giving this book to you/**Je te donne ce livre, Je vous donne ce livre**

young *adj.* **jeune**

your *poss. adj.* **ton, ta, tes, votre, vos**; your book/**ton livre, votre livre**; your mother/**ta mère, votre mère**; your books/**tes livres, vos livres**

you're welcome **de rien, il n'y a pas de quoi**

yourself *refl. pron.* **te, vous**; You wash yourself every morning, don't you?/**Tu te laves tous les matins, n'est-ce pas? Vous vous lavez tous les matins, n'est-ce pas?**

Z

zodiac **le zodiaque**

Answer Key

Leçons Préliminaires

1. La famille Paquet: Présentation (The Paquet family: Presentation)

Exercises, p. 2
I. 1. le père, une bonne épouse. 2. suis, mère, ai, bon. 3. suis, une soeur. 4. la fille, bon. 5. suis le. J'ai, famille. **II.** 3, 4, 1, 5, 2. **III.** 3, 5, 2, 1, 4. **IV.** 3, 4, 5, 1, 2.

Exercises, p. 3
V. 1. Janine. 2. Claire Paquet. 3. François Paquet. 4. Coco. 5. Pierre. **VI.** 1. la fille. 2. le frère. 3. la mère. 4. le chien. 5. le père.

II. Choses (Things)

Exercises, p. 4
I. 1. grand. 2. rond. 3. bonne. 4. petite. **II.** 1. petite. 2. bonne. 3. rond. 4. grand. **III.** 4, 3, 1, 2.

Exercises, pp. 4–5
I. 1. joli. 2. belle. 3. long. 4. jolie. **II.** 3, 1, 4, 2. **III.** 1. joli. 2. belle. 3. long. 4. jolie.

Exercises, pp. 5–6
I. 1. grand. 2. délicieux. 3. beau. 4. intéressant. **II.** 1. grand. 2. délicieux. 3. beau. 4. intéressant. **III.** 1. c'est un garage. est. 2. n'est pas. un. 3. c'est. beau. 4. c'est. est.

Exercises, p. 6
I. 1. confortable. 2. splendide. 3. charmante. 4. blanc. **II.** 4, 3, 1, 2.

Exercises, p. 7
I. 1. ouvert. 2. magnifique. 3. mignonne. 4. délicieux. **II.** 1. un parapluie, est. 2. n'est pas, est. 3. ce n'est pas, une. 4. un, délicieux.

Exercises, p. 8
I. 1. long. 2. noir. 3. beau. 4. grand. **II.** 4, 5, 1, 6, 2, 3.

III. Personnes (People)

Exercises, p. 9
I. 1. boit, lait. 2. danse. 3. un livre. 4. courent. **II.** 1. Le garçon boit du lait. 2. La jeune fille danse. 3. Le garçon lit un livre (possibly: Un garçon lit le livre). 4. La jeune fille et le garçon courent (possibly: Le garçon et la jeune fille courent).

Exercises, p. 10
I. 1. chante. 2. écrit. 3. arrête, autos. **II.** 1. (b). 2. (a). 3. (c).

IV. L'École: la salle de classe (The School: the classroom)

Exercises, p. 11
I. Column B: 1. Madame Duval est derrière le bureau. 2. Il est une heure. 3. Il y a une carte de France sur le mur. 4. La jeune fille lit un livre. 5. La jeune fille écrit une composition. 6. Le garçon est debout. 7. Le garçon lève la main.

Exercises, p. 12
II. 1. Non, madame (mademoiselle, monsieur), ce n'est pas le stylo. C'est le crayon. 2. Non, madame (mademoiselle, monsieur), ce n'est pas la feuille de papier. C'est le livre. 3. Non, madame (mademoiselle, monsieur), ce n'est pas

l'ordinateur. C'est l'horloge. 4. Non, madame (mademoiselle, monsieur), ce n'est pas un élève. C'est une élève. 5. Non, madame (mademoiselle, monsieur), ce n'est pas la chaise. C'est le banc. 6. Non, madame (mademoiselle, monsieur), ce n'est pas une élève. C'est un élève.

V. La Maison: la salle à manger (The House: the dining room)

Exercises, pp. 13–14
I. 1. C'est une fleur. 2. C'est une assiette. 3. C'est une tasse. 4. C'est une cuiller (OR cuillère). 5. C'est un verre. 6. C'est un couteau. **II.** 1. UNE CHAISE. 2. UNE ASSIETTE. 3. UN TAPIS. 4. UNE FOURCHETTE. 5. UN COUTEAU. 6. UNE NAPPE. 7. UN VERRE. 8. UNE TASSE. 9. UNE CUILLER. 10. UNE FLEUR.

VI. La Ville: dans la rue (The City: in the street)

Exercises, pp. 15–16
I. 1. C'est une dame. 2. C'est un homme. 3. C'est une petite fille. 4. C'est un garçon. 5. C'est un agent de police. 6. C'est une voiture. 7. C'est un immeuble. 8. C'est un autobus. **II.** 1. UNE VALISE. 2. UN PETIT CHIEN. 3. LE TROTTOIR. 4. LE MÉTRO.

STRUCTURES AND VERBS

Work Unit 1

Exercises, pp. 23–24
I. 1. (c). 2. (d). 3. (d). 4. (b). 5. (d). **II.** 1. Janine cherche dans la commode. 2. Madame Paquet cherche dans l'armoire. 3. Monsieur Paquet cherche sous la chaise. **III.** 1. Madame Paquet est la mère. 2. Janine est la fille (possibly: la soeur). 3. Pierre est le fils (possibly: le frère). 4. Coco est le chien (possibly: le petit chien).

IV. Un acrostiche

Exercises, pp. 25–26
I. 1. le. 2. la. 3. le. 4. la. 5. l'. 6. l'. 7. le. 8. le. 9. l'. 10. la. 11. le. 12. l'. 13. le. 14. la. 15. l'.

II. Word Hunt

Exercises, p. 26

III. A. 1. Le père est là-bas. 2. La mère est là-bas. 3. Le garçon est là-bas. 4. La jeune fille est là-bas. 5. L'ami est là-bas.

Exercises, p. 27

B. 1. La femme parle beaucoup. 2. L'homme parle beaucoup. 3. Le frère parle beaucoup. 4. La soeur parle beaucoup. 5. La famille parle beaucoup. **C.** 1. La table est ici. 2. Le chapeau est ici. 3. La maison est ici. 4. L'arbre est ici. 5. Le café est ici. **IV.** 1. Le chapeau est dans la cuisine. 2. Le chapeau est dans l'armoire. 3. Le chapeau est dans la maison. 4. Le chapeau est dans la commode. 5. Le chapeau est dans le garage.

Exercises, p. 28

I. 1. un. 2. une. 3. un. 4. un. 5. une. 6. un. 7. un. 8. un. 9. une. 10. un. 11. un. 12. une. 13. une. 14. une. 15. un.

Exercises, p. 29

II. Word Hunt

```
U  N  E  J  E  U  N  E  F  I  L  L  E  A
N  E  F  I  L  M  O  A  U  V  O  U  S  S
A  R  B  E  A  U  N  G  A  R  Ç  O  N  S
R  O  U  G  E  P  L  U  S  E  R  S  T  U
B  L  U  N  P  A  R  A  P  L  U  I  E  R
R  J  O  I  N  D  R  E  E  T  R  E  S  E
E  U  N  E  O  R  A  N  G  E  U  N  A  N
```

III. A. 1. Un homme cherche dans l'armoire. 2. Un garçon cherche dans l'armoire. 3. Un fils cherche dans l'armoire. 4. Une mère cherche dans l'armoire. 5. Un père cherche dans l'armoire.

Exercises, pp. 30–31

B. 1. Une femme mange dans la cuisine. 2. Une jeune fille mange dans la cuisine. 3. Un ami mange dans la cuisine. 4. Un chien mange dans la cuisine. 5. Une fille mange dans la cuisine. **C.** 1. Un homme quitte la chambre. 2. Une mère quitte la chambre. 3. Un père quitte la chambre. 4. Un garçon quitte la chambre. 5. Une jeune fille quitte la chambre. **IV.** 1. Monsieur Paquet cherche son chapeau. 2. Le chien est sous la commode. 3. Nous cherchons partout. 4. Je vais en ville acheter un nouveau chapeau. 5. Coco mange le chapeau. **V.** 1. le. 2. la. 3. la. 4. l'. 5. la. 6. le. 7. le. 8. le. 9. un. 10. une. **VI.** 1. Où est mon passeport? 2. Oui. Je cherche mon passeport. 3. Je cherche sous la chaise. Le voici!

Work Unit 2

Exercises, pp. 34–35

I. 1. (d). 2. (c). 3. (a). 4. (d). 5. (a). **II.** 1. oui. 2. non. 3. oui. 4. oui. 5. oui.

III. Mots croisés

IV. Un acrostiche

¹L	E	S	G	Â	T	E	A	U	X	
²E	T									
³D	E	S	S	E	R	T				
⁴É	C	L	A	I	R					
⁵J	O	U	R							
⁶E	S	P	É	R	E	R				
⁷U	N	E								
⁸N	O	N								
⁹E	S	P	R	I	T					
¹⁰R	O	S	B	I	F					

Exercises, pp. 37–38

I. 1. les garçons. 2. les fils. 3. les chapeaux. 4. les journaux. 5. les cieux. 6. les yeux. 7. les pères. 8. les voix. 9. les mères. 10. les chats. **II.** 1. la table. 2. le nez. 3. le genou. 4. la voix. 5. l'oeil. 6. le monsieur. 7. l'homme. 8. la jeune fille. 9. l'enfant. 10. l'arbre. **III.** 1. le père. 2. l'homme. 3. les eaux. 4. les fils. 5. les tables. 6. le journal. 7. les chevaux. 8. les oiseaux. 9. l'élève. 10. les pays.

Exercises, pp. 40–41

I. 7, 8, 5, 3, 6, 2, 1, 4. **II.** 1. au. 2. à la. 3. aux. 4. à l'. **III.** 1. du. 2. de l'. 3. de la. 4. des.

Exercises, pp. 41–42

I. 4, 6, 7, 2, 10, 9, 8, 3, 5, 1. **II.** 1. des. 2. de la. 3. de. 4. du. 5. de l'. 6. de l'. 7. de. 8. du. 9. de l'. 10. de la. **III. A.** Je voudrais avoir le jambon et le poulet. J'aime aussi le veau et la saucisse. Aussi, j'adore le gâteau et la glace. Voulez-vous apporter la viande ou les desserts? **B.** Pour moi, c'est bon pour la santé. Je n'aime pas le café. J'aime mieux l'eau minérale.

Work Unit 3

Exercises, p. 45

I. 1. (d). 2. (d). 3. (c). **II.** 1. oui. 2. non. 3. oui.

III. Word Hunt

D	U	C	A	F	É	D	E	S
U	M	O	N	S	I	E	U	R
P	D	U	O	D	E	L	A	O
O	C	A	U	J	A	I	M	E
I	D	C	S	P	O	I	D	U
S	E	L	A	V	O	S	N	E
S	L	A	V	I	A	N	D	E
O	E	D	O	E	L	A	E	A
N	A	E	N	A	U	E	A	E
D	U	L	S	O	M	O	N	S

Exercises, pp. 47–48

I. 1. Oui, j'ai du pain. 2. Oui, j'ai de la viande. 3. Oui, j'ai de l'eau. 4. Oui, j'ai des bonbons. 5. Oui, j'ai du beurre. **II.** 1. Non, je n'ai pas de café. 2. Non, je n'ai pas de viande. 3. Non, je n'ai pas d'eau. 4. Non, je n'ai pas de bonbons. 5. Non, je n'ai pas de beurre. **III.** 1. Oui, j'ai du bon café. 2. Oui, j'ai de jolis chapeaux. 3. Oui, j'ai de jolies jupes. 4. Oui, j'ai du bon vin. 5. Oui, j'ai de jolies cravates. **IV.** 1. Non, je n'ai pas de bon café. 2. Non, je n'ai pas de jolis chapeaux. 3. Non, je n'ai pas de jolies jupes. 4. Non, je n'ai pas de bon vin. 5. Non, je n'ai pas de jolies cravates.

Exercises, p. 49

I. 1. Oui, j'ai les mains sales. 2. Oui, j'ai le visage sale. 3. Oui, j'ai les pieds grands. 4. Oui, j'ai les yeux bruns. 5. Oui, j'ai les cheveux noirs. **II.** 1. Non, je n'ai pas les pieds grands. 2. Non, je n'ai pas le visage sale. 3. Non, je n'ai pas les mains sales. 4. Non, je n'ai pas le chapeau sur la tête. 5. Non, je n'ai pas les cheveux noirs.

Exercises, pp. 50–51

I. 1. Oui, je vais à l'école les matins. 2. Oui, je vais à la bibliothèque les après-midi. (Note: The French Academy writes *après-midi* with no *s* in the plural; but with *s* is acceptable.) 3. Oui, je vais au restaurant les soirs. 4. Oui, je vais au parc les après-midi. 5. Oui, je vais au café les soirs. **II.** 1. Non, je ne vais pas au cinéma les soirs. 2. Non, je ne vais pas à l'école les matins. 3. Non, je ne vais pas à la bibliothèque les soirs.

Exercises, pp. 52–55

I. 1. Il parle français. Il prononce bien le français. 2. Elle parle espagnol. Elle prononce bien l'espagnol. 3. Elle parle italien. Elle prononce bien l'italien. 4. Il parle anglais. Il prononce bien l'anglais. 5. Elle parle allemand. Elle prononce bien l'allemand. **II.** 1. Oui, j'ai cent dollars. 2. Oui, j'ai mille euros. 3. Oui, j'ai cent livres. 4. Oui, j'ai mille amis. **III.** 1. —. 2. l'. 3. —. 4. —. 5. la. 6. le. 7. les. 8. les. **IV.** 1. J'ai les sandwichs. 2. J'ai les éclairs. 3. J'ai la saucisse. 4. J'ai des dollars. 5. J'ai une jupe. 6. J'ai les chapeaux. 7. J'ai le dessert. 8. J'ai un gâteau.

V. Jeu de mots

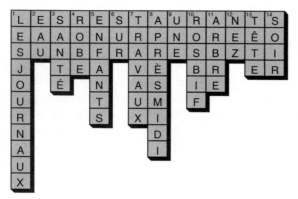

VI. J'ai les yeux bleus (bruns, gris, verts). J'ai les cheveux noirs (bruns, blonds, roux). J'ai les pieds grands (petits). J'ai le visage rond. J'ai les mains grandes (petites). **VII.** 1. Bonjour! Avez-vous du poisson aujourd'hui? 2. Avez-vous de la viande? 3. Avez-vous des saucisses? 4. Non, monsieur. Je regrette. Je ne veux pas (OR: Je ne désire pas) de viande. Je ne veux (désire) pas de saucisses. 5. Non, monsieur, je ne veux (désire) pas de poisson. Je regrette. 6. Non, monsieur, je ne veux (désire) pas de café. 7. Oui, oui. J'aime les éclairs et les tartes. **VIII.** 1. J'aimerais un grand gâteau au chocolat. 2. Avec ceci, j'aimerais deux éclairs et deux tartes aux pommes. 3. Oui, c'est tout, merci. **IX.** 1. Jacques est de France. Il parle français. Il prononce bien le français. 2. María est d'Espagne. Elle parle espagnol. Elle prononce bien l'espagnol. 3. Rosa est d'Italie. Elle parle italien. Elle prononce bien l'italien. 4. Ian est d'Angleterre. Il parle anglais. Il prononce bien l'anglais. 5. Marlena est d'Allemagne. Elle parle allemand. Elle prononce bien l'allemand.

Work Unit 4

Exercises, p. 58

I. 1. Janine et Pierre allument le téléviseur. 2. La mère et le père entrent dans le salon. 3. Pierre et Janine regardent dans les journaux. **II.** 1. oui. 2. non. 3. oui. 4. non. 5. non. **III.** 1. (b). 2. (c). 3. (b). **IV.** allument, marche, entrent, exclament, marche, regardez, demandent, mère, père.

Exercises, pp. 64–69

I. (a) 5, 3, 1, 2, 4. (b) 4, 5, 1, 2, 3. **II.** 1. Elle. 2. Il. 3. Elles. 4. Ils. 5. Ils. **III.** 1. Tu danses beaucoup. 2. Il danse beaucoup. 3. Elle danse beaucoup. 4. Vous dansez beaucoup. 5. Ils dansent beaucoup. 6. Elles dansent beaucoup. **IV.** 1. Je ne danse pas. 2. Tu ne danses pas. 3. Il ne danse pas. 4. Vous ne dansez pas. 5. Ils ne dansent pas. 6. Elles ne dansent pas. **V.** 1. Oui, je danse les matins; il danse aussi. 2. Oui, il cherche le chapeau; elle cherche le chapeau aussi. 3. Oui, elle étudie la leçon; j'étudie la leçon aussi. **VI.** 1. Non, je ne danse pas; il ne danse pas non plus. 2. Non, il n'étudie pas; elle n'étudie pas non plus. 3. Non, il ne cherche pas la balle; ils ne cherchent pas la balle non plus. 4. Non, elle n'écoute pas la musique; je n'écoute pas la musique non plus. 5. Non, je ne ferme pas la fenêtre; vous ne fermez pas la fenêtre non plus (possibly: nous ne fermons pas la fenêtre non plus). **VII.** 1. Je ferme. 2. Tu apportes. 3. Il étudie. 4. Elle parle. 5. Nous marchons. 6. Vous donnez. 7. Ils jouent. 8. Elles chantent. 9. Vous cherchez. 10. J'aime.

VIII. Word Search

IX. 1. Je ne parle pas. 2. Tu ne chantes pas. 3. Il n'écoute pas. 4. Elle n'oublie pas. 5. Nous ne jouons pas. 6. Vous ne désirez pas. **X.** 1. Nous désirons regarder le programme de sports. 2. Nous aimons les sports. 3. Si nous avons la permission de regarder le programme de sports, nous promettons de laver la voiture et nettoyer la salle de bains. **XI.** 1. Je désire danser ce soir. 2. Moi, je désire aller voir un film. **XII.** Je vais à la bibliothèque tous les jours. Je regarde la télé tous les soirs. J'étudie mes leçons de français tous les soirs aussi. **XIII.** 1. livres neufs 2. à prix réduits 3. vendeur 4. beaucoup de livres 5. beaucoup de personnes 6. regarder 7. acheter 8. parler

Work Unit 5

Exercises, p. 72
I. 1. (c). 2. (d). 3. (c). **II.** 1. non. 2. oui. 3. oui. 4. non. 5. oui. 6. oui. **III.** 1. choisit. 2. rougit. 3. finit. 4. finissent. 5. retentit.

Exercises, pp. 74–77
I. (a) 4, 1, 2, 3. (b) 3, 4, 2, 1. **II.** 1. Il . . . 2. Elle . . . 3. Elle . . . 4. Ils . . . 5. Ils . . . 6. Elles . . . **III.** 1. Ils finissent la leçon. 2. Tu finis la leçon. 3. Il finit la leçon. 4. Elle finit la leçon. 5. Vous finissez la leçon. 6. Elles finissent la leçon. **IV.** 1. Vous ne finissez pas le dîner. 2. Il ne finit pas le dîner. 3. Tu ne finis pas le dîner. 4. Elles ne finissent pas le dîner. 5. Ils ne finissent pas le dîner. 6. Nous ne finissons pas le dîner. **V.** 1. Oui, il finit le livre; je finis le livre aussi. 2. Oui, ils punissent les mauvais élèves; il punit les mauvais élèves aussi. 3. Oui, il choisit une nouvelle automobile; ils choisissent une nouvelle automobile aussi. 4. Oui, il obéit au garçon; ils obéissent au garçon aussi. 5. Oui, je finis la leçon aujourd'hui; elle finit la leçon aujourd'hui aussi. **VI.** 1. Non, il ne désobéit pas; je ne désobéis pas non plus (*possibly:* nous ne désobéissons pas non plus). 2. Non, je ne finis pas la leçon; il ne finit pas la leçon non plus. 3. Non, il ne choisit pas une auto; elle ne choisit pas une auto non plus. 4. Non, nous ne bâtissons pas une maison; ils ne bâtissent pas une maison non plus. 5. Non, je ne rougis pas (possibly: Non, nous ne rougissons pas); elles ne rougissent pas non plus. **VII.** 1. Je finis la leçon. 2. Tu saisis la balle. 3. Il accomplit les devoirs. 4. Elle bâtit une maison. 5. Nous choisissons un dessert. 6. Vous punissez le chien. 7. Ils rougissent facilement. 8. Elles désobéissent à leurs parents. 9. Je remplis le vase. 10. Vous finissez les devoirs.

VIII. Word Search

IX. A. Je ne finis pas le devoir parce que l'exercice est très dfficile. La leçon est difficile aussi. Je ne comprends rien. **B.** Monsieur Berty nous donne les leçons difficiles. Il veut punir les élèves parce qu'ils parlent trop en classe. Les exercices ne sont pas faciles!

Review Test: Work Units 1–5

Exercises, pp. 78–80

I. 1. la. 2. le. 3. l'. 4. les. 5. l'. 6. les. **II.** 1. une. 2. un. 3. une. 4. une. 5. un. 6. une. **III.** 1. les mères. 2. les journaux. 3. les voix. 4. les messieurs. 5. les yeux. 6. les fils. **IV.** 1. la table. 2. les eaux. 3. le nez. 4. les genoux. 5. le journal. 6. les pays. **V.** 1. au. 2. à l'. 3. à la. 4. aux. 5. à l'. 6. à la. **VI.** 4, 1, 5, 3, 2. **VII.** 1. J'ai du café. 2. J'ai de la vainde. 3. Je n'ai pas de café. 4. Je n'ai pas de bonbons. **VIII.** 1. E, S, C, L, E, I, S. 2. I, E, N, E. 3. O, S, R, A, N, I. **IX.** 1. Est-ce que vous parlez français? 2. Est-ce que Jacqueline regarde la télévision? 3. Est-ce qu'ils étudient la leçon? **X.** 1. Odette et Yvette chantent-elles bien? 2. Robert et Pierre jouent-ils à la balle? 3. Regardez-vous trop de télévision? **XI.** 1. J'aime la glace au chocolat. 2. Vous donnez des fleurs à la dame. 3. Je ferme la porte. 4. Michelle choisit une jolie robe. 5. Vous finissez les devoirs. 6. Nous bâtissons une maison. **XII.** 1. A. 2. C. 3. B. 4. C. 5. D. 6. A. 7. D. 8. A. 9. D. 10. A.

Work Unit 6

Exercises, pp. 83–84

I. 1. oui. 2. non. 3. oui. 4. oui. 5. oui. **II.** 1. vendez. 2. vends, dix. 3. vraiment. 4. joli. **III.** 1. Je vends ce vase pour dix euros. 2. La marchande vend beaucoup de vases. 3. Après un moment, la femme ajoute.

Exercises, pp. 85–89

I. 1. Il défend sa patrie. 2. Elle vend des vases. 3. Ils entendent la musique. 4. Ils vendent leur maison. 5. Il rompt la petite barrière. **II.** 1. Elle vend des livres. 2. Tu vends des livres. 3. Vous et moi (nous) vendons des livres. 4. Ils vendent des livres. 5. Vous vendez des livres. 6. Elles vendent des livres. **III.** 1. Nous ne vendons pas la voiture. 2. Je ne vends pas la voiture. 3. Tu ne vends pas la voiture. 4. Il ne vend pas la voiture. 5. Elles ne vendent pas la voiture. 6. Ils ne vendent pas la voiture. **IV.** 1. Oui, il répond à la lettre; je réponds à la lettre aussi (possibly: nous répondons à la lettre aussi). 2. Oui, il vend la maison; il vend la maison aussi. 3. Oui, il défend la patrie; je défends la patrie aussi (possibly: nous défendons la patrie aussi). 4. Oui, il est joli; il est joli aussi. 5. Oui, elle est au marché aux puces; elle est au marché aux puces aussi. **V.** 1. Janine étudie-t-elle dans la bibliothèque? 2. Cherche-t-elle le chapeau? 3. Finit-il la leçon? 4. Choisit-elle une jolie robe? 5. Répondons-nous à la lettre? 6. Vendent-ils la maison? **VI.** Elles attendent. 2. Nous vendons. 3. Je danse. 4. Ils écoutent. 5. Vous finissez. 6. Il répond. **VII.** 1. Est-ce qu'elle finit le livre? 2. Est-ce que Monsieur Berty vend la voiture? 3. Est-ce qu'elle choisit un joli chapeau? 4. Est-ce qu'il défend la patrie? 5. Est-ce qu'Hélène ouvre la boîte?

VIII.

¹L	E	T	É	L	É	V	I	S	E	U	R	
²L	E	P	A	R	A	P	L	U	I	E		
³L	E	P	O	U	L	E	T					
⁴L	A	P	O	R	T	E						
⁵L	A	T	A	B	L	E						
⁶L	E	V	A	S	E							

IX. 1. J'aime . . . 2. Vous chantez . . . 3. Janine étudie . . . 4. Je choisis . . . 5. Ils attendent . . . 6. Je vends . . . 7. Vous choisissez . . . 8. Nous finissons . . . **X.** 1. I dance, I do dance, I am dancing. 2. You finish, you do finish, you are finishing. 3. We sell, we do sell, we are selling.

XI. Word Search

N	N	O	I	L	V	E	N	D	O	U	I	N
I	L	S	P	E	R	D	E	N	T	I	C	I
E	L	L	E	S	I	M	P	O	R	T	A	N
L	U	I	E	L	L	E	A	T	T	E	N	D
E	L	L	E	S	P	E	R	D	E	N	T	O
E	J	E	R	E	N	D	S	A	L	O	R	S
V	O	S	S	E	T	M	O	I	S	O	N	T
N	O	U	S	R	É	P	O	N	D	O	N	S
U	E	A	I	P	N	A	C	E	G	L	I	L
A	E	I	T	U	D	É	F	E	N	D	S	T
V	O	U	S	R	É	P	O	N	D	E	Z	U

XII. J'aimerais aller à la foire. Mon amie Jacqueline va à la foire avec ses parents. Elle dit qu'on vend beaucoup de choses. Je voudrais acheter des cadeaux.

Work Unit 7

Exercises, pp. 92–93

I. 1. Le sport favori de Pierre est le football (possibly: Son sport favori est le football). 2. Il veut être toujours en forme parce qu'il est gardien de but dans son équipe à l'école. 3. Il mange seulement des aliments qui sont bons pour la santé. 4. Il se lève tôt (possibly: Il se lève avec le soleil). 5. Oui, Janine va jouer dans le match aussi. **II.** (Note: These are personal questions and you may answer in any number of ways.) **III.** 1. non. 2. oui. 3. oui. 4. non. 5. oui.

IV. Un acrostiche

¹L	E	N	T	E	M	E	N	T
²E	V	I	T	E	R			
³S	E	C	O	U	C	H	E	R
⁴S	E	L	E	V	E	R		
⁵P	O	U	R					
⁶O	U							
⁷R	É	P	O	N	D	R	E	
⁸T	A	R	D					
⁹S	E	L	A	V	E	R		

Exercises, pp. 98–104

I. 1. me. 2. me. 3. t'. 4. se. 5. s'. 6. nous. 7. vous. 8. s'. 9. se. 10. se. **II.** 8, 4, 9, 6, 2, 7, 1, 3, 5, 10.

III. Word Search

D	E	I	P	T	E	C	H	E	J
J	E	L	A	U	L	A	V	R	E
D	I	S	D	T	E	J	A	U	M
I	L	S	U	E	L	O	I	N	E
A	S	A	I	L	M	A	N	G	R
J	E	M	H	A	B	I	L	L	E
I	D	U	O	V	E	E	O	A	P
I	É	S	S	E	M	E	T	S	O
O	P	E	I	S	S	E	L	V	S
J	Ê	N	A	P	P	E	L	E	E
U	C	T	I	L	S	E	M	E	L
A	H	J	E	I	U	O	I	L	T
J	E	M	E	R	E	G	A	R	E

IV. 1. Je. 2. Tu. 3. Vous. 4. Ils, elles. 5. Il, elle. 6. Nous. 7. Vous. 8. Il, elle. 9. Ils, elles. 10. Je. **V.** 1. Oui, je m'amuse. 2. Oui, je me couche. 3. Oui, je me repose. 4. Oui, je m'habille. 5. Oui, je m'assieds. **VI.** 1. Non, je ne m'amuse pas ici. 2. Non, je ne me couche pas de bonne heure tous les soirs. 3. Non, je ne m'habille pas vite les matins. 4. Non, je ne m'appelle pas Jean-Jacques. 5. Non, je ne m'assieds pas ici. **VII.** 1. Se dépêche-t-il tous les soirs. 2. Je m'endors sur cette chaise. 3. Nous nous levons de bonne heure. 4. Il se lave vite. 5. Je m'amuse tous les jours. **VIII.** 1. Je m'habille dans ma chambre. 2. Ils s'amusent au théâtre les samedis (possibly: Les samedis soirs, ils s'amusent au théâtre). 3. Tu te reposes après le dîner (possible: Après le dîner, tu te reposes). 4. Je me couche de bonne heure. 5. Nous nous dépêchons pour aller à l'école. 6. Je me lave tous les matins (possibly: Tous les matins, je me lave). **IX.** 1. Est-ce que Robert s'amuse? 2. Est-ce que vous vous endormez vite? 3. Est-ce qu'ils se couchent tard? 4. Est-ce qu'Henri est absent aujourd'hui? 5. Est-ce qu'Alice se dépêche pour aller à l'école? **X.** 1. Se repose-t-elle après le dîner? 2. Vous levez-vous très tard le matin? 3. S'assied-elle devant la porte? 4. Nous dépêchons-nous? 5. Se couchent-ils tard? **XI.** 1. Pierre ne se couche-t-il pas de bonne heure? or: Est-ce que Pierre ne se couche pas de bonne heure? 2. Ne se lave-t-il pas soigneusement? or: Est-ce qu'il ne se lave pas soigneusement? 3. Ne s'habille-t-il pas vite? or: Est-ce qu'il ne s'habille pas vite? 4. Ne se dépêche-t-il pas? or: Est-ce qu'il ne se dépêche pas? 5. Ne se prépare-t-il pas à jouer au football? or: Est-ce qu'il ne se prépare pas à jouer au football? **XII.** 1. Je me lave. 2. Vous vous amusez. 3. Il s'endort. 4. Elle s'habille. 5. Nous nous couchons. 6. Tu t'amuses. 7. Ils se servent. 8. Elles s'endorment. 9. Je m'amuse. 10. Madame Paquet se dépêche. **XIII.** 1. Non. C'est ma première visite. 2. Oui. Le voyage est très agréable. Excellent. 3. Pour visiter le pays. 4. Non. Je ne suis pas seul. Je voyage avec mon frère. 5. Le service est parfait. Et les repas dans l'avion sont excellents. **XIV.** Je me couche de bonne heure (OR: tôt) tous les soirs. Je m'endors facilement. Je me lève avec le soleil. Je me lave. Je m'habille vite. Je m'amuse à Paris tous les jours. **XV.** Est-ce que tu t'amuses tous les jours? Moi, je m'amuse beaucoup ici. Te couches-tu tard ou tôt? T'endors-tu facilement? Moi, je m'endors facilement. Te reposes-tu quand tu es fatiguée? Moi, je me repose quand je suis fatigué(e). **XVI.** J'aime nager. J'aime la natation. Je vais à une piscine tous les jours. Voici une photo de la piscine. Elle est grande et belle. La natation est mon sport favori.

Work Unit 8

Exercises, pp. 107–108

I. 1. Madame Paquet aime beaucoup les ventes aux enchères. 2. Monsieur et Madame Paquet entrent dans la salle des ventes. 3. Elle lève la main pour chasser les mouches de son nez. 4. Madame paquet offre cent euros pour le fauteuil (sans le savoir, sans le vouloir, *or any acceptable answer*), quand elle lève la main pour chasser les mouches de son nez. 5. Tout le monde regarde Madame Paquet. **II.** (Note: These are personal questions and you may answer in any number of ways; they are "oui" or "non" questions to be answered in complete sentences in French.) **III.** 1. Monsieur Paquet parle à sa femme à voix basse. 2. Madame Paquet lève la main pour chasser les mouches de son nez. 3. J'ai cent euros. **IV.** 1. Ils entrent dans la salle des ventes. 2. Je n'aime pas ce fauteuil monstrueux. 3. Tout est si élégant dans cette salle. 4. Je veux une jolie petite table ronde.

Exercises, pp. 113–117

A. Cadinal numbers. I. 1. quatre. 2. sept. 3. douze. 4. dix. 5. dix-sept. 6. douze. **II.** 1. deux. 2. quatre. 3. six. 4. huit. 5. dix. 6. vingt. 7. vingt et un. 8. vingt-deux. 9. trente. 10. trente-sept. 11. soixante et un. 12. soixante-neuf. 13. soixante-dix. 14. quatre-vingts. 15. cent. **III.** (First column) 2, 4, 5, 3, 1; (Second column) 8, 9, 6, 10, 7. **IV.** 1. (c). 2. (a). 3. (c). 4. (d). 5. (c). **B. Ordinal numbers. I.** (First column) 3, 4, 1, 5, 2; (Second column) 7, 10, 6, 8, 9. **II.** 1. première. 2. premier. 3. second. 4. seconde. 5. deuxième. 6. quatrième. 7. cinquième. 8. neuvième. 9. dixième. 10. troisième. **III.** 3, 5, 4, 2, 1. **C. Cardinals, fractions, approximate amounts, ordinals, simple arithmetical expressions, weights and measures. I.** 1. deux. 2. soixante. 3. vingt-cinq. 4. deux cents. 5. huit cents.

II. Word Search

```
U  N  M  I  C ( T  R  E  N  T  E ) X
N  D  E ( C  I  N  Q  U  A  N  T  E )
M  T  R  C ( C  E  N  T ) A  I  N  E
( T  R  O  I  S  I  È  M  E ) U  N  E
O  M  I  N  L ( D  O  U  Z  E ) L  L
Q  C  I  Q  N  T  R ( M  I  L  L  E )
```

III. 7, 6, 8, 1, 10, 3, 5, 4, 9, 2. **IV.** 1. trois fois neuf font vingt-sept. 2. huit moins six font deux. 3. vingt divisés par cinq font quatre. 4. sept fois cent font sept cents. 5. quatre-vingts et dix font quatre-vingt-dix. **V.** 1. $3 \times 5 = 15$. 2. $12 - 10 = 2$. 3. $10 \div 2 = 5$. 4. $2 + 2 = 4$. 5. $9 \times 10 = 90$. **VI.** 4, 5, 7, 6, 2, 8, 3, 1, 10, 9. **VII.** Je veux partir parce que je n'aime pas les meubles ici. Les fauteuils sont laids. Les tables sont laides. Tout est monstrueux. Mille euros pour la lampe?! Deux cents euros pour la petite table?! Et il y a douze mouches dans cette salle!

Work Unit 9

Exercises, pp. 120–121

I. 1. (c). 2. (d). 3. (c). 4. (d). 5. (d). **II.** 1. oui. 2. oui. 3. non. 4. non. 5. oui. **III.** 1. J'ai quinze ans. 2. Quelle heure est-il? 3. Quelle est la date aujourd'hui? 4. Il est huit heures. 5. Il faut chercher dans le sac. **IV.** (Note: These are personal questions and you may answer in any number of ways.)

Exercises, pp. 125–128

I. 3, 4, 2, 1, 5, 6. **II.** 1. Il est trois heures et demie. 2. Il est dix heures moins dix. 3. Il est trois heures moins un quart. 4. Il est une heure et quart. **III.** 1. C'est aujourd'hui le premier octobre. 2. C'est aujourd'hui le dix novembre. **IV.** 1. Je me lève à six heures et demie du matin. 2. Je vais à l'école à huit heures du matin. 3. Je regarde la télévision à quatre heures de l'après-midi. 4. Je dîne à six heures du soir. 5. Je me couche à dix heures et demie du soir. **V.** 1. Les mois de l'année sont janvier, février, mars, avril, mai, juin, juillet, août, septembre, octobre, novembre, décembre. 2. Les jours de la semaine sont dimanche, lundi, mardi, mercredi, jeudi, vendredi, samedi. 3. Les saisons de l'année sont le printemps, l'été, l'automne, l'hiver. **VI.** 1. Non, ce n'est pas lundi; c'est aujourd'hui dimanche. 2. Non, ce n'est pas mardi; c'est aujourd'hui lundi. 3. Non, ce n'est pas mercredi; c'est aujourd'hui mardi. 4. Non, ce n'est pas samedi; c'est aujourd'hui jeudi. 5. Non, ce n'est pas jeudi; c'est aujourd'hui mercredi. 6. Non, ce n'est pas samedi; c'est aujourd'hui vendredi. 7. Non, ce n'est pas dimanche; c'est aujourd'hui samedi. **VII.** 1. Quel âge a-t-il? 2. Quelle heure est-il? 3. Quel âge a-t-elle? 4. Quelle est la date aujourd'hui? 5. Quelle heure est-il? 6. Quelle est la date aujourd'hui? 7. Quel âge ont-elles? 8. Quelle heure est-il? 9. Quel âge avez-vous? 10. Quel jour est-ce aujourd'hui? **VIII.** Salut! C'est moi. J'aimerais faire un voyage cet été. Veux-tu venir avec moi? J'aime voyager en avion. Et toi? Nous allons visiter La Martinique. Nous allons voir les monuments, faire des promendaes au bord de la mer jour et nuit. Si tu n'as pas assez d'argent, je vais payer pour toi. Tu acceptes? À bientôt!

Work Unit 10

Exercises, pp. 133–134

I. 1. C'est aujourd'hui vendredi. 2. Dans le concours de talents, Pierre va jouer le magicien. 3. Janine est l'assistante de Pierre. 4. Non, ils n'ont pas le chapeau haut-de-forme, le bâton, la cape, et le lapin. 5. Coco arrive (en courant) dans la grande salle avec le chapeau, le bâton, la cape, et le lapin. 6. Coco gagne le grand prix de talent. **II.** (Note: These are personal questions and you may answer in any number of ways.) **III.** C'est aujourd'hui vendredi. 2. C'est le grand jour du concours de talents. 3. Apporte-moi mon bâton; apporte-moi le lapin. 4. Je n'ai pas ta cape. 5. Et qui gagne le grand prix? Coco, naturellement! Parce qu'il a beaucoup de talent!

Exercises, pp. 135–136
I. A. -ER verbs. 1. donne, donnez, donnons. 2. apporte, apportez, apportons. 3. cherche, cherchez, cherchons. 4. aide, aidez, aidons. 5. chante, chantez, chantons. **B. -IR verbs.** 1. finis, finissez, finissons. 2. choisis, choisissez, choisissons. 3. bâtis, bâtissez, bâtissons. 4. punis, punissez, punissons. 5. obéis, obéissez, obéissons. **C. -RE verbs.** 1. vends, vendez, vendons. 2. attends, attendez, attendons. 3. descends, descendez, descendons. 4. réponds, répondez, répondons. 5. rends, rendez, rendons. **II.** 1. Ne chantez pas, Janine! 2. Ne finissons pas le travail maintenant! 3. Ne vendez pas la maison, Monsieur Paquet! 4. N'écoute pas la musique, Pierre! 5. N'attendez pas l'autobus!

Exercises, pp. 137–140
I. 1. Lavez-vous. 2. Assieds-toi. 3. Levez-vous. 4. Asseyez-vous. 5. Lavons-nous. 6. Lève-toi. 7. Ne te lave pas. 8. Ne nous levons pas. **II.** 1. Ne nous lavons pas! 2. Ne vous asseyez pas! 3. Ne te lave pas! 4. Ne t'assieds pas! 5. Ne vous lavez pas! 6. Ne te lève pas! **III.** 2, 4, 5, 1, 3. **IV.** 1. Z. 2. EZ. 3. EZ. 4. ISS. 5. EZ. 6. ONS. 7. DEZ. 8. PO, DE. 9. EN, EZ. 10. SS, EZ. 11. EZ. 12. A, Z. **V.** 1. Je voudrais acheter une plante. 2. C'est pour une amie. 3. Oui. C'est son anniversaire. 4. Oui. Je l'aime beaucoup. C'est combien? 5. Je l'achète. Voici l'argent. Merci beaucoup. Au revoir. **VI.** The five sentences you write will probably not be exactly the same as the following. 1. C'est le grand jour du concours de talents dans la grande salle de l'école. 2. Janine et Pierre sont dans le concours. 3. Pierre est le magicien et Janine est l'assistante. 4. Ils préparent leur représentation mais ils n'ont pas le chapeau haut-de-forme, le bâton, la cape, et le lapin. 5. Les spectateurs dans la grande salle crient: "Dansez! Chantez! Faites quelque chose!" 6. Tout d'un coup, Coco arrive sur la scène (on the stage) avec le chapeau haut-de-forme, le bâton, la cape, et le lapin! 7. Qui a gagné le grand prix? Coco, naturellement, parce qu'il a beaucoup de talent! **VII.** 1. Asseyez-vous, s'il vous plaît. 2. Ouvrez la bouche, s'il vous plaît. 3. Fermez les yeux, s'il vous plaît. 4. Fermez la bouche, s'il vous plaît. 5. Ouvrez les yeux, s'il vous plaît. 6. Levez-vous, s'il vous plaît. **VIII.** 1. Mais tu danses très bien. 2. Oui, c'est vrai. 3. Vas-tu au grand bal en ville avec Roger ce soir? 4. Avec mon ami Pierre. 5. C'est un film passionnant!

Review Test: Work Units 6–10

Exercises, pp. 142–146
I. Janine est au marché aux puces avec son amie Monique. OR: Monique est au marché aux puces avec son amie Janine. **II.** 1. Monsieur et Madame Durant vendent leur maison. 2. Le petit chien rompt la grande barrière. 3. Le professeur interrompt l'étudiant. 4. Janine rend le livre à la bibliothèque. 5. Nous entendons la musique. **III.** 1. ons. 2. e. 3. it. 4. s. 5. es. 6. issent. **IV.** 1. me. 2. te. 3. se. 4. me. 5. nous. **V.** 1. sept. 2. douze. 3. quatre. 4. vingt-cinq. **VI. A.** Il est cinq heures dix. **B.** Il est une heure. **C.** Il est six heures moins le quart (moins un quart). **D.** Il est sept heures et demie. **E.** Il est onze heures et quart. **F.** Il est quatre heures et quart. **VII.** 1. (c). 2. (b). 3. (c). 4. (d). 5. (a). **VIII.** 1. Wash yourself! 2. Let's sit down! 3. Get up! **IX.** 1. S, S, E, Z. 2. E Z. 3. I, S, S, E, Z. **X.** 1. Quel âge a Monsieur Durand? 2. Quel âge as-tu? 3. Quelle heure est-il? 4. Quel jour est-ce aujourd'hui? 5. Quelle est la date aujourd'hui? **XI.** 1. C. 2. D. 3. D. 4. A. 5. D. 6. A. 7. B. 8. A. 9. B. 10. B. **XII.** Note that each situation is a review of the situations in Work Units 6 to 10, as noted in each situation in this part of the review test. Before selecting four of the six situations for proficiency in writing, it would be a good idea to review what you said in the speaking proficiency exercises for the same situations. Then write what you said.

Work Unit 11

Exercises, p. 150
I. 1. (b). 2. (b). 3. (d). 4. (c). 5. (d). **II.** (Note: These are personal questions and you may answer in different ways.)

III. Un acrostiche

Exercises, pp. 152–155

I. 1. Oui, je lis beaucoup; elle lit beaucoup aussi. 2. Oui, j'apprends le français; elle apprend le français aussi. 3. Oui, j'ai de la glace; il a de la glace aussi. 4. Oui, je bois du jus d'orange; il boit du jus d'orange aussi. 5. Oui, je comprends la leçon; elle comprend la leçon aussi. 6. Oui, ils courent à l'école; nous courons à l'école aussi. 7. Oui, elles doivent écrire des compositions; je dois écrire des compositions aussi (possibly: Nous devons écrire des compositions aussi). 8. Oui, il dit la vérité; elles disent la vérité aussi. 9. Oui, elle écrit une lettre; elles écrivent une lettre aussi. 10. Oui, je suis dans le concours de talents à l'école; ils sont dans le concours de talents à l'école aussi. **II.** 1. Non, il ne lit pas beaucoup; je ne lis pas beaucoup; je ne lis pas beaucoup non plus (possibly: Nous ne lisons pas beaucoup non plus). 2. Non, elle ne met pas le vase sur la table; il ne met pas le vase sur la table non plus. 3. Non, je n'ouvre pas la porte; il n'ouvre pas la porte non plus. 4. Non, elle ne part pas à huit heures; il ne part pas à huit heures non plus. 5. Non, je ne peux (or: puis) pas aller au cinéma ce soir; ils ne peuvent pas aller au cinéma ce soir non plus. 6. Non, je ne prends pas le petit déjeuner à sept hueres; elle ne prend pas le petit déjeuner à sept heures non plus. 7. Non, je ne sais pas quelle heure il est; il ne sait pas quelle heure il est non plus. 8. Non, ils ne sortent pas ce soir; elle ne sort pas ce soir non plus. 9. Non, je ne viens pas ici tous les jours; il ne vient pas ici tous les jours non plus. 10. Non, je ne vois pas l'avion dans le ciel; elle ne voit pas l'avion dans le ciel non plus. **III.** 1. Ouvre-t-il la porte? 2. Est-ce qu'elle lit la lettre? 3. Prenez-vous du café? 4. Il ne fait pas la leçon. 5. Ecrivez-vous la date? **IV.** 1. Henri et Robert comprennent la réponse. 2. J'ai beaucoup de devoirs à faire. 3. Hélène et Marie sont-elles présentes aujourd'hui? 4. Michel et Jacques font-ils leurs leçons? 5. Je ne vois pas un taxi. **V.** 1. Nous voyons. 2. Je sais. 3. Ils font. 4. Ils partent. 5. Tu bois. 6. Janine devient. **VI.** 1. Ils comprennent bien aussi. 2. Elles écrivent bien aussi. 3. Ils vont bien aussi. 4. Elles lisent bien aussi. 5. Ils voient bien aussi.

Exercises, pp. 157–162

I. 1. Buvez! 2. Viens! 3. Dites! 4. Ecrivez! 5. Lisez! 6. Ouvre! 7. Sortons! 8. Soyons! 9. Buvons! 10. Revenez! **II.** 1. Dites la phrase. 2. Bois le lait. 3. Partez tout de suite. 4. Ferme la fenêtre. 5. Prends la valise là-bas. 6. Ecrivons la lettre. 7. Lisez le poème. 8. Sortons maintenant. 9. Revenez à l'heure. 10. Faisons la leçon. **III.** 7, 4, 6, 8, 3, 9, 1, 10, 5, 2. **IV. A.** 1. Bon! Alors, partez maintenant. 2. Bon! Alors, ouvrez la fenêtre. 3. Bon! Alors, faites la leçon. 4. Bon! Alors, écrivez une lettre. 5. Bon! Alors, lisez le journal. **IV. B.** 1. Bon! Alors, sortez maintenant. 2. Bon! Alors, soyez ici à dix heures. 3. Bon! Alors, faites le travail ce soir. 4. Bon! Alors, apprenez l'anglais. 5. Bon! Alors, parlez français. **V.** 1. C'est un objet d'habillement. C'est pour une femme. Qu'est-ce que c'est? (C'est une robe.) 2. C'est une partie du corps humain. Elle a cinq doigts. Qu'est-ce que c'est? (C'est une main.) 3. C'est un meuble. Vous dormez sur ce meuble. Qu'est-ce que c'est? (C'est un lit.) 4. C'est un fruit. Il a la couleur jaune. Qu'est-ce que c'est? (C'est une banane.) **VI.** 1. Il y a deux pièces dans l'appartement. 2. L'appartement est petit. 3. Le numéro de téléphone est 45-04-55-14. **VII.** 1. Il y a deux enfants dans cette photo. 2. Ils jouent ensemble. 3. Ils sont dans une chambre chez eux.

Work Unit 12

Exercises, pp. 166–167

I. 1. Ils ont quitté la maison à sept heures et demie pour aller à l'opéra. 2. Ils sont arrivés à l'opéra à huit heures. 3. Ils ont pris leurs places à huit heures et quart. 4. La repésentation a commencé à huit heures et demie. **II.** 1. oui. 2. non. 3. oui. 4. non. 5. non. **III.** 1. allée. 2. vu. 3. quitté. 4. arrivés. 5. entrés. 6. pris. 7. allée. 8. allé. 9. allé. 10. allée.

IV. Word Search

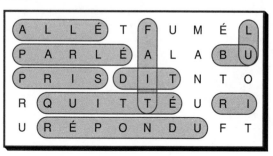

Exercises, pp. 170–173

I. A. 1. Oui, j'ai vendu la voiture. 2. Oui, j'ai acheté la propriété. 3. Oui, j'ai fini les leçons. 4. Oui, j'ai réussi la vente de la propriété. 5. Oui, j'ai fermé les portes et les fenêtres. **B.** 1. Non, elle n'a pas chanté hier soir. 2. Non, il n'a pas choisi une jolie cravate. 3. Non, je n'ai pas mangé l'éclair. 4. Non, ils n'ont pas étudié les leçons. 5. Non, nous n'avons pas fini le travail (possibly: Non, vous n'avez pas fini le travail). **C.** 1. Pierre a-t-il vu Madame Richy? 2. Hélène a-t-elle choisi une jolie robe? 3. Coco a-t-il mangé le gâteau? 4. Suzanne et Georges ont-ils navigué sur Internet? 5. Marie et Betty ont-elles voyagé en France? **D.** 1. Est-ce que Madame Paquet a acheté un beau chapeau? 2. Est-ce que Pierre a perdu sa montre? 3. Est-ce que Monsieur Paquet a fait un appel sur son téléphone portable? 4. Est-ce que Paul a mangé du chocolat? 5. Est-ce que Janine a bu un jus d'orange? **E.** 1. Madame Richy n'a-t-elle pas acheté une automobile? 2. Monsieur Richy n'a-t-il pas voyagé aux Etats-Unis? 3. Madame et Monsieur Armstrong n'ont-ils pas aimé le dessert? 4. Mathilde n'a-t-elle pas entendu la musique? 5. Joseph n'a-t-il pas choisi une jolie cravate? **F.** 1. Est-ce que Robert n'a pas dansé hier soir? 2. Est-ce que Joséphine n'a pas chanté ce matin? 3. Est-ce que Guy et Michel n'ont pas fini leurs leçons? 4. Est-ce que Françoise et Simone n'ont pas entendu la musique? 5. Est-ce que Charles n'a pas perdu son ami? **II.** 7, 10, 8, 9, 6, 3, 5, 2, 1, 4. **III.** 1. aimé. 2. quitté. 3. pris. 4. commencé. 5. parlé. 6. parlé. 7. mangé. 8. bu. 9. vu. 10. dit. **IV.** 1. I danced, I have danced. I did dance. 2. You finished, you have finished, you did finish. 3. We sold, we have sold, we did sell. **V.** 1. J'ai joué. 2. Tu as pleuré. 3. Il a fini. 4. Elle a choisi. 5. Janine a chanté. 6. Nous avons dansé. 7. Vous avez perdu. 8. Ils ont répondu. 9. J'ai étudié. 10. Il a parlé. 11. Robert a travaillé. 12. Marie et Bob ont dîné.

Exercises, pp. 176-184

I. A. 1. Oui, Janine est allée au cinéma. 2. Oui, Monique est allée à l'école. 3. Oui, Robert est allé au théâtre. 4. Oui, Pierre et Raymond sont allés au parc. 5. Oui, Anne et Béatrice sont allées au Canada. 6. Oui, Jacques et Jeanne sont allés à l'aéroport. 7. Oui, Monsieur et Madame Beaupuy sont allés aux Etats-Unis. 8. Oui, la mère est allée dans le garage. 9. Oui, le père est allé dans la cuisine. 10. Oui, la jeune fille est allée à la pharmacie. **B.** 1. Non, elle n'est pas arrivée à l'opéra à huit heures et demie. 2. Non, ils ne sont pas entrés dans le théâtre à huit heures. 3. Non, ils ne sont pas partis de bonne heure. 4. Non, il n'est pas resté à la maison. 5. Non, elle n'est pas sortie ce soir. **C.** 1. Yolande est-elle venue ce soir? 2. François est-il retourné à midi? 3. Les garçons sont-ils restés dans l'école? 4. Les jeunes filles sont-elles descendues vite? 5. Monsieur et Madame Paquet sont-ils rentrés à minuit? **D.** 1. Est-ce que John James Audubon est né aux Cayes à Haïti? 2. Est-ce que Napoléon Bonaparte est mort à Sainte-Hélène? 3. Est-ce que Marie-Antoinette est née à Vienne? 4. Est-ce que Jacques Chirac est devenu président de la République française en 1995? 5. Est-ce que Joséphine est née à la Martinique? 6. Est-ce que Marie-Antoinette est morte à Paris? 7. Est-ce que Joséphine est devenue impératrice en 1804? **E.** 1. N'es-tu pas resté à la maison? 2. N'est-elle pas tombée dans le jardin? 3. N'est-il pas parti ce matin? 4. N'êtes-vous pas arrivé à dix heures? 5. Ne sont-elles pas allées à l'école aujourd'hui? **II.** 4, 1, 2, 3, 10, 5, 6, 9, 7, 8. **III.** 1. I went . . . , I have gone . . . , I did go . . . . 2. She left, she has left, she did leave. 3. We arrived, we have arrived, we did arrive. **IV.** 1. Je suis allé. 2. Tu es venu. 3. Il est arrivé. 4. Elle est partie. 5. Jean est sorti. 6. Nous sommes entrés. 7. Vous êtes tombé. 8. Ils sont montés. 9. Elles sont allées. 10. Je suis descendu. 11. Michel est rentré. 12. Elle est morte.

V. Un ascrostiche

VI. 1. Suzanne a parlé. 2. Il est monté. 3. Elle est sortie. 4. Elle a compris. 5. Nous sommes arrivés. 6. Vous avez dit. 7. Elles ont lu. 8. Tu as fait. 9. Robert est resté. 10. Ils ont ri. 11. Je suis allé. 12. Madame Paquet a bu. **VII.** 1. apprendre. 2. devenir. 3. avoir. 4. couvrir. 5. croire. 6. comprendre. 7. permettre. 8. recevoir. 9. promettre. 10. vouloir. 11. devoir. 12. voir. 13. dire. 14. venir. 15. écrire. 16. être. 17. boire. 18. faire. 19. tenir. 20. lire. 21. ourvrir. 22. mettre 23. savoir. 24. mourir. 25. rire. 26. naître. 27. revenir. 28. paraître. 29. pouvoir. 30. prendre. **VIII.** 1. eu. 2. été. 3. fait. 4. fini. 5. su. 6. lu. 7. appris. 8. défendu. 9. choisi. 10. allé. 11. sorti. 12. saisi. 13. aidé. 14. bâti. 15. joué. 16. vu. 17. dansé. 18. vendu. **IX.** 1. être. 2. avoir. 3. avoir. 4. avoir. 5. être. 6. être. 7. avoir. 8. avoir. 9. être. 10. avoir. 11. avoir. 12. être. 13. être. 14. avoir. 15. être. 16. avoir. 17. être. 18. avoir. 19. avoir. 20. avoir. 21. être. **X.** 1. Il lit un bon livre. 2. Je vends la voiture. 3. Elle va à l'opéra. 4. Nous écrivons des lettres. 5. Vous arrivez tôt. **XI.** 1. Madame Paquet a eu un beau chapeau rouge. 2. Janine a bu un jus d'orange. 3. Pierre a mangé du chocolat. 4. Monique est allée au cinéma. 5. Jeanne et Joséphine sont entrées dans le théâtre. **XII.** 1. e. 2. —. 3. e 4. e. 5. s. 6. s. 7. —. **XIII.** 1. allée. 2. arrivés. 3. entrés. 4. allée. 5. allé. 6. allé. 7. allée. 8. retournée. 9. retourné. 10. retournée. **XIV.** 1. Hier soir, je suis allé(e) à l'opéra. J'ai vu l'opéra *Pelléas et Mélisande*. Claude Debussy a composé la musique. Pendant l'entracte, j'ai bu un jus d'orange et j'ai mangé du chocolat. **XV.** 1. Hier soir, Janine est allée à l'opéra. 2. Elle a vu la représentation de *Faust*. 3. Pendant l'entracte, elle a parlé avec un homme. 4. Elle a donné son programme et son stylo à l'homme pour son autographe. **XVI.** 1. Les jeunes hommes dans cette photo sont habillés en blanc. 2. Ils portent des bérets noirs. 3. Ils dansent La Danse des Sabres.

Work Unit 13

Exercises, p. 189

I. 1. Pierre a servi le dîner ce soir. 2. Il a servi le dîner pour la famille et les voisins. 3. Pierre commence à goûter le ragoût. 4. Monsieur Richy aime le ragoût. 5. Le ragoût est bien cuit (possibly: Il aime le ragoût bien cuit; or, il aime le ragoût parce qu'il est bien cuit). 6. Madame Paquet a fait le ragoût. **II.** (Note: These are personal questions and you may answer in different ways.) **III.** 1. Et comment! Il sent très bon. (Moi), j'ai grand faim (j'ai très faim). 2. Janine a raison. Il est brûlé. Je ne l'aime pas. Goûtez-en! 3. Je vais le goûter. 4. Madame Paquet rentre dans la salle à manger avec le dessert. 5. Est-ce que tout le monde aime mon ragoût? J'ai un dessert que j'ai fait aussi. Qui veut une crème brûlée? Goûtez-en!

Exercises, pp. 195–203

I. 1. Pierre la lit. 2. Janine l'écrit. 3. Michel l'apprend. 4. Christophe les fait. 5. Alexandre l'écoute. 6. Yolande le prononce. 7. Théodore le voit. 8. Monique la dit. 9. Joséphine l'attend. 10. Anne les mange. **II.** 1. Oui, elle la dit. 2. Oui, elle l'attend. 3. Oui, il la lit. 4. Oui, il les mange. 5. Oui, elle l'écoute. **III.** 1. Non, il ne la mange pas. 2. Non, elle ne le prononce pas. 3. Non, il ne l'aime pas. 4. Non, il ne la lit pas. 5. Non, elle ne les apporte pas. **IV.** 1. Oui, je la comprends aujourd'hui. 2. Oui, je la dis toujours. 3. Oui, je les fais maintenant. 4. Oui, je le lis tous les jours. 5. Oui, je l'écris en ce moment. **V.** 1. Oui, elle la connaît. 2. Oui, elle le connaît. 3. Oui, il les connaît. 4. Oui, elle les connaît. 5. Oui, il les connaît. **VI.** 1. Oui, elle me connaît. 2. Oui, il me voit. 3. Oui, elle nous aime. 4. Oui, ils les attendent. 5. Oui, il l'adore. **VII.** 1. Oui, je t'aime bien. 2. Oui, je l'aime bien aussi. 3. Oui, je l'aime bien aussi. 4. Oui, il m'aime bien.

5. Oui, elle m'aime bien aussi. **VIII.** 1. Oui, je t'aime. 2. Oui, il m'aime. 3. Oui, je l'aime aussi. 4. Oui, il m'aime. 5. Oui, elle m'aime. **IX.** 1. Bon! Alors, écrivez-la! 2. Bon! Alors, étudiez-les! 3. Bon! Alors, lisez-le! 4. Bon! Alors, buvez-le! 5. Bon! Alors, faites-les! **X.** 1. Bon! Alors, ne l'écrivez-pas! 2. Bon! Alors, ne les étudiez pas! 3. Bon! Alors, ne le lisez pas! 4. Bon! Alors, ne le buvez pas! 5. Bon! Alors, ne les faites pas! **XI.** 1. Pierre veut le lire. 2. Madeleine veut l'apprendre. 3. Paul ne veut pas l'écrire. 4. Philippe ne veut pas la manger. 5. Gertrude ne veut pas les apporter. **XII.** 1. Oui, j'en ai. 2. Oui, j'en bois. 3. Oui, j'en mange. 4. Oui, j'en mange. 5. Oui, j'en ai. 6. Oui, j'en ai. 7. Oui, il en vient. 8. Oui, j'en peur. 9. Oui, j'en mange. 10. Oui, j'en bois. **XIII.** 1. Non, je n'en ai pas. 2. Non, je n'en ai pas. 3. Non, je n'en ai pas. 4. Non, je n'en ai pas. 5. Non, je n'en ai pas. **XIV.** 1. Bon! Alors, buvez-en! 2. Bon! Alors, mangez-en! 3. Bon! Alors, écrivez-en! 4. Bon! Alors, buvez-en! 5. Bon! Alors, mangez-en! **XV.** 1. Bon! Alors, n'en buvez pas! 2. Bon! Alors, n'en mangez pas! 3. Bon! Alors, n'en écrivez pas! **XVI.** 1. Madame Paquet l'a préparé. 2. Monsieur Richy l'a mangé. 3. Pierre l'a servi. 4. Janine les a préparés. 5. Monsieur Paquet les a préparées. **XVII.** 1. Oui, il l'a servi. 2. Oui, elle l'a préparé. 3. Oui, il l'a mangé. 4. Oui, elle l'a écrite. 5. Oui, il les a faits. **XVIII.** 1. Non, il ne l'a pas préparée. 2. Non, il ne l'a pas fait. 3. Non, elle ne l'a pas lu. 4. Non, elle ne l'a pas mangé. 5. Non, il ne les a pas faits. **XIX.** 1. Mon frère Pierre l'a préparée. 2. Moi. Je les ai préparées. 3. Non, merci, papa. Je n'en veux pas. 4. J'en ai déjà mangé. 5. J'aimerais une tasse de thé avec le dessert, s'il vous plaît. Je ne bois pas de café. 6. Citron, s'il vous plaît, s'il y en a. 7. Oui, maman. Tout de suite. **XX.** 1. D'accord. La voici. 2. Non, je ne l'aime pas. Dis-moi, Pierre, as-tu fait (OR: est-ce que tu as fait) les devoirs de biologie pour demain? 3. Non. Je ne les ai pas faits. 4. Je ne les aime pas. Je ne les mange pas. Je n'aime pas la cuisine rapide. 5. Janine les a apportés. 6. J'aime les gâteaux. Je vais les manger tous. **XXI.** 1. Dans cette photo il y a des personnes qui mangent et boivent. 2. La serveuse porte une blouse blanche et une jupe noire (The waitress is wearing a white blouse and a black skirt). 3. Elle sert les clients (She is serving the customers). 4. Il y a des personnes assises aux petites tables rondes. 5. Je vois aussi des personnes qui marchent sur le trottoir. 6. Il fait beau aujourd'hui, n'est-ce pas? (The weather is beautiful today, isn't it?).

Work Unit 14

Exercises, p. 206

I. 1. Janine a prêté son téléphone portable à Suzanne. 2. Elle veut téléphoner à sa mère. 3. Paul prête son téléphone portable à Janine. **II.** 1. Elle m'a dit que tu l'as maintenant. 2. Je ne l'ai pas. Je l'ai donné à Monique. Va la voir. 3. J'ai donné le (téléphone) portable à Mimi. Mimi l'a donné à Raymond. 4. Je lui ai donné le (téléphone) portable. Va le voir.

III.

```
        3.
        P                6.
1.  2.  R   4.  5.       P
P   R   Ê   T   E   R
O   E   T   R   C   O
R   N   E   È   O   P
T   D       S   U   R
A   R           T   E
B   E           E
L               R
E
```

Exercises, pp. 209–212

I. 1. Janine lui donne le journal. 2. Madeleine lui donne le livre. 3. Gloria lui donne la fleur. 4. Robert leur donne la balle. 5. Monique leur donne les stylos. **II. A.** 1. Je lui parle. 2. Je lui parle. 3. Je lui parle. 4. Je lui parle. 5. Je lui parle. **II. B.** 1. Je leur donne les gâteaux. 2. Je leur donne les livres. 3. Je leur donne le ragoût brûlé. 4. Je leur donne les lettres. 5. Je leur donne le jus. **III.** 1. Oui, je vous parle. 2. Oui, je lui parle. 3. Oui, je vous parle. **IV.** 1. Bon! Alors, donnez-lui le gâteau! 2. Bon! Alors, donnez-lui le parapluie. 3. Bon! Alors, donnez-lui le bonbon. 4. Bon! Alors, donnez-lui le jus de fruit. 5. Bon! Alors, donnez-lui le ragoût brûlé. **V.** 1. Bon! Alors, ne leur donnez pas le chocolat! 2. Bon! Alors, ne lui donnez pas les devoirs! 3. Bon! Alors, ne lui donnez pas le billet! **VI.** 1. Bon! Alors, parlez-moi! 2. Bon! Alors, parlez-lui! 3. Bon! Alors, parlez-leur! **VII.** 1. Bon! Alors, ne me parlez pas! 2. Bon! Alors ne lui parlez pas! 3. Bon alors, ne leur parlez pas! **VIII.** 4, 5, 2, 6, 3, 1. **IX.** 1. Oui, j'y vais. 2. Oui, j'y vais. 3. Oui, j'y vais. **X.** 1. Bon! Alors, parlez-lui! 2. Janine veut leur parler. 3. Elle nous donne le chocolat. **XI.** 1. Anne, je t'ai prêté mes disques compacts au mois de septembre et aujourd'hui c'est le premier décembre. 2. Tu ne les as pas? Où sont-ils? 3. Je ne peux pas aller la voir. Elle est en vacances au Canada. 4. Non. Elle ne les a pas. Je lui ai parlé hier. 5. Elle m'a dit que tu les as. 6. Et, moi, je te dis que je ne les ai pas! Apparemment mes disques compacts sont perdus! Au revoir!

Work Unit 15

Exercises, pp. 217–218
I. 1. UN CHAMPIGNON. 2. UN FAUTEUIL. 3. UNE HORLOGE. 4. UNE GIRAFE. 5. UN KANGOUROU. **II.** 1. porte. 2. yeux, n'ai pas. 3. suis. 4. n'ai pas. 5. long, peux.

III.

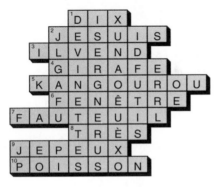

Exercises, pp. 219–221
I. 6, 3, 5, 1, 4, 2. **II.** 1. Qui. 2. Qui. 3. qui. 4. qui. 5. Que. 6. Qu'est-ce que. 7. Que. 8. Qu'est-ce que. 9. Qui. 10. Que. **III.** 1. Qui mange une pomme? 2. Que buvez-vous? 3. A qui parle Monique? (possibly: Qui parle à Roger?). 4. Qu'est-ce que vous dites? 5. Qu'est-ce que Janine écrit? 6. Qui a lancé la balle? 7. Que lit-elle? 8. Qu'est-ce que vous mangez? 9. Qu'est-ce que Pierre a servi? 10. Qui a fait le ragoût? **IV.** 1. Ne vois-tu pas que je parle à quelqu'un? 2. Non. Je ne lui parle pas. 3. Je ne lui parle pas en ce moment. Je lui ai parlé hier. 4. Je ne leur parle pas maintenant (en ce moment). Je leur ai parlé ce matin. 5. Je te parle, à toi. Va-t'en! **V.** Je regarde le tableau de Degas. C'est une danseuse de ballet au repos. Elle s'appelle Claudette. Elle est assise. Elle a la main droite sur un genou et la main gauche sur le pied. Le tutu qu'elle porte est joli. Elle se repose.

Review Test: Work Units 11–15

Exercises, pp. 223–227
I. 1. ma. 2. mais. 3. si. 4. on. 5. mis. 6. mon. 7. nom. 8. ai. **II.** Aimons! (Let's love!)

III.

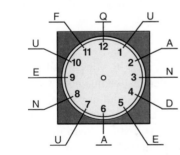

IV. 1. (c). 2. (b). 3. (a). **V.** 1. (b). 2. (a). 3. (c). 4. (b). 5. (a). **VI.** 1. (c). 2. (b). 3. (a). 4. (b). 5. (d). **VII.** 1. avoir. 2. être. 3. faire. 4. dire. 5. lire. 6. savoir. 7. comprendre. 8. mettre. 9. rire. **VIII.** 1. sont. 2. ai. 3. suis. 4. a. 5. est. 6. a. 7. a. 8. est. **IX.** 1. (a). 2. (c). 3. (a). 4. (c). 5. (d). **X.** 1. (a). 2. (a). 3. (a). 4. (b). 5. (a). **XI.** 1. Qui. 2. Qui. 3. qui. 4. qui. 5. Que. 6. Que. **XII.** 1. B. 2. A. 3. A. 4. B. 5. B. **XIII.** Note that each situation is a review of the situations in Work Units 11 to

15, as noted in each situation in this part of the review test. Before selecting four of the five situations for proficiency in writing, it would be a good idea to review what you said in the speaking proficiency exercises for the same situations. Then write what you said.

Work Unit 16

Exercises, p. 231
I. 1. vrai. 2. vrai. 3. vrai. 4. faux. 5. faux. 6. faux. 7. faux. 8. vrai. **II.** 1. professeur, géographie. 2. Paris. 3. port. 4. fleuve. 5. dans, classe. 6. au, bureau. 7. continuer, leçon. 8. poser. **III.** 1. Elle est professeur de géographie. 2. La Directrice (de l'école) entre dans la salle de classe. 3. Quand Madame Ravel quitte la salle, elle va dans le bureau de la directrice. 4. Robert a lancé un avion en papier contre l'horloge. 5. La leçon finit à trois heures.

Exercises, pp. 232–234
I. 5, 4, 2, 1, 3. **II.** Oui, cela est faux. 2. Oui, ceci est vrai. 3. Oui, c'est ça.

III. Word Hunt

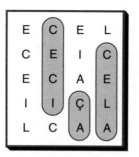

IV. Paris est un port sur la Méditerranée. Cela est vrai? Faux? (Faux) La Tour Eiffel est à Paris. Cela est vrai? Faux? (Vrai) Le quatre juillet est la fête nationale de la France. Cela est vrai? Faux? (Faux) Marseille est une ville dans les Alpes. Cela est vrai? Faux? (Faux). **V.** 1. C'est vrai. 2. C'est faux. 3. C'est vrai. 4. C'est vrai. 5. C'est faux. **VI.** 1. deux enfants 2. des robes d'été 3. des chemises à manches courtes 4. les chapeaux 5. (le) stationnement gratuit 6. (le) rabais de 20% 7. Annie est ma nièce. Demain c'est son anniversaire (de naissance)/birthday 8. Je vais lui donner un cadeau, une jolie robe d'été (un jouet, etc.)

Work Unit 17

Exercises, p. 237
I. MONSIEUR PAQUET: Moi, je ne veux pas y aller (possibly: Je ne veux pas accepter leur invitation; Non, nous n'acceptons pas leur invitation—or any acceptable response)…MONSIEUR PAQUET: Ils m'ennuient beaucoup. Je ne les aime pas. MONSIEUR PAQUET: (Note: In this last réplique of Monsieur Paquet, you may write any response that is acceptable from the dialogue on p. 236.) **II.** 1. entre eux et nous. 2. vous voir. 3. chez eux. 4. je ne les aime pas. 5. à l'invitation. **III.** 1. (d). 2. (d). 3. (a).

Exercises, pp. 238–242
I. 1. moi. 2. lui. 3. elle. 4. nous. 5. vous. 6. eux. **II.** 1. lui. 2. moi. 3. lui. 4. elle. 5. nous. 6. vous. 7. toi. 8. eux. 9. elles. 10. lui et moi. **III.** nous, moi, toi, vous, les, leur, les, les, les, moi, y. **IV.** 1. Eh bien, est-ce que nous y allons ou est-ce que nous n'y allons pas? 2. Quand je l'ai vue au supermarché hier, elle m'a parlé et je lui ai parlé. 3. Ils m'ennuient aussi. Mais si nous refusons leur invitation, tout est fini entre eux et nous. Tu sais cela. 4. Cela est vrai. Tu as raison. **V.** J'admire le tableau de Manet. C'est *Le Balcon.* Qui est le monsieur? Je ne sais pas. Est-il le mari de la dame à droite ou la dame à gauche? Les deux dames sont belles et le monsieur est beau. Quel beau tableau! **VI.** 1. à la plus sympa de toutes les mamans 2. de tout coeur. 3. Je te souhaite une joyeuse Fête des Mères. 4. Chez nous, j'ai appris la valeur de l'amour depuis mon enfance.

Work Unit 18

Exercises, p. 246
I. 1. La famille Paquet a une belle voiture grise. 2. Non, les grosses voitures neuves ne sont pas meilleures que la voiture de Monsieur Paquet. 3. Pierre veut le tournevis pour régler le moteur. Il veut enlever la vis et l'écrou. 4. Pierre les met dans la poubelle. **II.** (Note: There are personal questions and you may respond in different ways.) **III.** 1. oui. 2. oui. 3. non. 4. oui.

Exercises, pp. 248–249
I. 1. Non, j'ai une maison grise. 2. Non, j'ai un mauvais ordinateur. 3. Non, j'ai une belle pomme. 4. Non, j'ai une pêche douce. 5. Non, j'ai un vieux chapeau. **II.** 1. Oui, elle est petite; il est petit aussi. 2. Oui, il est furieux; elle est furieuse aussi. 3. Oui, elle est gentille; il est gentil aussi. 4. Oui, elles sont belles; ils sont beaux aussi. 5. Oui, elle est neuve; elles sont neuves aussi. **III.** 1. Non, elle n'est pas petite; il n'est pas petit non plus. 2. Non, il n'est pas mauvais; il n'est pas mauvais non plus. 3. Non, il n'est pas gros; elle n'est pas grosse non plus. 4. Non, il n'est pas muet; elle n'est pas muette non plus. 5. Non, ils ne sont pas étroits; elles ne sont pas étroites non plus. **IV.** 1. (d). 2. (c). 3. (c). 4. (b). 5. (b).

Exercises, pp. 251–253
I. 1. Oui, j'aime ma petite voiture neuve. 2. Oui, j'aime votre parapluie rouge. 3. Oui, j'aime votre maison blanche. 4. Oui, j'aime ton amie Monique. 5. Oui, j'aime mon petit frère. 6. Oui, j'aime ta jolie soeur. 7. Oui, j'aime vos jaquettes. 8. Oui, j'aime tes robes. 9. Oui, j'aime leurs gâteaux. 10. Oui, j'aime mon livre. **II.** 1. Oui, c'est ma voiture. 2. Oui, c'est mon chapeau. 3. Oui, c'est son livre à lui. 4. Oui, c'est ma maîtresse de français. 5. Oui, c'est leur maison. **III.** 1. Oui, ce sont mes stylos. 2. Oui, ce sont leurs crayons. 3. Oui, ce sont mes gâteaux. 4. Oui, ce sont vos (or: tes) pommes. 5. Oui, ce sont nos (or: vos) pêches. **IV.** votre, ma, votre, votre, vos, sa, son, nos, leurs. **V.** 1. Je mange ma pêche. 2. Il mange son sandwich. 3. Ils mangent leur chocolat. 4. Elles mangent leur soupe. 5. Je mange mes petits fours. **VI.** 1. Oui. Je veux y aller avec toi. Qu'est-ce que c'est? 2. Merveilleux! Je n'ai jamais vu un film français. 3. Okay. Je vais leur téléphoner tout de suite. 4. Je vais être là. 5. Nous allons à un café-restaurant pour avoir de la glace et de la pâtisserie. **VII.** 1. Les trois personnes jouent au foot. 2. Le jeune homme est l'entraîneur. 3. Un garçon a envoyé le ballon au fond des filets. 4. L'autre garçon est surpris! 5. Ils se sont bien amusés.

Work Unit 19

Exercises, p. 259
I. 1. lit, de l'horoscope, lui. 2. le meilleur. 3. plus forte. 4. le plus. 5. du moment, semaine, nouvelles. **II.** 1. faux. 2. vrai. 3. vrai. 4. faux. 5. vrai. **III.** 1. Pierre lit son horoscope. 2. Demain va être un jour parfait. 3. Une personne vous aime beaucoup. 4. Il y a un requin dans l'eau. 5. Le téléphone sonne.

Exercises, pp. 261–262
I. 1. Quel est votre (or: ton) nom? (possibly: Comment vous appelez-vous? or: Comment t'appelles-tu? or: Comment est-ce que vous vous appelez? or: Comment est-ce que tu t'appelles?). 2. Quelle est votre (or: ton) adresse? (Note: Please see page 260 in book for the expected "Quelle est votre adresse?" and "Quel est votre nom?".) 3. Quel âge avez-vous? (or: Quel âge as-tu? or: Quel est votre âge? or: Quel est ton âge?). **II.** (Note: These are personal questions, and you may answer in different ways.) **III.** 1. Quel. 2. Quelles. 3. Quels. 4. Quelle. **IV.** 5, 3, 1, 4, 2.

V. Word Hunt

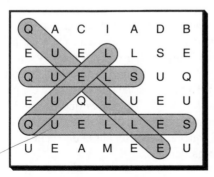

Exercises, pp. 263–264

I. A. 1. Je mange cette pêche. 2. Je mange ce gâteau. 3. Je mange ces petits fours. 4. Je mange cet ananas. 5. Je mange cette tomate. **I. B.** 1. Etudiez-vous cette leçon? 2. Etudiez-vous ce livre? 3. Etudiez-vous ces pages? 4. Etudiez-vous ces phrases? 5. Etudiez-vous ce poème? **I. C.** 1. Nous allons au cinéma avec ces jeunes filles. 2. Nous allons au cinéma avec cet ami. 3. Nous allons au cinéma avec cette amie. 4. Nous allons au cinéma avec ce jeune homme. 5. Nous allons au cinéma avec ces étudiants. **II.** 1. Bien! Je vous donne ce journal! 2. Bien! Je lui donne cette pomme! 3. Bien! Je leur donne ces pommes frites! **III.** 1. Je vais manger cet ananas et ces tomates. 2. Je vais écrire cette leçon et ces phrases. 3. Je vais boire ces vins et ces bières. 4. Je vais envoyer cette lettre. 5. Je vais acheter ce livre.

Exercises, pp. 266–271

I. 1. Non, il est moins grand que sa mère. 2. Non, elle est moins grande que son père. 3. Non, elle est moins intelligente que Janine. **II.** 1. Madame Paquet est plus grande que Janine. 2. Janine est moins grande que Pierre. 3. Mathilde est plus petite que Monique. 4. Suzanne est moins petite que Joseph. 5. Monsieur Richy est aussi grand que Monsieur Paquet. 6. Madame Paquet est aussi petite que Madame Banluc. **III.** 1. Non, ce n'est pas vrai. Janine est la plus intelligente du cours de mathématiques. 2. Non, ce n'est pas vrai. Suzanne est la plus grande du cours de français. 3. Non, ce n'est pas vrai. Simon est le moins grand de la famille. 4. Non, ce n'est pas vrai. Charles est le plus beau du groupe. 5. Non, ce n'est pas vrai. Hélène est la plus petite. **IV.** 1. Oui, cette phrase est moins facile que les autres; ces questions sont plus faciles que les autres aussi. 2. Oui, ce poème est plus difficile que les autres; cette leçon est plus difficile que les autres aussi. 3. Oui, cette voiture est plus belle que les autres; ces maisons sont plus belles que les autres aussi. 4. Oui, ce garçon est plus beau que les autres; ces jeunes filles sont plus belles que les autres aussi. 5. Oui, cette banane est plus délicieuse que les autres; ces gâteaux sont plus délicieux que les autres aussi. **V.** 1. plus. 2. grand. 3. aussi. 4. plus jolie. 5. le moins.

VI. Le Mot Mystère

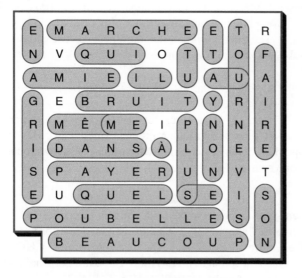

The mystery word is VOITURE; the scrambled letters that remain are, starting with the first line across: R, V, O, E, I, T, U.

VII. Bonjour! Vous désirez? Une chemise? Un cravate? Nous avons beaucoup de belles chemises. Voulez-vous regarder ces chaussettes? Elles sont vraiment jolies et elles ne coûtent pas beaucoup. C'est pour vous? Ou c'est pour une autre personne? C'est pour une soirée? Regardez! Vous avez choisi? C'est un grand plaisir de vous aider. **VIII.** 1. Il n'y a pas de problème. Dis-moi, est-ce qu'Anne est plus jolie que Monique? (OR: Dis-moi, Anne est-elle plus jolie que Monique?) 2. Dis-moi, mon père est-il plus grand que ton père? (OR: Dis-moi, est-ce que mon père est plus grand que ton père?) 3. Qui est le meilleur étudiant de notre classe de français? 4. Moi?! Tu penses que je suis le meilleur (la meilleure) étudiant(e) de notre classe de français?! 5. Merci! Maintenant, mangeons de la mousse au chocolat. C'est la meilleure. **IX.** 1. Je pense que *Le Penseur* est une oeuvre d'art magnifique. 2. Je pense, aussi, que cette statue est la plus belle de toutes les oeuvres de Rodin. 3. C'est une grande joie de la regarder.

Work Unit 20

Exercises, pp. 274–275
I. 1. oui. 2. oui. 3. non. 4. non. 5. non. **II.** 1. (d) 2. (a). 3. (c). 4. (b). 5. (c). **III.** 1. te coucher. 2. jeté. 3. toute. 4. meilleure. 5. plus. 6. moins.

Exercises, pp. 277–279
I. 1. distinctement. 2. seulement. 3. courageusement. 4. constamment. 5. patiemment. 6. fièrement. **II.** 1. Monsieur Richy aime beaucoup le ragoût brûlé. 2. Le professeur a bien parlé. 3. Janine a parlé constamment. 4. Elle est déjà partie. 5. Pierre a beaucoup mangé. **III.** 1. bien. 2. plus. 3. aussi . . . que. 4. plus . . . que. 5. moins. 6. le moins.

IV. Le Mot Mystère

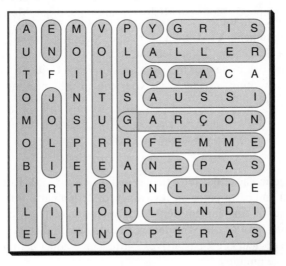

The mystery word is FRANCE; the scambled letters that remain are, starting with the third line across: F, C, A, R, N, E.

V. Silence! Robert, quel âge as-tu? Et toi, Debbie, quel âge as-tu? Vous savez, tous les deux, que vous n'êtes pas sages! Robert, tu es capricieux. Et toi, Debbie, tu es capricieuse. Vous avez abîmé tout! Cela suffit! (That's enough!). Pas de programme de télé ce soir! Robert, va te coucher. Debbie, va te coucher aussi! Maintenant! Vite! **VI.** 1. au plus sympa de tous les papas 2. de tout coeur 3. Je te souhaite une joyeuse Fête des Pères. 4. Je t'aime. 5. Chez nous, j'ai appris la valeur de l'amour depuis mon enfance.

Review Test: Work Units 16–20

Exercises, pp. 280–286

I.

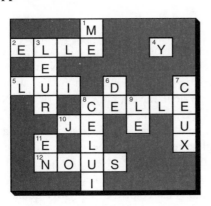

II.

III.

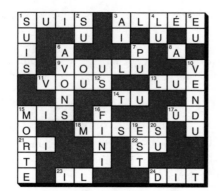

IV. 1. première. 2. grande. 3. bonne. 4. tout. 5. mauavaises. 6. toutes. 7. excellente. 8. studieuse. 9. jolie. 10. blanche.
V. 1. gentiment. 2. franchement. 3. affreusement. 4. amèrement. **VI.** 1. bien. 2. mal. 3. vite. 4. combien. 5. comment.
6. pourquoi. 7. où. 8. quand. 9. beaucoup. 10. assez. **VII.** 1. bien. 2. rapidement. 3. toujours. 4. aussi. 5. déjà. **VIII.**
1. B. 2. C. 3. B. 4. D. 5. A. **IX.** Note that each situation is a review of the situations in Work Units 16 to 20. Before
selecting eight of the ten situations for proficiency in writing, review what you said in the speaking proficiency
exercises for the same situations. Then write what you said.

Work Unit 21

Exercises, pp. 289–290
I. 1. Madame Paquet est malade. 2. Elle a mangé quelque chose qui lui a donné mal à l'estomac. 3. Elle est malade
depuis hier. 4. Le docteur lui donne un médicament. 5. Il doit partir parce qu'il va dîner (or: il doit partir pour aller dîner)
au Coq d'or. **II.** 1. Madame Paquet est malade depuis hier. 2. Absolument rien! 3. Pas même un oeuf à la coque! 4. Dis-
moi ce que tu manges et je te dirai ce que tu es! (or: Dites-moi ce que vous mangez et je vous dirai ce que vous êtes!).
5. Prenez ce médicament et ne mangez rien. **III.** 1. Le docteur n'est pas arrivé. 2. Madame Paquet est malade depuis
hier, n'est-ce pas? 3. Il est dans la chambre depuis quinze minutes.

IV. Mots-croisés

Exercises, pp. 293–298
I. 1. Non, je ne danse pas bien. 2. Non, mon père ne chante pas souvent. 3. Non, ma mère ne lit pas beaucoup. 4. Non,
mes amis n'écrivent pas bien. 5. Non, je ne fume pas. **II.** 1. Non, je ne parle jamais beaucoup. 2. Non, mon père ne boit
jamais beaucoup de lait. 3. Non, ma soeur ne travaille jamais beaucoup. 4. Non, mon ami n'étudie jamais beaucoup.
5. Non, je ne bois jamais beaucoup d'eau. **III.** 1. Non, Lucille ne mange rien. 2. Non, Guy n'écrit rien. 3. Non, je ne lis
rien. 4. Non, Madame Paquet ne fait rien. 5. Non, je n'étudie rien. **IV. A.** 1. Non, je n'ai rien dit. 2. Non, elle n'a rien
bu. 3. Non, mes amis n'ont rien étudié. 4. Non, je n'ai rien lu. 5. Non, je n'ai rien écrit. 6. Non, je n'ai rien bu. 7. Non,
elles n'ont rien mangé. **IV. B.** 1. Non, je n'ai jamais voyagé en Angleterre. 2. Non, je ne suis jamais allé au Canada.
3. Non, je n'ai jamais vu un film français. 4. Non, elle n'est jamais allée à l'opéra. 5. Non, il n'a jamais lu un journal
français. 6. Non, ils ne sont jamais allés en Espagne. 7. Non, elles n'ont jamais mangé un éclair. **V.** 1. Je sais que vous
êtes malade. 2. Madame Paquet est dans son lit parce qu'elle est malade, n'est-ce pas? 3. Je mange quand j'ai faim (or
possibly: Quand j'ai faim, je mange). 4. Le docteur va venir dans quelques minutes. 5. En une heure, le docteur est venu.
VI. 1. être. 2. avoir. 3. aller. 4. attendre. 5. dire. 6. prendre. **VII.** 1. Il est absent depuis lundi. 2. Elle attend le docteur

(or: Elle l'attend) depuis vingt minutes. 3. J'attends l'autobus (or: Je l'attends) depuis dix minutes. 4. Je travaille ici depuis le premier avril. 5. Je lis ce livre (or: Je le lis) depuis une heure. 6. Je lis ce livre (or: Je le lis) depuis ce matin. **VIII.** 1. Oui, il faut boire pour vivre. 2. Oui, il faut étudier pour apprendre. 3. Oui, il faut parler français dans la classe de français. 4. Oui, il faut parler espagnol dans la classe d'espagnol. 5. Oui, il faut faire les devoirs pour apprendre. **IX.** 1. J'ai déjà trouvé du travail pour l'été prochain. 2. Je vais vendre des téléviseurs dans un grand magasin. 3. Tu peux travailler avec moi. 4. Il faut parler avec Monsieur Dubois dans le grand magasin. 5. C'est une très bonne idée. Bonne chance! **X.** 1. Salut, Robert! Comment vas-tu aujourd'hui? 2. J'ai apporté une boîte de chocolats. 3. Dis-moi, Robert, comment est-ce que tu t'es cassé la jambe? (OR: comment t'es-tu cassé la jambe?) 4. Il a brûlé un feu rouge?! Quel idiot! 5. Ces chocolats sont délicieux! 6. Je les ai chetés chez Fauchon, derrière l'Église de la Madeleine. 7. Oui, c'est une très belle église. Dis-moi, Robert, combien de temps vas-tu rester dans l'hôpital? 8. Qui est venu te voir? 9. Je m'en vais maintenant (OR: Je pars maintenant). Je vais revenir demain. 10. À demain!

Work Unit 22

Exercises, pp. 302–303
I. 1. vrai. 2. faux. 3. vrai. **II.** (Note: This is free composition and you may write statements in French in different ways.) **III.** 1. Joseph et Joséphine sont allés (or: vont) au cinéma samedi. 2. Ils sont entrés (or: entrent) chez la chiromancienne. 3. Ils n'ont rien appris (or: n'apprennent rien) chez la chiromancienne. 4. François Paquet lui a payé (or: lui paye) dix euros pour les révélations.

Exercises, pp. 305–307
I. 1. Nous la changeons aussi. 2. Nous le corrigeons aussi. 3. Nous les appelons aussi. 4. Nous l'employons aussi. 5. Nous les achetons aussi. **II.** 1. Nous la lançons aussi. 2. Nous les avançons aussi. 3. Nous les levons aussi. 4. Nous la payons aussi. 5. Nous les mangeons aussi. **III.** 1. Janine et Monique sont allées au cinéma. 2. Nous avons voyagé aux Etats-Unis. 3. Madame Sétou a regardé fixement la main de Madame Paquet. 4. Madame Sétou a révélé les secrets de votre main. 5. Claire et François Paquet ont acheté des souvenirs. **IV.** 1. Nous arrangeons les fleurs. 2. Il achète une cravate. 3. Ils appellent la police. 4. Tu emploies le dictionnaire. 5. Nous prononçons le mot.

Exercises, pp. 309–312
I. 1. Oui, je vais faire un voyage au Canada. 2. Oui, elle va écrire une lettre. 3. Oui, il va jouer dans le parc. 4. Oui, ils vont voyager en Angleterre. 5. Oui, nous allons répondre à la question. **II.** 1. Non, je ne veux pas acheter une nouvelle voiture. 2. Non, il ne veut pas corriger les devoirs. 3. Non, il ne veut pas prononcer le mot. 4. Non, elle ne veut pas employer le dictionnaire. 5. Non, il ne veut pas fumer une cigarette. **III.** 4, 1, 3, 5, 2. **IV.** 1. Il n'y a pas un grand parc dans cette ville. 2. Il n'y a pas un arrêt d'autobus ici. 3. Il n'y a pas dix garçons dans la classe. **V.** 1. Oui, j'ai lu *Le livre de mon ami* d'Anatole France il y a trois mois. 2. Oui, il a vu Pierre il y a dix minutes. 3. Oui, je suis allé(e) en Californie il y a un an. 4. Oui, elles sont arrivées il y a une demi-heure. 5. Oui, elle est partie il y a une heure. **VI.** Il y a vingt membres dans le club à présent. Nous commençons l'année à l'école avec une surprise-partie. Nouns mangeons de la cuisine française. Nous arrangeons des programmes à l'école. Pendant l'été, nous voyageons ensemble, par exemple, au Canada. Nous corrigeons les devoirs des étudiants qui ont besoin d'assistance. Nous effaçons le tableau pour notre professeur de français. Madame Coty, et nous plaçons des fleurs dans un vase sur son bureau. **VII.** 1. Il y a trois enfants dans cette photo. 2. Ils sont dans un parc. 3. Ils jouent. 4. Il grimpe sur un arbre abattu. 5. Il est prêt à sauter. 6. Lui aussi, il grimpe sur un arbre abattu. **VIII.** 1. Il fait très chaud aujourd'hui. Je suis très fatigué. Et toi? 2. Je suis très fatiguée aussi. Allons prendre une glace à la vanille!

Work Unit 23

Exercises, p. 315
I. 1. Il est allé acheter une chaîne stéréo. 2. Janine a préparé un grand déjeuner. 3. Madame Paquet est allée chez le coiffeur. 4. Pierre a acheté une boîte de chocolats. 5. Monsieur Paquet n'a pas branché la chaîne stéréo sur la prise de courant. **II.** 1. non. 2. oui. 3. oui. 4. non. 5. oui. **III.** 1. Monsieur Paquet a acheté (or: achète) une chaîne stéréo. 2. Janine a préparé (or: prépare) le déjeuner. 3. Pierre est allé (or: va) chez un confiseur pour acheter une boîte de chocolats.

Exercises, pp. 318–322

I. 1. de. 2. à. 3. —. 4. de. 5. à. 6. —. 7. —. 8. à. 9. de. 10. de. **II.** 1. Oui, j'ai envie d'aller au cinéma; ils ont envie d'aller au cinéma aussi. 2. Oui, elle a besoin d'aller au supermarché; elles ont besoin d'aller au supermarché aussi. 3. Oui, je suis sorti(e) sans dire un mot; elle est sortie sans dire un mot aussi. 4. Oui, j'apprends à lire en français; il apprend à lire en français aussi. 5. Oui, j'ai horreur de manger dans un restaurant sale; ils ont horreur de manger dans un restaurant sale aussi. **III.** 1. (c). 2. (d). 3. (d). **IV.** 3, 5, 1, 2, 4. **V.** 1. (d). 2. (c). 3. (c). **VI.** 1. Oui. J'aime beaucoup le basketball. 2. Oui. C'est la meilleure équipe. 3. Oui. Il est superbe! 4. Nous allons gagner. 5. Bien sûr! Je vais venir. **VII.** 1. Monsieur Jacques Chirac, à gauche, est le président de la République Française. Il a été élu en 1995. 2. L'homme à droite est Monsieur François Mitterrand, l'ancien président. Les deux hommes viennent de sortir du Palais de l'Élysée, célèbre résidence du Président de la République, à Paris. **VIII.** 1. Anne-Marie et Pierre passent leur lune de miel à Paris. 2. Comme elle est jolie! Comme il est beau!

Review Test: Work Units 21–23

Exercises, pp. 323–326

I. 1. Je ne prononce pas. 2. Madame Paquet n'est pas grande. 3. Nous n'allons pas au cinéma. **II.** 1. quand. 2. parce qu'. 3. que. **III.** 1. elle. 2. depuis. 3. temps. 4. attend. **IV.** 1. (b). 2. (a). **V.** 1. J'ai besoin d'aller chez le dentiste. 2. Vous avez raison et j'ai tort. OR: Tu as raison et, moi, j'ai tort. 3. Nous n'avons pas peur de traverser la rue. 4. J'ai envie de dormir. 5. Il est intéressant d'aller à un musée. **VI.** 5, 4, 1, 3, 2. **VII.** 1. D. 2. B. 3. C. 4. B. 5. B. 6. A. 7. D. 8. B. 9. A. 10. C. **VIII.** Note that each situation is a review of the situations in Work Units 21 to 23. Before selecting six of the eight situations for proficiency in writing, review what you said in the speaking proficiency exercises for the same situations. Then write what you said.

Index

Numbers refer to pages.

MOVE TO THE HEAD OF YOUR CLASS
THE EASY WAY!

Barron's presents THE EASY WAY SERIES—specially prepared by top educators, it maximizes effective learning while minimizing the time and effort it takes to raise your grades, brush up on the basics, and build your confidence. Comprehensive and full of clear review examples, THE EASY WAY SERIES is your best bet for better grades, quickly!

0-7641-1976-1	Accounting the Easy Way, 4th Ed.—$16.99, Can. $24.50
0-7641-1972-9	Algebra the Easy Way, 4th Ed.—$14.95, Can. $21.95
0-7641-1973-7	American History the Easy Way, 3rd Ed.—$18.99, Can. $24.50
0-7641-3428-0	American Sign Language the Easy Way, 2nd Ed.—$16.99, Can. $21.50
0-7641-1979-6	Anatomy and Physiology the Easy Way—$16.99, Can. $24.50
0-7641-2913-9	Arithmetic the Easy Way, 4th Ed.—$14.99, Can. $21.99
0-7641-1358-5	Biology the Easy Way, 3rd Ed.—$14.95, Can. $21.95
0-7641-1079-9	Bookkeeping the Easy Way, 3rd Ed.—$16.99, Can. $21.50
0-7641-0314-8	Business Letters the Easy Way, 3rd Ed.—$14.99, Can. $21.00
0-7641-1359-3	Business Math the Easy Way, 3rd Ed.—$16.99, Can. $24.50
0-7641-2920-1	Calculus the Easy Way, 4th Ed.—$14.99, Can. $21.99
0-7641-1978-8	Chemistry the Easy Way, 4th Ed.—$16.99, Can. $24.50
0-7641-0659-7	Chinese the Easy Way—$16.99, Can. $24.50
0-7641-2579-6	Creative Writing the Easy Way—$14.99, Can. $18.95
0-7641-2146-4	Earth Science The Easy Way—$16.99, Can. $23.99
0-7641-1981-8	Electronics the Easy Way, 4th Ed.—$16.99, Can. $24.50
0-7641-1975-3	English the Easy Way, 4th Ed.—$14.99, Can. $21.99
0-7641-3050-1	Forensics the Easy Way—$14.99. Can. $21.99
0-7641-3411-6	French the Easy Way, 4th Ed.—$14.99, Can. $18.75
0-7641-2435-8	French Grammar the Easy Way—$16.99, Can. $24.50
0-7641-0110-2	Geometry the Easy Way, 3rd Ed.—$14.95, Can. $21.00
0-8120-9145-0	German the Easy Way, 2nd Ed.—$14.95, Can. $21.00
0-7641-1989-3	Grammar the Easy Way—$14.95, Can. $21.00
0-7641-3413-2	Italian the Easy Way, 3rd Ed.—$14.99, Can. $21.99
0-8120-9627-4	Japanese the Easy Way—$18.99, Can. $24.50
0-7641-3237-7	Macroeconomics the Easy Way—$14.99, Can. $21.00
0-7641-9369-4	Mandarin Chinese the Easy Way—$21.99, Can. $25.99
0-7641-2011-5	Math the Easy Way, 4th Ed.—$13.95, Can. $19.50
0-7641-1871-4	Math Word Problems the Easy Way—$16.99, Can. $21.50
0-7641-2845-0	Microbiology the Easy Way—$16.99, Can. $21.99
0-8120-9601-0	Microeconomics the Easy Way—$16.99, Can. $24.50
0-7641-2794-2	Organic Chemistry the Easy Way—$14.99, Can. $21.99
0-7641-0236-2	Physics the Easy Way, 3rd Ed.—$16.99, Can. $24.50
0-7641-2892-2	Precalculus the Easy Way—$14.95, Can. $21.95
0-7641-2393-9	Psychology the Easy Way—$14.95, Can. $21.95
0-7641-2263-0	Spanish Grammar the Easy Way—$14.99, Can. $21.99
0-7641-1974-5	Spanish the Easy Way, 4th Ed.—$14.95, Can. $21.95
0-8120-9852-8	Speed Reading the Easy Way—$16.99, Can. $21.95
0-7641-3410-8	Spelling the Easy Way, 4th Ed.—$14.99, Can. $21.99
0-8120-9392-5	Statistics the Easy Way, 3rd Ed.—$14.99, Can. $21.00
0-7641-1360-7	Trigonometry the Easy Way, 3rd Ed.—$14.95, Can. $21.00
0-8120-9765-3	World History the Easy Way, Vol. One—$16.99, Can. $24.50
0-8120-9766-1	World History the Easy Way, Vol. Two—$16.99, Can. $24.50
0-7641-1206-6	Writing the Easy Way, 3rd Ed.—$14.95, Can. $21.00

Barron's Educational Series, Inc.
250 Wireless Boulevard • Hauppauge, New York 11788
In Canada: Georgetown Book Warehouse • 34 Armstrong Avenue, Georgetown, Ontario L7G 4R9
www.barronseduc.com $ = U.S. Dollars   Can. $ = Canadian Dollars

Prices subject to change without notice. Books may be purchased at your local bookstore, or by mail from Barron's. Enclose check or money order for total amount plus sales tax where applicable and 18% for postage and handling (minimum charge $5.95 U.S. and Canada). New York, New Jersey, Michigan, Tennessee, and California residents add sales tax. All books are paperback editions.

(#45) R 8/07

DATE DUE

~~APR 2 0 2010~~			
~~MAR 1 6 2011~~			
~~APR 0 6 2011~~			
OCT 2 4 2011			
JUL 1 9 2012			
OCT 0 1 2013			
JUL 2 8 2015			
NOV 06 2017			